The Face of the Other and the Trace of God

DATE DUE

WITHDRAWN

PERSPECTIVES IN CONTINENTAL PHILOSOPHY
John D. Caputo, series editor

1. John D. Caputo, ed., *Deconstruction in a Nutshell: A Conversation with Jacques Derrida.*
2. Michael Barber, *Ethical Hermeneutics: Rationality in Enrique Dussel's Philosophy of Liberation.*
3. Michael Strawser, *Both/And: Reading Kierkegaard—From Irony to Edification.*
4. James H. Olthuis, ed., *Knowing Other-wise: Philosophy at the Threshold of Spirituality.*
5. James Swindal, *Reflection Revisited: Jürgen Habermas's Discursive Theory of Truth.*
6. Richard Kearney, *Poetics of Imagining: Modern and Postmodern.* Second edition.
7. Thomas W. Busch, *Circulating Being: From Embodiment to Incorporation—Essays on Late Existentialism.*
8. Edith Wyschogrod, *Emmanuel Levinas: The Problem of Ethical Metaphysics.* Second edition.
9. Francis J. Ambrosio, ed., *The Question of Christian Philosophy Today.*

THE FACE OF THE OTHER
AND THE TRACE OF GOD

Essays on the Philosophy
of Emmanuel Levinas

edited by

JEFFREY BLOECHL

Fordham University Press
New York
2000

ISSN 1089–3938
Perspectives in Continental Philosophy, No. 10

Library of Congress Cataloging-in-Publication Data

The face of the Other and the trace of God : essays on the philosophy of
Emmanuel
Lévinas / Jeffrey Bloechl, editor.—1st ed.
    p.   cm.—(Perspectives in continental philosophy; no. 10)
    Includes bibliographical references and index.
    ISBN 0-8232-1965-8 (hc)—ISBN 0-8232-1966-6 (pbk)
    1. Lâvinas, Emmanuel.   I. Bloechl, Jeffrey, 1966–   II. Series.
B2430.L484 F32 2000
194—dc21   99-049540

Printed in the United States of America
00 01 02 03 04   5 4 3 2 1
First Edition

CONTENTS

ACKNOWLEDGMENTS

Although all of the essays in this volume are published here for the first time in English, several have appeared previously in other languages or have been delivered as lectures. Didier Franck's text was published first as "Le corps de la différence," in *Philosophie* no. 34 (1992). Paul Moyaert's "Phenomenology of Eros" is the text of a paper given at a conference on Levinas's work held in Leusden in 1987, and published as "Fenomenologie van de eros" in *Emmanuel Levinas over psyche, kunst en moraal,* ed. H. Bleijendaal et al. (Baarn: Ambo, 1991). An earlier version of Rudolf Bernet's "The Encounter with the Stranger" was read before a gathering of Eastern and Western philosophers in Hong Kong in April 1996. Portions of Jeffrey Bloechl's "Ethics as First Philosophy and Religion" have been taken from a lecture given in April 1997 at Vytautas Magnus University in Kaunas, Lithuania. Adriaan Peperzak's essay is a revised version of a paper given at a conference held in Aachen and Simpelveld in 1982, and published as "Das Bedeutung des Werkes von Emmanuel Levinas für das Christliche Denken" in *Verantwortung für den Anderen -und die Frage nach Gott,* ed. H. H. Henrix (Aachen: Einhard Verlag, 1984). Jean-Luc Marion's homage to Levinas is the unpublished text of a lecture given at the Sorbonne in 1996; parts of it have since appeared in his book *Etant donné* (Paris: P.U.F., 1997). Rudi Visker's contribution is a revised version of his "De prijs van de onteigening: Levinas, God en het trauma," which appeared in *De God van denkers en dichters* (Amsterdam: Boom, 1997). Portions of John Caputo's "Adieu—sans Dieu" were given at the annual meeting of the Eastern Division of the American Philosophical Association in December 1997. The contributions by Franck and Marion were translated from the French by Jeffrey Bloechl. The contributions by Moyaert, Burggraeve, and Visker were translated from the Dutch by Jeffrey Bloechl. Peperzak's contribution was translated from the German by Gregory Renner. Both translators thank the authors for the generous help and attention. The editor also wishes to thank Jonathan Lawrence, for countless improvements on the final text, and John Caputo, for graciously inviting it into his series on contemporary Continental thought.

EDITOR'S NOTE

The reader will notice from the following list of abbreviations as well as bibliographical information for each contribution in this volume that English translations have been cited in, by far, most but not quite all possible instances. Owing to the technical difficulties always involved in reading and explicating a complex thinker, several contributors have sometimes preferred to work and argue directly from Levinas's French. In my "Acknowledgments" I have already expressed my gratitude to them for taking up the extra work this has implied for an English rendering.

Levinas is notoriously difficult to translate even from his own lexicon and perspective into one's own, and quite apart from the challenge of his terse, yet lyrical French. This is due mainly to his use of capital letters—as well as irregular refrain from doing so—precisely with some of his most important sets of concepts: (impersonal) "other"/(personal) "other," "being"/"beings," and what is rendered variously as "infinity" and "the infinite." There is no clear rule for when to capitalize these words within Levinas's own work, and considerable discord on the point among his interpreters. Needless to say, decisions especially about *autre* and *autrui* are already enough to imply a specific interpretation of much of his argument as a whole, and whether one intends it or not. It is with this in mind that I have sought a middle path between a wish to remind the reader of Levinas's extreme definitions of those terms and, of course, a responsibility to preserve the intentions of each author contributing to the volume. What has resulted is a general tendency to capitalize all instances of the word "Other" (whether *autre* or *autrui*)—except, of course, in secondary literature—wherever it seems necessary to clarify that it is indeed Levinas's particular definition at stake. A similar practice has been followed regarding the Heideggerian distinction between "Being" (*Sein*) and "beings" (*Seiende*), which, however, is additionally complicated by Levinas's own growing insistence on reducing *Sein* to a lowercase, verbal "being" (*être*). As for Levinas's *l'infini* (infinite, infinity), it has seemed advisable to simply leave each author's practice wholly intact, whether discussing Levinas's own thinking or his glosses on Descartes.

Reflection on Levinas's work is far from exempt from difficulties surrounding the problem of gendered language. This is hardly the place to attempt anything more than a brief mention of themes and debates which have preoccupied entire essays, if not books. Levinas's philosophy provokes such discussion on at least two main levels— that of the life of the subject or human being, and that of philosophizing itself, in its discursive aspect. Regarding the former, the basic nature of Levinas's objection to Husserl and his lineage has been to associate the degree of primacy always accorded to *Seinkönnen* with a "virile subjectivity" promoting violence. Feminists have not been slow to borrow from this notion, if also with considerable nuance and a frequent unwillingness to move from that active virility to a passive femininity on record in the "Phenomenology of Eros" appearing in *Totality and Infinity*. As for the status of Levinas's own philosophy, Derrida put a sharp edge on this question already in a remark near the end of "Violence and Metaphysics" (1963), which claims that Levinas's internal critique of Western philosophy itself obeys conditions that only a man could have adopted.

These two strands in Levinas's thought and in turn the interpretation and critique of that thought make the issue of gender and language exceptionally complex in a manner lying at the heart of his position, not least where everything comes to bear on the crucial but notoriously enigmatic concept "Other." Here, where it has been a matter of collecting, in some cases translating, and in rare cases editing the work of others engaging Levinas, sensitivity to the reader has been tempered perhaps to a greater degree than elsewhere by sensitivity to the intentions of the author: I have endeavored to render gendered pronouns in a neutral manner, without, however, distorting points essential to the arguments of Levinas or his interpreter, as the case may be.

ABBREVIATIONS

The following abbreviations are in use throughout this volume and refer to works by Levinas. Other abbreviations are occasionally employed by individual authors, with the necessary indication provided in an endnote.

AE	*Autrement qu'être ou au-delà de l'essence.* The Hague: Martinus Nijhoff, 1974.
CPP	*Collected Philosophical Papers.* Trans. A. Lingis. The Hague: Martinus Nijhoff, 1987.
DE	*De l'existence à l'existant.* Paris: Vrin, 1947.
DVI	*De Dieu qui vient à l'idée.* Paris: Vrin, 1982.
EDE	*En découvrant l'existence avec Husserl et Heidegger,* 3rd ed. Paris: Vrin, 1974.
EE	*Existence and Existents.* Trans. A. Lingis. The Hague: Martinus Nijhoff, 1978.
GCM	*Of the God Who Comes to Mind.* Trans. B. Bergo. Stanford: Stanford University Press, 1998.
HAH	*Humanisme de l'autre homme.* Montpellier: Fata Morgana, 1972.
OB	*Otherwise Than Being or Beyond Essence.* Trans. A. Lingis. The Hague: Martinus Nijhoff, 1981.
TA	*Le temps et l'autre.* Montpellier: Fata Morgana, 1979.
TeI	*Totalité et Infini.* The Hague: Martinus Nijhoff, 1961.
TI	*Totality and Infinity.* Trans. A. Lingis. Pittsburgh: Duquesne University Press, 1969.
TO	*Time and the Other.* Trans. R. A. Cohen. Pittsburgh: Duquesne University Press, 1987.
TrO	"The Trace of the Other." Trans. A. Lingis. In *Deconstruction in Context,* ed. M. C. Taylor, 345–59. Chicago: University of Chicago Press, 1986.

INTRODUCTION

Jeffrey Bloechl

Rather than summarize each contribution in this volume, I wish only to say a few things about their relation to one another, which of course does require me to mention briefly what each author has set out to do. My original intention as editor was simply to gather some older works perhaps less known in the Anglo-American world, augmented by some newer ones. To this I have added the idea of mixing contributions by authors on both sides of the Atlantic, with the obscure aim of asking whether there might be different trends or currents in reading Levinas. A more important dimension to this volume more or less imposed itself with the arrival of the contributions: as the table of contents clearly shows, Levinas can and often is read with greater attention to either the I–Other relation or to that other Other which the tradition has called "God." However, as many essays collected here make plain, this difference in orientation, whatever its justifications, need not be exclusive. This is no doubt more significant than any possible divide across the Atlantic.

The order in which the contributions appear also has a certain logic. Among those which are more focused on the I–Other relation, Didier Franck's "The Body of Difference" not only comments on a benchmark position established at the onset of Levinas's independent philosophy but also analyzes, and to some degree deconstructs, the manner in which Levinas found his way past Heidegger's fundamental ontology. As many commentators have urged, what is condensed and assumed in *Totality and Infinity* (1961) was worked out in great detail more than fifteen years earlier, in the texts presented here by Franck. Accordingly, Paul Moyaert's reading of the provocative phenomenology of eros appearing in *Totality and Infinity* can be situated already after the fact of that move past Heidegger. Let the reader be warned in advance: Moyaert's essay is no mere commentary on Levinas, but the sketch of an ethics which contests the one he finds contained within fifteen pages of Levinas's first great work. Some of the themes emerging there (corporeality, desire, vulnerability) are taken up again by Rudolf Bernet, who returns the discussion to Husserl—a Husserl who, moreover, proves unexpectedly, to some at least, subtle and resourceful on such matters. This touches on a hidden benefit from any reading of Levinas: one always returns to his various discussion partners with a more penetrating sense of their independent positions. This is also the style of Robert Bernasconi's intricate reading of Levinas and some critics on the difference between otherness as strange and otherness as alien. Having first given the floor to three of those critics—Derrida, Ricoeur, and Francis Jacques—Bernasconi then allows Levinas the right to respond powerfully, but with the result of better exposing a still deeper problem which Bernhard Waldenfels will have best understood and addressed. Bernasconi's essay moves between *Totality and Infinity* and *Otherwise Than Being or Beyond Essence* (1973). Michael Newman remains close to the latter book, along with some of its supporting essays. This was the period in which Levinas's philosophy of God emerged, both through an extension of already familiar ideas on infinity and exteriority, and through a renewal of his dialogue with Husserl, now specifically on time and sensibility. Knitting these two poles together, Newman's piece is also an occasion to gather the numerous strands of I–Other analysis hitherto dominating Levinas's work, thus opening discussion of the place that God has perhaps always occupied there. My own essay begins at nearly this same point, tracing Levinas's definition of the ethical relation outward into its more classically religious background or horizon. However, whereas Newman may be said to focus on defining the ethical relation which that religion seems to support, my own interest is more with situating that religion with respect to the forms of thinking from which it takes its distance, and then exploring its existential implications.

Those last two contributions of the first section of this volume are recognizably transitional, moving already from the ethical relation toward the question of God. The second section nonetheless starts anew, wishing above all to state some basic facts and explore some key connections before taking up debate and appropriation. Roger Burggraeve's contribution begins by reviewing some biographical information concerning Levinas's particular Jewish identity, which he himself termed "*mitnagged*" in origin and "intellectualist" in form. From there, Burggraeve moves quickly to Levinas's relation to Scripture, as learned at the hand of Chouchani (incidentally, also the teacher of Elie Wiesel),[1] and then to an exploration of the spirituality which this involves. Adriaan Peperzak's essay dovetails neatly with Burggraeve's but is far more exploratory in nature, sketching the contours of a Christianity at the far reaches of Levinas's ethical critique of metaphysical theology. Whereas Burggraeve calls for an intellectual lay Christianity paralleling Levinas's intellectual lay Judaism, Peperzak tries to reawaken a mysticism purged of foundations and totalization. The knot between a non-foundational religion, the non-totalizable community which this implies, and thus a non-violent concern for others, is also to be found in Merold Westphal's attempt to read Levinas partly in line with Augustine and Kierkegaard, but against a certain Hegel. It is probably Kierkegaard whom we associate most readily with the idea that, properly understood, a divine command is the sole event which can open us from universalization into a truly ethical singularity. Westphal finds this thought in Augustine's talk of an opening within our conscience to an otherness which memory can never recapture. The resonances between Levinas and Kierkegaard have often been noted; Westphal awakens us to the unmistakable echo of Augustine in Levinas's notion of an immemorial past (see Newman). The language of memory and immemorial moves away from the philosophical terminology of question and answer, and closer to the religious terminology of appeal and response. From this angle, Levinas's thinking on God presents itself as an approach to a Word voiced before memory and immune to recollection. If a philosophy of this immemorial Word is thus a philosophy which moves beyond, or better beneath, foundations, then the postfoundational thinking par excellence will be religious. This has long been the strategy of Jean-Luc Marion, who not only reformulates it here, and in updated form, but also with pains to state his debt to Levinas. A nearly opposite tack is taken by Rudi Visker, in a tour de force which draws mainly on a constructed dialogue between Levinas and Freud to assert that what emerges from the explosion of transcendental philosophy, itself possibly the last good candidate for foundationalism, is not religion at all, at least not in anything like its classical forms (see Westphal), but in fact something more like sheer pluralism with a weak option for paganism, but in any event reducible to, if I may invoke a word dropped at the end of my own essay, materialism. This possibility represents an appropriate point of departure for the final contribution to this volume, John Caputo's meditation on Derrida's *adieu* to Levinas. More than a good-bye, Derrida's final word is also wrapped up in a discrete network of associations anchoring the eulogy itself in a prolonged argument with Levinas that began with the question of the closure of metaphysics, moved through the implications for time and writing, and has now become explicitly political but also religious. To date, Levinas's political philosophy has received far too little attention, a state of affairs which is only now changing, with the appearance of collected essays in that direction.[2] It is not necessary to agree with the specifics of Derrida's analysis, and still less with his own politics, to be won over to the view that there is nonetheless a lurking political dimension to Levinas's entire *oeuvre*. Indeed, if it is true, as Caputo and Derrida suggest, that the question of the political is inextricable from the question of the religious, then this last essay serves not to close the book on Levinas, neither here nor elsewhere, but instead to convoke yet another reading of the claims set forth over more than fifty years and retraced here, in the present volume.

NOTES

1. On Chouchani, see S. Malka, *Monsieur Chouchani: L'enigme d'un maître du XXe siècle* (Paris: Ed. J.-C. Lattès, 1994). For a statement of his importance to Levinas, see E. Levinas, *Difficile Liberté: Essais sur le judaïsme* (Paris: Albin Michel, 1976), 373.

2. See, e.g., E. Levinas, *Alterité et transcendence* (Paris: Fata Morgana, 1995).

I
Relations with Others

1

The Body of Difference

Didier Franck

*Is there a path leading from originary time to the meaning of Being?
Is time itself manifest as the horizon of Being?* Heidegger poses these
two questions at the end of the existential analytic, where they interrupt *Sein und Zeit,* announcing the section entitled "Time and
Being," at the threshold of which fundamental ontology breaks off
provisionally but also, as it has happened, definitively. Can one, in
spite of this solution of continuity and the unachieved status of a
universal phenomenological ontology, still engage these questions,
describing the movement of thought which bears them and to which
they are opened and delivered?

In order to move from originary time to the meaning of Being, it
would be necessary for the former to be the condition of the possibility of comprehending the latter, as that toward which Being as such
is projected—in short, time must be the horizon of Being. But to ask
whether this is indeed so is to question beyond Being, rejoining the
Platonic theme of the *epekeina tes ousias.* Furthermore, to exceed
Being toward that which opens comprehension of it is to return to
the origin of the ontological difference, since to comprehend Being is
to comprehend *its* difference with beings. To conduct oneself beyond
Being is thus to found the ontological difference already at work
throughout the preparatory analytic of *Dasein,* which at that point
remains unfounded. The section "Time and Being" would thus have
had as its aim establishing the ontological difference in transcending
Being toward its horizon.[1]

This program was never carried out, and Heidegger eventually
renounced it. Is this to say that he struck up against insurmountable
difficulties in the way of achieving his goal? Is it impossible—and if
so, why—to deduce the ontological difference from a description of
the manner that *Dasein,* which is this very difference (since it is the

being that comprehends Being), occurs in Being by comprehending Being? In other words, can one describe the movement which, going from existence to the existent, makes ontological knowledge itself possible? All of these questions inherited from fundamental ontology are in the background of a book which Levinas published in 1947, entitled *De l'existence à l'existant*. Thus, we will attempt to respond to some of them by following his path to the Other.

Levinas has always claimed a Platonic heritage. "My teaching," he declared in 1987, "remains, in the final account, quite classical; it repeats, as in Plato, that it is not that consciousness founds the Good but that the Good calls to consciousness."[2] This claim does not close the book on philosophical research and enterprise. To the contrary, "the Platonic formula placing the Good beyond being is the most general and empty indication which guides them." This last phrase comes from the "Avant-Propos" of *De l'existence à l'existant*, the first moment in the philosophical itinerary of which *Autrement qu'être ou au-delà de l'essence* is undoubtedly the final accomplishment. Thus, the considerable evolution which Levinas's thinking has undergone is such that we may consider *De l'existence à l'existant* the first step in a project whose necessity was strong enough and deep enough to guarantee and assure an inner consistency.

It goes without saying that the Platonic formula situating the Good beyond Being is difficult to interpret. We will not involve ourselves in that exercise since for the moment all that matters is the specific sense which Levinas has given to it. "It signifies," he writes in the same "Avant-Propos," "that the movement which conducts an existent toward the Good is not a transcendence by which the existent is elevated to a superior existence, but a departure from being and the categories which describe it: an *ex-cendence*." This version of the *epekeina tes ousias* calls for several remarks. First, by "existent," Levinas indicates the being which we are, *Dasein*. But, as we will see, "existence" and "existent" also translate *Sein* and *Seiende*, Being and beings in general. Thus, for Levinas, the word "existent" designates the very beings (*étants*) whose modes of Being (*d'être*) Heidegger takes great pains to differentiate—an ambiguity testifying to an assimilation of *all* ontological structures to *categories*, a move which requires further explanation.[3] Second, if the movement beyond Being is not a transcendence toward a superior existence but a departure from Being, this implies on one hand that the transcendence of *Da-*

sein is not, as Heidegger maintains, the truth of the *epekeina tes ousias,* and that the *agathon* is not the source of possibility as such.[4] On the other hand, it also implies that the distinction between authentic and inauthentic existence is understood in terms of a distinction between the superior and inferior, which thus supposes a hierarchy within Being. Third, to this transcendence which is only a movement internal to the Same, the movement and the mobility of the Same, Levinas opposes a movement radically otherwise, a veritable departure from Being and its truth, a movement which never returns to the Same, an exodus without hope of return, or an *evasion,* as the 1935 essay bearing that title puts it, also proposing the neologism *excendence,* the motif of a departure from Being which "expresses the movement toward the Creator [*traduisait l'élan vers le Créateur*]" and necessitates the conclusion that "every civilization which accepts Being, the tragic despair which it bears, and the crimes that it justifies, deserves to be called barbarous."[5]

If there must be evasion, if the existent must exceed Being toward the Good if it is to find salvation and happiness, this is because it first has "a foot in Being," has already taken *position.* Without this taking of position, no excendence would be possible, which is why Levinas can evaluate Being and affirm that "it is better to be than not to be." Since excendence therefore proceeds from Being to the Good, it is necessary first of all to fix and understand the *terminus a quo,* the position of this existent in the existence which it is called to depart from. As the "Avant- Propos" states, the "present work limits itself" to clarifying this theme. This limitation, in turn, confers upon *De l'existence à l'existant* a preliminary status with respect to all of Levinas's subsequent work, since the movement by which an existent enters into a contract with existence precedes that by which that existent evades existence; to describe the position of the existent in existence is to describe the springboard for excendence, determining the meaning that Being is to receive when summoned to appear before the Good.

De l'existence à l'existant begins with a review of the difference between that which exists, the existent, and the very event of existing, existence. This difference which Heidegger raises and deposits at the beginning of *Sein und Zeit* is immediately understood by Levinas in terms of a difference between verb and substantive, or substantive participle. A grammatical interpretation of the ontological difference is presupposed throughout the work of Levinas, for whom the enduring grandeur of Heidegger's thought resides in having reawakened and restored the verbal sense of Being.

However, as the history of philosophy readily shows, the difference between Being and the being, between verb and substantive, is difficult to maintain because thought slips imperceptibly from being where a being is, to a Being which is the eminent cause of all beings. Where does this confusion come from? "The difficulty of separating Being and 'the being' and the tendency to see one in the other are certainly not accidental. They derive from the habit of situating the instant, atom of time, beyond every event." What does this mean? Being and the being must be distinguished without being separated: Being is the being of a being, and when we affirm of a being that it is, this implies that "the being has already made a contract with being" upon which it exercises "the same domination as the subject exercises on the attribute." Now this singular domination is accomplished "in the instant which, under phenomenological analysis, is irreducible [*indécomposable*]." Everything depends on how one understands this. Either the instant is conceived as a pure present state and Being is canceled by the being, or it is an event and the verb distinguishes itself from the substantive, manifesting the ontological difference. "One can ask oneself," writes Levinas, "whether this adherence of 'the being' to Being is simply given in the instant, whether it is not accomplished in the very *stance* of the instant, whether the instant is not the event itself by which in the pure act, in the pure verb to be, in *being in general*, a 'being' is posed, a substantive which is rendered its master; whether the instant is not the 'polarization' of *being in general*." But how to derive this event from the instant? "Commencement, origin, birth display a dialectic where this event at the heart of the instant becomes meaningful." In fact, when a being surges forth from Being—and from where could it do so if not from Being which, at this level, has an unquestionable priority—it is necessary to assign it a cause, but above all "to explain what in it receives existence" (*DE* 16/*EE* 18)—or so says Levinas, substituting *existence* for Being (*être*). Now what can this reception (*accueil*) of Being by a being mean, if not an act of that being on Being, and thus the mastery of the subject, *it*, over its attribute, *is*? It is thus by studying this dialectic that it will be possible to render to the instant its dramatic character as event. This, however, would not be possible without also defining a sense of "being in general" that becomes the Being of a particular being thanks to this "inversion" (*DE* 18/*EE* 18) which is the event of the instant, where what is first—Being (*l'être*)—becomes an attribute of what is second: a being. Hence does Levinas's project take the following course: accede to Being in general in order to analyze the position of the existent in existence.

This program issues from fundamental ontology, which "has defended perhaps only this one sole thesis: Being is inseparable from the comprehension of Being" (*TeI* 15/*TI* 45). Heidegger conceives of this as existence and being-in-the-world. Yet should we not dissociate existence and being-in-the-world? In fact, with the exception of mythology, when we do speak of a disruption of the world, or an end to the world, we designate a moment in which the world ceases to be coherent and our relations are interrupted. The residue of this quasi-reduction is neither the pure ego nor death as possibility of impossibility, but naked existence, the fact that one is and that there is Being (*être il y a*). Being-in-the-world is thus not synonymous with existence, since the disappearance of the former does not affect the latter. "In the situation of the end of the world, there is posed the primary relation which attaches us to Being." This relation does not join two substantives, but a substantive to a verb, an existent to existence. The end of the world manifests the fact of Being and that the existent exists in and through participating in it, taking up existence in an assumption preliminary to all commerce with the world, an "event of birth" anterior to being-in-the-world, and which, "considered in the context of economic life, where instants are equivalent and compensate for one another, occurs in all moments" (*DE* 26–27/*EE* 22).

To exist is thus to adhere to existence. But in order to distinguish the existent and existence, is it not necessary to view that adherence of one to the other as a cleavage? In other words: where are we to discover this adhesion of the existent to existence *in statu nascendi*? In fatigue and indolence, which are not in the first place contents of consciousness offered to reflection but attitudes of the existent toward existence. True fatigue is intransitive, without object, because it is weariness itself. To be tired is to tire of Being, and what tires is precisely existence. Fatigue is thus, in the modality of refusal, the proof of an unremitting obligation to be. "Existence in weariness is like the reminder of a commitment to exist, with all the seriousness and all the harshness of an interminable contract" (*DE* 31/*EE* 24). If being fatigued is at once to exist and to refuse to exist, to exist in abdication or in discharging oneself from existing, then weariness brings to light, with the movement by which the existent takes up existence, a cleavage between them which in the same stroke testifies to a contract binding them together. Let us note in passing how the meaning of the word *contract*, whose use Levinas does not justify, is unstable and indecisive, that is to say contradictory, since one of the contracting parties, the existent, derives from the contract, while the other, existence, is by nature without the possibility of subscribing to it or imposing it. Being does not enter into a covenant. In short, is it legitimate to speak of a contract, which moreover cannot be terminated, where the free and reciprocal consent to obligation among two or more parties is in principle impossible, and where all juridical reference is excluded since it is a matter solely of the position of the existent in existence and of the ontological difference? One can doubt it, and this doubt is not without importance, for to speak of a *contract* between the existent and existence, between a being and Being, is ultimately to subordinate the question "Why is there Being rather than nothing?" to the question "I have the right to be?" (*DVI* 257/ *GCM* 171)—a subordination which all, or almost all, of Levinas's work tries to sustain.

Indolence is also an attitude of the existent with respect to existence. It is indolence of existing. What does this mean? "Indolence concerns the beginning, as if existence were not there already, but preexisted the beginning in an inhibition" (*DE* 33/*EE* 26). Indolence is a hesitation to exist, the beginning of existence, but in the mode of retention. What, then, is it to begin to exist? The instant of the beginning can reveal itself only in that "there is already something to lose, for something is already possessed, if only this very instant itself" (*DE* 35/*EE* 27). The instant of the beginning maintains with itself a relation of possession, it is and it has, it belongs to itself and it takes itself up, and it is relative to the weight of existence that indolence has meaning. Existence is a burden, said Heidegger, without the analytic of *Dasein* having been able to render an account of its split into being and having.[6] Indolence and fatigue thus manifest, by way of a de-phasing, the contractual relation between the existent and existence. Nevertheless, whereas fatigue does apprehend existence and thus chafes at having "shouldered" it, indolence refuses that "shoul-

dering" itself (*DE* 39/*EE* 29).[7] But to speak of the existent's relation
to existence as one of "body to body" (*corps à corps*)—is this not to
suggest that the existent has a position in existence by virtue of having a body?

If the non-differentiation of Being and beings is provided by the
obliteration of the dramatic character of the instant, the task of grasping the meaning of a phenomenon within the general economy of
Being must begin by examining the instant of its event. "To scrutinize
the instant," writes Levinas, "to seek the dialectic which occurs in a
dimension hitherto unsuspected—such is the essential principle of
method that we have adopted" (*DE* 42/*EE* 30). It would only be at
great risk of misunderstanding for one to approach the thought of
Levinas, which always describes what it does, without close attention
to the support it receives from this method inherited—not merely
taken over, but transformed—from Husserl and Heidegger: a method
which consists in treating substantives as verbs or states of being as
events, and to which, finally, despite the presence of numerous gaps
of varying amplitude, he will always remain faithful. Accordingly, we
take up the analysis of fatigue, placing ourselves in the instant of its
event.

Fatigue is present as a kind of numbness (*engourdissement*), a
"constant and increasing lag [*décalage*] between the being and what
it is still attached to, like a hand which little by little releases something that it finds tiring to lift, releasing it in the same instant that it
tries to hold it" (*DE* 42/*EE* 30). Fatigue is not relief or relaxation pure
and simple, but, still bound to what it releases, a displacement of self
upon self, "a dislocation of the *I* from itself" (*DE* 50/*EE* 35). There is
fatigue only at the heart of an effort which "lunges forward out of it
and falls back on it" (*DE* 44/*EE* 31). What, then, is dramatic relation
between the "thrust" (*l'élan*) and fatigue, the relation whose very
tension constitutes effort? Effort is a thrust beyond oneself which
fatigue holds back: "in the advance over oneself and over the present,
in the ecstasis of the thrust which anticipates and bypasses the present, fatigue marks a delay with respect to oneself and to the present"
(*DE* 44/*EE* 31). Effort, delay with respect to oneself in the advance
over oneself, articulates thrust and fatigue, with fatigue conditioning
thrust, which projects itself forward only to be thrown back. Effort
thus cannot be reduced to a pure thrust which knows no fatigue; it
does not find its temporal meaning in the ecstasis of the future, but

is an "effort of the present that lags behind the present" (*DE* 45/ *EE* 31). The ecstatic temporality which flows from the future is thus submitted to a temporality of originary delay of which Levinas will eventually deploy all virtualities. Consequently, the account of fatigue will not have completed the existential analytic but in fact overturned it.

However, no account of the temporal structure of effort would be complete without describing its relation with the instant. To exert oneself is to exert oneself in duration. Every effort is a step-by-step engagement in duration. This is not continuous: in musical duration, for example, each note appears only to immediately disappear. The duration of effort is not that which Bergson and Husserl have analyzed. Its essential movement proceeds in fits and starts. "The duration of effort is made up entirely of stops." The instant of effort is thus neither that of a melody which is never present because it always passes and vanishes, nor that of the thrust which anticipates the future, but simply an ineluctable present. Effort is "caught up in the instant as an inevitable present." Effort accomplishes the stance of the instant; "in the midst of the anonymous flow of existence, there is stoppage and positing" (*DE* 48/*EE* 34).

This definition of the instant of effort—and through it Levinas also applies himself to an account of the dynamism of the thrust toward authentic possibility (*la possibilité propre*)—permits a deduction of the notions of act and activity, situating them in the general economy of Being. If effort accomplishes the instant, to act is not to struggle with matter but to take up a present. And this present is not an intratemporal now, a substantive, but a "function" (*TA* 32/*TO* 52), an event of existence by which something is born from itself, the event of a departure from self and return to self, the very work of identity. In effect, to act is to assume existence, and this assumption both flows from existence and returns to it, as the existent appears in subjugating it.

Effort, correlate of the act, is always an effort upon fatigue, which is fatigue of existing, and "the lag of the existent behind existing." Now this "lag" (*retard*) constitutes the present which effort takes up. To act is to take up a present lagging behind itself, and without this lag the relation of the existent to existence would not appear. In this way, fatigue, as the present lagging behind itself, makes possible a description of the "hypostasis," the transmutation of the verbal into the substantive, or of existence into an existent, thus in the same stroke also yielding a deduction of the ontological difference. Levinas draws the necessary conclusion: "If the present is thus constituted by the taking charge of the present, if the time-lag [*décalage*] of fatigue creates the interval in which the event of the present can occur, and if this event is equivalent to the upsurge of an *existent* for whom *to be* means *to take up Being*, the existence of the existent is essentially act" (*DE* 51/*EE* 35). Indeed, even when inactive the existent is always active. What is the meaning of this originary activity through which alone the worldly opposition of action and inaction has meaning? Echoing Husserl's reference to an archi-immobile ground which he calls "Earth"—absolute where I live my body and relative to which I can move or come to a rest—Levinas understands this primary sense of activity as "the act of positing oneself on the ground," as an abiding (*repos*) insofar as this is "not pure negation but the very tension of position, the bringing about of a *here*" (*DE* 51–52/*EE* 36). The event of abiding is thus the very surging of a being on Being: the "hypostasis." *De l'existence à l'existant* attempts only to clarify the implications of this localization, the *here* which posits itself and abides.

However, this interpretation of act as assumption of the present raises another problem. Whereas in assuming the instant through effort we engage ourselves in the existence which is event and pure verb, in the concrete world we are involved with things, with substantives. In other words, the ontological function of the act cannot be identical with its occurrence in the world.

Objects in the world are objects of intentions. How are we to understand this? According to Levinas, the notion of intention must not be taken, as it has by Husserl, "in a neutralized and disincarnate sense," but "in its ordinary sense, with the sting of desire which animates it" (*DE* 56/*EE* 37). Setting aside our reservations at this disincarnation of Husserlian intentionality, let us describe Levinas's sense of intention characterizing our being-in-the-world. When, for example, I desire something to eat, I know perfectly well what I want, and I am wholly present to what I desire, "without ulterior references." It is not only that an intention is aimed at an object, but also that the object is at our disposal. If the world is what is given to us, this implies that we receive it, that objects are destined to us, offered to our intentions, and possessed even before being desired.

In the world, desire is in a certain sense always at its end. To eat is thus to have an experience of "complete correspondence between desire and its satisfaction," a "full realization of its intention" (*DE* 65/ *EE* 43). Daily bread is not, as Heidegger thought, a tool ready to hand,[8] not something *in order to . . .* which refers to something else and finally to care for Being, but the very consummation of the intention. It is not that we eat *in order to* live, but that eating simply is living, so that intention defines being-in-the-world because it has an end. Intention, or consciousness, is always "sincere," for it "describes a closed circle where it remains by effacing every ulterior finality" (*DE* 68/*EE* 44–45). The world, which is this circle, is not a complex of tools but an ensemble of nourishments—"these are the nourishments which characterize our existence in the world" (*TA* 46/*TO* 63). Being-in-the-world is not care but enjoyment, and it is "before" being-in-the-world that we can implicitly comprehend, without the light of sincerity, the verbal sense of existence. Consequently, everyday being-in-the-world, far from being a fall into inauthenticity, permits one "to extract oneself from anonymous being" (*DE* 69/*EE* 45).

Being-in-the-world is this "extraction" because the intention thanks to which the ego possesses the given preserves a distance from it. While the existent is "enthralled" (*envoûté*) by the existence which "adheres to it," the world offered to the intention "leaves the ego a freedom with regard to it," such that existence is always a burden which encumbers us and which we must always be concerned with, a burden deposited and yet also still present in that way, like "left luggage." Tending toward things, the ego can also withdraw from them and, in the world, has "an inside and outside" (*DE* 73/*EE* 47; cf. also 36/27). That by which one person refers to another is meaning, or "luminosity." Light is constitutive of the world, since through it the object, "while coming from without, is already ours in the horizon which precedes it" (*DE* 76/*EE* 48). Intention and light, being-in-the-world is knowledge, and this in the manner of a relating oneself to things and events without attaching oneself to them— freely keeping one's distance, one's reserve. The *epoche* is therefore no longer the avenue to a pure extramundane ego, but rather the mode of being of an intramundane ego. This makes it understandable that for Levinas being-in-the-world is, "at the heart of being, the possibility of detaching oneself from Being" (*DE* 79/*EE* 50), how the hypostasis as consciousness and consciousness as intention, light, and knowledge, is an evasion of existence in the verbal sense, a "resistance to anonymous being" (*DE* 80/*EE* 51).

But why resist anonymous being? We cannot respond to this question without describing the verbal sense of existence which is the "central notion" (*DE* 80/*EE* 51) of the work whose course we are following. However, to the degree that this existence is not confused with being-in-the-world, it is necessary first to show that we can depart from the world, or disinterest ourselves in it. Art, understood as exoticism in the proper sense of the term, is this possibility. Art removes things from the order of use. Whereas perception gives us mundane objects, art "departs from the level of perception in order to reinstate sensation," and "instead of arriving at the object, the intention gets lost in the sensation itself" (*DE* 85/*EE* 53). Sensation leads away from the object; it is not material offered to apprehension but "the impersonality of the *element*" (*DE* 86/*EE* 53). Deforming their luminous and rational forms, which convert exteriority into interiority, art—and it is above all modern art to which Levinas refers—transports objects into an exteriority without a correlative interiority. It discovers "the materiality of Being" (*DE* 92/*EE* 57), "it brings about an absolute existence in the very fact that there is something which is not in its turn an object or a name" (*DE* 91/*EE* 57). The exoticism of art thus manifests in the unformed world the "formless proliferation" (*DE* 92/*EE* 57) which precedes it.

If art reveals the absoluteness of the fact of existing, it still does not describe it and does not yield an analysis of the idea. To do this, we must begin by imagining that everything is annihilated. The return of all existents, of all substantives, to nothingness is an event. But then, what are we to think of this nothingness itself? Is it an ultimate substantive, a final state? Is it not, to the contrary, the privileged moment in which it is necessary to deploy the method which approaches states as events? What occurs when one treats nothingness as an event? Nothing more than this: something is happening. Now this "something is happening" does not refer to a substantive; its indeterminateness is not that of a subject. "Like the third person impersonal pronominal of a verb, it designates not the poorly understood author of an action, but the character of the action itself, which somehow has no author. This impersonal, anonymous, yet inextinguishable 'consummation' of being which murmurs in the depths of nothingness itself, we shall designate with the term *there is* [*il y a*].

The *there is*, inasmuch as it resists an impersonal form, is 'being in general' " (*DE* 93–94/*EE* 57).[9]

The *there is* thus designates existence without existents, the pure verbality of the verb of verbs. Three reasons can have motivated Levinas's choice of this expression. The first would be that *il y a* is a locution which signifies Being; it says Being without repeating the word itself. The second would be that in French *il y a* can have the status of a preposition, and since it is a matter here of describing the position of the existent in existence, it would indeed be necessary to invoke pre-position. The third and most important reason, however, would be that in understanding Being as *il y a*, Levinas is able to point toward impersonality, anonymity, and neutrality. As determined by the expression *il y a*, Being is conceived outside of all relation to the being—thus as Being in general. Having adopted this expression, Levinas never reconsiders it. It recurs regularly throughout his subsequent work, including in the first lines of *Autrement qu'être ou au-delà de l'essence*. Accordingly, the determination of Being as *there is* represents the constant ontological premise by which Being can be subordinated to the Good and ontology to ethics.

Can one have an experience of the *there is*? "Were it not for the fact that the term experience is inapplicable to a situation which involves the absolute exclusion of light, we could say that night is the very experience of the *there is*" (*DE* 94/*EE* 58). In this night which can in fact take place during the day, things no longer have contour or form, and names have lost their deictic power. Nothing is given anymore, but that universal absence is an unavoidable presence: "nothing responds to us but this silence; the voice of this silence frightens us like the infinite spaces which Pascal speaks of" (*DE* 95/*EE* 58). But there is more. The night engulfs and submerges the ego itself. To accede to the *there is* is to accede to Being which is no longer the attribute of any being, to existence of which no existent is the master. To be exposed to the night is to be deposed of oneself—the *there is* is not an "*en soi*" but a "*sans soi*" (*TA* 27/*TO* 49)—it is to be brought back to "what cannot disappear, to the very fact of being in which *one* can participate, for better or worse, without having taken the initiative, anonymously" (*DE* 95/*EE* 58). In opening us to Being, the night revokes our capacity to say *I*. The *one* is no longer the pronoun declining the identity which existence forfeits to the existent, but a *one* which, following upon the monopolization of that existent by the existence in which it participates, has lost all identity. With this, one of the major contributions of the existential analytic is reversed.

How does one participate in the night of the *there is*? Participation here must not be understood in the Platonic sense but rather in that which Lévy-Bruhl has given to it. According to that latter sense, the separation between the one who participates and that in which one participates is effaced: "one term *is the other*" (*DE* 99/*EE* 60). When the existent participates in existence, it *is* the verb and loses all its substantiveness. This participation arouses horror, since it "strips" the subject of his or her subjectivity. Participation in the *there is,* horror "turns the subjectivity of the subject, his particularity as a *being,* inside out" (*DE* 100/*EE* 61). Horror is thus revelation of the *there is* just as anxiety is the revelation of nothingness, of being. But this analogy is only functional, and one misses in Levinas's thought attention to the fact that for Heidegger horror is close to anxiety.[10] For Heidegger, horror is preliminary to anxiety since whereas the first is grasped through absence of self, the second manifests the true self. Horror takes hold by depriving the existent of a self. Anxiety confronts the existent with its self. The former is a quasi-psychotic dispossession of self, the latter is the principle of individuation. Horror does not suppose the self to which anxiety attests in its truth. For Levinas, horror is anterior to the ontological difference which anxiety accomplishes in all its propriety. Horror of Being thus precedes anxiety before Being, and this priority signifies, in the final account, the priority of the analysis of the hypostasis over the analytic of *Dasein.* In this respect, to understand what distinguishes horror from anxiety is, within the horizon of the project of deducing the ontological difference, to measure the scope of the transformation worked upon Heidegger's fundamental ontology by the ontology of Levinas.

But Levinas speaks without differentiation of both horror at Being (*l'horreur de l'être*) and horror of Being (*l'horreur d'être*) (cf. *DE* 102 and 103 n/63 and n).[11] Are these the same thing? Should we not rather distinguish them? Horror at Being signifies a horror before the abstract Being of all beings, whereas horror of being signifies horror of being a being. The horror of life must not be confused with the horror of living—a parallel justified by Levinas's remark that "life appears as the prototype of the relation between existence and the existent" (*DE* 29/*EE* 23). Where, then, does the assimilation of these two horrors come from?

If horror reveals the *there is*, horror at Being and horror of Being must be correlatives of, respectively, the evil in Being (*mal de l'être*) and the evil of Being (*mal d'être*) which Levinas opposes in his introduction to *De l'existence à l'existant*. Evoking the relation of the existent to existence, he writes that it "constitutes an event whose reality and in some sense surprising character manifest themselves in the disquiet in which it occurs," and adds that "the evil in being, the evil of matter in idealist philosophy, becomes the evil of being" (*DE* 19/*EE* 19). Leaving aside our reservations at this "evil of matter," a concept which is rather more Plotinian than idealist in *stricto sensu*, let us note that only this identification of the evil in Being (*mal de l'être*) with the evil of Being (*mal d'être*) makes it possible to confuse horror at Being (*l'horreur de l'être*) with horror of Being (*l'horreur d'être*). And Levinas himself confirms this when, still in his introduction, he defines the whole of his project as follows: "We shall try to place in question the idea that evil is defect (*défaut*). Does being contain no other vice than its limitation and nothingness? Is there not a sort of underlying evil in its very positivity? Is not anxiety over being (*l'angoisse devant l'être*)—horror at being (*l'horreur de l'être*)—just as primordial as anxiety over death? Is not fear of being as primordial as fear for being? It is perhaps even more so, for the former may account for the latter" (*DE* 20/*EE* 20). The assimilation of horror at Being to horror of Being, and the primacy of this latter over anxiety, thus depends on the thesis that Being is functionally vicious and malignant.

However, this interpretation of Being, while supporting all of Levinas's work, is never justified. To be sure, Levinas dedicates himself to exceeding ontology toward ethics, but insofar as he will not have demonstrated that "being is evil" (*TA* 29/*TO* 51)[12]—insofar as the malignancy of Being which renders *ethically* necessary an excendence toward the Good will not have been *ontologically* established— the entire effort risks promoting a false departure and ruinous evasion. But is such a demonstration possible? Nothing could be less certain. If, in stating that "the being is" I affirm the mastery of that being (*l'étant*), as subject, over Being (*l'être*) as an attribute, then in stating that "Being is evil" I affirm the mastery of Being over evil. Placed in the position of the subject, Being will always be something other than evil, so that to say "being is evil" will never equate with "evil is being." To be sure, Being is not yet the Good, but it is also no longer evil. The being of evil is not the evil of Being; to admit, as for example Schelling did, that evil is founded in Being is not to admit that Being founds nothing but evil or that evil is the foundation of Being. The functional malignancy of Being in general, of the *there is*, is undemonstrable, and the proposition "Being is evil," which in any event cannot be taken for a speculative proposition since this would be to substitute the ontology of Hegel for that of Heidegger, both supports itself and annuls itself.[13]

The foregoing objections do not touch on the determination of Being as *there is*, but on the qualification of its neutrality as inhuman.[14] The neutrality of Being is not a violent neutralization of humanity, and "accepting being," if this is even meaningful, is not an act of "barbary." Can one thus accede to the *there is* otherwise than through horror? It can appear through poetry, says Levinas, appealing to Shakespeare, on whom "the whole of philosophy is but a meditation," and to Poe, for whom "the horror at being buried alive," at being brought back to the heart of nothingness, constitutes the fundamental emotion.[15] We entrust to Yves Bonnefoy the task of manifesting the *there is* wholly otherwise:

Let us imagine that this human society—in which we today declare that ontology has only been a dream, that the "main pillar" is only a simple mass of vapors, sometimes even toxic, the person nothing but a mask which, as the Latins already knew, concealed only an absence— is, by some disastrous event, reduced to a handful of survivors harshly tested from moment to moment by a constant tide of peril. In these moments of scarcity and haste, the survivors would decide upon a course of action and distribute tasks, but the first decision, taken without even thinking, in the new and incontestable evidence of lived experience, would be that *there is being [il y a de l'être]*: could such beings, under that crumbling rock, doubt that the relation to oneself, even if nothing else founds it, is original and self-sufficient? And the horizon around them, however ruined and unsuited to nourish dreams, *would be*, from the very first, how it had been forgotten that something could be, from which it follows that in that presence one could all at once recognize *that which is*, that which responds to our simple needs, that which is taken up in our project, which permits exchange, and which must have first occurred in finding its place in language: in short, the aspects of a place, the instruments of labor, tomorrow perhaps the elements of a feast—one will thus say bread and wine. Being is the first-born of need.[16]

The situation imagined by Bonnefoy is almost identical to that which Levinas imagined. Between these two cases, it is a matter of envisioning the end of the world, interpreted as everyday and economic in the limited sense of the term. Still more, Bonnefoy, by granting right to nihilism, as the volatilization of Being, distinguishes the *there is Being* from *that which is*—thus Being from beings, with the latter recognized only in the horizon of the former, determined as presence—also manages to heed the ontological difference. And yet, the contrast between the two descriptions could not be more vivid. According to Bonnefoy, the *there is Being* is given by a tacit decision made in the light of evidence. A diurnal *there is* is therefore possible, which proves not only that the *there is* is not necessarily restricted to horror, which on the contrary it brings to an end, but also that the *there is* itself—Being—is not essentially "horrifying."[17]

Let us return more directly to the analysis of the hypostasis and to the deduction of the ontological difference. The impossibility of supporting existence is patent in the experience of insomnia. "One watches when there is nothing to watch and despite the absence of any reason to keep watching" (*DE* 109/*EE* 65). Though without any object, and even because of that, the vigilance of insomnia rivets us to the unrelenting work of Being. Accordingly, this is an insomnia and a watchfulness of the *there is*. However, to attribute vigilance to Being is not to endow it with consciousness, "for one must ask whether vigilance defines consciousness, or if consciousness is not rather the possibility of tearing itself loose from vigilance" (*TA* 29–30/ *TO* 51). In other words, vigilance is mine only through participation in Being. "In insomnia, it is not *my* vigilance in the night, it is the night itself which watches. It watches" (*DE* 111/*EE* 66). Insomnia is thus an event which, when it arrives, does not arrive to *me*, an event which does not strike a subject as such, but the subject in its subjectivity. To be sure, it is difficult to fulfill an intuition of meaning such that "it watches," but this is because anterior to the ego capable of intuition it is no longer a matter of a phenomenon in the proper sense of the word. "Here, description," says Levinas, situating his work in relation to that of Husserl, "makes use of terms whose consistency it tries precisely to go beyond; it stages *personages*, whereas the *there is* is their dissipation. This is the index of a method where thought is invited beyond intuition" (*DE* 112/*EE* 66). This invitation, however, is not to the Kantian Idea in which intuition is postponed infinitely, for Levinas's description of the scene suggests a backstage. Such a method exceeds the strict limits of descriptive phenomenology even while appealing to it. But is this not also true of Husserl's analyses of time, the Other, and the body, and is not phenomenology, in the twists and turns of its development, characterized by the fact that it never ceases to take distance from itself, but with the gaps which thus emerge belonging to it in the end?

Insomnia without subjectivity is primary. The question is thus how the subject arises. Awakened, consciousness participates in the vigilance of the *there is*. But then it only participates there, and always preserves the possibility of sleeping again. "Consciousness is the possibility of sleeping" (*TA* 30/*TO* 51). Still, is it not paradoxical to define consciousness by the unconscious? Everything depends on the manner in which their relation is conceived. The unconscious, the discovery of which gives evidence of "a considerable intellectual upheaval" (*DE* 57/*EE* 38), is not the absolute contrary of consciousness. The one communicates with the other. In fact, bound to effort, consciousness cannot fail to tire and fade into unconsciousness. "In its very intentionality, it can be described as issuing from an underlying depth, like the power which the poet Vorge de Jules Romains has called the power of 'breaking camp from the inside' [*f . . . le camp par l'intérieur*]."[18] Hence are we not to separate this withdrawal of consciousness toward the unconscious and its emergence back out of it, and not only because "reservations murmur in the very activity of thought" but above all because the present of effort "catches up with itself in a lag behind itself, or accomplishes a retreat, a rebound, in the simplicity of its stroke" (*DE* 116/*EE* 68). Levinas thus attributes to consciousness, as a "fading away at the very point of its luminosity" (*DE* 117/*EE* 68), the temporality which Freud reserves for the unconscious. Consciousness is therefore not a function of the unconscious, but the unconscious is the power of consciousness.

Far from being incompatible with Descartes's position on the matter, this interpretation of consciousness restores to it, against Heidegger's critique, a phenomenological truth. In effect, the *cogito* signifies that I am a thing that thinks, *sum res cogitans*. Levinas comments, "the word *thing* is here admirably precise. The most profound teach-

ing of the Cartesian *cogito* consists in discovering thought as substance, that is to say as something that is posited. Thought has a point
of departure. There is not only a consciousness of localization, but
also a localization of consciousness which is not in turn reabsorbed
into consciousness, into knowledge" (*DE* 117/*EE* 68). Consciousness
is thus *here*, and this *here* does not presuppose the objective space
which, to the contrary, it makes possible. But if consciousness is also
possibility to sleep, is there then an essential bond between sleep
and place? To attest to such a bond phenomenologically requires one
to reach that place after awakening, having left sleep. To sleep is to
suspend all activity. However, this suspension does have one condition, since in order to go to sleep one must first lie down. And "to lie
down is precisely to limit existence to a place, to position." The place
where I finally lie down in order to sleep is neither geometric and in
that sense "somewhere" nor the place of a bed taken up as a tool, but
simply "a base, a *condition*" (*DE* 119/*EE* 69), an establishment and a
manner of being. Consciousness thus occurs from position. There is
no position of consciousness, nor indeed of the unconscious, because
consciousness is position and the unconscious belongs to it. "The
localization of consciousness is not subjective but the subjectivization
of the subject" (*DE* 118/*EE* 69). The subject constitutes itself as substance in positing itself and resting on a base, and it is in and as
position that it sets a foot in being. Ecstasis is then no longer the
event by which the existent takes up existence, rehabilitating substance, or better substantiality: Levinas has assumed a means to assimilate, as we have already seen, existantialia (of *Dasein*) with
categories, calling into question another central distinction in fundamental ontology.

As the seat of the subject, the *here* of this base is essentially different from the existential *there*. The *there* of being-there, of *Dasein*,
implies the world and is a mode of temporalization, whereas "the
here of position precedes all comprehension, every horizon, and all
time" (*DE* 122/*EE* 71). Before characterizing this pretemporal position any further, it is necessary to underline the importance of an
affirmation which marks the abandoning of phenomenology, the horizon of which is the vital element, and which signifies, already before
Heidegger saw it, the irreducibility of the spatiality of the existent to
ecstatic temporality.[19] This said, one wants to know: from where does
the base receive its status as base? From the body which takes posi-

tion there. To conceive of the *here* as base is to make of the body "the very future of consciousness." The body is not a posited thing, a substantive, but position itself, an event. The body "is the irruption in anonymous being of the very fact of localization" (*DE* 122/*EE* 71). Originarily localizing or spatializing, the body "is the manner in which man engages himself in existence, the manner in which he posits himself." It is thus in the body and through the body that is accomplished "the very transformation of the event into a being" (*DE* 123/*EE* 72), of the verb into a substantive. The body is the event of positing, hypostasis, "a term which, in the history of philosophy, designates the event by which the act expressed by a verb becomes a being designated by a substantive" (*DE* 140–41/*EE* 82), in short, the ontological difference *in statu nascendi*. As position, the body is body of difference.

But what does it mean that the position of the body is prior to time? Position is "the very event of the instant as present" (*DE* 124/*EE* 72). What does this mean? Ordinarily, time is conceived as an infinite sequence of events. But if the instant is inscribed in the order of time between the before and the after, it can also occur purely from out of itself. "This way for the instant to occur is to be present." Without a past because it is initial, and without a future because it is evanescent, the present instant issues from itself and refers only to itself. It severs the line of time as duration, and this caesura creates a situation in which "there is not only being in general but also a being, a subject" (*DE* 125/*EE* 73). It is because it is of itself in both origin and end that the present instant is the event of position, hypostasis.

This description of the present instant no longer comprehends it within the temporal horizon or as if the relation between Being and time were evident. The instant subordinated to time is a matter of indifference, but the present instant is central. Now if the present is central, if it is the instant par excellence, this is because before being bound to equivalent instants preceding or succeeding it, it is the act by which the existent conquers existence. The event of the instant is not relative to other instants, but to Being. Taken in itself, in its discontinuity and according to its proper drama, outside of time, the present instant is "a relation with Being, an initiation into Being" (*DE* 130/*EE* 76).

As relation to Being, the present instant is always a beginning, a birth. But if to begin is to come to oneself in departing from nowhere, there is no prenatal instant and the paradox of the beginning determines the present instant itself "of which the point of departure is contained in the point of arrival, as a rebound movement [*un choc en retour*]" (*DE* 131/*EE* 76). The present instant which arrives and recoils back into itself is thus articulated as internally dephased.

The relation to Being occurring in the instant is absolute; duration cannot affect it, since the initial character of the present, where the being breaks from Being, is a function of its evanescence. How, then, to describe the absoluteness of the relation between the existent and existence accomplished in the instant? This relation is absolute because nothing can destroy its "definiteness" (*DE* 133/*EE* 78). The instant cannot release itself from Being since it is in taking charge of Being that it is constituted. Abstracting from its relation to time, it is in itself that the present has charge over Being. But the fact that Being is taken charge of in the instant implies that that instant occurs as a return to itself since, as pure beginning, it is lag behind itself recaptured by itself. The self-reference of the present which is present thus signifies an identification: "The return of the present to itself is the affirmation of the I already bound to itself, already folded back onto a *self*" (*DE* 135–36/*EE* 79). The present as event of the origin turns back into a substance originally possessed, back into an *I*. The *I* is thus the definitive mode in which is effectuated the taking up of existence in the present. This is why "it *is*, and yet remains inassimilable to an object" (*DE* 136/*EE* 79).

How does this self-reference of the present instant found itself on the positing of which it is the event? The present instant is a stop: it interrupts the flow of time in proceeding from itself, and the relation with Being which it accomplishes is definitive. And the present cuts through duration because its constitutive "contact" with Being has no place in the passage from one instant to another. "The essential in the instant is its *stance*" (*DE* 133/*EE* 77). What is signified in this halt, or better, what is the event of this stance? "The 'halt' of the present is the very effort of positing in which the present rejoins and assumes itself" (*DE* 137/*EE* 80). The effort of positing must not be confused with the effort directed on the world, since this latter presupposes it. If the world poses resistance to effort, "the spot trampled in a subject's taking position sustains the effort not only as resistance, but also as base, as condition for the effort" (*DE* 138/*EE* 81). The subject is not anterior to the position which, resisting the effort of which it is at the same time the condition, surges precisely there where it acts. Positing is thus an act without transcendence, and "this effort which does not transcend constitutes the present or the 'I' " (*DE* 138/*EE* 81), since this is an effort which makes possible all effort, and since all effort assumes the instant as lag behind itself recaptured by itself, or in short, as reference to itself. The existent is thus no longer an ecstatic being outside itself, but a substance folded back on its base of departure, with transcendence henceforth founded in "the non-transcendence of position" (*DE* 173/*EE* 100) the event of which is the body.

Comprised as substance and substantive, subjectivity holds the *there is* and the verb in its power. The existing subject is master over its attribute, existence. Does this amount to saying that it is free? In the world, the ego is free because, keeping a distance from objects, it can always detach itself from them. The freedom of intentional consciousness is that of "non-engagement" and "refusal of the definitive" (*DE* 143/*EE* 84). However, this remains a conditioned freedom, for it "does not spare me from what is definitive for my very existence, from the fact that I am always with myself" (*DE* 144/*EE* 84). Freed from the *there is,* the existent is chained to itself. It is definitively alone, refuses all multiplicity. The ego is the captive of the self, and "the impossibility for the ego not to be itself marks its tragic function" (*DE* 143/*EE* 84). Is time not therefore called to break this solitude founded on the relation to Being accomplished in the present instant, and to deliver us from the "tragic in Being" (*le tragique d'être*), as assimilated to what is "tragic about Being" (*le tragique de l'être*) (*DE* 134/*EE* 78 and 147/86)?[20] But is the time where nothing is definitive the relation with the other person?

This question plays a pivotal role in the general economy of Levinas's project. In effect, if the other person is necessary for the constitution of time, recourse to ethics is an ontological exigency. Ethics would then, and for ontological reasons, articulate itself upon ontology—whose reign it would thus extend and to which it would remain subordinate. This is why, when it is a matter of exceeding Being toward the Good, it does not suffice to refer ontologically to ethics. The necessity of the passage beyond Being must be justified, before all else, ethically. In other words: the Good is the *terminus ad quem* of excendence because Being is evil.

The thesis that Being is evil, presupposed the whole length of Levinas's thought, reappears precisely at the moment when time is called to break the solitude of the hypostasis. "Solitude," he thus writes, "is accursed not of itself, but by reason of its ontological significance as something definitive. Reaching the other person is not justified of itself. It does not shake me out of my boredom. Ontologically, it is the event of the most radical breakup of the very categories of the ego, for it is for me to be elsewhere than in myself, it is to be pardoned, to not be a definitive existence" (*DE* 144/*EE* 85). To say that solitude is an evil by reason of the definitive contact with Being of which it is the event, and that to be faced by the other person is to be pardoned from Being, since the other person breaks what is definitive about my being: is this not to say that the ego is in fault only for being and that Being is evil? It is thus beginning from the identification of Being and evil that time can and must be thought as relation to the other person.

In order to do this, we are to begin by returning to the ego which remains identical to itself through its many states. What is the meaning of this identity? It is not that of a substance modified by its accidents, for such would be to remand substantial identity to an infinite regression. The identity of the ego is that of knowledge, as the relation of interiority to an exteriority which does not alter interiority. The *I* is identical to itself because the variation of what affects it does not penetrate its reserve (*quant-à-soi*) and does not concern its being, because it is consciousness. The subject is therefore substance because, positing itself without ever becoming Other, it is not engaged by the changing of its accidents—in short, because it is free. "The freedom of the 'I' is its substantiality" (*DE* 149/*EE* 87).

However, the identity of the *I* must not be abstracted from the event of identification accomplished by position and the present. Now, if the substantial subject is free, it is—in the self-reference of the present, prisoner of itself. At the instant of its initiation in Being, the subject is thus free and not free, taking charge and taken in charge. But this charge can be a charge only within the horizon of a possible discharge. Consequently, it is necessary that, as freedom, the present is conceived as presentiment, as hope of freedom. "The thought or the hope of freedom explains the despair which characterizes the engagement in existence in the present" (*DE* 152/*EE* 88–89).

But is to hope also to open up a future? In order to answer this question, it is necessary first to describe the drama proper to the instant of hope, thus specifying the manner in which it aims at time. Hope is not the expectation of a happy future; expectation can be certain, hope would not be. Nor is it relative to a future insofar as compensating for present suffering, for this would presuppose an equivalence between instants, and thus an economic time exterior to the subject, where all pain merits repayment. Hope is meaningful as hope only when hope is no longer permitted, so that in saying that Abraham hoped against all hope, St. Paul will have defined not only faith but the act of hope.[21] The "irreparable" is the "natural atmosphere" of hope, and "what is irreparable in the instant of hope is that it is even present" (*DE* 153/*EE* 89)—in other words, that it is a relation to Being. To hope is to hope for the present, to hope for the reparation of the irreparable, and since the irreparable is the evil of Being, "the true object of hope is the Messiah or salvation" (*DE* 156/ *EE* 91).

If to hope is to hope in the present instant for redemption from the evil of Being of which that same instant is the event, the need for salvation proper to the present instant can find its response only in another instant, an instant to come, in time. The future is thus not an invitation to die, but a "resurrection of the present" (*DE* 157/*EE* 92). How are we to understand this? Since the relation to Being that is accomplished in the instant is definitive, the instant to come hoped for in the present instant, as its deliverance, must free the existent from the definitive character of its relation to Being; it must untie the knot to Being which constitutes the instant as present. "What is called 'the following instant' is an annulment of the unimpeachable commitment to existence made in the instant, the resurrection of the 'I' " (*DE* 157/*EE* 92). How can this resurrection which the subject hopes for as its freedom be produced? To resurrect is to start again as an Other. From where comes this alterity which the subject captive of itself is in principle incapable of, and which must save it from the evil of Being that is consubstantial with the solitude of its hypostasis? If the whole of the subject is found here, in the present instant, then resurrection can come only from an other person who can pardon me of the evil that I am. This is why the irruption of the other person signifies the rupture of the ego, for to be otherwise than oneself is to be pardoned of Being and to no longer be a definitive existence. Freedom thus consists "in having one's being *pardoned*" (*DE*

161/*EE* 94), in being absolved by the other person of the evil simply in Being. In *Totalité et Infini,* Levinas will say more pointedly that the pardon is the time whose primary event is constituted by resurrection (*TeI* 259–60/*TI* 283). Time is thus no longer knotted to Being, but to the other person; it is no longer the horizon of Being but, beyond Being, the relation to the Other [*autre*] and to the Good.

The analysis of hypostasis aims at determining the meaning of a being within the economy of Being, and of deducing their difference. However, this task, required by the fundamental ontology which simply deposits the difference between beings and Being at its threshold (cf. *DE* 141/*EE* 83), was also impossible for it, since the deduction of the ontological difference as position implies, by extension, a critique of the entire existential analytic and, beyond that, the subordination of Being to the Good. In this respect, to deduce the ontological difference is to justify the incomplete status of *Sein und Zeit.*

As necessary as it is, Levinas's enterprise is not without difficulties. In interpreting the difference between Being and beings in terms of a distinction between the verbal and the substantive, does he not— and this is the first difficulty—reduce the ontological difference to another difference which in fact derives from it? This objection would be admissible if the verbal sense of Being were itself conceived grammatically as the noun of an action or a noun which adds to its meaning a temporal sense. This, however, it certainly does not do, since time frees us from purely verbal Being, and since "the function of the verb does not consist in naming, but in producing language, that is, in bringing forth the seeds of poetry which overwhelm 'existents' in their position and in their very positivity" (*DE* 140/*EE* 82).

The second difficulty pertains to the "dialectical" character of the method employed by Levinas. Being "has its own dialectic," and analysis has as its object the dialectic of the instant, effort, time, and the social relation (cf. *DE* 42/*EE* 30, 44/31, and 160/93; and *TA* 18/*TO* 39–40). But if dialectic is at once both the form and the content of description, can Levinas attack the ontology of Heidegger without falling into that of Hegel? Without any doubt, since by defining dialectic as "delayed evidence"[22] and as originary delay, Levinas turns dialectic itself back against Hegel. In effect, if the system of science rests on the apprehension of the true not as substance but as subject, then the analyses of the position of the subject, its substantiality, and its freedom will all be preliminary to it. In short, Levinas's criticisms apply not only to the ontology of Heidegger but also, by a sort of ricochet, to that of Hegel.

The third and final difficulty is of a wholly different order, and ultimately concerns the thought of Levinas in its entirety. Regarding the analysis of hypostasis, which is also an ontology of birth and nomination, since the present instant is the beginning of a subject whose substantivity renders it susceptible to a proper name: is it necessarily bound to the unacceptable determination of Being as evil? In other words, is it possible, and under what conditions, to dissociate the deduction of the ontological difference from the understanding of Being as malignancy? As we have already shown that the *there is*, or *Being*, could be removed from the darkness of horror and submitted to the light of decision, it is a matter here of knowing whether *time* can be the resurrection of the *I* without being the pardon of evil, or if, returning the *I* to consciousness and consciousness in turn to position, the body can be resuscitated beyond good and evil.

It is certainly not without use to measure the stakes of this last question. By understanding time as pardon, Levinas accomplishes the subordination of Being to the Good, founds the ontological difference on resurrection, and opens the dimension in which all of his later work will be deployed. But the determination of time as pardon implies something more. Time is relation to the other person because it is the other person who can pardon me of Being. Now, that the Other could do so in fact means nothing else than that he or she does. Since the *I* is temporal, it must therefore be the case that the pardon of the evil of Being has been accorded once and for all. But then, if the object of hope is here the Messiah, is this not to make Christ the fundamental event of time? In short, the interpretation of time as pardon, which presupposes the identification of Being and evil, implies in turn the recognition of Christ as the Messiah. And hence, in seeking the possibility of a resurrection of the body beyond good and evil, one must not only free the deduction of the ontological difference from Levinas's unjustifiable thesis on Being, but also and above all engage in a general explication of revelation and sacred history.

Does this not lead back to eternal recurrence and the transvaluation of values? Is not the eternal return decided in the instant not in fact "the creation of a superior body,"[23] with that superiority valued at the dawn of new values issuing from the transvaluation of ancient Jewish and Christian values? In conceiving subjective identity in line with the body and the body as a hierarchy of forces commanded by modifiable values, has Nietzsche not opened the possibility of a resurrection beyond good and evil which, preserving the deduction of the ontological difference whose movement we have just followed, also delivers us from a morality all the more surely founded on the evil and horror of being when elevated to the rank of first philosophy?

NOTES

1. See M. Heidegger, *Die Grundprobleme der Phänomenologie* (1927), *Gesamtausgabe* [GA], Bd. 24, pp. 324 and 399ff. (trans. A. Hofstadter, pp. 228 and 282ff.).

2. E. Levinas, "Dialogue sur le penser-à-l'autre," in *Entre Nous: Essais sur le penser-à-l'autre* (Paris: Grasset, 1991), 240.

3. Levinas has proposed several translations of the pair *Sein/Seiende*, the study of which could serve as the guiding thread for an interpretation of his entire project.

4. M. Heidegger, *Vom Wesen des Grundes*, in *Wegmarken*, GA, Bd. 9, pp. 160ff.

5. E. Levinas, *De l'évasion* (1935) (Montpellier: Fata Morgana, 1982), 73, 97, 98.

6. Cf. M. Heidegger, *Sein und Zeit* (Tübingen: Niemeyer, 1957), 134, 284, 345.

7. Translator's note: Where the English translator, lacking a closer approximation, is forced to write "shouldering" existence, Levinas has employed the expression "corps à corps," which is plainly close to the concern announced in Franck's title, "Le corps de la différence." It is bodiliness, he immediately proposes, which permits Levinas to claim an advance beyond the aporias in the analytic of *Dasein* opening the thinking of ontological difference. This line of thought is resumed in the closing pages of the essay.

8. Cf. Heidegger, *Sein und Zeit*, 245.

9. Reading "manière" [translated here as "somehow"] rather than "matière."

10. Cf. M. Heidegger, "Nachwort zu: 'Was ist Metaphysik?' " in *Wegmarken*, GA, Bd. 9, p. 307.

11. In its first publication, the analysis of horror was entitled *L'horreur d'être*, in *Deucalion* I (1946), p. 149. (Translator's note: Franck's distinction is lost in Lingis's rendering of both as "horror of being.")

12. The full passage reads: "Being is evil not because it is finite, but because it is without limits." Levinas reproaches Heidegger for envisioning nothingness as end and limit. But if this were the case, it would signify the finitude and limitation of Being, since Heidegger reprises Hegel's thesis that pure Being and nothingness are the same thing, founding it on the finitude of Being. Cf. *DE* 105/*EE* 64 and *Was ist Metaphysik?* in *Wegmarken*, *GA*, Bd. 9, p. 120; trans. by D. F. Krell in M. Heidegger, *Basic Writings*, ed. D. F. Krell (New York: Harper and Row, 1977), 110.

13. At this point we rejoin, from a different path, the reservations formulated by J.-L. Chrétien in "La dette et l'élection," in *Emmanuel Levinas*, ed. M. Abensour and C. Chalier (Paris: L'Herne, 1991), 262ff.

14. Cf. the preface to the second edition of *De l'existence à l'existant*.

15. Cf. ibid., 91/57; on Shakespeare cf. *TA* 60/*TO* 72–73; on Poe, cf. *Deucalion* I (1946), p. 148ff.

16. Y. Bonnefoy, "La présence et l'image," in *Entretiens sur la poésie (1972–1990)* (Paris: Mercure, 1990), 195. Levinas uses the expression "there is being" (*il y a de l'être*) in *De l'évasion*, 70.

17. As one hears at *AE* 208/*OB* 163.

18. Translator's note: "*f . . . le camp*"—*Foutre le camp*—is a (profane) argot expression meaning "to leave in great haste" or "to flee rapidly." My thanks to Didier Franck for this clarification.

19. Cf. Heidegger, "Zeit und Sein," in *Zur Sache des Denkens* (Tübingen: Niemeyer, 1969), 24; trans. A. Hofstadter, in M. Heidegger, *Poetry, Language, Thought* (New York: HarperCollins, 1985). For an extended analysis, see my *Heidegger et le problème de l'espace* (Paris: Minuit, 1986).

20. Translator's note: this distinction is to be understood in correspondence with the earlier distinction between "horror of Being" and "horror at Being"; Lingis proposes "tragic in Being" and "tragic involved in Being," respectively.

21. Cf. Romans 4:18.

22. E. Levinas, *Sur Maurice Blanchot* (Montpellier: Fata Morgana, 1975), 10.

23. Cf. F. Nietzsche, *Thus Spoke Zarathustra*, "On the Child and on Marriage," and 1881, note 11 (141) (Colli-Mollinari enumeration).

2

The Phenomenology of Eros: A Reading of *Totality and Infinity*, IV.B

Paul Moyaert

I WILL LIMIT MYSELF to a fragmentary reading of the chapter from *Totality and Infinity* entitled "The Phenomenology of Eros," a chapter which, the existence of numerous commentaries and annotations notwithstanding, still can appear as ambiguous and incomprehensive as the very play of eros and desire for the beloved which it both evokes and describes.

The existential phenomena that Levinas takes up are not alien to philosophical discourse. However, in his analysis he does show how in these recognizable experiences there is at work an existential logic which escapes the conceptual framework of a certain ontology and which dislocates from inside out a certain conception of the ego's relation to itself and to the Other (*TeI* 250/*TI* 272). In the same way, an analysis of how parents devote themselves to their children shows that that responsibility cannot be measured in terms of autonomous freedom, cannot be founded in a free decision one takes upon oneself, and by definition cannot be limited to what one, as a parent, has in his or her own power. The child invokes a responsibility in life—in my life—that reaches further than my life. In the child, I as his or her parent relate myself to an independent and alien future which takes its course without me and which does not coincide with my own controllable future; I am related to a future that reaches infinitely further, to the far side of my own life and death; I am related to a future without a final point of arrival in any present moment.

Erotic desire, such as Levinas describes it, must be distinguished from the love which occurs simply as caring for another person: the erotic relation involves being in love with the Other in a way perhaps best expressed by the phrase "madly in love." Erotic desire must also be distinguished from the ecstatic passion that excludes all reciprocity with the beloved and is consumed only with desire for an unreachable Other—even though the momentary intensity of erotic pleasure points at the same time to the dizzying possibility, but also sometimes destructive dynamic, of an impassioned desire.

I. EROTIC DESIRE AND BEING IN LOVE

To be in love is to no longer be oneself. The other person has suddenly completely taken over the place of one's own ego. The penetrating and obsessive presence of the Other seizes the ego in such a way and to such a degree that it loses all independence. The ego is so full of the Other that it is no longer itself. All at once, I am no longer anything without the Other who is everything to me and who means everything to me. The Other is everything and I am nothing. Nothing in my life has meaning without the Other. This is why someone in love is so intensely—to the point of madness—dependent on the Other. One is so captivated by the beloved that one can think of nothing and no one else; one can no longer sleep or eat. In those moments of delightful folly, everything in me and of me, everything that distinguishes and separates me from the Other, is too much for me. It is in this way that someone caught up in an overly forceful passion can desire to no longer exist. But the contrary can also come about. Just as the Other is everything for me, I want at the same time to see the perfect and unique Other as my fascinated prisoner, that is to say, to see that the beloved is completely under my spell. When one has fallen in love, self-destruction and hetero-aggression are never far off. The least degree of remoteness or resistance in the Other might therefore be already enough to leave me feeling worthless and superfluous. If the Other whom I love wants nothing to do with me, then nothing else has any meaning. This aggressive devalorization of oneself can also strike back in aggression and even hate against this Other who no longer supports or answers to the image I have of unique perfection.

The lover lives in a totally disordered world. He or she no longer recognizes the distinction, so important for every intentional act, be-

tween what is relevant and irrelevant, interesting and futile, significant and insignificant. The lover inhabits a world on the hither side
of this distinction, a disordered world in which this distinction has
lost its structuring function. The lover knows not one moment of rest,
cannot remain still before a single detail in the face of the beloved,
and loses all feel for harmony, all sense of balance. The smallest disturbance and the least hesitation immediately take dramatic and extraordinary proportion. In love, the relation to the beloved is of a
fundamentally different nature than the relation to beauty, "to a
weightless grace" (TeI 240–41/TI 262–63). According to Lacan,
whom I read on this point as the echo of Levinas, to behold beauty
is for one's gaze to turn inward, to come to a stop.[1] The harmony of
the beautiful radiates peace and makes the eyes close. This peace is
not granted to the lover.

In this fascinated, even ecstatic being-outside-oneself, the lover is
not aimed at a concrete, corporeal Other, but rather captivated only
by a delightful image from which it is impossible to get free. Moreover, the object of love is idealized to such a degree that it is a matter
here of an almost supernatural, supersensible Other. This excessive,
quasi-incorporeal perfection transports the lover into ecstasy.

But this is precisely why one becomes so completely confused by
that Other, for there is an intimate relationship between the self and
the Other. As Freud and Kierkegaard understood, in the Other who
remains beyond reach one beholds and adores the representation
of one's own narcissistic completion. This kind of love draws on a
narcissistic identification with the love-object whereby the ego loves
itself in the Other and finds in the Other the complementary substitute for its own self. Levinas, too, discerns the fundamental immanence and underlying natural relation with the beloved (TeI 232/TI
254). He also speaks of a relationship with a "sister soul" such that
every union with the beloved in a certain respect stands always already under the sign of an incestuous reunion with oneself.[2] For that
matter, this interpretation is also partly justified by the ambiguity of
an enjoyment which, in spite of all else, circles out from but also back
into itself. But at the same time, the erotic crosses through every
attempt to reduce one's relation to the beloved to the moment of
amorous blindness. While from a psychological perspective erotic
desire can draw on a fascination with the idealized and ideal love-
object, erotic love already involves another relation to the beloved,

because it is precisely this concrete, individual, corporeal Other that one desires, and no one else.[3] One is no longer exclusively attached to a captivating image but aims at a physically incarnate Other. In contrast with being in love, eros, as Levinas understands it, already presupposes having been arrested and disturbed by the vulnerability of the human face. Or, in contrast with the love of a concrete person, there is a kind of love in which one is captivated by the wholly unreachable Other (e.g., in hysteria) or by God (e.g., in mystical love).[4] A love-relation is distinguished by a hypersensitive attention for the concrete, which is of another nature than the restless obsession of an amorous subject. In love, one is concerned for the Other, full of compassion for the beloved's vulnerability; one feels with the Other in a manner which cannot be reduced to pity. One is through and through softness and sensitivity for the rhythm of the beloved's breathing, the lines in his or her face, the slope of the cheeks, and the moist blink of the eyes. In this sensitivity for barely perceptible details, one is attached to something in the Other by which he or she withdraws from and escapes a captivating image or representation, "soliciting what ceaselessly escapes its form" (*TeI* 235/*TI* 257).

II. THE INTRIGUE OF THE PERSONAL AND THE IMPERSONAL IN EROS

In eros, one is not moved exclusively by the supernatural beauty of the beloved, but by the *sublime beauty which already submits to the weight of a body.* One is attracted by something in and of the physically incarnate face by which the beloved's unreal and inaccessible beauty is already tangible and in play. One is attracted by the possible clouding of the Other's pure gaze, by the already all too carnal, troubled surface of a facial expression which is still fragile, by all the bodily signs indicating that the beloved has already lost perfect self-control.

The erotic originates not in fascination with the inaccessible or unreachable as such, but in the softening and the caresses which are its physical expression. This softening is a sensitivity for the concrete, the ultra-concrete, for the tender, for what is so fragile and vulnerable that the lover seems to give way, even to pull back in his or her drive to make the feminine available to touch (*TeI* 233–34/*TI* 256–

57). The intrusive and also seductive weakness of the feminine cannot be touched without either anxiety or reticence. It is as if the lover is apprehensive before what he or she is already also attracted to: apprehensive at the betrayal of a secret no longer able to protect itself, at the profanation and indecent contamination of what is taboo, at the defilement of what just now was so untouched, so virginal and pure, and at tarnishing what is at risk of losing its grace.

The vulnerable is vulnerable only in tension with what threatens to overflow the fragile from inside out. In this vulnerability, the feminine seems to be able to rise up before succumbing to the carnal violence of anonymous drives. The tender lies on an ungraspable and ambiguous line between, on the one hand, an exorbitant nudity and an excess of being, and on the other hand, a non-being that is too weak and too volatile to be able or even willing to uphold itself. "In the caress . . . the body already denudes itself of its very form, offering itself as erotic nudity" (*TeI* 235–36/*TI* 258). The erotic takes place in the *infinite transition* between the face that remains present in disappearing and the already impersonal underside that breaks through in the ripple of facial expressions, or in the *infinite between* of the face and its disfiguration. Sexual pleasure is as it were the repetition and lifelike *mise-en-scène* of the irresistible cycle of life and death to which each of us separate organisms is subject. "An amorphous non-I sweeps away the I into an absolute future where it escapes itself and loses its position as subject" (*TeI* 237/*TI* 259).

The erotic withdraws itself and maintains itself in a world that no longer has anything in common with this world. The desire for unconditional physical contact with the Other erases the distinctions between interesting versus repulsive and attractive versus repugnant. In this momentary transgressive movement, nothing remains of distinctions which retain their power in the order of the profane. In the dimension beyond the face, the feminine speaks not a single word which is true. However, the falling away of all seriousness is not at all ponderous or burdensome. Animal playfulness and the frivolity of erotic nudity are comprised of precisely this (*TeI* 241/*TI* 263). Caresses pass over into obscene words which have nothing more to signify. The feminine laughs at the otherwise all-important distinctions between sincerity and acting as if, between seriousness and play. One laughs at philosophers who offer deadly serious descriptions pointing to an order in which the serious is nevertheless totally absent. So, too, does the rather strained behavior of the lover who, while making love, sometimes begins to act as if his or her life or I do not know what stake depends on it, sometimes appear particularly funny or ludicrous.

As a transcending movement, the caress goes past the face (*TeI* 242/*TI* 264). It brings us into contact with, on the one hand, what still lies beyond the face, and on the other hand, what the face has left behind, that is to say, *with the bare fact of human existence. The erotic, as the most intimate and personal communication with the physical Other, is at the same time contact with the impersonal in the Other.* For in the obscenity of extravagant nudity, every recognizable and distinct form of the Other stands at the brink of disappearing. In nudity, everyone is the same. This is why someone who is naked can be so vulnerable (the transcendence that lies beyond the face is not a deeper reality or source of meaning, and still less does it take on the form of a hidden richness). Beyond the face, all significant differences disappear and an inhuman and unbearable anonymity threatens to return. But in contrast with the irrepressible and all too direct relation with what Levinas calls the *il y a*, the erotic contact with the nocturnal underside of our existence does not strike us with panic, anxiety, or disgust. This is possible only because the impersonal and amorphous non-ego of cries, respiration, muscles, flesh, and blood, its proximity notwithstanding, at the same time also remains at a distance, with its all too intrusive presence continuing to point to the human face that blurs. Without this far-reaching support from a recognizable face, the otherwise too brutal and too immediate contact with the impersonal exterior would take on monstrous and hideous forms. In the endless turnover of the discontinuous (the differentiated) into a gaping continuity (the indifferent), and in the infinitely futural passage of the formed into the formless, there must always remain a trace of what is on the brink of disappearing. In the almost nothing or almost no more of blurring and fading, the face must remain visible. Disfiguration supposes the face (*TeI* 240/*TI* 262); penetrating indiscretion implies respect for the face (*TeI* 241/*TI* 264), and far-reaching, disenchanting profanation supposes what already exists as radiance and significance (*TeI* 244/*TI* 266–67).

III. THE ESSENTIAL AMBIGUITY OF LOVE: AUTO-AFFECTION AND TRANSCENDENCE

In caressing (touching, feeling, stroking), the hand loses its instrumental meaning and its mastery. The I who caresses is not an I who is in control of oneself. For to touch the Other also means to be touched from outside by that Other. In feeling the Other, which is also being felt by the Other, the ego-subject is taken hold of by what it feels and also by that feeling itself. The I finds itself no longer in the position of an untouched third person or an unmoved outsider: one loses control over oneself. In feeling, one's passivity and activity are entangled in one another: feeling and being felt, stroking and being stroked, sucking and being sucked. Physical attraction to the Other is thus always at the same time also auto-affection, but without the self in that circuit ever occupying either its proper starting point or its ultimate end point. The subject comes loose from itself but at the same time remains bound to itself. "Love does not transcend unequivocally" (*TeI* 244/*TI* 266). The touching hand is not directed to grasping or possessing the Other. Stroking does not seek possession; in possession, pleasure as such has already exhausted itself. Pleasure means being possessed by the Other's being-outside-itself. Feeling is not liberated in touching or by stroking; rather, it spirals endlessly downward, drawn powerlessly into an abyssal depth. In the unclosed circuit between the self and the Other, the caress circles emptily and in vain, fed by an insatiable hunger. In this dynamic which can be neither stopped nor stanched, the subject is turned fruitlessly inside out: *one is passionately grasped by the incomprehensible.* In this intrigue, it is no longer possible to say who feels whom and who is caressed by whom. Together, the two lovers form a confused and self-enclosed unity, and so, in their self-satisfaction, close themselves from the rest of the world. Any reference to a possible exterior standpoint has disappeared.

Still, this does not go all the way to a fusion in which each lover in his or her separate independence is taken up into a higher unity. Whereas in pleasure I *am* in a sense the Other, the Other still remains irreducibly separate from me. It is precisely this inconquerable separation in unity—a proximity in distance and a distance in proximity—which accounts for the keenness of desire and the momentary intensity of pleasure.

In pleasure, one is *outside oneself:* one no longer belongs to oneself, but is in and of the Other. Nothing remains hidden; one abandons oneself to the Other. The physical I becomes an outside without depth, without interiority. But at the same time, the Other, as feminine, also withdraws from pleasure, fully back into him- or herself, into mystery (*TeI* 254/*TI* 276). The Other withdraws from pleasure as animal self-satisfaction, as pure egoistic voluptuousness, escaping me in the very moment of unconditional surrender. Pleasure is therefore not mutual and complementary fulfillment of two lovers. The Other is swallowed up by a pleasure that does not permit itself to be shared. And this is a pleasure that the one who experiences it does not control. It is as if the Other enjoys me only in him- or herself, and in spite of me. Precisely this loss of all control constitutes this pleasure. All possible "knowledge" and control over that which the Other now will ultimately take pleasure in—a recurring fantasy in perversion— means the destruction of pleasure. In the paroxysm of pleasurable abandon, one is no longer present to oneself in person. One loses concern with one's own image. One is no longer interested in seeing how the Other actually enjoys him- or herself or how one might be seen by the Other (who would take the position of the third person, by which one could then identify oneself). One therefore goes to the extreme in an irresistible, impersonal play of drives.

Erotic pleasure is characterized by *complicity between a mutual dependence and a unilateral drivenness of the respective partners* (of a self-abandon and egoistic voluptuousness which can no longer be controlled). Sexual pleasure does not seek the discharge of tension, and aims even less at the release of desire (*TeI* 244/*TI* 266). It is rather the case that such a release overtakes enjoyment, making—at least in a certain respect—a brusque and unwanted end to the ecstatic being-outside-oneself of pleasure. In that release, one falls back on oneself without the promise of an impossible satisfaction having been redeemed. Pleasure is pleasure in and desire for the pleasure of the Other (*TeI* 244/*TI* 266), that is to say, the pleasure of the Other who is taken outside of him- or herself by pleasure in my physical being-there. In this dependence, one still remains attached to oneself in auto-affection: pleasure for oneself through the fact that the Other enjoys me, while the enjoying subject at the same time almost loses itself in the transcending movement which this involves. Without this play, pleasure is not possible. But the reciprocal independence which it involves is interesting only when both partners take their pleasure separately and despite the Other (in other words, it is unbearable to me for the Other to offer him- or herself non-egoistically, so that I may enjoy myself), and also despite oneself (in other words, because it is stronger than oneself). Love is not interesting unless one loves to be loved and desires to be loved. "I love fully only if the other loves me" (*TeI* 244/*TI* 266). Thanks to that love, I can enjoy the fact that I am worthy of love and desirable. However, this play of desire is also interesting only on the condition that the Other does not love me merely because I desire to be loved. In other words, that play must escape my control. Hence is it so that the loving abandon to an Other does not rest simply on the possible response the beloved may make to it. In this sense, love is also a relation in which I always relate myself to the possibility that the Other will *not* love me in return. "In love . . . unless one does not love with love, one must resign oneself to not being loved" (*AE* 153/*OB* 121).

This mutual dependence and the auto-affective component inseparably bound up with it are meaningful only when reciprocity as such is not directly aimed at and is not bent into a reflexive intentionality. This mutual dependence must go together with an egoistic drive by which one's abandon to the Other no longer depends on the beloved's possible response. Erotic pleasure is destroyed when one tries to stay in control and remain at the point where pleasurable effects can be brought about in the Other. At such a moment, the reciprocity is in fact interrupted, and one has already taken the position of an outsider who surveys the play in which one is involved.

This problematic is central not only for clinical psychology as it studies love relations which have already become ill, but also in the Sartrean analysis of masochism and sadism. While it seems to me that Levinas's phenomenology of eros can be read as a thinly disguised critique of Sartre, this does not mean that it renders the Sartrean description superfluous. To the contrary. Just as Freud describes the countless destinies of wanting to be loved (narcissism), so Sartre describes the destinies of love-relations in which the circuit of *reciprocal physical incarnation and dependence* ("*la double incarnation réciproque*") *is interrupted to the extreme* and the play with the Other is reduced to a play of imaginary *fascination*. In contrast with what Levinas describes as erotic desire, masochism and sadism are essentially and exceptionally puritanical (incorporeal) affairs.

In masochism, I want to see to an extreme degree how the disincarnate gaze of the Other is fascinated by my object-ness for him or
her. The masochist yields before a desire to touch the Other, so that
both the Other and the masochist are drawn into the play of impersonal drives in which there is no longer a person present to him- or
herself left standing. The masochist is afraid of disappearing as a person, and even wishes to fall under the impulsion of his or her own
objectionable, abject, and infantile object-ness, and identifies with
the Other who despises and mistreats the masochist for his or her
fear and ridiculous behavior. But this Other must not become *flesh
and blood* through this identification. The Other must remain in the
position of a disincarnate gaze. He or she must remain at a distance,
and is not to be comprehended in or through his or her own corporeality. For precisely this reason, anyone can in principle occupy the
imaginary position of that disincarnate gaze. The Other thus takes
only the position of, as it were, *outsider.* In contrast to the description
of Levinas, masochism thus displays once again a central reference
to a third (the outsider), with whom the masochist identifies.

In sadism, to the contrary, one wishes not to be swallowed up and
drawn into one's own corporeality. The sadist wishes to be absolutely
present to his or her own unassailable mastery; the sadist wishes, in
other words, to fall under the impulsion of his or her own mastery,
which is reaffirmed through subjective reactions of pain, horror,
panic, and anxiety in the Other. The sadist identifies with the victim:
the victim's desperate cries are impressive evidence of the sadist's
own absolute power. The sadist thus reduces the Other to a pure
object; or better, compels the other person to an extreme confrontation with his or her object-ness. The sadist cannot bear for the Other,
as person, to disappear in his or her corporeality. In contrast with
Levinas's account of erotic desire, in which the Other, as person,
disappears into the impersonal outside of his or her physical existence, Sartre's sadist exercises an extreme compulsion on the Other,
as person, to continue to react—including, and above all, at the point
where he or she almost ceases to be a person.

The difference between the phenomenology of eros (Levinas) and
the analysis of perversion (Sartre) can also be summarized as follows:
First, as opposed to what is sometimes asserted in some handbooks
of psychiatry, neither the individual ego (masochism) nor the Other

(sadism) is ever reduced to a purely manipulable and impersonal object. Such perversions are not possible without a basic recognition of the Other as a person. Perversion is a typically human phenomenon. Animals are neither sadistic nor masochistic. In perversion, one aims above all and to an extreme degree at the subjective reactions of the Other as a person. In sadism, one does not permit the Other to disappear into the impersonal exterior of his or her existence: the victim must *realize* what it means for the inaccessible Other to be reduced to an object. Sadism breaks down as soon as the Other succumbs to torture and no longer reacts as a person. The masochist wants to see what it means to no longer mean anything to the Other: the masochist is fascinated by his or her object-ness for the Other. Perversions are thus characterized by an endless (imaginary) dissociation between the Other's consciousness (the gaze) and his or her corporeality. In Levinas's phenomenology of eros, it is no longer the distant, lucid, and neutral gaze which is central, but the gaze which clouds and breaks down under the caress.

The lack of respect for the Other consists here in a extreme demand and compulsion exercised on him or her to continue to react as a person. From the perspective of this problematic, it is understandable how the description of eros in *Totality and Infinity* is important for the analysis of the ethical relation. For the sensibility of the face is seen there to consist in the fact that one *can* be touched by the Other even at the point where he or she is almost no longer a person—the face that manifests itself in the proximity of an irrecusable decline, this face becomes truly intrusive and obsessive only at the very brink of the impersonal *il y a*—as if the possible disappearance of all recognizable and comparable properties confronts one with the irreplaceable singularity of the Other. Ethics finds its foundation in this limit-experience.

Second, ambiguity comprises the very essence of the erotic. The erotic consists of the ambiguous play of loving and being loved, immanence and transcendence, and so forth. Perversion is the consequence of an urge to free oneself of this ambiguity. This isolates the existential paradox of perversion: the attempt to break out of the play of mutual dependence leads directly into perversion. It is from this perspective that Sartre must be read. Sartre never alleged that sadism and masochism are the ultimate truth of human love-relations.

He only shows what the truth of love-relations is where the circuit of mutual dependence and physical incarnation is radically interrupted.

IV. EROTIC DESIRE AND PASSION

In contrast with erotic love, passion does not in principle aim at a possible reciprocity with the beloved; in passion, one is consumed to an extreme degree by a desire for the inaccessible Other. Passion is an extreme form of love. Like love, passion does not involve attraction to a concrete, physical Other. In a passionate love-relation, one is drawn to an absolute that is not of this world, or to an Other who is so absolute that he or she remains inevitably untouchable and out of reach. Such a relation stands from the very beginning exclusively under the sign of an impossible love and a love that a priori excludes all possible reciprocity. As such, passion is not so much borne by a physical consumption as it bursts out in a sometimes almost unbearable *self-consuming flame:* a desire which is never interrupted by the possibility of physical liberation, but only *consumed by that desire itself.* Passionate love is thus characterized by a paradoxical existential logic. On the one hand, one does everything possible to abolish the distance separating one from an unreachable Other. One leaves everything behind. Ultimately, it is nothing other than the self-enclosedness of existence and life itself that makes an ultimate union impossible. But on the other hand, the passionate lover also seeks the very separation that causes him or her to suffer, as if seeking at one and the same time both the separation itself and the possibility of overcoming it. On the one hand the lover says that he or she will never love anyone else, while on the other hand finding it unbearable for this Other to answer to his or her desire: "ni sans toi, ni avec toi"—neither without you nor with you. In passion, desire is described only in terms of "dying of not dying," that is to say, an almost dying from not being able to die of desire. As such, passion is the extreme example of a desire without future, without fecundity.

NOTES

1. J. Lacan, *The Four Fundamental Concepts of Psycho-Analysis* (Seminar XI), ed. J.-A. Miller, trans. A. Sheridan (New York: Penguin, 1977), 86.

2. Levinas refers explicitly to the myth of Aristophanes, told in Plato's *Symposium* 189c–193d.

3. In this connection, see also R. Scruton, *Sexual Desire* (London: Weidenfeld and Nicolson, 1986).

4. P. Moyaert, *De mateloosheid van het christendom* (Nijmegen: SUN, 1998), Part 3, "De christelijke Liefdesmystiek: De omvorming van een passioneel liefdesverlangen in een liefde zonder begeerte."

3

The Encounter with the Stranger: Two Interpretations of the Vulnerability of the Skin

Rudolf Bernet

I

THE ENCOUNTER WITH THE Other has become a central issue in European philosophy of the last fifty years. This "issue" is, however, hardly more than a common name for a great variety of questions. Contemporary philosophical debates on rationalism versus relativism, universalism versus particularism, transculturalism versus multiculturalism, and so forth can be said to circle around the question of the Other as an emblematic figure representing difference, plurality, and strangeness. Political issues concerning the assimilation or integration of strangers, the politics of gender, the treatment of the poor by the rich, of the disabled by the healthy, of non-Europeans by Europeans, and so forth also seem to demand a properly philosophical competence in what looks like their common root, that is, the encounter with the Other. We all know from experience, however, that philosophy, far from giving a pacifying answer to these political debates, is itself a battlefield. There is disagreement, not only between different philosophical systems, but also about the relations between the different philosophical disciplines and their competence in the questions of the Other. Granted that the encounter with the Other is a central philosophical issue, what comes first: ethics, metaphysics, or epistemology? And what is the most appropriate attitude: respect, understanding of a difference in the mode of being, or insight into a reality as it is in itself?

The least one can say, therefore, is that the question concerning

the encounter with the Other can have different meanings, both inside and outside philosophy. The interests, methods of approach,
doctrines, and also the meaning of the words themselves have become so diverse that one eventually wonders what one is talking
about. Our situation is not unlike the one Husserl found himself entangled with at the beginning of his philosophical career and which
gave birth to phenomenology as a return to the things themselves. As
we discover the meaning of the expression "encounter with the
Other" shifting (*schwankend*) to such an extraordinary degree, it
seems useful to follow Husserl and search for the missing clarity
through a phenomenological analysis of how the Other or different
sorts of Others appear to me in themselves and from themselves.

Unfortunately, the appeal to a Husserlian phenomenology does
little to simplify matters. This is so not only because Husserlian phenomenology is itself a complicated matter, but also and mainly because it has been widely doubted whether the Other can even
become a phenomenon without betraying his essence, that is, his
alterity. What appears to me, it is said, has to adapt itself to my mental framework in order to be apprehended by me. What is given to
me is therefore the Other-for-me and not the Other-in-himself. Phenomenology, as an inquiry into the *logos* that allows phenomena to be
given, fixes in advance the conditions (modes of horizon, rationality,
discourse) the Other has to meet in order to mean anything to me.
Phenomenological openness is a determinate openness; it unfolds a
horizon that is necessarily limited, and it involves a form of violence
that some do not hesitate to call a mode of imperialism or coloniza-
tion of the Other. As long as I (or We) occupy the center of the space
where the Other comes to appear, we are not equal and I (or We)
can be rightly accused of failing to respect the Other's otherness. The
least one can say therefore is that phenomenology, far from providing
a simple and clear answer to the question concerning the encounter
with the Other, is itself put into question by the advent of the Other.

There is still more to discourage us in advance in our audacious
attempt to say something meaningful about the encounter with the
Other from a phenomenological perspective. Why is it that nowadays
one speaks indifferently of the "encounter with the Other" and the
"encounter with the stranger," as if these expressions would have
exactly the same meaning? Is the difference between the Other and
the Same just the same as the difference between the self and the

stranger, or as the difference between a place where I am at home and a place that is abroad? Why do we have the feeling that the difference between the self and the stranger is about something more concrete and more narrow than the difference between the Same and the Other? However, what does "narrow" mean? One is inclined to say that it refers to the limited extension of space with respect to a particular standpoint. What is narrow is around me and close by and thus differs from what is wide and therefore extending far away from me. The difference between the self and the stranger is thus not only more narrow than the difference between the Same and the Other, it seems to be precisely about what is narrow and near and what is wide and far away. It thus involves the idea of a limit, of a border that separates what, because it is near and narrow, belongs to myself and what is too far away and too wide to be grasped or appropriated by me and which therefore remains strange to me.

Having initially been at a loss in our attempt to account for the encounter with the Other, we are now more than eager to seize and exploit the clue provided by the concept of a limit or *border* separating the self from the stranger. But precisely what would function as the border separating myself from the stranger? And what sort of border would it be? Would it be possible to cross this border, and how far, and what kind of crossing would be permissible without the risk of the border becoming inoperative or disappearing? Would this border do away with the violence in the encounter with the stranger, or would it rather enforce and legitimate this violence? And eventually: what deserves our highest respect—the border, or the person of the stranger?

Speaking of a border presupposes a body that has an inside and an outside. Without forgetting that social and political institutions can also be considered bodies and that all systems of order and their functioning in terms of inclusion and exclusion have a physical side, let us rather concentrate on the human body, that is, my body. The border of this body is the skin. My body is, in the irreverent words of Lacan, "a bag (made out) of skin (*sac de peau*)." Even a tight and thick skin has small and large holes that one can adequately call "openings." There are natural openings as well as artificial or forced openings called "wounds." Natural openings are still subject, however, to being forced and wounded. The natural openings allowing for a passage and exchange between the inside and the outside of a body cannot prevent the violence of a traumatic intrusion or expulsion.

My encounter with the Other is therefore a matter of *skin* where the organic porosity, the sensitivity, and even the color of the skin play an important role and contribute to the mode, the frequency, and the quality of the encounter. This is to say that the skin which at the same time separates me from the Other and mediates our encounter cannot be reduced to its mechanical and objective qualities. The skin of a living organism is not just a membrane; it is alive and has a life of its own. Its behavior cannot be explained solely in terms of external stimuli causing it to always react in the same way (according to the principle of constancy). Rather, the skin "responds" to what affects it from the outside and the inside, and its dynamic behavior further includes an expressive representation of the meaning of this response.

Does all of this mean that my encounter with the Other is a matter of two "bags of skin" getting in touch with each other and letting pass something from one bag into the other, by way of natural or forced openings? The first difficulty with this picture is the fact that somebody (or rather no-body) pretends to say what a human encounter is without referring to his own experience of such an encounter. The objective description of how two Others get involved with each other cannot count as an answer to the philosophical question concerning the possibility and meaning of the difference and the encounter between a self and a stranger. A second, more serious difficulty questions whether it is indeed true that I am a bag of skin that possibly encounters a stranger that is another bag of skin. This question or objection has been raised by all phenomenologists, Husserl and Levinas included. To be more precise: they do not necessarily object to the idea that I am a bag of skin, but rather the idea that I am that bag of skin in and for myself, even before I encounter the Other. Phenomenologists, in short, have also wondered what was inside the bag.

Considering myself to be a bag of skin with an inside and an outside presupposes that, while dwelling and sheltering inside my skin, I can nevertheless look at it from the outside and grasp the self-enclosed surface of my body as a totality or form (gestalt). However, elementary empirical observation already shows that this is not the case, and that at least a mirror is required in order to apprehend my body from the outside as a perceptive gestalt. The apprehension of myself as a bag of skin, far from being an originary form of self-awareness preceding the encounter with the Other, actually already presupposes an external view of my body. The holes in my skin are not openings that precede the encounter with the Other as its conditions of possibility; quite to the contrary, they presuppose an Other looking at me. If they are called "windows," then the one who looks through them from the inside at once meets the Other looking into them from the outside. My skin is thus no ordinary bag, but a twisted surface where the inside is an outside, in the manner of a Moebius strip.[1] It is a surface that both protects me and exposes me. Given this paradoxical nature of my skin, my encounter with the Other can still be given two different philosophical interpretations. The first interpretation will insist on the fact that my encounter with the Other is actually the experience of an original entanglement. The second interpretation will insist on the need to do away with all concerns for the gestalt of bodies in my encounter with the "face" of the Other. The first interpretation can be found in Husserl and Merleau-Ponty; the second is found in Levinas.

II

What we have learned so far is that my encounter with the Other has to cross the border of my skin. My skin has the "mechanical" property of being permeable and the "psychological" property of being sensible to what affects it. We have also learned that this skin is a border of my body that comes to exist for me only when it has been crossed from both sides. This required us to say that my skin at the same time protects and exposes me, that it defends me against the Other and at the same time makes me extremely vulnerable to the gaze of the Other and the demands it expresses. This vulnerability need not be a traumatic one, provided one can show that it belongs to my skin in a manner analogous to the manner it belongs to the skin of the Other. Unlike a one-sided vulnerability that turns me into a "hostage" of the Other, reciprocal vulnerability and exposure create a form of community. The entanglement between me and the Other that follows from reciprocal dependency is the concern of what we have called the first interpretation of the vulnerability of the skin.

It is worth noting that this first interpretation promotes an understanding of the dependency of the self on the Other that cannot properly be called "alienation." Alienation (*Entfremdung*) presupposes that something that first has been my own is taken away from me by the Other and thus becomes strange (*alienus*) to me. We have seen that the skin covering the totality or gestalt of my body, quite to the contrary, has never been entirely my own, that it was already at the beginning me-for-the-Other. Husserl will insist, however, on the fact that this "me-for-the-Other" is still for me. This is to say that it is me and only me who experiences my skin as being surrounded and pierced by the look of the Other. And more than this, Husserl will also stress that the Other is similarly for me. What is the meaning of this word "similarly"? It certainly cannot mean that the Other in himself is just as much for me as my skin (my "me-for-the-Other") is for me. Is it then to say that the Other *appears* to me just as my skin appears to me? But if the mode of their appearing is the same, why then speak of a "similarity"? There must be a difference for there to be similarity, and accounting for this difference might well show that "similarity" is not the right word here.

What, then, is the difference between me appearing to the Other and the Other appearing to me? Or more precisely, between me apprehending myself as being looked at by the Other and me apprehending the Other as being looked at by me? Or again, between the experience of my skin and the experience of the Other's skin? The answer that immediately comes to mind is that I experience my own skin from both the inside and the outside, while the skin of the Other is given to me only from the outside. But such an answer is no good, since it conflicts with our earlier insight that a skin always and at the same time has an inside and an outside and that therefore the givenness or appearing of the skin of the Other cannot be reduced to the outside it presents to me. However, this answer has it right when it suggests that the inside of the Other's skin is not given to me in the same way as the inside of my own skin. We thus cannot help but claim that the inside of the skin of the Other is both given and not given to me. Or better, it is given to me *as* not being able to be given to me; the outside of the Other's skin makes visible that its inside is and must remain invisible for me.

Husserl and Merleau-Ponty have devoted long and brilliant analyses to the clarification of this paradoxical mode of givenness, and even Heidegger, in one of his last seminars, suggested that phenomenology has the task of thinking the appearing of the invisible (*Phänomenologie des Unscheinbaren*).[2] With an eye already trained on the second interpretation (the one found in Levinas), what we must retain from these analyses is that the visible and the invisible in the appearing of the Other's skin are not given in the same way and therefore cannot be said to form a unity which would be a totality or gestalt. What presents itself as invisible and inaccessible in the appearing of the Other can *in principle never* be made visible and accessible to me. It is a lack I never can fill up by moving around the Other or by penetrating into his intimacy. It therefore also becomes highly problematic to say that the skin of the Other has two "sides," as if we could turn it inside out like a glove. The way the Other is for-himself can never be reduced to the way he is for-me. And, as we will see momentarily, the way the Other is for-himself (or the way I am for-myself) does not do away with all invisibility. For it is not certain that what I cannot see in the Other coincides with what he can see in himself. This is to say, even our two perspectives on him taken together—the sum of how the Other looks to me and how he sees himself—might not form a totality or gestalt.

Let us first return to the question concerning the alleged "similarity" between the way I apprehend my skin as being for-the-Other and the way I apprehend the Other's skin as being for-me. According to Husserl, the two apprehensions have at least in common that they are both mine. I am at the source (*archè*) of both apprehensions, and both are governed by the same rational rules (*logos*), that is, the rules applying to all my rational activities. The two apprehensions remain different, however, insofar as my apprehension of my body as being both experienced by me from the inside and looked at from the outside by the Other is more fundamental than (but not necessarily prior to in time) my apprehension of the Other's body as expressing his inner life. Why is this so? Because I can, by means of my imagination, transpose myself into the standpoint of the Other (*Hineinversetzen*) who looks at me from the outside, while I cannot pretend to know in a similar manner the inner life of the Other merely on the basis of how it becomes visible for me through its bodily expression. In other words, the invisibility of my back and the invisibility of the Other's inner life do not have (for me) the same meaning and the same "degree" of absence. This is why Husserl speaks of an "*analogy*" between the two apprehensions rather than a "similarity," "resemblance," or "mirroring."[3] I grasp the Other's expressive body according to the rules (*ana logon*) that govern my apprehension of my own expressive body, and not the other way around. As long as both apprehensions are mine, as long as I am the *archè* of both apprehensions, that "other way around" makes no sense, and the second interpretation (put forward by Levinas) must mean something else than a mere reversal in the primacy of one perspective over the other.[4] Needless to say, the (transcendental) primacy of the apprehension of my two-sided or folded skin does not conflict with what we said about an (equally transcendental) entanglement between both perspectives (me on the Other and the Other on me). Quite to the contrary, it allows for a proper understanding of how, appearing in the same light, I and the Other can live in a common world.

But what happens when we do *not* live in a common world, that is, when the Other is and remains a *stranger* to me? Sticking to Husserl and his conception of an analogous apprehension of the Other, one would then have to say that there must be a strangeness in myself the understanding of which guides me in my apprehension (or appresentation) of the Other's strangeness. Several of Husserl's texts seem to be willing to go this far.[5] What would then be the possible (transcendental) meaning of a strangeness I encounter in myself? It must be something in myself that does not come from myself and that is governed by other rules, by another *logos* than the one presiding over the activities that have their source (*archè*) in me. Where in my "sphere of ownness" is there a place for such a strangeness that is governed by a *logos* that has its source in the Other? Husserl's French readers in particular have claimed, already for more than a generation, that this place is what Husserl has called "*Ur-Hyle*."[6] The realm of the strange in me is therefore passivity, and more precisely, the passivity of what affects me without being a sedimented result of my former activities and without my being able to fully appropriate it to myself.

III

The time has come to move on and consider the second interpretation and its contribution to the question concerning the meaning of the encounter with an Other who is a stranger. In fact, the way to this second interpretation is already prepared by the first interpretation, where it has led us to speak of the invisible and the strange in myself. Delving more deeply into their meaning and emphasizing the *anarchic logos* at work in them, the second interpretation, found in Levinas, will, however, definitely dismiss the conception of an egologically centered analogy. But instead of moving the center from me to the stranger, it will come up with an analysis of two decentered subjects locked into a one-directional relation of demand asking for a "substitution" and prohibiting permutation and reciprocity. Moving thus from the Other to the stranger, cognitive and ontological questions are subordinated to the ethical obligation of respecting the stranger's alterity and of being concerned with the misery it implies.

The totality of the skin of my body as it looks from the outside is indeed invisible to me, but we can hardly say that it is strange to me. An invisible exteriority need not remain strange to me. Husserl is certainly right when he claims that the invisible side of my body which is visible to the Other can be reappropriated by me. Matters would be entirely different if the Other would be the cause of my invisibility rather than its compensation. If the Other would make a claim on me which, while irremediably concerning me, would forever remain strange to me, then the possibility of my apprehending the Other's body as a visible totality or gestalt would fade altogether. When the Other makes a claim on me, there is no point in studying what his body looks like and what sort of inner life it expresses. Apprehending the form of the Other's body instead of responding to the infinite demand his "face" expresses would be both a theoretical and ethical fallacy. There is also no point in turning the fact that my external invisible is more visible than the Other's internal invisible into the basic meaning of our encounter. It no longer matters whether the Other's claim or appeal comes from his inside or his outside, so long as it comes from him and affects me in a way I could not foresee. It is not my outer invisibility but only the radical *passivity* of my exposure to an appeal that obliges me to respond which truly counts as a strangeness in me.[7] "In me"? How can we still refer to this strangeness as a mere part of myself when it means that I ought to be entirely for-the-stranger?

It is worth emphasizing once more that Levinas's interpretation does not oppose itself directly to Husserl's, as if arguing that my encounter with the Other takes place on his ground instead of mine. What Levinas wants to show is that there is no ground whatsoever for this encounter. The encounter brings together two individuals who have lost a firm ground to stand on. The Other, as "an orphan, a widow, a stranger," does not dwell in the *oikonomia* of a household; he is not an owner protecting his property and appealing to others to make it fructify. It is neither with the logic of his mind and the cultural traditions governing his life—nor his economical or political power, but with the lack of all this, thus with his poverty, nakedness, and suffering, that he lays a claim on me. *This appeal coming out of a lack makes me in turn lacking.* It pierces my skin in a way that I am turned inside out, depriving my interiority of its protective skin, leaving it to hemorrhage in a way nobody has the power to stanch. In other, more sober words, nothing in me has prepared me for the appeal that comes over me from the Other. My mode of thinking, my clever anticipations and calculations are of no use and out of order when I am struck by the vulnerability of the "face" of the Other. The Other's imploring eyes shatter all objectifying looks directed at his gestalt, they pierce his skin and penetrate into mine. No skin is thick enough to make them stop their demanding. When skins are pierced on both sides and when fronts are overrun, it clearly makes no sense to continue to consider the encounter between two people as a matter of two opposites meeting, or of "con-frontation." This is why Levinas instead speaks of the Other's *"proximity"* to me, making clear at once that this does not mean a "fusion" between him and me.[8]

This proximity does away with distance and protection, with opposition and confrontation, but not with difference and separation. It leads to a mode of encounter that is necessarily traumatic because it is immediate, that is, without mediation of any sort, and without transcendental conditions preparing in advance for its advent. This is to say that the encounter with the stranger cannot be reduced to a form of understanding him and especially understanding him *as being* such and such. It is an encounter without the assistance of categories *a priori* (be they universal or relative to a particular cultural framework); what is at stake in it is a truth that is prior to any communal *logos* or neutral being. It is striking that all these preliminary statements about the seemingly simple and positive notion of "proximity" have been formulated in a negative and rather complicated manner. The reader of Levinas is familiar with this impression and knows from experience that the second interpretation of the vulnerability of the skin mainly consists in a criticism of the first interpretation and thereby falls short of characterizing positively a mode of the encounter that it pretends to be prior to any other. It is as if Levinas were trying to say something that cannot be stated in philosophical terms. This might explain why he cannot dispense with critically referring to Husserlian transcendental philosophy, to Hegelian universalism, to Heideggerian existentialism, and to structuralism without, however, making great efforts to do justice to them. Nonetheless, these criticisms deserve all our attention because they alone can permit us to decide whether the second interpretation is truly independent from the first, and whether it can or cannot be reconciled with it.

Levinas repeats ceaselessly and with innumerable variations that Husserl's transcendental philosophy of consciousness reduces the Other to an intentional object of representation.[9] In his view, this disrespectful objectification of the Other amounts to a form of egoism—one which is, to be more precise, both theoretical and ethical. The theoretical egoism consists in reducing the Other to a possible object of experience *for me,* in anticipating the Other's advent in the horizon of my own expectations. Levinas stresses convincingly that the Other's existence is more than a possibility for my thought and that the Other's presence is something else than an intuitive fulfillment of my anticipations. The ethical egoism that goes with this consists in turning the Other into a field of application of a form of responsibility that first concerns what I owe to myself as a rational ethical agent. For Levinas responsibility is, quite to the contrary, a matter of response, of obeying a command that comes from the Other and not from me, my superego, or a universal law that has no face. The alternative to such a theoretical and ethical egoism is therefore *passivity,* a passivity older than my egological subject and prior to both *my* activity and passivity. Speaking in this context of a dispossession or a decentering of myself is a merely provisional way of speaking, addressing itself to those still thinking in terms of transcendental subjectivism. Levinas prefers to speak the language of debt, or guilt (*dette*), of the essential shortcomings in my infinite responsibility for the Other's sufferings. This infinite responsibility is again something other than the finitude or inadequacy in my way of answering the Other's imperative demand. The language of finitude is said to come out of an ontological egoism in which finitude is said to be about the limits of what I can and cannot do and not about what the Other requires from me. Accepting its own finitude is an authentic way for *Dasein* to be for-itself instead of offering itself entirely to the Other or, rather, sacrificing its *Jemeinigkeit* in a face-to- face with the Other.[10]

Another detour leading to a provisional understanding of Levinas's basic concerns takes the road of a criticism of the philosophy of history (supposedly the one to be found in Hegel). This philosophy of history is said to think in terms of a reason where the logic of universal concepts becomes an instrument of power and domination. Its imperialism is guided by a will of expansion which suppresses all limits and comes to rest only when the uniform reign of the universal is attained. What, according to Levinas, is particularly unethical in such a philosophy of history is the fact that the individual person is sacrificed on the altar of universal reason. In such a view, individual suffering no longer counts; or, put more cynically, it is a necessary price to be paid for the Idea of universal humanity to be realized on earth. It is easy, then, to understand why Levinas dismisses irenic metaphysical humanism just as much as the battlefields of a philosophy of history. They both subsume the concrete individual person under the reign of abstract universal Ideas and thereby empty ethical responsibility of its very meaning. For Levinas, all ethics is necessarily rooted in a face-to-face relation with an Other who is unique and singular, that is to say, not comparable to a third Other. My responsibility for the Other thus allows for no delegation and also for no justification in terms of a universal principle. It is neither in the name of a universal law nor in the name of my rational will, but only in the name of this Other in this situation that I must sacrifice or "substitute" myself for his misery.

What these criticisms of transcendental subjectivism and dialectical rationalism suggest is that only Levinas's interpretation of the vulnerability of the skin is *pure* enough to account for the necessarily ethical meaning of the encounter with the Other. Pure vulnerability means unavoidable traumatism, exposure without protection, obeying a command one cannot understand, responsibility without end or limit, forced and therefore humble generosity, a guilt that is infinite because it is about all I have *not* done, and so forth. The purity of this vulnerability is thus due to the suppression of all limits and mediations in my encounter with the Other. The debate between Husserl's and Levinas's interpretations of the vulnerability therefore concerns the limits or borders of my skin, its naked exposure or protective dressing, its immediate and unrestricted affectability or its recognizable gestalt allowing for analogy and attention to what different skins might have in common. The debate on the skin is thus simply another way of repeating the debate on subjectivity—on a first, a second, and a third subject—involved in my encounter with the Other.

Reducing all authentic modes of encounter with the Other to a pure—that is, unmediated and nonreciprocal—"face to face" is not far from being an untenable position. Levinas is ready to concede this and consequently develops a theory of justice where the Other is referred to an other Other, or "third person (*le tiers*)," and where the presence of this third with distinct but equal demands, thus competing with those of the first Other, requires me to measure and apportion what I give to each. He also says that the face of the Other bears the trace of God and that the command expressed by the face of the Other comes from God: "Thou shall not kill!" However, none of this changes anything about the fact that the anarchic origin of ethics is the "one for the Other" and that justice and God cannot be approached independently from this primitive duality. On the other hand, appealing to the mediating role of the universal is just as untenable a position as doing away with all mediation. It is an offense to the Other's alterity and exteriority, to his unicity and his need for immediate assistance. If one wishes to amend the intransigent purism of an ethics in which the face of the Other takes me into an immediate and helpless rapture, then one will have to invoke other forms of mediation than those suggested by Kant and Hegel. There seems more promise in what Husserl said about analogy in difference, about sharing the same light in one's appearing, and about worldly borders that separate what we have in common and what must remain strange. But such an appeal to more subtle forms of mediation rejected by Levinas has its price, and it might be precisely an unwillingness to pay this price that has led Levinas to adopt his purist interpretation of the vulnerability of the skin. What, then, is the price for this mediation, for a limitation of responsibility to the measure of finitude and for an encounter with an Other who must not necessarily be considered an absolute stranger? The price to be paid is nothing else than giving up the claim of ethics to be *prima philosophia*.

IV

Returning to Husserl's interpretation of the vulnerability of the skin in order to make out how far it can go in order to meet the exigencies of Levinas, we are led back to the phenomena and to a phenomenology that is less and less present in the later work of Levinas. According to this first interpretation, the encounter with the Other is mediated by the *light* in which we both appear or do not appear. Without pretending that we appear in the same way or that the invisible entangled with my way of appearing is of the same nature as the Other's invisible, the two ways of partial or finite appearing are said to be ana-logous. The common *logos* presupposed in this *analogia* is thus light. This light illuminates an open field of visibility that we call "world." One is therefore entitled to claim that we appear in a common world, even if we do not appear totally in this world and even if we might not have this world totally in common. With this reference to the world, a new mode of our being enters into consideration: not only appearing, but also belonging or dwelling. Despite the fact that we can appear in the same way pretty much anywhere, we do not belong just anywhere. Where we belong or dwell is our home, our "homeworld." Whereas the light might be the same in all different homeworlds, the natives of these different homeworlds are not. They are born into a different civilization, they have different values, and also skins of a different color. It is thus not merely arbitrary geographical borders which separate homeworlds from each other (removing them does not make all of us dwell in the same world). Each of them is unique and, in this sense at least, incommensurable with all others. But can one not say also that natives of different homeworlds have at least an analogous way of being attached to their homeworld and of being curious about foreign homeworlds?

The light to which Husserl appeals is a *transcendental* light. This transcendental light is a communal light that allows particular homeworlds to appear in their irreducible difference. Transcendental philosophy does not equate or assimilate different homeworlds; it does not say living is the same in different homeworlds; it does not make us leave our homeworlds and move into a universal world. Its stress on analogy is the mark of its respect for difference. It differs, however, from Levinas's ethics by its refusal to see the unicity of the stranger and the facticity of being born into a particular homeworld as precluding the possibility of a *logos* that would allow us to *say* the difference. In other words, it refuses to subscribe to the contention put forward by Levinas that the *logos* either belongs to one person or to nobody, that it is either absolutely singular or absolutely universal.

By now it will have become clear that the difference between the two interpretations of the vulnerability of the skin ultimately concerns nothing else than the understanding of *subjectivity.* According to Levinas, the subject or the self originates from the absolute passivity of being affected by the appeal of this Other who is present in this particular situation and with this concrete need. The subject's response to this traumatic proximity of the imploring and commanding face of the Other must be substitution, the gift of itself or the giving away of its self. Husserl sees the subject as a transcendental subjectivity that shares with the Other the light of a *logos* allowing the alterity of the Other to appear and to be expressed. He contends that the subject has access to a *logos* allowing for an understanding of what it means for the Other to dwell (in the same way or differently) in his homeworld. However, since this *logos* is of a transcendental nature, it in no way entails an empirical uniformity. Furthermore, the transcendental subject has but a finite access to this *logos.* This is to say that the transcendental subject, when speaking out about the Other's way of dwelling in a (common or strange) homeworld, experiences the resistance of a limit, and also that it is taken by a desire to push this limit further back.

The finitude of the transcendental subject also means that there is no ground for believing that my finitude and the Other's finitude are in any way reciprocal or reversible so as to compensate for each other's shortcomings and lacks. Even if I can see the Other's back that he cannot see, *my* seeing it has another meaning than does *his* incapacity to see it. My seeing does not fulfill his lack of seeing; his heterogeneity to me prevents me from providing an intuitive fulfillment to his unsatisfied intentions. Put in ethical terms: I can never give the Other precisely what he needs, I cannot do away with his imperfection and finitude. My response to the Other's appeal is always inadequate because it is a response to finitude coming out of another

finitude. Being imperfect myself, I cannot be the perfection the
Other is missing in himself. Beside the impossibility of fully understanding the Other and of adequately fulfilling his needs, the finitude
of the transcendental subject thus also means that I have a finite
understanding of my own finitude. I do not only miss seeing my back,
I also miss having a clear view of all my imperfections, lacks, and
desires. Neither the Other's view of me nor my fullest substitution
for the Other's sufferings can do away with this experience of a lack
in understanding what, precisely, I lack. Quite to the contrary, the
acknowledgment of my imperfect insight into my imperfections
forms a necessary condition for me to be able to do something for the
Other. And doing something for him might turn me into a better
ethical person, but it does not remove any of my ontological imperfections.

At this point, it can be safely concluded that such an account of a
finite transcendental subject encountering the sufferings of the Other
cannot be charged with appealing to a universal reason with no concern for the Other's singularity and one's own vulnerability. Its difference with Levinas must lie elsewhere. In the meantime, we have
also learned that this difference has to do with the egological character of the finite transcendental subject and with an ontological understanding of its ethical responsibility.

We have seen that the *egological* character of the subject, once it
is determined in a transcendental way, cannot mean that I impose my
view on the Other or turn him into an object for me. This egological
character is also compatible with an originary form of passivity and
thus allows for the possibility of the Other's revealing myself to myself, contributing in an essential way to the appearing to myself of
who I am. If my self is a finite self revealed by the Other, my finitude
cannot have a meaning that would belong exclusively to me. It is
always related to the Other, and this in a twofold way: to the Other
that has revealed me to myself and to my way of responding to this
Other. This insight into myself that comes from the Other is thus
without an origin which can be assigned by intuition; it comes from
an Other who for essential reasons escapes my insight, since he is
other than and prior to my finite insight into myself. This insight into
myself, in addition to being finite, is therefore also anarchic. It remains, however, an insight into myself, into my own being, and not
into the Other, and it remains my insight and not the Other's insight.

Similarly, my insight into the Other, even if it is said to come after the Other has revealed myself to myself and to be therefore more of a response, still is mine. Far from overlooking my original entanglement with the Other and far from denying what I owe the Other, far from being a narcissistic incorporation of the Other into myself or an equally narcissistic expulsion of the Other out of myself, emphasis on the fact that an insight or an experience is mine is precisely a way of avoiding con-fusion. My skin, even if it is more like a lunar landscape composed of holes than a tight membrane with some openings, even if it is turned inside out rather than being a solid barrier separating an inside from an outside, still remains my skin and not the skin of the Other.

It is difficult to understand why this rather trivial emphasis on an *ontological* separation between me and the Other should stand in the way of ethics. To give the egological character of the transcendental subject the ontological meaning of mineness (*Jemeinigkeit*)—to assert that I can make the difference between what is my existence and what is the Other's existence—is far from concluding necessarily to some form of ethical egoism. Even if what is mine is never solely mine, it remains the case that only I can give it away. In a similar fashion, my finitude does not preclude infinite engagement for the Other. Had not Husserl already shown that infinite tasks, tasks which require an effort without either an end or final satisfaction, and infinite responsibility, responsibility for what transcends and eludes me forever, belong to the very essence of a finite transcendental subject? Then why is it that Levinas thinks egological finitude to be an inadequate determination of the ethical subject? True, egological finitude does not yet account for ethical goodness, but why should it preclude such an account? Why, if not to satisfy the metaphysical claim that ethics and not ontology is *prima philosophia*?

We have seen that on ontological grounds it might not be too difficult to undermine this claim to convert ethics into first philosophy. However, it would be more fruitful if we could also show that this claim itself is superfluous for the legitimate concerns of Levinas, and that it might even turn against these very concerns. Needless to say, to show this properly would require separate inquiry. But it is possible, by way of conclusion, to discern some hints in this direction in what has already been said.

The genuinely ethical or nonmetaphysical motive for the second interpretation's claim for ethics to be *prima philosophia* is the *epek-eina tes ousias*, the Good beyond Being. That the Good transcends Being means that the Good, rather than belonging to Being as one of its perfections, comes to Being as an unforeseen and undeserved gratuitous gift. It also means that I, as an ethical subject, must go beyond care (*Sorge*) for my own being and give myself away for the sake of the Other. Ethics is thus a matter of a gift without an ontological origin and goal, of a gift without reservation and limit, of a gift that has no common measure with an intersubjective exchange or an invisibility shared by different finite subjects. In Levinas's view, the concern for my own life, for the accounts of what is my own and what belongs to the Other, for a clear distinction between my activity and my passivity, for intermediaries and measure in my relation to the Other—all are out of order in ethics. Renouncing these concerns amounts to conceiving of myself as the Other of the Other and to considering all Others (including myself) to be strangers.

The least one can say is that this is an extreme view on ethical life. It is not difficult to imagine other forms of ethical life (friendship, love, etc.) which, while being unquestionably ethical, do not fit into this picture. One can therefore question whether such a hyperbolic discourse can count as a philosophical foundation for all manifestations of the Good and for all forms of ethical life. Can giving oneself away for the Other, without reservations and limit, be the paradigm, the norm, and even the ideal of ethical life? Asking this question is not just a matter of promoting a trivial form of ethical realism. Quite to the contrary, this question is about ontological and ethical stakes which philosophical thought cannot disregard.

As to the *ontological side*, it must be stressed once more that the life I am giving away is and remains *my* life. It is not the life of a complete stranger, and it is not necessarily a gift addressed to a complete stranger. Turning all Others (including myself) into strangers is ontologically unacceptable and ethically unnecessary. I must have something in common with the life I am giving away, and I must have something in common with the Other to whom I offer the gift of my life. What I have in common with my life is not a merely sensible "enjoyment" (*jouissance*), and what I have in common with the Other is not just universal reason or an "abstract (form of) humanism." Transcendental phenomenology exhibits forms of experience and intersubjective community that are neither empirical nor formally universal.

Turning now to the *ethical side* of the question, the concern for a possible mediation in my relation to the Other becomes a concern for *a measure* or *a limit* to the Other's demand and to my response. Does the face of the Other always command me in a traumatic way to sacrifice my life for him? Does he have the right to ask so much of me? Does God, the trace of whom the Other bears on his face, command me to renounce my guilty existence for the sake of God and the Other? Conversely, why must the gift I owe the Other be the sacrifice of my life? Is there then no limit on what I can be asked to give, no limit I may transgress in an excess of generosity without being obliged to do so? Is nothing of what I give ever enough, so long as I have not given myself entirely?

NOTES

1. Editor's note: a Moebius strip is a loop of paper twisted once and closed into a ring.

2. M. Heidegger, *Vier Seminare: Le Thor 1966, 1968, 1969—Zähringen 1973* (Frankfurt a.M.: V. Klostermann, 1977), 137.

3. E. Husserl, *Cartesian Meditations: An Introduction to Phenomenology,* trans. D. Cairns (The Hague: Martinus Nijhoff, 1960), 110.

4. See section III below.

5. E. Husserl, *Cartesian Meditations,* §§ 43–44 (esp. p. 94). Cf. also E. Husserl, *Zur Phänomenologie der Intersubjektivität: Texte aus dem Nachlass. Dritter Teil: 1929–1935,* ed. I. Kern (The Hague: M. Nijhoff, 1973), 102ff., 357.

6. Cf. *Ms.* A VII 13, p. 67, and *Ms.* C 3, p. 77b (unpublished manuscripts at the Husserl Archive–Leuven).

7. This passivity is then a *susceptiveness,* even if also, as Levinas puts it, "pre-originary." Cf. *AE* 160/*OB* 124–25.

8. As the relation in which I am assigned to a responsibility which is precisely "despite me" (*AE* 180/*OB* 141), the proximity of the Other is the ultimate condition of an individuation and an ipseity that neither I nor the Other can reach and control (cf. already *TeI* 223/*TI* 245).

9. This is asserted as early as "L'Oeuvre d'Edmond Husserl" (1940), *EDE* 48, and is restated, with some nuance, after a rereading of Husserl's texts on consciousness of internal time, at *AE* 42/*OB* 33.

10. Cf. the explicit reference to this effect at *AE* 162–63/*OB* 126.

4

The Alterity of the Stranger and the Experience of the Alien

Robert Bernasconi

I

THE ACCOUNT THAT Levinas gives in *Totality and Infinity* of the face-to-face relation with the Other (in the sense of the other human being) has now achieved classic status. Its basic characteristics are familiar. First, the face-to-face is not a relation, if that means that it forms a totality. Hence Levinas prefers to use the word "relation" only with some qualification, as when he calls the face-to-face a relation *sui generis* or a "relation without relation" (*TeI* 52 and 271/*TI* 80 and 295). The terms of the face-to-face absolve themselves from the relation insofar as they are both absolute within it (*TeI* 35–36, 195/*TI* 64, 220). Second, because the face of the Other is accessible only "starting from an I" (*TeI* 195/*TI* 220), the face-to-face is inaccessible from the outside. In consequence, it cannot be made the subject matter of impersonal reason. Third, the face-to-face has an ethical significance. If the I in its separation is the absolute starting point, then the Other is also absolute in the sense of transcending, exceeding, or overflowing this starting point in such a way as to call the I into question. The Other puts me in question in such a way that I find myself responsible for the Other, for whom I can never do enough. This is the asymmetrical character of the relation. I demand more of myself than I would ever have the right to demand of the Other (*TeI* 24/*TI* 53). These three claims about the face-to-face are now virtually synonymous with the proper name "Levinas." It is as if mentioning Levinas's name in philosophical circles today amounts to summoning this account of alterity. The alterity in question is preeminently the alterity of the stranger. Although Levinas evokes other "figures" of alterity—the widow, the orphan, the hungry, and the teacher—the stranger creates the distance or "separation" that introduces the ethical: "The strangeness of the Other, his irreducibility to the I, to my thoughts and my possessions, is precisely accomplished as a calling into question of my spontaneity, as ethics" (*TeI* 13/*TI* 43). Nevertheless, the alterity of the Other does not depend concretely upon his or her having come from far away. The face is abstract (*HAH* 57/*CPP* 102). The strangerhood of the Other, his or her alterity, is not relative to me.

But can one make sense of an alterity that is not relative? This is one of the most powerful questions that Derrida poses to Levinas in "Violence and Metaphysics." He appeals to the full force of the Western tradition to say that the Other is other only as other than myself. The Other cannot be absolved of a relation to an ego from which it is other; it cannot be absolutely Other.[1] To establish the point, Derrida draws most heavily on Plato's *Sophist.* The precise details of his interpretation are not clear, but all readers will recognize the general outline that gives rise to the consideration that the Other is always other than. In the *Sophist,* Plato's Eleatic Stranger asks about the meaning of the Same and the Other (254e). The Stranger proposes that the Same and the Other are two new classes to be added to the three others: being, motion, and rest. It is in the course of the discussion of the question of whether "the other" and "being" are two names for one class that the Stranger introduces the distinction between beings that are absolute (*kath'auto*) and beings that are relative (*pros alla*) (255c). The status of the Other as a fifth class is secured on the basis that the Other is always relative to some Other (*to d'heteron aei pros heteron*) (255d). The standard interpretation of this passage is that the Other is always other than. Or, to put it another way, the expression "a is other" is, unlike the expression "a exists," an incomplete expression.[2] These considerations underlie, without exhausting, the questions Derrida addresses to Levinas's account of alterity. "The Stranger in the *Sophist,* who, like Levinas, seems to break with Eleatism in the name of alterity, knows that alterity can be thought only as negativity, and above all, can be *said* only as negativity, which Levinas begins by refusing; he knows too, that differing from Being, the other is always relative, is stated *pros eteron,* which does not prevent it from being an *eidos* (or a *genre*, in a nonconceptual sense), that is, from being the same as itself" (*ED* 186/*WD* 127). Derrida notes Levinas's refusal to assimilate the Other to the Stranger's account of the *heteron* (*ED* 186/*WD* 127), while questioning Levinas's ability to do so. Taking up the analyses of Husserl's Fifth *Cartesian Meditation,* Derrida concludes that it might be better to recognize the Other as an alter ego than as absolutely Other: "The other, then, would not be what he is (my fellow man as stranger) if he were not alter ego" (*ED* 187/*WD* 127).

The questions that Derrida poses to Levinas in the section entitled "Of Transcendental Violence" were largely invited by the first section of *Totality and Infinity,* "The Same and the Other" (*le même et l'autre*), whose "aridity" and "labor" Levinas concedes at the same time that he insists it sets "the horizon of this whole research" (*TeI* xviii/ *TI* 29). In those pages, Levinas already addresses Derrida's concern that the absolutely Other is always other than the ego and so not absolutely Other. In the course of explaining how the Cartesian notion of the idea of Infinity enables him to describe "the relation with a being that maintains its total exteriority with respect to him who thinks it" (*TeI* 20–21/*TI* 50), Levinas claims that he has the tools with which to dismiss the Platonic objection. "To affirm the presence in us of the idea of infinity is to deem purely abstract and formal the contradiction the idea of metaphysics is said to harbor, which Plato brings up in the *Parmenides* (133b–135c, 141e–142b)—that the relation with the Absolute would render the Absolute relative" (*TeI* 21/ *TI* 50). This notion of Infinity is borrowed from Descartes, but, on Levinas's terms, Descartes's idea of infinity remains abstract and formal at another level, until it achieves its concretization in a description of "the infinite distance of the Stranger" (*TeI* 21/*TI* 50). Levinas gives this account of the concretization of the stranger as a face: "The face of the Other at each moment destroys and overflows the plastic image it leaves me, the idea existing to my own measure and to the measure of its *ideatum*—the adequate idea. It does not manifest itself by these qualities, but *kath'auto*. It *expresses itself*" (*TeI* 21/*TI* 50–51). In other words, Levinas believes that he has circumvented the problem that, according to Plato, would arise if the Other were always *pros heteron,* because in the face-to-face the stranger does not present him- or herself in terms of qualities, but as exceeding my idea: the stranger is *kath'auto.* I will return to the question of whether one can indeed find in the alterity of *l'étranger* as *kath'auto* an adequate response to the account of alterity given by Plato's Stranger in the *Sophist,* or whether one must look elsewhere in Levinas's writings to resolve this difficulty. First, however, it is necessary to examine Levinas's decision to formulate his thought in Plato's language.

If Levinas expresses his thought in terms of the Same and the Other, *autos* and *heteron,* it is not because he believes them adequate to describe the face-to-face. Already in *Time and the Other,* albeit in the context of a discussion of eros, Levinas puts this pair of terms aside. "To the cosmos, which is Plato's world, is opposed the world of the mind (*l'esprit*) in which the implications of eros are not reduced to the logic of genera where the ego (*moi*) is substituted for the *same,* and Others (*autrui*) for the other (*l'autre*)" (*TA* 89/*TO* 94, translation modified).[3] When in "Violence and Metaphysics" Derrida recalls these lines, he is particularly interested in the way Levinas returns to categories that he seemed to have rejected previously (*ED* 164/ *WD* 111). Derrida continues:

> Now, in *Totality and Infinity,* where the categories of Same and Other (*Autre*) return in force, the *via demonstrandi* and the very energy of the break with the tradition is precisely the adequation of Ego to the Same and of the Other (*Autrui*) to the Other (*Autre*). Without using these terms themselves, Levinas often warned us against confusing *identity* and *ipseity,* Same and Ego: *idem* and *ipse.* This confusion, which in a certain way, is immediately practiced by the Greek concept of *autos* and the German concept of *selbst,* does not occur as spontaneously in French; nevertheless, in spite of prior warnings, it returns as a kind of silent axiom in *Totality and Infinity.* (*ED* 161–62/*WD* 109, translation modified)

Levinas could overlook the distinctions between identity and ipseity, Same and Ego, *idem* and *ipse,* on which he had previously insisted, only because he had come to see the inner connection between the Greek philosophies that did not make the distinction and the modern philosophies of subjectivity that did. Derrida explains:

> If, formerly, interiority, the secret, original separation, had permitted the break with the classical use of the Greek concepts of Same and Other, the amalgamation of the Same and of the Ego (both homogenized with the concept of the finite totality) now permits Levinas to include within the Same a condemnation of both the Greek and the

most modern philosophies of subjectivity, the philosophies most careful to distinguish, as did Levinas previously, the Ego from the Same and the Other (*Autrui*) from the Other (*Autre*). (*ED* 162/*WD* 109–10)

Derrida emphasizes that he does not want to understand this merely as another case of a philosopher abandoning an earlier position. Both stages are necessary and constitute a complex process by which both Greek substantiality and modern subjectivity are contested simultaneously. "Without close attention to this double movement, to this program which seems to contest its own condition and its own initial stage, we would miss the originality of this protest against the concept, the state and totality: it is not made, as is generally the case, in the name of subjective existence, but against it. Simultaneously against Hegel and against Kierkegaard" (*ED* 162/*WD* 110). If Levinas in this context returns to a language he had earlier discarded, it is, according to Derrida, a consequence of "the necessity of lodging oneself within traditional conceptuality in order to destroy it" (*ED* 165/ *WD* 111). These statements provide the context of Derrida's discussion of Levinas's notion of alterity and complicate our sense of what can otherwise be too easily read as a critique. They also draw attention to the fact that Levinas in the first section of *Totality and Infinity* borrows the language of the Same and the Other from Plato's *Parmenides* and the *Sophist* in order to show what that language presupposes and yet at the same time excludes.

Levinas is concerned not just with Plato but with a tendency on the part of both classical and modern metaphysics to exclude knowledge of the other being *kath'auto* (*TeI* 36/*TI* 64–65). He sees a certain continuity between Plato, for whom, in the *Parmenides*, knowledge of the One modifies the One such that it loses its certainty, and Heidegger, for whom, in *Being and Time*, disclosure takes place with respect to a project (*TeI* 37/*TI* 64). In neither case is there a possibility of a "manifestation *kath'auto*" in which the being tells itself to us independently of every position that we take with regard to it (*TeI* 37/*TI* 65). Levinas finds this possibility realized in the face as the coinciding of the expressed with the one who expresses. But even though Levinas's initial aim is to show that Plato's notion of form does not transfer from the realm of things to the face (*TeI* 37/*TI* 66), Plato soon proves to be a valuable ally. Plato catches sight not only of the non-nostalgic structure of desire (*TeI* 34/*TI* 63), but also of that speech in which the speaker comes to his or her own assistance (*TeI* 37, 43/*TI* 66, 71). Furthermore, Levinas finds in Plato's idea of the transcendence of the Good over Being the basis for a pluralist philosophy in which the plurality of Being would neither disappear into the unity of number nor be integrated into a totality (*TeI* 53/*TI* 80).

Next to Plato, the most important figure for understanding the relation of Levinas's account of alterity to traditional conceptuality is Husserl. The pages of *Totality and Infinity* in which Levinas offers his account of the Other as *kath'auto* are also the pages in which he gives his most explicit statement of his objections to Husserl's theory of intersubjectivity. I shall next turn to the debate between Husserl and Levinas. It is often said that Derrida is never more critical of Levinas than in the context of his reading of Husserl, but that assessment seems to derive from the idea that Derrida takes Husserl's side against Levinas.[4] In order to clarify Derrida's strategy and keep the larger issues in view, I shall have to show that that is not the case. In my third section, I shall propose that the chapter on "Substitution" in Levinas's *Otherwise Than Being or Beyond Essence* can be understood as a response to some suggestions by Derrida in "Violence and Metaphysics." At the same time, I shall argue that *Otherwise Than Being* provides an answer to some of Levinas's other critics— specifically, Francis Jacques and Paul Ricoeur, who, like Derrida, have attempted to turn the dialectic of Same and Other back on Levinas precisely in the context of juxtaposing Levinas's account of alterity with that of Husserl. In an effort to take the debate further, in the final section I will turn to the work of Bernhard Waldenfels, who has not only identified certain flaws in the critiques of both Jacques and Ricoeur, but has also offered an account of the experience of the alien that serves to highlight certain features of Levinas's discussions that are all too often ignored.

II

The *Cartesian Meditations* are one of the places where Husserl is concerned to refute the charge that his phenomenology amounts to a transcendental solipsism.[5] The specific question Husserl addresses in his Fifth Meditation—and the question to which he believes he has found the answer—is that of how I can constitute in myself another ego so that I experience what is constituted in me as nevertheless other than me (*Hul* 154/*CM* 126). "How can my ego, within its peculiar ownness, constitute under the name, 'experience of something other,' precisely something *other*—something, that is, with a sense that excludes the constituted from the concrete make-up of the sense-constituting I myself, as somehow the latter's analogue?" (*Hul* 126/*CM* 94). In other words, how are we to understand the fact that the ego has intentionalities in which it wholly transcends its own being (*Hul* 135/*CM* 105)?

Husserl proposes that in order for there to be alterity, the intentional relation to it must involve a certain mediacy: "if what belongs to the other's own essence were directly accessible (*in direkter Weise zugänglich*), it would be merely a moment of my own essence, and ultimately he himself and I myself would be the same" (*Hul* 139/*CM* 109). Husserl calls this particular mediacy (*Mittelbarkeit*) by the name *appresentation*. Appresentation is explained as a kind of making co-present distinct from presentation as such. It plays a role throughout everyday experience in the case of both organic and physical bodies. For example, the reverse side of an object is not given in perception, but it is appresented in an "analogical apperception" which can subsequently be confirmed simply by walking around the object in question. Similarly, it is by "analogizing transfer" that, for example, scissors are recognized at first glance *as* scissors (*Hul* 141/ *CM* 111). Nevertheless, there is an important difference between apperceptions within the primordial sphere and those that present themselves with the sense of alter ego. As with physical objects, an organic body is presented and it is recognized by an appresentation of an organic body, an appresentation that works by analogy and not by inference. But what is peculiar about the appresentation of an organic body as opposed to a physical body is that it takes place by a "transfer from animate organism" (*Hul* 140/*CM* 110). A body is presented, but it is only on analogy with my own body that it is recognized as an organic body. Similarly, at another level, my identification of the other ego as such is derived from my own case by a process of analogizing which Husserl calls "empathy" (*Einfühlung*). Only through empathy, as a form of alienation, is the alien constituted. It is by making myself Other that there is an Other. Husserl explicates the expression "alter ego" in the following way: "the ego involved here is I myself, constituted within my own primordial ownness"

(*Hul* 140/*CM* 110). And yet Husserl will also say that the alter ego is appresented as other than mine (*Hul* 148/*CM* 112). The ego and the alter ego are given in an original pairing or coupling and form a unity of similarity (*Hul* 142/*CM* 112). The Other is an intentional modification of my ego, a "mirroring" of my own self (*Hul* 142/*CM* 115).

In spite of Husserl's orientation in terms of the "here and there" such that the body of the Other is not a reduplication of my own body, the parallel he draws between appresentation of the Other's body and of the Other's ego raises the question of whether Husserl avoids conceiving the Other as simply a reduplication of the ego. Can the I as accounted for by Husserl ever be surprised by the alter ego? Does this adventure ever risk becoming "dangerous," as Levinas puts it in his chapter "Substitution" (*AE* 126/*OB* 99)? Although Levinas's objections to Husserl in *Totality and Infinity* could be more specific, their general thrust could not be clearer: Husserl fails to secure the genuine alterity or otherness of the Other because the Husserlian constitution of the Other is only a variation of the constitution of the object.

> The constitution of the Other's body in what Husserl calls "the primordial sphere," the transcendental "pairing" of the object thus constituted with my own body itself experienced from within as "I can," the comprehension of this body of the Other as an *alter ego*—this analysis dissimulates, in each of its stages which are taken as a description of constitution, mutations of object constitution into a relation with the Other—which is as primordial as the constitution from which it is to be derived. The primordial sphere, which corresponds to what we call the same, turns to the absolutely other only on call from the Other. *Revelation* constitutes a veritable inversion of *objectifying cognition*. (*TeI* 39/*TI* 67, translation modified)

So far as Levinas is concerned, Husserl attempts to constitute the Other, the basis of objectivity, in a purely subjective process. Levinas himself, by contrast, insists that the relation to the Other is not just a modification of intentionality, but a reversal of it. Levinas appeals to Descartes's Third Meditation to develop the alternative (*TeI* 185/*TI* 219). In Descartes, the Infinite is not an object which I can constitute: God is a thought I cannot think or contain. The idea of God exceeds me, so that if it can be said that I think God, it is only because God thinks himself in me. In this way, Levinas returns to Descartes to correct Husserl's *Cartesian Meditations*.

In "Violence and Metaphysics," Derrida faithfully records Levinas's adaptation of Descartes's argument to challenge Husserl's transcendental constitution of the Other. Levinas uses Descartes to support his claim that Husserl's *Cartesian Meditations* presupposes "that whose genesis it allegedly traces" (*ED* 156/*WD* 105–6). Derrida questions the alleged priority of the asymmetry of radical alterity by asking if it was not made possible by an underlying symmetry. This symmetry would be transcendental, whereas in Derrida's understanding, Levinas situated the asymmetry at the empirical level. Derrida, appealing to Hegel, argues in favor of a doubling of empirical symmetry: "The other, for me, is an ego which I know to be in relation to me as an other. Where have these movements been better described than in the *Phenomenology of Spirit*? The movement of transcendence toward the other, as invoked by Levinas, would have no meaning if it did not bear within it, as one of its essential meanings, that in my ipseity I know myself to be for the other" (*ED* 185/*WD* 126). Alongside the empirical asymmetry by which the Other is Other to me, there is another empirical asymmetry by which I am Other to the Other. Together they constitute a "strange symmetry," "the transcendental symmetry of two empirical asymmetries" (*ED* 185/*WD* 126) that, according to Derrida, goes unrecognized in Levinas: "[its] trace appears nowhere in Levinas' descriptions" (*ED* 188/*WD* 128).[6] Derrida writes: "Dissymmetry itself would be impossible without this symmetry, which is not of the world, and which, having no real aspect, imposes no limit upon alterity and dissymmetry— makes them possible, on the contrary" (*ED* 184/*WD* 126).

The argument in favor of symmetry is particularly marked in Husserl's account in the difference of levels that is recorded in the *Cartesian Meditations*. My ego is given to me in self- presentation, whereas the Other's ego is given in an appresentation not open to fulfillment by presentation: I experience another's psychic life with merely secondary originality, because that Other's psychic life is essentially inaccessible to me in direct perception (*Hul* 148/*CM* 119). But Husserl does not regard such an account of the constitution of the Other to be complete, for it lacks reference to "the constitution of higher levels of intermonadic community" (*Hul* 156–59/*CM* 128–31). As my understanding of someone penetrates his or her horizon of ownness, I come to recognize that that person experiences me as his or her Other. In the case of a plurality of Others, I find that they are experienced also by one another as Others. "I can experience any given Other not only as himself an Other but also as related in turn to *his* Others and perhaps—with a mediatedness that may be conceived as reiterable— related at the same time to me" (*Hul* 158/*CM* 130). Husserl calls the open community of a plurality of monads mutually for one another by the name "transcendental intersubjectivity" (*Hul* 156/*CM* 130). He describes this "mutual being for one another" as entailing "an objectivating equalization of my existence with that of all others (*eine objektivierende Gleichstellung meines Daseins und des aller Anderen*)" (*Hul* 157–58/*CM* 129). In his study of the Fifth *Cartesian Meditation,* Ricoeur describes this stage in terms that immediately show its relevance to Derrida's discussion of Levinas: "For good or bad, it seems sure that one must renounce the asymmetry of the relationship me-Other required by the monadic idealism in order to account for this objectifying equalization required by sociological realism."[7] What Derrida calls "transcendental symmetry" seems to correspond to what Husserl calls "objectifying equalization." It was already implicit in Husserl's description at the beginning of the Fifth *Cartesian Meditation* of what had to be accounted for: "I experience them (these alter egos) at the same time as subjects for this world, as experiencing it (this world that I experience) and, in so doing, experiencing me too, even as I experience the world and others in it" (*Hul* 123/ *CM* 91). Of course, this passage would not satisfy Levinas's conception of alterity, but it helps to explain the basis of Derrida's challenge to it. Derrida seems, at least at first reading, to be not only contesting Levinas's interpretation of Husserl, but also calling into question the coherence of Levinas's account of the face-to-face.

However, on closer examination, it emerges that Derrida's argument is not suited to such a purpose. When addressing the question of whether Levinas does justice to Husserl, Derrida tends to take Husserl's statements of purpose at face value as if one need not question whether Husserl had accomplished what he set out to do. Furthermore, another strand of Derrida's argument points in another direction. Derrida takes Husserl's affirmation of the irreducibly *mediate* nature of the intentionality aiming at the Other as Other to be evidence that Husserl does indeed recognize the "radical *separation* of the absolute origins, the relationship of absolved absolutes and

nonviolent respect for the secret: the opposite of victorious assimilation" (*ED* 183/*WD* 124). This is to judge Husserl by Levinas's standards and to find him meeting them. The debate shifts, almost
imperceptibly, from the task of challenging the coherence of Levinas's enterprise to the question of the language that would better
preserve the result. Derrida's surprising contention is that Husserl's
phrase "alter ego" says alterity better than Levinas's appeal to "the
absolute Other." Whereas Levinas denies that the "theoretical idea
of another myself" is adequate to the Infinite (*TeI* 56/*TI* 84), so that
the notion of the Other as alter ego reduces the Other to a *modification of myself* (and we have seen language suggestive of this in Husserl), Derrida insists that the notion of the alter ego alone manages
to secure for the Other *its irreducibility to my ego.* Husserl insists
that one recognize the Other as Other only as a transcendental alter
ego. According to Derrida, Levinas's refusal to recognize this has a
serious consequence: "To refuse to see in it [the Other] an ego in this
sense is, within the ethical order, the very gesture of all violence. If
the other was not recognized as ego, its entire alterity would collapse" (*ED* 184/*WD* 125). This objection belongs to Derrida's resistance to Levinas's use of the notion of the "absolutely other." The
Other cannot be the Other of the Same except by being itself the
same, that is, an ego.

Ultimately, therefore, what Derrida wants to save from Husserl's
analyses is the notion of the alter ego. According to Derrida, Levinas
understands the *alter* as a modification of my real (empirical) identity
(*ED* 187/*WD* 127). To make the Other immediate is to reduce the
Other to the Same so that it is not the Other, and to make the Other
absolutely Other is either to say something nonsensical or to oppose
the Other to the Same and so fail to establish genuine otherness.
Otherness is maintained only in the contradiction *alter ego* which
states that "the absolute of alterity is the same." The distance between Levinas and Derrida is therefore not as great as it first appeared to be. Derrida quotes Levinas's early work *Existence and
Existents,* where Levinas rejects the phrase *alter ego:* "The Other as
Other is not only an *alter ego.* He is what I am not" (*DE* 162/*EE* 95,
cited at *ED* 184/*WD* 125). Derrida's response is that "The other is
absolutely other only if he is an ego, that is, in a certain way, if he is
the same as I" (*ED* 187/*WD* 127). Derrida's conclusion is not that
Levinas is guilty of breaking the rules of logic with the result that he

ends up talking nonsense, although it might indeed seem that this is his argument. Rather, he complains that Levinas's rejection of the notion of the alter ego follows "formal logic" in spite of the fact that he also claims repeatedly not to be bound by it (e.g., *TeI* 77/*TI* 104). Derrida therefore accepts the "impossibility of translating my relation to the Other into the rational coherence of language." And he acknowledges that "one may no longer draw inspiration from *within* the coherence of the *logos*" (*ED* 187/*WD* 128). His quarrel with Levinas is ultimately not that Levinas fails to recognize that there can be no "absolute Other" so much that he is inconsistent in allowing talk of the "absolute Other" while rejecting the phrase "alter ego." Furthermore, although both phrases are incoherent in terms of the *logos,* Derrida suggests that "alter ego" says better what Levinas *wants to say* with his expression "absolutely Other." In the same way, Derrida also underlines that his own call for "the transcendental symmetry of two empirical asymmetries" relies on a formula that is logically absurd (*ED* 184/*WD* 126).

It should be clear that at the time of "Violence and Metaphysics" the issue between Levinas and Derrida is more about the appropriate language for saying the Other than about the validity of Husserl's account. In "Violence and Metaphysics," Derrida does not offer a defense of Husserl, but restricts himself to showing that Husserl's text is not vulnerable to Levinas's criticisms. Derrida writes, "Far from thinking that the fifth of the *Cartesian Meditations* must be admired in silence as the last word on this problem, we have sought here only to begin to experience and to respect its power of resistance to Levinas' criticisms" (*ED* 194 n/*WD* 316 n. 51). After all, one would not expect Derrida, even in 1964, to be engaged in a straightforward defense of Husserlian constitution. Only three years later, in *Speech and Phenomena,* he would say that "The very concept of constitution must itself be deconstructed."[8] Furthermore, Levinas himself subsequently finds within Husserl's Fifth *Cartesian Meditation* what he had previously said Husserl neglects: in "Notes on Meaning," an essay first published in 1981, Levinas observes how, according to Husserl, I constitute the Other in appresentation on the basis of the perceived behavior of a body analogous to the one I inhabit. He then comments: "What we take to be the secret of the other man in appresentation is precisely the reverse side (*envers*) of a meaning other than knowledge: awakening to the other man in his identity, an identity indiscernible for knowledge, thought in which the proximity of the neighbor signifies, commerce with the Other which cannot be reduced to experience, the approach of the first comer" (*DVI* 244).[9] Further light is thrown on this "reverse side" of Husserl's discussion by the "Preface" Levinas wrote to Geraet's dissertation on Merleau-Ponty. There Levinas refers to the Fifth *Cartesian Meditation* as "the *authentically Husserlian* possibility for leaving idealism."[10] Levinas remarks that a hasty reading would expect from this text a proof of the existence of the Other and that it would find evidence, particularly in the discussion of my body's "original coupling" with the body of the Other, that Husserl lost himself in the realm of transcendental empiricism. But then Levinas asks if empathy (*Einfühlung*), far from presenting itself as a form of knowledge, is not the *non-constituted event* of substitution and of proximity, such that this event is already presupposed by "knowledge of the Other" (cf. *AE* 161/*OB* 125).

When Derrida responds to Levinas's attempt to think infinity as a positive plenitude, he appropriately employs the formula used by the Stranger in the *Sophist* to describe non-being: it is inexpressible, unspeakable, and irrational (*aphtheggon te auto kai arreton kai alogon*) (238e). However, it is apparent from the context that Derrida does not employ the formula in order to reject Levinas's thought, but rather to expose the conditions that render it possible: "Perhaps Levinas calls us toward this unthinkable-impossible-unutterable beyond (tradition's) Being and Logos. But it must not be possible either to think or state this call. In any event, that the positive plenitude of classical infinity is translated into language only by betraying itself in a negative word (in-finite), perhaps situates, in the most profound way, the point where thought breaks with language. A break which afterward will but resonate throughout all language" (*ED* 168–69/ *WD* 114). In the next section, I shall try to show that in *Otherwise Than Being or Beyond Essence* Levinas finds just such a resonating break in the non-constituted event of substitution.[11]

III

Early in *Otherwise Than Being*, Levinas concedes to Derrida that negativity would be insufficient to the task of saying being's Other.

But he contests Derrida's claim, introduced on the authority of the Eleatic Stranger, that alterity can be thought and said only as negativity (*ED* 186/*WD* 127): "The philosopher finds language again in the abuses of language in the history of philosophy, in which the unsayable and the beyond being are conveyed before us. But negativity, still correlative with being, will not be enough to signify the *other than being*" (*AE* 10/*OB* 9, translation modified). Such abuses of language are a recurrent theme in *Otherwise Than Being*. So, for example, Levinas writes that "The anarchical is possible only when contested by language (*discours*), which betrays, but conveys, its anarchy, without abolishing it, by an abuse of language" (*AE* 127 n/*OB* 194 n. 2).

Derrida also writes by means of such abuses of language. In 1967, in an addition to the revised version of "Violence and Metaphysics," he referred to an unheard-of graphics that inscribes the relations between the philosophical and the nonphilosophical (*ED* 163/*WD* 110–11). This is called for because without such ruses the only language available is that of Western metaphysics. But in contrast to the questioning characteristic of "Violence and Metaphysics," Derrida's return to Levinas in 1980 barely conceals an admiration for the title *Otherwise Than Being or Beyond Essence:*

> In a singular comparative locution that does not constitute a phrase, an adverb (*otherwise*) immeasurably wins out over a verb (and what a verb: to be) to say something "other" that cannot make nor even modify a noun or a verb, nor this noun-verb which always amounts/returns to *being*, in order to say something else, some "other" thing that is neither verb nor noun, and especially not the simple *alterity* that would still submit the *otherwise* (that modality without substance) to the authority of a category, an essence or being again.[12]

With this formulation, Derrida's objections to Levinas's language, if they were indeed objections, have taken a backseat. In *Adieu: à Emmanuel Levinas,* Derrida even feigns surprise that Levinas concedes that the ontological language of *Totality and Infinity* was not definitive, even though it was probably Derrida himself who convinced him of this.[13]

In *Otherwise Than Being,* Levinas insists that being must be understood on the basis of *being's Other* (*AE* 21/*OB* 16). The opening sentences of the book mark the difference between what Plato calls *heteron* and what Levinas calls "being's Other" by posing a question which would make no sense if they were identical: "If transcendence has a meaning, it can only signify the fact that the *event of being,* the *esse,* the *essence,* passes over to what is the other of being. But what is *being's Other*? Among the five 'genera' of the *Sophist* a genus opposed to being is lacking, even though since the *Republic* the beyond essence was a question" (*AE* 3/*OB* 3, translation modified). As with *Totality and Infinity,* Levinas sets out from Plato in an attempt to leave Plato behind. On this occasion, however, Levinas does not employ the dialectic of the Same and the Other to do so. He directly distances himself from that effort: "The proximity of the one to the other is here conceived outside of ontological categories in which, in different ways, the notion of the *other (autre)* also figures" (*AE* 19/*OB* 15). The renewed effort to avoid ontological language is combined with a difference of emphasis that ultimately places the analysis on a different level.

In *Otherwise Than Being,* the attempt to go beyond essence proceeds less with reference to the alterity of the other human being than to subjectivity. "The essence claims to recover and cover over every ex-ception—negativity, nihilation, and already since Plato, non-being, which 'in a certain sense is.' It will then be necessary to show that the exception of the 'other than being,' beyond non-being, signifies subjectivity or humanity, the *oneself (soi-même)* which repels the annexations by essence" (*AE* 9/*OB* 8). Levinas establishes a list of some of the cases where this subjectivity which breaks with essence has been recognized within the history of philosophy. I repeat here the list given in "No Identity" because it is slightly fuller than the one found in *Otherwise Than Being:*

> These are marvellous moments: the One without being of Plato's *Parmenides;* the *I* that breaks through in the *cogito* when all being is in shipwreck, but before the I is rescued into being, as though the shipwreck has not taken place; the Kantian unity of the "I think" before its reduction to a logical form, which Hegel will reduce to a concept; Husserl's pure ego, transcendent in immanence, on the hither side of the world, but also on the hither side of the absolute being of the reduced consciousness; the Nietzschean man shaking the world's being in the passage to the overman. (*HAH* 94/*CPP* 147)

This list seems designed to counter any attempt, such as Derrida's, to declare the other than being foreign to the tradition of Greek philosophy. In *Totality and Infinity*, Levinas approaches the One in Plato with suspicion. It inaugurates the traditional focus on unity as a totality from which only the Good, as the *epekeina tes ousias*, seems to escape (*TeI* 75–76/*TI* 102). Yet in subsequent texts, and especially the chapter on "Substitution" from *Otherwise Than Being*, the One in the first hypothesis of Plato's *Parmenides* serves as an important model for saying how the subject in the accusative is expelled from being (*AE* 140/*OB* 110). To Derrida's question addressed to *Totality and Infinity*, "why does Levinas return to categories he seemed to have rejected previously?" (*ED* 164/*WD* 111), one must add a further question addressed to *Otherwise Than Being*: why does Levinas seemingly turn away from the absolute Other to focus once more, as he had done in *Existence and Existents*, on subjectivity?

Levinas's notion of substitution offers a response to Derrida's questions about his use of the language of alterity.[14] Levinas does not accept that it is necessary to conceive the Other under the form of an ego. Rather, he says that I am Other, and yet, in clear contrast to Husserl, Other without alienation (*AE* 139/*OB* 109). This takes place in giving, which is in turn possible only because of corporeality: "the body . . . makes me other without alienation" (*AE* 181/*OB* 142).[15] The most telling sentence runs as follows: "In substitution, my being that belongs to me and not to another is undone, and it is through this substitution that I am not 'another,' but 'me' " (*AE* 163/*OB* 127). This is the meaning of the "contradictory trope of the-one-for-the-other" (*AE* 126/*OB* 100). Substitution of the one for the Other is not the psychological event of compassion, but a putting oneself in the place of the Other (*AE* 186/*OB* 146). Or, more precisely, it is the asymmetry of responsibility. Substitution is my responsibility for everyone else, including their responsibility: "No one can substitute himself for me, who substitute myself for all" (*AE* 162/*OB* 136). My responsibility for the responsibility of the Other constitutes that "one degree of responsibility more" (*AE* 150/*OB* 117).

That substitution is, at least in part, a response to the questions raised by Derrida in "Violence and Metaphysics" is confirmed in the transformation that Levinas's thought undergoes. In "Violence and Metaphysics," Derrida writes that "According to Levinas, there would be no interior difference, no fundamental and autochthonous alterity within the ego (*dans le Moi*)" (*ED* 162/*WD* 109). Derrida's development of the problematic relies on that claim, which is incontestable as a reading of *Totality and Infinity*. But in *Otherwise Than Being* it is expressly contradicted. The notion of substitution amounts to saying that "the other is in me and in the midst of my very identification" (*AE* 160/*OB* 125). The only reason why this does not amount to a recantation of Levinas's earlier thought is that "substitution" operates not at the level of the ego (*le moi*), but of the self (*le soi*), such that the whole notion of identity has to be rethought to the point where Levinas refers to "the unjustifiable identity . . . expressed in terms such as ego, I, oneself" (*AE* 135/*OB* 106). Levinas can now compare the self to a stranger, and he thereby bridges the distance that had previously separated the Same and the Other. "To revert to oneself is not to establish oneself at home, even if stripped of all one's acquisitions. It is to be like a stranger, hunted down even in one's home, contested in one's own identity and one's very poverty" (*AE* 117/*OB* 92). Where previously Levinas found that in the relationship with another I found myself rich (*EDE* 193/*TrO* 350–51), now the metaphors are reversed. Of course, the change in the metaphors is not what is important here, except as an indication of the philosophical transformation that underlies it. The measure of that transformation is found in the way it serves to respond to some of the leading criticisms of Levinas.

To the end, Levinas persists with the language of the absolutely Other, retaining it as the preferred terminology for introducing his thought. I would be tempted to call it his exoteric doctrine, but *Otherwise Than Being* cannot be conceived of in this way simply because it is under-read. The earlier, more familiar formulation is, one suspects, not judged by him to be wrong so much as incomplete, and so ultimately misleading. Of course, it had already proved misleading in Levinas's very first attempts to formulate it, as Simone de Beauvoir showed when, discussing Levinas's *Time and the Other,* she discerned in his application of the language of alterity to describe women a veiled privilege of the masculine.[16] The discussion of the feminine in *Totality and Infinity* confirms, if there was ever any doubt, the limits of Levinas's perspective on this point, but it cannot be reduced to de Beauvoir's conclusion that because for him (Levinas), "He is the Subject, he is the Absolute—she is the Other." As everyone now knows, the Other is also absolute. But there is always a question as to whether the language of alterity is not in certain circumstances complicit with various forms of exoticism. Nor is the language of substitution free of danger. Taking responsibility for the Other sounds like paternalism, or perhaps identification, and Levinas's legitimation of such a language could easily be perverted to that end. This is why one has to hope that if the terminology of substitution ever becomes as widespread as that of absolute alterity, the chain of thought that led to it will not be forgotten, as it alone can safeguard against misinterpretation.

IV

I have now shown how certain passages from *Otherwise Than Being* can be read as a response to Derrida. These same passages have an impact on other readings, especially those that set out from the account of the face given in *Totality and Infinity* but fail to recognize the extent to which *Otherwise Than Being* goes beyond that perspective. If I now take up the objections leveled against Levinas by Francis Jacques and Paul Ricoeur, it is not so much to answer them point by point, as if this were a standard philosophical dispute for which the rules are known in advance, as to further show the radicality of *Otherwise Than Being*. Even though both Jacques and Ricoeur are aware of the later book, they do not appear to have seen the extent to which it has shifted the ground on which the debate must be held. To the question of whether or not Levinas manages to escape from the classic dialectic of the Same and the Other, Jacques responds that he only inverts the standard arguments with the result that ultimately "the philosophical narcissism of the ego" is left intact.[17] In *Oneself as Another*, Ricoeur takes another route through the same territory. Unlike Derrida, who at least appears to set Husserl and Levinas at odds with each other, or Jacques, who eventually minimizes their differences, Ricoeur seeks to combine the two. He can do this because for him the movement from the ego toward the alter ego maintains a priority in the genealogical dimension, whereas in the ethical dimension the priority is held by the movement from the Other toward me.[18] Ricoeur argues that there is no contradiction in holding the movement from the Same to the Other and from the Other to the Same to be "dialectically complementary" (*SA* 393/*OA* 340).

Both Jacques and Ricoeur thus return us to the difficult question of "relation" in Levinas. Jacques believes that the idea of relation

"has the power to confirm each person in his or her positive difference": "If the relation is fundamental . . . it would be inconsistent
(and a technical mistake) to make the self into the subject of a relation
of which, in fact, it is simply one pole—on exactly the same level as
the other, with neither privilege nor dissymmetry between them"
(*DeS* 156/*DS* 129). It is clear that although Jacques directs this argument primarily against proponents of the primacy of the self, of which
Levinas is definitely not one, it is formulated in such a way that it can
readily be applied to Levinas as well. And this is what he immediately
attempts to do when he claims that the absurdity of the concept of
absolute alterity is that it leads to a reinforcement of the primacy of
the self (*DeS* 157/*DS* 129). Jacques locates this moment in Levinas at
the point where the latter claims that radical heterogeneity is possible "only if the Other is other in relation to a term whose essence is
to act as a way into the relation, to be the Same, not relatively but
absolutely" (*DeS* 169/*DS* 141). Jacques maintains that Levinas is led
to this claim by the tension between his ethical theme and his debt
to the phenomenological method, which cannot free itself from the
primacy of the intentional ego (*DeS* 180/*DS* 152). According to Jacques, Levinas's often accurate descriptions run counter to his metaphysics of separation and radical exteriority (*DeS* 169/*DS* 141).
Accordingly, what he sees is a refusal on Levinas's part to renounce
the egological primacy of the I (*moi*), even though the transcendental
approach has been found inadequate to the encounter with the other
human being. It makes no difference to Jacques that the egological
"for oneself" has been transformed into a "for-the-other."[19] As he
sees it, Levinas remains a victim of the idea of intentionality because
"it is as if for Levinas intersubjective relations always started from
the self (*moi*)" (*DeS* 170/*DS* 142). Ultimately, separation in Levinas
works not "in favor of difference," but "to the advantage of the self
(*moi*)" (*DeS* 170/*DS* 143). Jacques's response is not surprising, given
the nature of his philosophical commitments. In certain respects, his
position approximates the negative critique that some readers have
mistakenly located in "Violence and Metaphysics," although Derrida's essay, as I tried to show above, has a more complex aim.

Whereas Jacques judges the dialectic of the Same and the Other
to be undermining insofar as it makes my relations with Others "a
matter of constitution or problematic encounter" (*DeS* 173/*DS* 145,
translation modified), Ricoeur attempts to exploit this dialectic in

order to keep the self from occupying the place of foundation (*SA* 368/*OA* 318). Ricoeur's objection to Levinas's "re-working of the 'great kinds' of the Same and the Other" (*SA* 368/*OA* 336) arises from the lack of complementarity in Levinas's treatment of the relation of the Same to the Other and of the Other to the Same. He notes first that Levinas thinks of the relation as an "irrelation": "the initiative of the Other . . . establishes no relation" (*SA* 221/*OA* 188). "Because the Same signifies totalization and separation, the exteriority of the Other can no longer be expressed in the language of relation" (*SA* 388/*OA* 366). Ricoeur claims that Levinas is at an impasse "unless the preeminently ethical movement of the Other toward the self is made to intersect with . . . the genealogical movement from the self toward the Other" (*SA* 391/*OA* 339). In a move reminiscent of "Violence and Metaphysics," Ricoeur insists that Levinas's attempt to derive responsibility from the Other must be made to intersect with Husserl's attempt to derive the alter ego from the ego (*SA* 382/*OA* 331).[20] According to Ricoeur, Levinas needs to be supplemented by Husserl here because Levinas's own account of separation renders unthinkable the distinction between the self (*soi*) and the I (*moi*) (*SA* 391/*OA* 339). More specifically, Ricoeur argues that Levinas's account of separation does not provide him with an appropriate account of the self because it is doubtful that an interiority determined solely by the desire for retreat could ever be receptive to what is addressed to it from elsewhere.[21]

Ricoeur's own attempt to negotiate the distinction between the self and the I involves a two-pronged conception of otherness that corresponds to the distinction between the Same as *idem* and the Same as *ipse* (*SA* 382/*OA* 331).[22] These are the same terms that, as Derrida noted in "Violence and Metaphysics," Levinas had already introduced in *Time and the Other*, only to reject them fifteen years later in *Totality and Infinity*. Ricoeur himself understands the reason for this change as a consequence of the larger picture behind Levinas's analyses. Levinas's work is "directed against a conception of the identity of the Same, to which the otherness of the Other is diametrically opposed, but at a level of radicality where the distinction I propose between two sorts of identity, that of *ipse* and *idem*, cannot be taken into account" (*SA* 387/*OA* 335). According to Ricoeur, Levinas refuses the distinction between *idem* and *ipse* after the 1940s "because, in Levinas, the identity of the Same is bound up with an ontology of totality," but it is an ontology which Ricoeur himself has "never assumed or even come across" (SA 387/OA 335). In other words, Ricoeur ultimately separates himself from Levinas on the basis of a dispute over the nature of the history of Western philosophy. That is also what separates Ricoeur from Derrida, even though Ricoeur's own arguments against Levinas are remarkably similar to observations already made in "Violence and Metaphysics." That is also why it is highly significant, now that I am about to turn to the work of Bernhard Waldenfels, that the latter has expressed surprise at Ricoeur's denial of the pervasiveness of such an ontology of totality.[23] For Waldenfels, this blind spot is the basis for Ricoeur's claim that "foreignness—as in both classical Greek and modern thought—belongs as a relative foreignness not to a first but to a second philosophy."[24] Although Waldenfels focuses on the full range of what is covered by the experience of the alien and thus does not directly engage the same complex set of ethical issues that organize Levinas's thought, he has identified what is problematic in the interpretations of Levinas by both Jacques and Ricoeur. Waldenfels recognizes that both Jacques and Ricoeur mischaracterize Levinas's philosophy to the degree that they tend to represent his thought as an inversion of Husserl's. The Other is not for Levinas a negative figure of the I, but a figure of excess that breaks up our thinking.[25]

In the course of his account of the experience of the alien, Waldenfels alludes to Levinas's account of an encounter with the Other, but he does not give this encounter a unique status.[26] Nor does he suppose that Levinas was himself trying to give an account of the experience of the alien. And yet Waldenfels's analyses do throw light on some of the issues raised by Levinas. I shall limit myself here to two of them: the sense in which Levinas's enterprise remains phenomenological, and Levinas's characterization of alterity.

For all the differences between Husserl and Levinas, Waldenfels's essay "Experience of the Alien in Husserl's Phenomenology" enables us to juxtapose the former's more classically phenomenological analysis with Levinas's somewhat different approach.[27] Waldenfels's inspiration comes from Husserl's paradoxical characterization of the experience of the Other as a "verifiable accessibility of what is originally inaccessible" (Hul 144/CM 114). It is this that enables Waldenfels's Husserl to come closer to Levinas than might otherwise be the case. Waldenfels also finds a certain asymmetry in Husserl's account of the relation.[28] Nevertheless, Waldenfels also recognizes that whereas Husserl's account of the original non-originality in which the Other shows him- or herself can be characterized as a co-presenting, Levinas explains that the "absence of the Other is precisely his or her presence as Other" (*TA* 89/*TO* 94). Waldenfels comments: "This little step from co-presence to absence is not nothing, and it certainly becomes clear here how the non-phenomenality of the phenomena must still reveal itself phenomenally if phenomenology is not to turn into some form of metaphysics or post-metaphysics" (*EF* 49/*EA* 25). Levinas always starts from the phenomena but, as he elaborates his thought, invariably departs from a description of experience in an effort to uncover what he sometimes calls the "enigma" (*EDE* 203–17/*CPP* 61–73).[29] There is a further important difference between Waldenfels's project and that of Levinas. If one examines the discussion of the alien in *Order in the Twilight*, one finds, even within this more systematic presentation, a respect for the concrete character of the alien lacking in Levinas. Although Levinas, in *Totality and Infinity*, invokes the face as the concretization of the Infinite, he shows little or no interest in the concrete Other, but aims instead for an abstract Other. I have tried to show elsewhere that this has problematic consequences for the way in which Levinas can address the question of racism.[30]

Waldenfels also helps to clarify the distinction between *idem* and *ipse*, sameness and selfhood. Indeed, he claims that it suggests a parallel contrast between two senses of the Other. Diversity (*diversité, Verschiedenheit*) corresponds to "sameness" as alienness or foreignness (*étrangeté, Fremdheit*) corresponds to "ownness."[31] If, as Derrida suggested in "Violence and Metaphysics," German fails to distinguish between two different senses of *selbst* that present themselves more readily to a French speaker, then Waldenfels seems to respond by saying that the French *autre, autrui,* or *alterité,* corresponding to the English notions of the Other and alterity, fail to distinguish between what is readily identified as different to a German speaker. The idea here is that the alien is not simply an Other (*heteron, aliud*) that arises through demarcation from the self, as in Plato's *Sophist* (*TF* 20–21). The radically alien is grasped only as excess (*TF* 37). Waldenfels insists on distinguishing between, on the one hand, "the relational" whereby something determines itself in relation (*Bezug*) with an Other, and, on the other hand, "the relative" which

is only for me or for us (*TF* 37 n). Taking us back to the original
problem posed by Derrida, Waldenfels denies that otherness could
ever be total.[32] But he also employs this as the basis for an ethical, as
well as logical, objection. Waldenfels recognizes that ethnocentrism
remains intact so long as the alien is regarded *only* in contrast to
the own.[33] However, Levinas refuses to decide between an absolute
alterity and an alterity that starts only from me. He does not respect
the distinctions that might free him from this problem: "The alterity,
the radical heterogeneity of the Other, is possible only if the Other
is Other with respect to a term whose essence is to remain at the
point of departure, to serve as *entry* into the relation, to be the same
not relatively but absolutely. *A term can remain absolutely at the
point of departure of relationship only as I (Moi)*" (*TeI* 6/*TI* 36). This
reaffirms the abiding problem of reading *Totality and Infinity* so long
as one remains rooted in traditional conceptuality as secured by Plato
in the *Sophist*.

The question of whether and in what sense the face-to-face can be
understood as an experience also penetrates to the heart of the question of how *Totality and Infinity* is to be read. On the one hand,
there are passages in which Levinas appears to be offering a concrete
description. On the other hand, much of the language of *Totality and
Infinity* seems to explicitly evoke a transcendental reading. Jacques,
in identifying a tension between Levinas's ethics and his phenomenology, and Ricoeur, in calling for the ethical movement of the Other
toward the self to intersect with a genealogical movement in the opposite direction, both attempt to negotiate this question. I have discussed the problem of reading *Totality and Infinity* elsewhere, trying
to show that it is impossible to sustain the idea that it is a defense of
the empirical against the transcendental.[34] This also has an impact on
Derrida's presentation of Levinas as supporting a notion of encounter
against the Husserlian concept of constitution. Indeed, Derrida's
strategy was in part to draw certain implications from this notion of
encounter. For example, he wrote that "it is impossible to encounter
the alter ego (in the very form of the encounter described by Levinas), impossible to respect it in experience and in language, if this
other, in its alterity, does not *appear* for an ego (in general)" (*ED* 181/
WD 123). More generally, Derrida presents the notion of encounter
as "prey to empiricism" and hence as implying "a time and an experience without 'other' *before* the encounter," which is what Husserl

excludes: "The *Cartesian Meditations* often emphasize that in *fact, really,* nothing precedes the experience of Others" (*ED* 181 n/*WD* 315–16). So far as Derrida is concerned, Levinas refuses the very transcendental phenomenology his thought presupposes (*ED* 195/ *WD* 133). This is perhaps because Derrida equates transcendental discourse with a certain conception of subjectivity that Levinas does indeed refuse. In any case, Derrida portrays Levinas as offering an empiricism of the encounter that he cannot account for. But this is to ignore, as Ricoeur also seems to do when proposing Husserl as a necessary supplement to Levinas, the Cartesian structure governing the central sections of *Totality and Infinity,* whereby the I is first in the order of knowledge, whereas the Infinite is first in the order of being.[35]

After seeing the problems to which Levinas is led by the language of alterity, Etienne Feron asks whether Derrida was not misguided to identify the opposition between the Same and the Other as the basis of Levinas's thought.[36] Feron proposes instead that the concreteness of the face would have been more appropriate, but this not only leads to the question as to how concrete the face is in Levinas, but also overlooks the extent to which Levinas needed to take up the language of Same and Other to show the inadequacy of traditional terminology. Nevertheless, with the notion of substitution Levinas radically transforms the classic opposition of the Same and the Other and thus the language within which his own thought is framed. This is why, more than twenty years after *Otherwise Than Being or Beyond Essence,* Derrida can still be taken by surprise by Levinas's notion of substitution and above all its status as an a priori. Derrida even expresses some doubt as to whether it has a place in Levinas's discourse.[37] Levinas finds in the notion of substitution an alterity other than that of the absolutely Other, seemingly without reverting to the relative alterity of the stranger, as proposed by the Stranger in Plato's *Sophist.* To this extent, Levinas does not submit to traditional conceptuality, or what in *Totality and Infinity* he had already renounced under the name "formal logic." The notion of substitution contests the application of the logic of identity to the self. This is especially clear in Levinas's essay "No Identity," where the biblical "I am a stranger on the earth, do not hide from me your commandments" (Psalm 119) is understood as consonant with a certain interpretation of Rimbaud's "I is an other." Rimbaud's formula does not mean "alteration, alienation, betrayal of oneself, foreignness with regard to oneself and subjection to this foreigner" (*HAH* 91/*CPP* 145). It amounts to substitution as the extreme point of "a subjectivity incapable of shutting itself up" (*HAH* 100/*CPP* 151). Because the idea of the subject as a hostage, substituting for everyone "by its very non-interchange-ability," is so novel (*HAH* 99/*CPP* 150), I hesitate to declare that it leaves intact the problems of a certain ethnocentrism that the earlier formulations seem ill-equipped to avoid. However, this is merely one instance of the larger claim that this essay sought to demonstrate: that the criticisms directed against Levinas's notion of alterity have tended to focus on *Totality and Infinity* and have been insensitive to the larger strategies of that book, let alone its qualified status after the publication of *Otherwise Than Being or Beyond Essence*.

NOTES

1. J. Derrida, *L'écriture et la différence* (Paris: Seuil, 1967), 185; trans. A. Bass, *Writing and Difference* (Chicago: University of Chicago Press, 1978), 126. Cited henceforth as *ED* and *WD*, respectively.

2. S. Rosen, *Plato's Sophist* (New Haven: Yale University Press, 1983), 270.

3. The exact same passage is found at *DE* 164/*EE* 95.

4. For example, C. Norris, "Ethics and Alterity: Derrida on Levinas," in *Truth and the Ethics of Criticism* (Manchester: Manchester University Press, 1994), 47–51.

5. E. Husserl, *Cartesianische Meditationen,* Husserliana I (The Hague: Martinus Nijhoff, 1973), 89; trans. D. Cairns, *Cartesian Meditations* (The Hague: Martinus Nijhoff, 1970), 89. Cited henceforth as *HuI* and *CM*, respectively.

6. This alleged blindness is exaggerated by Derrida. In *Totality and Infinity,* Levinas explicitly acknowledges the sense in which "I myself can feel myself to be the Other of the Other" (*TeI* 56/*TI* 84). Although it is true that Levinas tends to refer to the face-to-face as primary and to the symmetrical relation between individuals as derivative, such a formulation of this kind, which appears to place the face-to-face within an ontological hierarchy, is not unproblematic, as he subsequently acknowledged. The question of symmetry is, in Levinas, a question of justice, and it is in the context of the discussion of justice that he (and later, Derrida) explores it.

7. P. Ricoeur, "La Cinquième *Méditation Cartésienne*," in *A l'école de la*

phénoménologie (Paris: Vrin, 1986), 218; trans. E. G. Ballard and L. Embree, *Husserl: An Analysis of His Phenomenology* (Chicago: Northwestern University Press, 1967), 136.

8. J. Derrida, *La voix et la phénomène* (Paris: P.U.F., 1967), 94 n; trans. D. Allison, *Speech and Phenomena* (Evanston: Northwestern University Press, 1973), 85 n. See also the further implicit reference to *Speech and Phenomena* added to "Violence and Metaphysics" for re-publication in 1967, *ED* 178/*WD* 121.

9. The same passage can be found in a text that corresponds to no single publication in French: "Beyond Intentionality," in *Philosophy in France Today*, ed. A. Montefiore (Cambridge: Cambridge University Press, 1983), 109.

10. E. Levinas, preface to T. F. Geraets, *Vers une nouvelle philosophie transcendentale* (The Hague: Martinus Nijhoff, 1971), xiii.

11. "The recurrence of the oneself . . . is already constituted when the act of constitution first originates" (*AE* 133/*OB* 105).

12. J. Derrida, "En ce moment même dans cet ouvrage me voici," in *Textes pour Emmanuel Levinas*, ed. F. Laruelle (Paris: Jean-Michel Place, 1980), 29; trans. R. Berezdivin, "At This Very Moment in This Work Here I Am," in *Re-Reading Levinas*, ed. R. Bernasconi and S. Critchley (Bloomington: Indiana University Press, 1991), 18.

13. J. Derrida, *Adieu: à Emmanuel Levinas* (Paris: Galilée, 1997), 112.

14. That certain of Derrida's arguments in "Violence and Metaphysics" apply only to *Totality and Infinity* and not to *Otherwise Than Being* has already been argued in F. Ciaramelli, "Levinas' Ethical Discourse between Individuation and Universality," in Bernasconi and Critchley, *Re-Reading Levinas*, 83–105, esp. 90. However, Ciaramelli's focus is very different from mine.

15. On the gift, see R. Bernasconi, "What Goes Around Comes Around: Derrida and Levinas on the Economy of the Gift and the Gift of Genealogy," in *The Logic of the Gift*, ed. A. Schrift (New York: Routledge, 1997), 256–73.

16. S. de Beauvoir, *Le deuxième sexe* (Paris: Gallimard, 1949), 1:15 n; trans. H. M. Parshley, *The Second Sex* (New York: Knopf, 1953), xvi n.

17. F. Jacques, *Différence et subjectivité* (Paris: Aubier, 1982), 157; trans. A. Rothwell, *Difference and Subjectivity* (New Haven: Yale University Press, 1991), 130. Cited henceforth as *DeS* and *DS*, respectively.

18. P. Ricoeur, *Soi-même comme un autre* (Paris: Seuil, 1990), 386; trans. K. Blamey, *Oneself as Another* (Chicago: University of Chicago Press, 1992), 335. Cited henceforth as *SA* and *OA*, respectively.

19. See Levinas's response to Jacques's criticisms, as posed by François Armengaud, in "Sur la philosophie juive," *A l'heure des nations* (Paris: Minuit, 1988), 213; trans. M. B. Smith, *In the Time of the Nations* (Blooming-

ton: Indiana University Press, 1994), 181–82. Jacques has subsequently restated his position in "E. Levinas: Entre le primat phénoménologique du moi et l'allégeance éthique à l'autrui," *Etudes phénoménologiques* 6, no. 12 (1990): 101–40.

20. Ricoeur agrees with Levinas that the constitution of the thing tacitly remains the model for Husserl's account of the constitution of the Other, but he nevertheless believes that the failure of the Fifth *Cartesian Meditation* at the foundational level does not detract from its power to show the paradoxical character of the Other's mode of givenness in appresentation (*SA* 383–85/*OA* 332–33).

21. Ricoeur acknowledges the radical difference between the notion of separation and that of substitution, although I doubt that the latter should be interpreted as the "contrary" of the former (*SA* 392/*OA* 340). Even though I disagree with Peter Kemp's suggestion that Ricoeur's interpretation of the self in Levinas fits *Otherwise Than Being* better than *Totality and Infinity*, I would agree that it is hard to see how Ricoeur can claim to have done justice to both works. Cf. P. Kemp, "Ricoeur between Heidegger and Levinas," *Philosophy and Social Criticism* 21, nos. 5–6 (1995): 56.

22. The distinction between the self and the I is not, of course, identical with the distinction between *ipse* and *idem*, but Ricoeur grafts the latter onto the former (*SA* 30/*OA* 18).

23. B. Waldenfels, "The Other and the Foreign," *Philosophy and Social Criticism* 21, nos. 5–6 (1995): 122.

24. Ibid.

25. B. Waldenfels, "Dialogische Untersuchungen: Francis Jacques's 'Weg von der Intersubjectivität zur Interlokution,'" *Philosophische Rundschau* 36 (1989): 226. See also Waldenfels, "The Other and the Foreign," 121.

26. See, for example, B. Waldenfels, *Topographie des Fremden* (Frankfurt a.M.: Suhrkamp, 1997), 180. Cited henceforth as *TF*. Elsewhere, Waldenfels does question Levinas's notion of responsibility, but this goes beyond the present inquiry. See B. Waldenfels, "Response and Responsibility in Levinas," in *Ethics as First Philosophy*, ed. A. Peperzak (New York: Routledge, 1995), 39–52.

27. B. Waldenfels, "Erfahrung des Fremden in Husserl's Phänomenologie," *Profile der Phänomenologie, Phänomenologische Forschungen* 22 (Freiburg: Alber, 1989), 39–63; trans. A. J. Steinbock, "Experience of the Alien in Husserl's Phenomenology," *Research in Phenomenology* 20 (1990): 19–33. This is theme is present already in Waldenfels's *Das Zwischenreich des Dialogs* (The Hague: Martinus Nijhoff, 1971), 44–51.

28. Ibid., 57–58/29–30.

29. In his discussion of Husserl in "Violence and Metaphysics," Derrida

repeatedly asserts a certain priority of phenomenology over the metaphysics of alterity (e.g., *ED* 173, 184, 195/*WD* 118, 125, 133). Without trivializing the richness of Derrida's argument, it is important to recognize that in his own way Levinas does respect the appropriateness of phenomenology as a starting point, consistently beginning from it but also going beyond it. It may be that Levinas did not give full depth of thought to the conditions governing such a procedure until Derrida did so, but it is a mistake to suppose that he needed to wait for Derrida to tell him that this was his own modus operandi.

30. Given the role of anti-Semitism in Levinas's life and its motivating role in the development of his philosophy, this is a serious concern. See R. Bernasconi, "Was ist der Dritte? Überkreuzung von Ethik und Politik bei Levinas," trans. Antje Kapust, in *Der Anspruch des Anderen,* ed. B. Waldenfels and I. Därmann (München: Wilhelm Fink, 1998), 87–110.

31. See also B. Waldenfels, *Ordnung im Zwielicht* (Frankfurt a.M.: Suhrkamp, 1987), 122–23; trans. D. Parent, *Order in the Twilight* (Athens: Ohio University Press, 1996), 76.

32. B. Waldenfels, "Response to the Other," in *Encountering the Other(s),* ed. G. Brinker-Gabler (Albany: State University of New York Press, 1995), 37.

33. B. Waldenfels, "Experience of the Other: Between Appropriation and Disappropriation," in *Life-World and Politics,* ed. S. K. White (Notre Dame: Notre Dame University Press, 1989), 71.

34. R. Bernasconi, "Rereading *Totality and Infinity,*" in *The Question of the Other: Essays in Contemporary Continental Philosophy,* ed. A. Dallery and C. E. Scott (New York: State University of New York Press, 1989), 23–40.

35. See R. Bernasconi, "The Silent Anarchic World of the Evil Genius," in *The Collegium Phaenomenologicum: The First Ten Years,* ed. J. Sallis, G. Moneta, and J. Taminiaux (Dordrecht: Martinus Nijhoff, 1988), 257–72.

36. E. Feron, *Emmanuel Levinas: De l'idée de transcendence à la question du langage* (Grenoble: Jerôme Millon, 1992), 267.

37. Derrida, *Adieu: à Emmanuel Levinas,* 199 n.

5

Sensibility, Trauma, and the Trace: Levinas from Phenomenology to the Immemorial

Michael Newman

EVEN IF THE RELATION with the Other is supposed to be unmediated, and thereby to have a traumatic character, as Emmanuel Levinas claims (*AE* 179–85/*OB* 141–45), that would not by itself be enough to derive from it an ethical responsibility.[1] There are many kinds of trauma which do not make any kind of ethical claim, which therefore cannot be derived from the structure per se of trauma, unless one were to suppose that the only real trauma were the trauma of the other *person*, of a personal Other rather than a non-personal alterity. If this is not the case—and it would indeed be a hard argument to sustain in its exclusivity—then there must be something else that enables a specifically ethical claim, one of responsibility, to be derived from the traumatic way in which the subject is affected by the Other, and indeed constituted as subjectivity in that affection. It is my contention that the role of this "something else" is taken by what Levinas calls "illeity," and that this also means that the term "God" is an indispensably structural necessity of his philosophy. Whether this be its advantage or its undoing is not my concern here; rather, it is important to grasp exactly what is at stake, which for our purposes is the issue of what it is according to Levinas that makes the relation with alterity one of ethical responsibility. This assignation is linked by Levinas to the memory of that which cannot be made present, the "immemorial," hence the continuing importance of Levinas's disturbance of phenomenology and its language of description. A crucial passage which, early on in Levinas's work, brings these topics together comes from the section "Subjectivity and 'Illeity'" in the essay "Phenomenon and Enigma." Of the enigma that the Other poses for being and its phenomenality, Levinas writes,

> The signifyingness of an enigma comes from an irreversible, irrecuperable past which it has *perhaps* not left, since it has already been absent from the very terms in which it was signaled ("perhaps" is the modality of an enigma, irreducible to the modalities of being and certainty). We hear this way to signify— . . . this way of leaving the alternatives of being—under the third person personal pronoun, under the word *He* [*Il*]. The enigma comes to us from Illeity [*Illéité*]. The enigma is the way the Ab-solute, foreign to cognition, because it does not lend itself to the contemporaneousness that constitutes the force of time tied in the present, because it imposes a completely different version of time. . . . [I]n the trace of *illeity*, in the enigma, the synchronism falls out of tune, the totality is transcended in another time. This extravagant movement of going beyond being or transcendence toward an immemorial antiquity we call the idea of infinity. The Infinite is an unassimilable alterity, a difference and ab-solute past with respect to everything that is shown, signaled, symbolized, announced, remembered, and thereby "contemporized" with him who understands. (*EDE* 214/*CPP* 71)

The question to be posed is simple even if its implications are not: why does Levinas need the word "illeity"? Why does he need more than the relation of the responsible subject to *autrui*, the personal Other? My contention will be that illeity is needed as a stand-in for the Law in order to "convert" the traumatic relation with *autrui*, constitutive of subjectivity, into an ethical relation of responsibility. Its role in the later philosophy therefore exceeds that which it has in *Totality and Infinity*, where illeity primarily assures the possibility of a transition from ethics to justice, from the *à deux* of the ethical relation to the "third," the Other of the Other and all the Others, although the structure of the problem remains constant: how to move from the singular to the general, or derive a general claim from a singular relationship, without reducing the former to the latter, a problem that remains to be laid out even if it is claimed, rightly, that the second state is already in the first, or even precedes it. Precisely because Levinas does not want to subsume the singularity of the ethical relationship, its articulation with the Law remains somewhat obscure in the philosophical writings, particularly given the amount of work that the term "illeity" is expected to do. As he writes in the above passage from "Phenomenon and Enigma," one of the senses of illeity is the Infinite, and it will be my argument that it is from this connection that we may derive an idea of what other than the relation with *autrui* is needed to make the singular relation an ethical one.

Published in 1965,[2] "Phenomenon and Enigma" anticipates the developments in Levinas's thinking that will result eight years later in *Otherwise Than Being or Beyond Essence*. What will come to the fore meanwhile is an emphasis on the language of trauma in order to evoke the way in which sensibility is always already affected by the Other. While this terminology intensifies the problem to which we have pointed, a consideration of the traumatic im-mediacy of the relation with the Other will enable the significance of diachrony, the non-coincidence of my time with that of the Other, the way in which synchrony is disturbed by alterity, to be further specified. The emphasis on the reference to transcendence of the trace, in its distinction from the immanent referral of the sign and the anticipations of presence, implies, as we shall see, a linking of responsibility to a past that cannot be recuperated.[3] It is with the implications of this change in temporal valency that we will begin. In addition to the question of time, this turn coincides in the development of Levinas's thinking with an articulation of the trace of the "immemorial" with the question of ethical language,[4] and we shall return to this issue as we approach the conclusion of our discussion.

The transition from the "ethical transcendental philosophy"[5] of *Totality and Infinity* to the discussion of subjectivity in relation to the *trace* of the Other in *Otherwise Than Being or Beyond Essence* involves a shift in emphasis from the future to the past, even if, as we have seen, the notion of the immemorial was already present in earlier writings. *Totality and Infinity* is a book about the modes of alterity and the relation of the Other to the Same. Remaining in a certain sense faithful to phenomenology, it comprises first a description of the genesis of a subject to whom an Other can appear as Other, and then a series of analyses—which might still be described as "eidetic"—of the modes of presence of the Other: as face, in eros, in fecundity, in filiality and fraternity. This "phenomenology" is complicated by the fact that the terms of the relation to be described are absolute; that is to say, they absolve themselves from the relation.

Thus the Other does not appear against a horizon, or within a system of references, but rather in its own light.[6] For Levinas this means that the Other is not present to me according to the act of synthesis that *I* perform: the Other's presence depends neither on my initiative nor on an act. Nor is the Other's manifestation mediated by an impersonal middle term, which is how Levinas interprets Heideggerian Being (*TeI* 36–38/*TI* 64–66).

Following Husserl's emphasis on the role of retention in the constitution of the present, and a tradition going back at least to Kant, Levinas tends in *Totality and Infinity* to think of the modality of the past as that of the formation of the level of the Same, of the identity of the subject, and of representation within the subject's horizon. While that which is gathered in memory is the "same," that which comes from the future is the "new," the Other. Indeed, it could be said that insofar as *Totality and Infinity* is a "phenomenology" of the Other, the emphasis must be on the future, even if already that future, as future of the Other, must break with my present, and thereby joins the past that I cannot recuperate in representational memory, "this future in which memory will lay hold of a past that was before the past, the 'deep past, never past enough'" (*TeI* 145/*TI* 170). Phenomenology is only the culmination, according to Heidegger—and this is taken over, to be criticized, by Levinas—of a tradition in which truth is determined as the unveiling of Being, and therefore as knowledge. The priority of the future follows from the anticipation involved in the journey toward truth as unveiling (*TA* 19/*TO* 41).

By contrast, we read very little of the future in *Otherwise Than Being*. Indeed, in the later book the temporal stress seems to be largely on the modality of the past, albeit not on a past representable in memory, but rather on the "immemorial." This is consistent with the emphasis of *Otherwise Than Being* on the topic of subjectivity, since traditionally the subject is constituted as identical in relation to the continuity of its past. *Otherwise Than Being* returns to the least satisfactory aspect of *Totality and Infinity*, the discussion of the kind of subject who can have an experience of alterity. Whereas in *Totality and Infinity* this subject is first of all described as becoming "separated," then engaging in an ethical relation, while all along such a relation must already have been presumed in the description of separation, the subject of *Otherwise Than Being* is from the start—indeed before the start, before any beginning—in a relation with the Other, and described as such. This being the case, there is no longer any need for an independent analysis of the phenomenon of the Other, especially since there can be no mediated access to the Other which could be analyzed from a point of view independent of the subject constituted by and passible to the Other: any such attempt would reduce the Other to the Same since it would be employing a third-person standpoint to turn the Other into a theme. To a degree such mediation is unavoidable in a philosophical work that requires concepts—but philosophy is also obliged by Levinas to "reduce" this objectivating standpoint, just as, equally, in the other direction the Saying must be betrayed in the Said (*AE* 8/*OB* 6).

If objectification is dependent on memory—both retention and representing memory—what kind of account of the past would be required by an analysis of subjectivity saturated from the start by an unobjectifiable alterity? It will be my argument that the discussions of the "immemorial" in *Otherwise Than Being* provide just such an account. Furthermore, I will argue that the notion of the "immemorial" is required for the turn from phenomenology to ethical language. This turn is linked to the conception of the ethical relation as a "traumatism," already present in Levinas's early account of time and in *Totality and Infinity* but receiving more emphasis in *Otherwise Than Being*. If the relation with the Other constitutes subjectivity in the first place, it cannot be the act of a subject—and since Levinas conceives intentionality as always act, it cannot be an intentionality either. Furthermore, the Other approaches the subject without context or horizon, as "stranger," and without any reasons, in the sheer contingency of the particular "neighbor" who just happens to be near. The status of the Other is thus "absolute" in the strict sense, absolved from any relation to world, context, culture, home, symbolic order, rituals, and from any order of reason. Hence the abstraction of the terms Levinas uses for the other person. "Traumatism" figures the undergoing (*épreuve*) of the absolute status both of the Other and of the relation itself, a relationship which is not chosen, and which cannot be anticipated or controlled by the subject.

We thus have a triple task: first, to follow Levinas's account of subjectivity, focusing in particular on the role of trauma and the immemorial; second, to show the role of the immemorial in the turn from phenomenology to ethical language via an account of time as having a structure that is at once traumatic and messianic; and third, to consider whether a further element is needed in addition to the traumatic structure of the way the subject is affected by the Other in order that the passivity of sensibility is at the same time ethical responsibility. Levinas sets up the problem of the relation between phenomenology and ethical language in "Language and Proximity." We will first offer a reading of parts of that essay, and of Levinas's reworking of Husserlian time-consciousness, before going on to discuss the account of subjectivity given in the chapter on "Substitution," where the notion of proximity provides a way of approaching the approach to the "traumatic" relation to the Other.

I. FROM INTENTIONALITY TO PASSIVITY

In the first section of his essay "Language and Proximity" (*EDE* 217–36/*CPP* 109–26), Levinas wants to show that the phenomenological account of ideal objects, meaning, and temporality depends on a condition in relation to the particularity of the ethical relation—utterance, signifyingness, or what in *Otherwise Than Being* will be called the "Saying"—which the commitment to universality conceals. That is, taking the section as dealing with the relation of *logos* (signs) to being (events), one conception of the *logos* conceals another. According to the tradition culminating with Husserl, "Logos as speech is entirely one with logos as rationality" (*EDE* 217/*CPP* 109). In this view, "communication is simply derivative of the logos which animates or bears thought" and "is made possible by the break which the logos consummates with the particularisms of the thinker and of experience, a break which links up with universality" (*EDE* 217–18/*CPP* 109–10). For the tradition, then, communication depends on the universality achieved by the *logos* in "synchronizing" events or being and identifying themes. Levinas will displace this conception of communication with one—supposedly "older" and perhaps no longer describable as communication which would correlate its terms—in which the singularity of the subject is exposed before any thematization.

If in the philosophical tradition the particular is grasped through the mediation of ideality and the universal, Levinas asks whether "behind discourse [the 'thinking utterance' in which 'the universal precedes the individual'], there does not lie hidden a philosophical thought distinct from discourse and refractory to its prestiges and pretensions, and whether there it does not aim at the singular which discourse cannot express without idealizing" (*EDE* 222/*CPP* 113). However, thought involves identification, and identification proceeds from a structure of loss and re-finding which in turn involves a minimal distance between the feeling and the felt. The felt is necessarily objectified through being lost and found again, this movement of losing and re-finding being the very structure of time, "such that what shows itself must have already been lost in order to be found again by consciousness (consciousness being this permanent losing and finding again—this *anamnesis*). Then, if what shows itself, be it the singular, by virtue of its essence still has to be identified, because of this loss, then the singular too in these rediscoveries will be an ideality" (*EDE* 222/*CPP* 113–14). Levinas is interested in the origin of the noetico-noematic structure of intentionality: if for Husserl this would be the auto-affection of absolute consciousness, for Levinas it would be a hetero-affection.[7] However, given the structure of thought and this structure of time, it would seem to be unavoidable that singularity be approached through ideality, and thereby lost. Language and universality are born in this very movement of "running after what has already escaped through the original flowing of time" where "identification is born by a discourse consubstantial with consciousness" (*EDE* 222/*CPP* 114). Consciousness is thus inherently identificatory, and is born of loss of the immediate in the gap between sensing and sensed, and thereby of both a passivity and an "active" attempt to recoup what was given in it: "This consciousness is, to be sure, without a subject; it is a 'passive activity' of time, which no subject could claim to have initiated, a 'passive synthesis' of what 'passes,' which is born in the flow and divergency of time, an anamnesis and a rediscovery and consequently an identification, in which ideality and universality take on meaning" (*EDE* 222–23/*CPP* 114). This movement can be related to the auto-affection of absolute consciousness in Husserl's account of internal time-consciousness. However, to say that absolute consciousness precedes the constitution of the transcendental ego is not necessarily to say that it is a consciousness without a subject.[8]

Levinas wants to distinguish "a-thematic consciousness that takes place as time" from "an objectifying consciousness." He places intentionality on the side of the latter, implying (contra Husserl's account

of the double intentionality of time) that "pre-subjective" consciousness is not an intentionality: it is a consciousness with neither subject
nor intentionality, and as "a-thematic" it also does not have an object.
So what is left? Nothing other than "a passivity more passive still
than any passivity that is simply antithetical to activity, a passivity
without reserve, the passivity of a creature at the time of creation
when there is no subject to assume the creative act, to, so to speak,
hear the creative word" (*EDE* 223/*CPP* 114). And he adds that "consciousness as the passive work of time which no one activates cannot
be described by the categories proper to a consciousness that aims at
an object," recalling Husserl's dictum with regard to absolute time-
consciousness that for this names are lacking.

The absolute passivity of the creature, the non-coincidence with
itself, with its origin, is that which retention aims to recuperate.
Through retention the instant is "meant as identical" (*EDE* 223/*CPP*
114–15), and is supposed to be recovered from its loss. Even if retention precedes the self-identical subject, it is already an ur-intentional-
ity insofar as it "means" or aims at the instant which is sinking away,
attempting to salvage it from its irredeemable loss by means of an
anamnesis, an identification of the instant as identical with itself,
even before any recourse to verbal signs. In contrast, Levinas's model
for a "true" passive synthesis will be aging, in which the subject is
affected by time in such a way that the loss is irrecoverable.

Husserl's aim with his notion of "passive synthesis" was to trace
back the presuppositions of the various configurations of universal
judgments to an antecedent world of individuals.[9] In his earlier approach, these individuals were constituted by the apprehension of
the given data, which were united in this apprehension into an object. Synthesis is therefore at this stage predicative. Later Husserl
came to understand the data—*hyle* or sensations—as themselves the
result of a synthesis, thus introducing a distinction between predicative and pre-predicative, or active and passive syntheses. It should
be noted here that, according to Husserl in *Experience and Judgment*,[10] the passive synthesis is a synthesis of association (§ 81, p.
321).

Levinas in his appropriation—indicated as such by his scare-
quotes around "passive work"—appears to blur a fine distinction
upon which Husserl insists concerning association, "the unique character of the synthesis of like with like": "Its peculiarity lies in the fact

that, though it indeed very much resembles a synthesis of identity, it is still not one. It resembles such a synthesis so much that as we pass from like to like we often simply say: 'This is surely the same thing.' But the like are two distinct objects, and not one and the same" (*Experience and Judgment*, § 81, p. 321).

Whereas Levinas seems to assume that synthesis, as an act, is necessarily a synthesis of identity, Husserl appears to be proposing here a synthesis of association which is *not* a synthesis of identity. But Husserl is assuming that those items which are to be associated are already objects, hence would be the result of a synthesis preceding the passive synthesis which would associate them. And furthermore, Husserl never lets go of the assumption that the passive syntheses— the habitualities and associations—are sedimented *acts*, and can therefore be recovered as acts by the subject. This recoverability of the act will be the very basis of moral responsibility for Husserl, for otherwise the subject might deny responsibility for acts which devolved from habits and customs. The subject must be able to reappropriate the passive synthesis as its own work. Responsibility, for Husserl, would be the very movement from the passive to the active, whereas Levinas's approach to responsibility moves from the active, through the passivity of activity ("passive *synthesis*"), to a passivity more passive than any passivity that is the opposite or deprived form of activity, in other words, a passivity that can no longer be synthesized, and therefore which is no longer subordinate to activity. The passivity more passive than the passivity of activity will be neither a passive activity ("passive synthesis") nor a reactive passivity, one that would be *relative* to activity. The paradox that is difficult to grasp here is that Levinasian "passivity" is related to the normal sense of passivity and at the same time incommensurable with it, as if at the point at which passivity becomes hyperbolic a rupture takes place. The move from the passivity of activity to a passivity without reserve is therefore not a smooth one: it is rather at once a relation and an absolute rupture—a *rapport sans rapport*—which will require the intervention of the other person and the diachronic rather than synchronic conception of time. We will return to the question of time after having considered the relation of sensibility to language.

II. PROXIMITY AND ETHICAL LANGUAGE

According to Levinas, the ethical relation with the Other is fundamental, in that it is prior to, and the basis of, the relation to beings and the world. It is surely a problem to show that one level, the ethical, is foundational of the other, the ontological and epistemological, when there is—where there can be by definition—no common or mediating term between them or common ground beneath them.[11] Fundamental, but not ontological? Even to describe the ethical relation as "fundamental" is to thematize and objectify it, which is perhaps why Levinas claims ethics as "first philosophy" rather than ground. However, the ethical must have some bearing on the sphere of ontology, otherwise how could it affect actual relations with Others in the world? Eventually the move "back" from ethics to ontology and phenomenology will be a question of justice and of the "third" where the mediating term will be referred, not to an underlying identity between the other two terms, but to the unmediatable "*Il*" or God. The need for justice will arise out of a complication of the ethical relation, the demand of the third in addition to my relation with *autrui*. Justice is thus preceded by ethics, hence the need, in the order of exposition, to characterize the ethical relation first. But equally the third person will have always already been there, "in the eyes of the Other" (*TeI* 188/*TI* 213),[12] so, just as the ethical relation is itself an interruption, in turn there was never an uninterrupted ethical relation. Eventually, justice will provide a means of redescribing by reference to the ethical precisely those universally mediated relations which conceal the ethical, and yet which equally, it must be said, are needed by the ethical, among them intentionality and universal logical or theoretical language.

It is to such a concealment that Levinas turns in the fourth section of "Language and Proximity," which hinges on a distinction between intentionality as a form of cognition and contact as a form of proximity. With each is associated a different mode of language: with intentionality, language as the universal communication of messages; with proximity, an "original language" which is "pure communication" as the communication of communication, of the heterogeneity that makes communication more than mediation, that is, the ethical relationship "itself" insofar as the latter involves response and Saying before the communication of a thematized content. At issue is the possibility of a transcendence which, as ethical transcendence, is not a knowing. However, it is not enough simply to state a distinction as if it were self-evident. We also have to ask on what evidence the distinction is based, and what is the relation between its terms.

It is through sensibility, which Levinas distinguishes from consciousness, that ethical transcendence will be attained, as opposed to the cognitive transcendence toward the object of phenomenological intentionality, for which consciousness is always "consciousness of. . . ." The contrast is made by Levinas from the start: "The immediacy of the sensible is an event of proximity and not of knowledge" (*EDE* 225/*CPP* 116). Not only is the immediacy of sensibility to be contrasted with the "mediation of the ideal, or of kerygmatic language," but also with "sensible intuition" where "the sensibility is already subordinated to the disclosure of being." In other words, sensibility is a matter neither of *logos* (in its identifying, mediating apophantic sense) nor of being. However, sensibility is not, either, a mere opacity, a block to cognition.

Levinas has characterized consciousness as the minimal distinction between the sensing and the sensed. This means that consciousness has an intentional structure. Sensation broken down into the relation between the sensing and the sensed falls under a cognitive theoretical model, even if the sensed is not necessarily an object (*EDE* 226 n. 1/*CPP* 117 n. 8). That is, for Levinas both the ultimacy of theoretical intentionality in Husserl and the critique of such ultimacy in Heidegger remain captive of a model of comprehension (as, for example, would be the case with the "moods" [*Stimmungen*] of *Being and Time* as modes of knowledge). According to such a model, *"Every transcendence is conceived as a knowing"* (*EDE* 226/*CPP* 117, emphasis in source). At issue is not only that intentionality, even if without an object, presupposes a subject, but the kind of subject that is involved here, namely, a subject that is *detached.* It is this detached subject that is then the basis of the conception of transcendence as a knowing, that is, as a kind of spanning of a distance, by contrast with proximity as contact. This structure seems to call for the metaphor of sight: "the structure of openness, discerned in all sensibility, resembles the structure of sight, in which the sensibility is invested as a knowing" (*EDE* 226/*CPP* 117). At stake here is the misapprehension that results from the application of the cognitive model to the ethical relation with the other person.

Can we say that we have had an experience of the Other as Other? Would, for example, touching the Other or being touched by the Other be an "experience"? Not, it would seem, for Levinas, insofar as experience is to be conceptualized as intentionality with a noetico-noematic structure (*EDE* 226 n. 2/*CPP* 117, n. 10), thus involving neither contact nor proximity, but distance between the sensing and the sensed. An experience refers back to the subject, as, for example, in the transcendental apperception of the "I think" which for Kant must accompany my experience. Contact, Levinas appears to be saying, must precede any self-reference, and needs to be described not according to the categories of experience (eidos, profiles, etc.) but as signification or expression. Contact is not a quality in the sense of nearness or distance, qualities being linked with manifestation. To speak of signification with respect to the caress is precisely to avoid talk of manifestation when it comes to the relation with Others in their otherness: "In contact things are near, but are so in a quite different sense from the sense in which they are rough, heavy, black, agreeable, or even existing or non-existing. The way in which they are 'in flesh and bone' [the usual translation of Husserl's *'leibhaft gegeben'*] does not characterize their manifestation, but their proximity" (*EDE* 227/*CPP* 118). Contact is concerned neither with qualities nor with existence as such. Although Levinas refers here to "things," it would seem that contact must strictly speaking be limited to the relation with other people, and may only be extended to things through metaphor from the relation with *autrui*. The passage above is preceded by the sentence: "To approach, to neighbour [*voisiner*], is not tantamount to the knowing or consciousness one can have of approaching" (*EDE* 227/*CPP* 118), as if "to know" were dependent on, derivative from, "to neighbour." "The sensed is defined by this relationship of proximity. It is a tenderness: from the face to the nudity of the skin—the one in the context of the other, taking its whole meaning in this context—from the pure to the troubled" (*EDE* 227/*CPP* 118, translation modified).

III. ONE-FOR-THE-OTHER:
THE TRAUMATIC ORIGIN OF ETHICS

The paradox of Levinasian ethics is the "conversion"—which would of course take place before rather than after the event—of what would appear to be a contingent relation with the neighbor into a responsible one, without any choice or decision on my part being involved. Just as I cannot choose to become obsessed, in the relation with the other person something befalls me before I have time to make a choice. The ethical relation thus exceeds both anticipation and memory. Hence, as we shall see, the necessity for something like the thought of the trace of the immemorial.

The aim of the last section of "Language and Proximity," entitled "It Is Only a Word," is to detach a "transcendence outside of intentionality." This transcendence, as we have seen, arises in the conjunction of language—properly understood—with sensibility. Levinas asks the rhetorical question: "would language involve a positive and antecedent event of communication which would be an *approach* to and a *contact* with the neighbour, and in which the secret of the birth of thought itself and of the verbal statement that bears it would lie?" (*EDE* 235/*CPP* 125). The reply is in the affirmative: "The contact . . . [is] the ethical event of communication which is presupposed by every transmission of messages. . . . This contact transcends the I to the neighbour, and is not its thematization; it is the deliverance of a sign prior to every proposition, to the statement of anything whatever. . . . The first word says only the saying itself before every being and every thought in which being is sighted and reflected" (*EDE* 236/*CPP* 125–26).

By contrast with the tradition that would seek the origin in an idea or form, Levinas's originality is to link the "first word"—the immemorial word, we might say—with sensibility such that sensible passibility and language are inseparable: the "caress is dormant in sensorial or verbal contact; in the caress proximity signifies. . . ." Further, this language is ethical language. Sensibility is thus rendered ethical—responsibility—at its core. But how does "contact" become ethical? Why is the relation with the Other necessarily an ethical one first of all, one that demands responsibility? Contact points in two directions: to the body or sensibility, and to a certain absence. "An inordinate absence that is infinity, in an absolute sense, invisible, that is, exterior to all intentionality. The neighbour, *this face and this skin in the trace of this absence,* and consequently in their distress as forsaken, and in their unimpeachable right over me, obsesses me with an obsession irreducible to consciousness, which has not begun in my freedom. Am I in my egoness qua I anything but a hostage?" (*EDE* 235/*CPP* 125, my emphasis).

The neighbor is both face and skin, but is these "in the trace of this absence," the trace of the absence that is infinity. The only true transcendence for Levinas is ethical transcendence: the transcendence is toward *autrui in the trace of an absence. Autrui* is thus disallowed from possession (in the sense of an object of knowledge) and fusion (in the sense of a nostalgia or ascent toward oneness). In this sense infinity functions not unlike being in the ontological difference: the Other approaches in the trace of infinity; things are disclosed in the withdrawal of being. This only goes to show that non-objectifiability, non-possessability, or the impossibility of a total grasp or final comprehension, is not yet ethical. It is the association of infinity with the Saying which differentiates transcendence within immanence, phenomenological transcendence, from ethical transcendence: "For the saying in being said at every moment breaks the definition of what it says and breaks up the totality it includes. . . . [I]t interrupts the totality by its very speaking" (*EDE* 236/*CPP* 126). The saying which says the saying is the ethical relation with *autrui,* "this primary transcendence that breaks the Logos." An enigma for "coherent thought"—that is, thought which synchronizes and thematizes and makes present—"This first saying is to be sure but a word. But the word is God" (*EDE* 236/*CPP* 126). Language is "a sign that says the very fact of Saying," but the trace, Levinas has remarked, is not a sign left by an absent being. There is no negative theology here, since the absence is not a negation, nor even negativity that would protect as a secret that which it shelters, but that which makes possible the exposed positivity of the ethical relation as religion where the rebinding is responsibility. For Levinas to name this saying of the saying "God" is to say that transcendence not toward but beyond being, *autrement qu'être,* where it rejoins the ethical relation. A relation—named, with increasing tension: approach, contact, substitution, hostage—with the positive Other, *autrui,* is in the trace of an *absolute* alterity. By themselves none of the terms cited that name the relation with *autrui* are ethical. "God" and "trace" name the "something else" that makes the relation an ethical one, to *ordain* or *elect* the subject to responsibility—it is here that religious language comes to supplement the pathological and the relational. This conversion occurs not within being but *an-archically,* in an *immemorial* time, as a *trauma.* This also means that its temporality is not causal or sequential. The trace of the immemorial past will always already have broken open the present; the present just is, as we have seen from the hints given of Levinas's interpretation of time-consciousness, a breaking, in infraction or im-pression. But there will also need to be a way back, a redemption of ontology, which is not simply a "forgetting" of the trace.

Levinas begins the first section, "Principle and Anarchy," of the chapter in *Otherwise Than Being* on "Substitution" by contrasting consciousness with sensibility understood as proximity. Consciousness is based on a principle or *arché*, while proximity is an-archic. The identity of the subject will not be based on an *arché* or ground, but rather the anarchic will in turn be linked with an immemorial obligation that will constitute the unicity of the subject. This obligation will make itself felt in a substitution that will have the character of a trauma. Both subjectivity and the ethical—indistinguishable for Levinas—will thus be shown to have a traumatic origin. This conception of the traumatic origin of the ethical distinguishes Levinas's approach from all previous theories of ethics, whether based on knowledge, the virtues, love of the neighbor, rational self-consistency and respect for others as free rational agents, the calculus of pleasure, or belonging to an ethical community with shared values. Substitution is Levinas's an-archic answer to all these principles and grounds.

This chapter first appeared as a paper, in 1968.[13] The main addition to it as it makes its way into *Otherwise Than Being* is the formulation of substitution as *"l'un-pour-l'autre"*: "Signification is the contradictory trope of the one-for-the-other. The one-for-the-other is not a lack of intuition, but a surplus of responsibility. My responsibility for the other is the *for* of the relationship, the very signifyingness of signification [*la signifiance même de la signification*], which signifies in saying before showing itself in the said. The one-for-the-other is the very signifyingness of signification" (*AE* 127/*OB* 100). The account of signification in "Language and Proximity"—the communication of communication—is linked here with an account of subjectivity as, not primarily self-identity, but substitution. The notion of the one-for-the-Other makes clear that the alterity for which the subject is responsible is the alterity of *autrui*. The subject is thus constituted in relation to a *personal* rather than a non-personal alterity such as a "culture" or a "world." However, we shall see that the subject cannot *only* be constituted as ethical in relation to a singular, personal Other (*autrui*), but that a further condition is required to maintain the *otherness* of this Other, and to prevent its collapse into the identity of the alter ego.[14]

The "one-for-the-Other" is not a *being* for or with Others but, as

Levinas describes it, a "contradictory trope" whereby "adjacency in proximity" becomes "an absolute exteriority" (*AE* 127/*OB* 100), an exteriority which is "absolute" as exterior to being. The "one-for-the-Other" could be understood as an answer to the question of how a relation with a singularity is possible, given that a singularity is by definition absolute, since if it in turn were constituted by relations it would no longer be a singularity. The relation with a singularity can only be unmediated: "Proximity is thus *anarchically* a relationship with a singularity without the mediation of any principle, any ideal-ity. What concretely corresponds to this description is my relation-ship with my neighbour" (*AE* 127/*OB* 100). However, we need to recognize that the mediation Levinas is rejecting serves not a single but a double role. On the one hand, it makes possible relationships with entities on the basis of a third term which is symbolic or univer-sal: relationships with things and with other people are mediated through categorial properties. These are ontological relations, and, clearly, precisely what Levinas wishes to distinguish, as the reduction of the Other to the Same, from the ethical by contrasting the an-archic with mediation through universal principles. On the other hand, it could be argued that the necessity to pass through media-tions imposes a detour which prevents a fusion with the object or the other person (the night in which all cows are black), thus arguably *preserving* the latter's otherness.

One possible line to take is that, although fusion is opposed to mediation, both depend on the same premise, which is a notion of presence linked with a certain conception of temporality: of the living present as the moment of mediation. So, for Levinas to say that the relationship with the singular Other, *autrui*, is "anarchic" has a dou-ble sense: first, it is not mediated by any principle or ground, includ-ing being; and second, it involves a temporality which is not that of a synchronization of the past and future with the present. Its temporal-ity is one of "lapse," of falling away, of an irrecoverability. Moreover, that which is irrecoverable will not be a past present, nor an entity which was present but is now past, but rather "something"—Levinas will say a "passing"—that was never present in the first place. Such a "passed" would fall away from retention. That this could happen to any event we might say is the result of the finitude of human capacity, the contingent limits of memory. Could not such a past, while falling away from retention (the past which constitutes the *internal* differ-

ence of the "extended present"), still be represented? Not if it had
never been present in the first place, if its modality were never that
of being, but, from the start, of a "passing." If the *Urimpression*,
which as we have shown is for Levinas irreducible to the identity of
a repetition, is now to be associated with this "passing," how can it
be said to affect the immanence of the presence?

IV. THE IMPRESSION OF TIME

The articulation of sensibility, language, and time is through the
"trace." The issue of the trace arises through thinking of time in relation to the transcendence of the Other, although this does not necessarily imply that this alterity is a personal Other. However, Levinas's
aim in *Time and the Other*[15] is "to show that time is not the achieve-
ment of an isolated and lone subject, but that it is the very relationship of the subject with the Other [*autrui*]" (*TA* 17/*TO* 39). The
conception of time as constituted through the affect of the transcendent Other involves, in its elaboration, reading Husserl's account of
time-consciousness according to the structure of trauma. Rather than
acting through auto-affection, consciousness is primordially passive.
In death the subject's active relationship with the world reverses into
passivity (*TA* 59/*TO* 72), where "we are no longer able to be able
(*nous ne pouvons plus pouvoir*)" (*TA* 62/*TO* 74). Just as death cannot
be grasped, so the "future is what is in no way grasped. The exteriority of the future is totally different from spatial exteriority precisely
through the fact that the future is absolutely surprising" (*TA* 64/*TO*
76). Thus passivity is the condition for the possibility of the event,
which as that which comes to us is related to the future, and also to
the Other, such that the "other is the future. The very relationship
with the other is the relationship with the future" (*TA* 64/*TO* 77).

The question arises of how to "welcome" this event of the Other:
"How can the event that cannot be grasped still happen to me?"
(*TA* 65/*TO* 77). Levinas's question here is how can the absolutely
transcendent future, the future of the Other, affect the present, given
"the absolute impossibility of finding in the present the equivalent of
the future, the lack of any hold upon the future" (*TA* 71/*TO* 80)? "The
future that death gives, the future of the event, is not yet time. In
order for this future, which is nobody's and which a human being

cannot assume, to become an element of time, it must also enter into relationship with the present, but without losing its transcendence. What is the tie between two instants that have between them the whole interval, the whole abyss, that separates the present and death, the margin at once both insignificant and infinite, where there is always room for hope?" (*TA* 68/*TO* 79). This "impossible" relationship, in which the transcendent affects the subject without losing its absolute transcendence, is ethics: "Relationship with the future, the presence of the future in the present, seems all the same accomplished in the face-to-face with the other. The situation of the face-to-face would be the very accomplishment of time . . ." (*TA* 68–69/*TO* 79). This means that the relation to the Other has a messianic structure: the present is broken open (opened to the event, to the future) by that which it cannot grasp or anticipate, that in relation to which it is in effect passive.

If this were applied to Husserlian time-consciousness it would shift the emphasis from the past (retention which is emphasized insofar as Husserl is concerned with the constitution of the continuum, with the identity of subject and object) to the future (as Heidegger had already done), but also, as Levinas sees it at least, from possibility to impossibility, and from activity to passivity. Levinas suggests this himself in his later commentary on Husserl's time-consciousness lectures in the essay "Intentionalité et Sensation" (1965),[16] where he writes, drawing attention to the *Urimpression*, that the lectures "insist first of all on the impressional sources of all consciousness" (*EDE* 151), and that the "*après-coup*" of consciousnesses becoming conscious is the very "after" of time in relation to the "event" of the *Urimpression* (*EDE* 154). It is unclear whether the distinction Levinas is drawing here is between "sensing [*Empfinden*]" and perception, or between conscious and unconscious. For Husserl, the *Urempfindung* (another word for *Urimpression*) is not unconscious but rather a kind of quasi-intentionality of consciousness that is the correlate of the Now.[17] To the contrary, Levinas here opens up the possibility of treating the *Urimpression* as unconscious, while associating consciousness with objectifying perception. The fact that, for Husserl, the "longitudinal intentionality" is non-objectifying is at the very least underplayed if not ignored altogether. What Levinas does is emphasize the iterative structure of temporalizing intentionality, such that the interpretation of "iteration"[18] may be extended to sug-

gest traumatic repetition. Consciousness is produced as the afteref-
fect of an (unconscious?) impression, as the repeated attempts to
recover from a blow. If this implied an opposition of *Urimpression*
and retention it would go against Husserl's account, which emphasizes the way in which temporalization occurs through their difference.

Temporalization involves distancing, the very production of intentionality, "a minimal distance between the sensing and the sensed,"
and "a return of time on itself, a fundamental *iteration*" (*EDE* 153), a
structure which would seem on the face of it to be that of the Ulyssean circle of departure and return, except that what sets it in train—
the affect of the Other in the *Urimpression*—means precisely that the
circle cannot be closed and that each moment is *also* departure without return: a hetero-affection that generates a recurrence, which is
both the opening of the subject to the Other, and a return that is not
a closure but constitutes it as responsibility for the Other. In other
words, time is temporalized not as re-*presentation* of the impression,
but as "lapse" and "dispersion" (*EDE* 162), with presence-to-self
across this irrecoverable "first gap," the non-coincidence of consciousness with an affection that it can neither anticipate (protention)
nor recuperate (retention). Iteration has to do with the continuing
impossibility of closing the circle which is motivated *from the start*
by the Other, with the imputation of responsibility in the very constitution of subjectivity rather than to a pre-given subject.

It is Levinas who here already insists that perception itself, intentionality (if interpreted as objectifying perception), has this *après-
coup* structure with respect to the *"proto-impression,"* which is itself
"non-idéalité par excellence" (*EDE* 155). The "unforeseeable novelty
of the contents which surge forth in this source of all consciousness
and all being" is, according to Husserl cited by Levinas, "original
creation (*Urzeugung*)" which "merits the name of absolute activity,
of *genesis spontanea*";[19] "but," Levinas adds—and this is his crucial
interpretative move—"it is at the same time loaded beyond all expectation, all anticipation, all source of germination and all continuity
and, as a result, is wholly passivity, receptivity of an 'other' ['*autre*']
penetrating into the 'same,' life and not 'thought' " (*EDE* 156). The
structure of consciousness just is time-consciousness if the *Urimpression* is taken as impression by the Other: consciousness is an act that
attempts to recuperate, to catch up with, the affection in the trace of

the Other that undoes it, which, as absolutely past/passed, withdraws from all coincidence and adequation (and is therefore immemorial). "*L'acte est donc postérieur au matériau de l'objet constitué. . . . la conscience est retard sur elle-même, une façon de s'attarder à un passé*" (*EDE* 155). The Other cannot be grasped as at once on the other side and on the hither side of consciousness, infinitely removed yet immediately close to the point of obsession: "*Essentiellement 'impressionnelle' n'est-elle pas possédée par le non-moi, par l'autre, par la 'facticité'?*" (*EDE* 162).

The new is not an autonomous or free surging forth, but comes after having been affected in passivity by the advent of the absolutely Other or *autrui*. The role of retention in Husserl would then be taken over by the "assuming" of the Other who comes from the future, the whole problem being that of a "relation without relation [*rapport sans rapport*]," of transcendence *before* identity. Retention becomes, in effect, the secondary response to and assuming of responsibility in relation to an "impressional" trauma of time and the Other (although it could equally be argued that the primacy of the impression depends on the "supplement" of the retention). So rather than being extended beyond the Now to include retention and protention, and synthesized by an intentionality, as it is in Husserl, the presence of the present is supposed to be in a certain sense broken open, and in *Time and the Other* Levinas sees this as being accomplished by the future.

What would happen, then, if, through the ultra-passivity of the *Urimpression,* this "other" future were put in communication with the "immemorial" past? Why should one need to think this? Perhaps we can understand this development in relation to the problem of recuperation. If the "assuming" of the "other future," the future of the event, were to be purely in terms of "memory"—whether retention or representation—would this not be to reduce again the transcendent to immanence? Auto-affection would triumph over hetero-affection. We could interpret the moment of retention in time-consciousness as an "assuming" of the *Urimpression* while continuing to be affected by (future) *Urimpressionen.* If this assuming is not to reduce transcendence to immanence, it would have to be not only non-objective or non-objectifying, but also not in relation to a presence. That is, the non-present would have to be received *as* non-present: taking the place of retention would have to be a certain "memory" of a "trace" of a past that was never present. And since such a "past"—"retained" in a retention that was not a retention of a past-present but a response to the non-present alterity of the Other—is precisely that of the moment of affection, of *Impression,* by the Other, that is, of that which is "to come [*à venir*]," it is equally to do with a *rapport sans rapport* with the future (of the Other). If the Other is taken to be never *present* as such in his or her alterity (where "present" is understood as reduction to immanence since there is also for Levinas an ultra-presence of transcendence, a superlative present that is incomparable), then the *Urimpression* must *already* be a trace, so that the retention as trace-of-the-impression is the trace of a trace. The trace is thus absolutely—and paradoxically—primary,[20] and "memory" becomes the response to or receiving of an immemorial affection which as having-never-been-present-as-such is no different from the future to come. The affection of time is thus not an auto-affection but a hetero-affection with a structure that is at once traumatic and messianic whereby the immanence of the present is broken open by the absolutely Other. Yet more is needed if that Other is to be specified as *autrui:* the account of time will need to be related to an account of subjectivity as responsible in the absolute sense that Levinas means by substitution and sacrifice.[21] In *Otherwise Than Being* the traumatic-messianic account of time will be extended into a description of responsible subjectivity.

V. THE ANARCHIC TRACE:
PASSIVITY, PASSIBILITY, PASSION

The problem Levinas sets out to solve in his account of time is to describe how the present of the subject is affected—disturbed—without that which affects it being reduced to the present, and (self)-presence, that it affects by marking it as always already broken open. With the turn to the immemorial in an account of subjectivity affected by that which it cannot recuperate in the presence of any present or representation, the trace, as the way in which transcendence affects the immanence of the subject, comes to have a crucial role in preventing substitution from collapsing into identification. Whereas the trace in Derrida introduces non-presence into the present of the *Augenblick,* the Levinasian trace preserves the irreducibility to the Same of the otherness of the personal Other. With that in mind, let us return to the account of subjectivity in *Otherwise Than Being* to follow Levinas's crucial description of the "absolute exteriority" of "adjacency in proximity":

> Incommensurable with the present, unassemblable in it, it [adjacency in proximity, *attenance dans la proximité*] is always "already in the past" behind which the present delays, over and beyond the "now" which this exteriority disturbs or obsesses. This way of passing [*passer*], disturbing the present without allowing itself to be invested by the *arché* of consciousness, striating with its furrows the clarity of the ostensible, is what we have called a trace. Proximity is thus *anarchically* a relationship with singularity without the mediation of any principle, any ideality. What concretely corresponds to this description is my relationship with my neighbor. (*AE* 127/*OB* 100)

The "trace" is the way in which the transcendent, the absolutely Other, affects immanence. But how, then, is this to be described philosophically, in the language of the *logos*? Levinas adds the following footnote: "If the anarchical were not signalled in consciousness, it would reign in its own way. The anarchical is possible only when contested by language, which betrays, but conveys [or 'translates'], its anarchy, without abolishing it, by an abuse of language [*qui trahit, mais traduit, sans l'annuler, son anarchie par un abus de langage*]" (*AE* 127 n. 2/*OB* 194 n. 2).

What is at issue is the status of the trace, its relation to the ethical relation, and its consequences for a possible discourse on and of ethics. The trace, in the first quotation, is the way "exteriority" has of "passing" and disturbing the present and consciousness: the trace is a "furrow" in presence, an absence not *of* but *in* presence, yet not an absence left by a (past) presence which could in principle be represented. In the passage, "exteriority" appears to refer to "proximity," as if the neighbor or *autrui* in proximity *were* the exteriority concerned. But, on the other hand, it is *not* unequivocally claimed that that trace is the trace of *autrui*. There is thus an ambiguity in the text: is or is not the trace the trace of the Other as *autrui*?

The ego cannot conceive (i.e., anticipate, grasp) what "touches" it; rather, what touches the ego exercises a mastery over it:

> Anarchy troubles being over and beyond these alternatives. . . . In the form of an ego, anachronously *delayed* behind its present moment, and

unable to recuperate this delay—that is, in the form of an ego unable to conceive what is "touching" it, the ascendency of the other is exercised upon the same [*l'emprise de l'Autre s'exercise sur le Même*] to the point of interrupting it, leaving it speechless. . . . This inversion of consciousness is no doubt a passivity—but it is a passivity beneath all passivity. It cannot be defined in terms of intentionality, where undergoing is always also an assuming, that is, an experience always anticipated and consented to, already an origin and an *arché*. (*AE* 128–29/*OB* 101)

This structure is temporalized as the delay in reflection: the ego cannot grasp what is present in the very present of its occurrence, and is therefore unable to appropriate what affects it. Anticipation is already too late: something has slipped in. This will become the traumatic character of the relation with the Other. Once again, we can interpret this in relation to Husserl's account of time-consciousness, where the "living present" is supposed to involve an "*Urimpression*": at the origin there is not an act of the ego but a passivity, an impression.[22] If the subject can go no further back than the *Urimpression*, this means that at the origin there is something which the subject cannot appropriate. By maintaining the absolute passivity of the *Urimpression* as a primordial having-been-affected, a passivity not recuperable by an activity (including an auto-affection), Levinas makes of this "origin" a disturbance of the present and of presence, a disturbance which cannot be recovered or synchronized in the present.

If anything, the move in the final paragraph of the first section of the chapter on "Substitution" appears indeed to be toward the identification of *autrui* with the anarchic. However, even here the identification of the an-archic with *autrui* is not complete. It is not in *autrui* as such that the anarchy "takes form" but in "*responsibility* for another" (my emphasis). When Levinas writes, "It is *as though* persecution by another were at the bottom of solidarity with another" (*AE* 129–30/*OB* 102, my emphasis), what is the force of the "as though [*comme si*]"? How does "persecution by" *autrui* become "responsibility for" *autrui*? This is the central question of the "Substitution" chapter, and therefore of *Otherwise Than Being* as a whole. "Persecution" by the Other suggests an unmediated, traumatic, virtually psychotic, relation with the Other.[23] How does such a relation become "responsibility"? Is it so immediately (in terms of both temporality and mediation)? Or is there a need for a term other than "me"—passive, passible subjectivity, corporeality—and *autrui*, the other person without qualities, for the trauma to give over to ethical responsibility? In asking the question himself—"How can such a passion take place and have its time in consciousness?" (*AE* 130/*OB* 102, translation modified)—Levinas is perhaps not only saying that this passion is not conscious, but also that there must be a further condition which makes the passion possible, beyond *moi* and *autrui*.

VI. THE ASSIGNATION OF RESPONSIBILITY

The relation of subjectivity to *autrui* is developed in the section entitled "Recurrence," which in *Otherwise Than Being* is abbreviated from "La récurrence et l'en deçà" in the Brussels paper. This change, while serving to maintain the ambiguity of recurrence, also makes it more obscure. At issue in the section is the relation of the "outside"—which, we have seen in "Principle and Anarchy," leaves a trace—to the "hither" or "this side" of sensibility, before representation. It could be said that we are concerned here with the sensible affect of the trace.

Levinas's account of recurrence can be situated in relation to a number of attempts in French philosophy since the impact of Husserl in France to excavate a constitutive level beneath that of the transcendental ego. The two main directions of such attempts—following different tendencies in Husserl—are, first, to remove from constituting consciousness any residue whatsoever of positivity so that the subject is supposed to be pure negativity (Sartre); and second, to discover a layer of irreducible positivity in the life-world and/or the body (Merleau-Ponty) in such a way that, taking a cue from Heidegger's rethinking of the relation of "man" to Being, constitution takes place outside the transcendental subject, although of course that positivity is not necessarily substantial, but might involve some kind of process. Indeed, both directions arise from the dissolution of the conception of subject as substance which begins with Kant and is carried through by Hegel. The act of self-identification, elaborated most clearly by Fichte—whether direct, as in the transcendental apperception of the "I think" which must accompany all my representations in Kant, or mediated, as in the return to self though otherness in Hegel—replaces the conception of the subject as a created or thinking substance. Levinas's conception of recurrence amounts to a repudiation of this tradition of the dissolution of substantiality of the subject for the sake of its spontaneity or its work of negation, which culminated in the self-appropriating movement of self-consciousness: "The reduction of subjectivity to consciousness dominates philosophical thought, which since Hegel has been trying to overcome the duality of being and thought, by identifying under different figures, substance and subject. This also amounts to undoing the substantivity of substance, but in relationship with self-consciousness" (*AE* 131/ *OB* 103).

Rather than simply undoing the substantivity of substance, Levinas will produce a different account of substance as "hypostasis" which will occur before or on "this side" of consciousness. The underlying support which is subjectivity will consist in responsibility which, as absolute, will include responsibility for the responsibility or freedom of the Other. Thus Levinas will maintain the importance of subjectivity against those who, also working against the idealist tradition, would dissolve it. Moreover, he will base that subjectivity on a re-worked notion of substance which ceases, in substitution, to be onto-logical (at least, according to Levinas's self-understanding), while rejecting completely the priority of consciousness and self-consciousness. Having situated Levinas's project, we now turn to his alternative to identity in the characterization of the subject.

The subject according to Levinas is absolutely passive, backed up to itself, uneasy in its skin, accused, assigned prior to any act, exiled from itself, and "like a sound that would resound in its own echo." These are the various figures Levinas uses to characterize the aspect of subjectivity that is "older" than the ego. Consciousness is, as Kant showed, based on self-consciousness. As Levinas puts it, "It already rests on a 'subjective condition,' an identity that one calls ego or I" (*AE* 130/*OB* 102). Referring implicitly to Heidegger and Sartre, Levinas writes, "It is true that, when asking about the meaning of this identity, we have the habit either of denouncing in it a reified sub-stance, or of finding in it once again the for-itself of consciousness" (*AE* 130/*OB* 103). Against what he sees as this idealist teaching, Levinas wants to draw notice to the "*who* or the *me*" which is "nonrela-tion, but absolutely a term [*non-relation, mais absolument terme*]": non-relational, insofar as unmediated, including through qualities, but absolutely a term, insofar as *assigned*, thus the "term of an irre-

versible assignation" (*AE* 130/*OB* 103). That assignation is "non-relational"—that is, unmediated—means that there is no way out of the
assignation, including the way of an economy of reciprocity, reciprocal recognition, and exchange. Assignation of responsibility comes to
its stopping point, its terminus, in the subject who is "backed up
against itself, its feet to the wall" (*AE* 132/*OB* 104, translation modified), because there is no escape from the accusation or assignation
of responsibility.[24]

Levinas describes this condition not in terms of abstract morality
but as a condition of sensibility—"twisted over itself in its skin, uneasy in its skin, in itself already outside of itself" (*AE* 132/*OB* 104,
translation modified). It is not that being in one's skin, incarnate,
precedes the accusation, being outside of oneself, but that incarnation
is already a being outside oneself without being the exile of the soul
in the body. Nor is this a dispersion of moments which could be
recuperated in a return to identity or subjective synthesis of identification: "The uncancellable recurrence of the oneself in the subject
is prior to any distinction between moments which could present
themselves to a synthesizing activity of identification and assemblage
to recall or expectation" (*AE* 132/*OB* 104). Which is to say that recurrence is not a feature of the self as a synthesizing agent.

At issue in all this is the *immediate* relation of the "outside" or
beyond being to the "hither side [*l'en deçà*]" of sensibility. A key
move in *Otherwise Than Being* is to demonstrate that ethics is not an
idea or ideal but is immediately sensibility. For Levinas *sensibility
just is possibility to the "outside,"* and thus transcendence is not transcendence out of sensibility but the transcendence of sensibility in
its very constitution, which, insofar as sensibility is passivity and transcendence in passivity, calls for the language of the creature and of
createdness or dependency.

If sensibility or corporeity just is possibility, being able to be affected, this affect can only be from an "outside," since auto-affection
would close up the possible subject into a circle, rendering it impassi-
ble, even if only because all-inclusive. This is the basis of Levinas's
critique of circular ontologies, and the Ulyssean movement of return,
which are a denial of possibility to the outside. Similarly, the priority
of the *cogito* could be seen as stemming from a stoic tradition, seeking to locate the center of the subject outside the sphere of affect.
And if, in Levinas, the "outside" is identified as *autrui,* then sensible

passibility is response to the other person, and the way is open to the ethicization of the sensibility. This sensible possibility as *immediate* response also becomes traumatic, hence Levinas's characterization of the ethical relation as a "traumatism." But not only are there traumas that are not linked with an ethical claim, such as those resulting from a sudden accident, but it is also far from clear that the fact that the relation with the other person is traumatic makes it evidently an *ethical* relation. We will have to see whether a further condition is required.

VII. TRAUMA, THE OTHER PERSON, AND THE LAW

For Levinas the self is at once in its skin and outside itself, assigned, passive, yet responsible. Maternity is one of the ways in which he deformalizes this condition. And, referring to Leibniz's formula "the ego is innate to itself," Levinas writes in a crucial passage:

> The self involved in maintaining oneself, losing oneself or finding oneself again [*Le se du "se maintenir" ou du "se perdre" ou du "se retrouver"*—note that these are terms of the movement of the idealist ego, activities rendered *passive* by the emphasis on the reflexive pronoun] is not a result, but the very matrix [*la matrice*] of the relations or events that these pronominal verbs express. The evocation of maternity in this metaphor suggests to us the proper sense of the oneself (*soi-même*). The oneself cannot form itself; it is already formed with absolute passivity. . . . This passivity is that of an attachment that has already been made [*déjà nuée*], as something irreversibly past, prior to all memory and all recall. It was made in an irrecuperable time which the present, represented in recall, does not equal, in a time of birth or creation, of which nature or creation retains a trace, unconvertible into a memory. Recurrence is more past than any rememberable past, any past convertible into a present. The oneself is a creature, but an orphan by birth or an atheist no doubt ignorant of its Creator, for to know it would again be to take up its commencement. The recurrence of the oneself refers to the hither side of the present in which every identity identified in the said is constituted. It is already constituted when the act of constitution first originates. (*AE* 132–33/*OB* 104–5)

To begin the exegesis of this passage somewhat indirectly, we now know why the "ego is in itself like a sound that would resound in its own echo" (*AE* 131/*OB* 103). We could approach this metaphor through a contrast with Husserl, whose account of time-consciousness begins with a question concerning the relation of the duration of a sound, or melody, to the duration of consciousness. Consciousness is not punctual but temporal, and this temporality is stretched to include retention and protention. But at the same time the priority of the present, as living present, is maintained. The question has been all along how the sound is *present* to consciousness, and how the (absent) past of the sound is *present* as past, and the not-yet of the future *present* as future. Thus we could say that for Husserl the ego is like a sound—his example of a temporal object in *On the Phenomenology of the Consciousness of Internal Time*—a sound that is present to itself. For Levinas, by contrast, the ego is like an echo, or, to be more precise, like a sound that is its own echo, that can never be present except as echo, in other words, in relation to a non-presence, something with which it can never catch up. Perhaps the metaphor is exceeded when we say that the sound of which the ego is an echo can never have been present in its fullness, is always already apprehended as echo. Echo is a response, a doubling which calls without Narcissus hearing her as his Other. Narcissus, as the ego constituted in reflection and self-appropriation, does not hear Echo except as an echo of himself. Echo is the trace of the Other, ungathered into memory, immemorial, the trace of an assignation forgotten in the self-appropriation of the ego, a constitution already constituted before any act. The subject, as echo, has its center or source outside itself, and it is this very disappropriation that makes the subject feel itself as in itself, "backed up against itself." Were the subject content, satisfied with itself, it would hardly feel its containment, but would rather expand to include everything in its narcissism. It is thus the "outside" that makes possible an "inside" or interiority, while this inside, the interiority of the ego, thus remains the echo of the outside that constitutes it. If this constitution could be appropriated by the ego, it would cease to be an echo, since the origin would be present to that which originated from it. To say that this origin is "immemorial," then, is to say that the subject can never be other than an echo, primordially a response to that which it cannot appropriate. But this is still not necessarily to claim that the "outside" is *autrui*. Or if it is, we still need to know how it is that *autrui* cannot be appropriated, why the trace of the Other that echoes in being is "older" than being—the trace of the immemorial. What is the condition for the unappropriability of the Other?

The singularity-without-qualities of the subject is derived from its being unable to evade or be substituted in its infinite responsibility as response to the accusation. For Levinas this infinite responsibility is never detached from the condition of sensibility. The "deformalization" to materiality of this absolute passivity is "maternity" as "the complete being 'for the other,' " and the "very signifyingness of signification" (AE 137/OB 108). Levinas may be thinking here of maternity as self-sacrifice, sacrifice of the self to the Other at its center. As with filiality and fecundity, the metaphor is problematic. It does, however, concretize and indeed extend the signification of the expression "in one's skin" (dans sa peau): the "body is not only an image or figure here; it is the distinctive in-oneself of the contraction of ipseity and its breakup" (AE 138–39/OB 109). Levinas's account of corporeality is the "other side" of the metaphysical thought of the Infinite in me as more than I can contain. The skin tightens against an ever-inflating responsibility. And just as I am my skin, I cannot step out of it and slough off my responsibility: the "irremissible guilt with regard to the neighbor is like a Nessus tunic my skin would be" (AE 139/OB 109).

The question to be posed again, however, is whether the passivity of incarnation is necessarily ethical; that is, whether it will be possible to derive responsibility from passivity, contrary to the traditional account of ethics which would see it as deriving from the free acts of the autonomous subject, of the self-subjection of the subject to the universal law one gives oneself. The answer is to be provided through an account of what it means to undergo a relation which one cannot assume in the active sense. "The active source of this passivity is not thematizable. It is the passivity of a trauma, but one that prevents its own representation, a deafening trauma, cutting the thread of consciousness which should have welcomed it in its present, the passivity of being persecuted" (AE 141/OB 111). To say that the source of this passivity is not thematizable is to say that it cannot be anticipated, is not the noema of an intentional act. This also means that it does not fall within a horizon of meaning-giving (Sinngebung) whether through the transcendental ego or being, which implies further that this source cannot be related to anything else. Because nonrelational in terms of relations of mediation and anticipatory projection, the subject undergoes the source of its passivity as a trauma.

The function of the category of "trauma" here is to enable the transition from "recurrence" to "persecution." Unlike recurrence, persecution implies an Other, a persecutor. Since the relation of the persecuted to the persecutor is that of a trauma, a relation without relations, the passivity of the persecuted is "absolute" (*AE* 141/*OB* 111).

The final step is to determine this passivity as responsibility. Since the passivity is absolute, rather than a limited passivity that would be determinate with respect to activity, it must include responsibility for the persecutor; absolute passivity admits neither exception or qualification: "This passivity deserves the epithet of complete or absolute only if the persecuted one is liable to answer for the persecutor" (*AE* 141/*OB* 111). The "ethical" conversion here is from the from-the-Other to the for-the-Other, from persecution to responsibility. Subjectivity is the locus of this conversion. The locus of the subject, however, is dis-inter-ested—literally, "not in being"—a *non-lieu*. If ethical responsibility is not referred to a place in being, this also means that it is not possible to hide: exposure is without recourse to concealment or the play of veiling and unveiling. Temporally the "transfer" does not occur as a causal sequence where something becomes something else, but has always already happened. It is both "traumatic" (non-horizonal, not present, not in being) and "immemorial" (not in the synchronized time of the *logos*). From the perspective of ontology, subjectivity is a paradox, "the *other in the same* [*l'autre dans le même*]." Existentially, this is described as "persecution." Through the "transfer," persecution may be understood to have already been total responsibility. As such, it is irreducible to intentionality which is as act depending on self-possession in the present and an impersonal discourse of thematization: "subjectivity taken as intentionality is founded on auto-affection as an auto-revelation, source of an impersonal discourse" (*AE* 142/*OB* 111). Contrary to being an auto-affection, the "uniqueness of the self is the very fact of bearing the fault of another" (*AE* 143/*OB* 112). This bearing of the fault of the other is "expiation."

It would seem from this summary that the face-to-face with the Other is not enough per se to ordain the subject to responsibility. The "turn" or crux in *Otherwise Than Being* is when subjectivity becomes responsibility.

Responsibility for another is not an accident that happens to a subject, but precedes essence in it, has not awaited freedom, in which a commitment to another would have been made. I have not done anything and I have always been under accusation—persecuted. The ipseity, in the passivity without arche characteristic of identity, is a hostage. The word *I* means *here I am* [*me voici*], answering for everything and everyone. Responsibility for the others has not been a return to oneself, but an exasperated contracting, which the limits of identity cannot retain. Recurrence becomes identity in breaking up the limits of identity, breaking up the *principle* of being in me, the intolerable rest in itself characteristic of definition. (*AE* 145–46/*OB* 114)

Recalling the account of creation as the breath of life being breathed into Adam, Levinas writes, "*By* the other (*l'autre*) and for the other, but without alienation: inspired. Inspiration which is the psyche. But the psyche which can signify this alterity in the same without alienation, in the guise of incarnation, as being-in-one's-skin, having-the-other [*l'autre*]-in-one's- skin" (*AE* 146/*OB* 114–15, translation modified).

On the one hand, recurrence has now been linked with the implantation of the Law in such a way that the recurrence cannot involve a reappropriation by the subject of that which is recurred to.[25] On the other hand, recurrence is connected with the relation with the Other. By using the term *autre* rather than *autrui*, Levinas leaves indeterminate whether these are the same or different relations—an indeterminacy which may well be irreducible, in that the Law and *autrui* may be neither the same nor separable. In any event, both could be said to involve the trace of the immemorial. It is the implication of Levinas's account of sensibility that there is no distance between the subject and the Law on the one hand and the other person on the other hand: the relation with both has a traumatic structure. Does this mean that the Law is identified with the other person? It seems not, insofar as the other person is ordained to my responsibility in the trace of "illeity": "It is the trace of a relationship with illeity that no unity of apperception grasps, ordering me to responsibility" (*AE* 214/*OB* 168). There must be something other than the Other that prevents the Other from being reduced to immanence, that renders the Other unappropriable, and thereby, equally, sustains desire as well as responsibility.

As responsibility, substitution is not simply an indifferent replacement of one term by another. Hence Levinas's recourse to the language of sacrifice. A sacrifice, as self-sacrifice, refers beyond ontology and is prior to any deliberated act of commitment. If it is not a free and premeditated commitment, though, what is it that makes a self-sacrifice ethical? What is it that ordains or commands the sacrifice? The "what . . . ?" question is perhaps illegitimate here, since such a question is ontologically determined. However, we can at least suggest that what makes substitution ethical sacrifice is not *what* it *is*, but *that* it is in the trace.

> It is because in an approach, there is inscribed or written [*s'inscrit ou s'écrit*] the trace of Infinity—the trace of a departure, but trace of what is inordinate [*dé-mesuré*], does not enter into the present and inverts the *arché* into anarchy—that there is forsakenness of the Other [*délaissement d'autrui:* abandonment, relinquishment, renunciation], obsession by him, responsibility and a Self [*Soi*]. The non-interchangeable par excellence, the I, the unique one, substitutes itself for others. Nothing is a game. Thus being is transcended. (AE 148–49/OB 116–17)

In the footnote to this passage it is stated that it is the Infinite "which addresses the other to my responsibility." So the approach is not simply the approach of another person, but the approach of what makes the Other an *Other* in the sense of transcendence, which is the trace of the departure and of what is beyond measure, the departure or passing of the beyond measure, counterpart of the Infinite as the more-in-me-than-I-can-contain,[26] in both cases fracturing the immanence of being and creating a hollow out of which the Other comes to me as the one for whom I am absolutely responsible but with whom I can never identify. We should remember that for Levinas the Infinite is not inclusive, an unlimited totalization, but rather transcendence and disturbance of the immanent totality. And it equally follows from the emphasis on transcendence that if this is an ethics of affectivity and passibility, it is not a morality of empathy, of identity with the feelings of the Other, since one way or another these would have to be mediated in order to communicate themselves, and thereby reduce the Other to the immanence of an alter ego. How, then, without a "reducing" mediation, can there be any kind of relation with the traumatically Other, a relation that does not depend on identity or identification, reducing the Other to the Same,

yet which allows the "conversion" of trauma to responsibility? Without some kind of relation there would be no ethics, only the traumatic
repetition of non-relation. "Substitution" is central to *Otherwise
Than Being* because it just is that relation, strictly "impossible" in
ontological terms, and it is thanks to "illeity" that the trauma of the
Other is substitution, where the unique may substitute for the Other,
indeed is unique in this very substitution. *Autrui* is ordained to my
responsibility in the withdrawal of the Infinite, yet at the same time
the Infinite is not the unattainable, an onto-theologically "hidden
God," since it is also both the Other in me that constitutes me as a
singular, singularly responsible subject—yet an Other that infinitely
exceeds its container and in its very immemoriality is more present
than any presence—as well as concrete, everyday relations with the
Other and with Others. Thus, in this double sense, the Infinite is the
inappropriable par excellence. Both in *distinguishing* the face from
Infinity and in indicating their necessary *relation,* the face being face
only as or in the trace of Infinity, Levinas is first of all distinguishing
the Other for whom I am responsible from the object of desire, and
desired identification or fusion, and showing the way in which the
unappropriability of the desired, figured by the Infinite in its sheer
positive excess, commands me to responsibility before any decision
or distance can be taken.

The unpossessability or unappropriability of the desired, as Infinity, combined with its absolute proximity, is a condition that allows
the other person to be ordained to my responsibility. Both this structure and that which is required for it in turn to be possible need to
be understood. The excess of the Other in the subject is not "shut up
in itself like a state of the soul" but is "given over to the other" as
Saying ("God and Philosophy," *DVI* 121/*CPP* 169). That is to say,
ethical language is the form of "mediation" that does not reduce its
terms. The Saying is a testimony that does not include or comprehend that to which it testifies: "And the only pure testimony is that
of the Infinite. This is not a psychological wonder, but the modality
in which the Infinite *comes to pass,* signifying through him to whom
it signifies, understood inasmuch as, before any commitment, I answer for the other" (*DVI* 122/*CPP* 170). It is crucial here that the
other person is *not* the object of my desire, but rather in the trace as
the addressee of a testimony to the Infinite. In a sense, then, the
Other as the one for whom I am responsible lies in a falling short of

my desire before an infinity that I cannot contain, which marks my finitude by breaking open the self-relation of my immanence, which has in turn only been made possible by that breaking-open, such that it has always already taken place—in the "non-place" of the immemorial. Thus my finitude is not an impossible relation with a Nothing, a being-towards-death in my solitude as a relation with something that is more my own than anything else, but a relation with the excessiveness in proximity of the infinitely Other.[27] I am finite, for Levinas, not primarily with respect to my death, but with respect to the infinitude of the Other. The proximity to that which cannot be contained is also a relation with a passing, with the trace in its structure of erasure.[28] Notwithstanding their difference, *both* these structures—the relation with death and with the infinitely Other as and in the trace—have this in common, that they are "impossible" relations or non-relations: I can appropriate neither my death nor the infinitely Other in myself. Neither can be the object of an intentional experience (nor, Levinas would presumably say, of a non-objectifying intentionality), and both are received in passivity. However, while being-towards-death invites an orientation, in throw-ness, toward the future of the project as the authentic temporal mode of existence, for Levinas subjectivity is constituted in the immemorial "non-place" of substitution where the traumatic absolute of singularity is, in the trace of illeity, already responsibility.

CONCLUSION

Levinas is sometimes read as implying either that the Law is nothing else than the relation with the Other or that the relation with *autrui* is beyond the Law. Yet in order that the traumatic relation of the subject with the Other involve an ethical responsibility, it is clear that the other person and the Law have equally to be distinguished in order to prevent an identificatory or mimetic relation—ultimately a fusion—with the other person. It is thanks to "illeity"—the trace of the immemorial, the diachronic impossibility of synchronizing the time of the Other with my time—that the Other cannot be reduced to myself nor I merge with the Other. This distinction inheres in the opening up of a non-presence within the present, an "immemorial," whereby the present is affected by the trace of what it cannot recuperate. It is only in relation to the trace of the immemorial that the trauma of the Other is rendered "ethical." Illeity marks the difference not within immanence but as the difference of immanence and transcendence, and as such assumes the structural role of the Law, although in bringing the Law into such close proximity with *autrui* Levinas tends to underplay its neutrality, even if this is hinted at in the echo in the word *illeity* of the *il y a,* thereby linking the name, the "*Il,*" with the indifference of un-negatable being, thus marking the site of a trauma other than that of subjectivity's passibility to *autrui.*[29]

In separating me from the Other, and in thereby preventing substitution from collapsing into identity, in making substitution possible, the Law ordains the Other to my responsibility. And it does so not prior to or independently of the relation with the Other, but in and as that very relation. The role of the Law in the constitution of subjectivity as responsibility is suggested in the talmudic reading "The Temptation of Temptation," where Levinas claims that the "apparently upside-down order" of the Israelites' response to the gift of the Torah, "We will do and we will hear" (Exodus 24:7), whereby the Law is accepted before it is known (to know the Law you have to already be a subject of the Law), placing passivity prior to both *praxis* and contemplation, "reveals the deep structure of subjectivity" and "the meaning of inspiration."[30]

> The impossibility of escaping from God—which in this at least is not a value among others—is the "mystery of angels," the "We will do and we will hear." It lies in the depth of the ego as ego, which is not only for a being the possibility of death, "the possibility of impossibility," but already the possibility of sacrifice, birth of meaning in the obtuseness of being, of a subordination of a "being able to die" to a "knowing how to sacrifice oneself."[31]

We find an exact homology here with the structure of the relation to the Other in the discussion of "substitution" in *Otherwise Than Being:*

> In this substitution, in which identity is inverted, this passivity more passive still than the passivity conjoined with action, beyond the inert passivity of the designated, the self is absolved of itself. Is this freedom? It is a different freedom from that of an initiative. Through substitution for others, the oneself escapes relations. . . . Outside of any

mysticism, in this respiration—the possibility of every sacrifice for the other—activity and passivity coincide [*se confondent*]. (*AE* 146/*OB* 115)

Substitution for the Other and the Law are inseparable—"The face of the other in proximity, which is more than representation, is an unrepresentable trace, the way [*façon*] of the Infinite" (*AE* 149/*OB* 116)—but this does not mean that the Law is identical with the other person. As "immemorial," both substitution as the being affected by the other person, and the receiving of the Law, involve the same *nachträglich* temporal structure, yet are also distinct from each other, and must be if the ethical is not to veer into perverse enjoyment. Hence the necessity that the approach be in the trace as an irreducible yet always already erased mark, in immanence, of the transcendence of the Other. However, the dependence of ethical assignation on something other than the personal Other opens up, within the ambiguity of illeity, an undecidability in the affect of alterity, between the transcendence of *autrui* and the immanence of *il y a*, the un-negatable "there is."

NOTES

1. My approach to Levinas has been profoundly affected by discussions I had in Leuven while on a fellowship there from 1992 to 1994, in particular with Rudolf Bernet, Paul Moyaert, Philippe Van Haute, and Rudi Visker, as well as by a continuing dialogue with Robert Bernasconi. I also wish to thank Rebecca Comay for her reading and suggestions.

2. E. Levinas, "Énigme et phénomène," *Esprit* 33, no. 6 (June 1965): 1128–42.

3. See E. Levinas, "La trace de l'autre" (originally published in 1963), in *EDE* 187–202; trans. A. Lingis, "The Trace of the Other," in *Deconstruction in Context*, ed. M. C. Taylor (Chicago: University of Chicago Press, 1986), 345–59. For two excellent discussions of the trace in Levinas, see E. S. Casey, "Levinas on Memory and the Trace," in *The Collegium Phaenomenologicum: The First Ten Years*, ed. J. Sallis, G. Moneta, and J. Taminiaux (Dordrecht: Kluwer, 1988), 241–55; and Jill Robbins, "Tracing Responsibility in Levinas's Ethical Thought," in *Ethics as First Philosophy*, ed. A. Peperzak (New York: Routledge, 1995), 173–83. Memory and the trace are also the subjects of my forthcoming book, *Traces of Memory and Forgetting: Heidegger, Levinas, Derrida*.

4. For a subtle discussion of this issue, see Paul Davies, "On Resorting to an Ethical Language," in Peperzak, *Ethics as First Philosophy*, 95–104.

5. See Theodore de Boer, "An Ethical Transcendental Philosophy," in *Face to Face with Levinas*, ed. R. A. Cohen (Albany: State University of New York Press, 1986), 83–115.

6. Even if it is also so that, whereas an eidetic phenomenological analysis moves from the concrete to its formal essence, the descriptions in *Totality and Infinity* move from formal structures to their "deformalization" in the ethical life of the subject.

7. See E. Levinas, "Intentionalité et Sensation" (1965), reprinted in *EDE* 145–62, esp. 151–56.

8. For a discussion of this issue, see R. Bernet, *La vie du sujet* (Paris: P.U.F., 1994), 297–327.

9. Cf. E. Husserl, *Formal and Transcendental Logic*, trans. D. Cairns (The Hague: Martinus Nijhoff, 1969), § 83.

10. E. Husserl, *Erfahrung und Urteil*, ed. Ludwig Landgrebe (Hamburg: Felix Meiner, 1954); trans. J. S. Churchill and K. Ameriks, *Experience and Judgment* (Evanston: Northwestern University Press, 1973).

11. Cf. Kant, *Critique of Practical Reason*, trans. L. W. Beck (New York: MacMillan, 1956), Book 1, chapter 3, pp. 74–92.

12. See R. Comay, "Facies Hippocratica," in Peperzak, *Ethics as First Philosophy*, 223–34; and J. Derrida, *Adieu: à Emmanuel Lévinas* (Paris: Galilée, 1997), 63: "le tiers n'attend pas, il est là, dès la 'première' épiphanie du visage dans le face-à-face" ("the third does not wait, he is there from the 'first' epiphany of the face in the face-to-face").

13. E. Levinas, "Substitution," *Revue Philosophique de Louvain* 66 (October 1968); *Basic Philosophical Writings*, ed. A. Peperzak, S. Critchley and R. Bernasconi (Indianapolis: Indiana University Press, 1996), 80–95.

14. Levinas sees the Husserlian alter ego as a reduction of the Other to being, understood in terms of analogy.

15. Levinas's *Le temps et l'autre* was first delivered as a series of four lectures in 1946–47 in Paris at the Collège Philosophique founded by Jean Wahl. It originally appeared in J. Wahl, *Le Choix, Le Monde, L'Existence* (Grenoble and Paris: Arthaud, 1947).

16. Rudolf Bernet draws attention to the importance of Levinas's interpretation of Husserl in this essay in his introduction to Husserl, *Texte zur Phänomenologie des inneren Zeitbewußtseins (1893–1917)* (Hamburg: Felix Meiner Verlag, 1985), lxiii–lxv.

17. Cf. J. B. Brough, "The Emergence of an Absolute Consciousness in Husserl's Early Writings on Time-Consciousness," *Man and World* 2 (1972): 314.

18. Levinas: "Il faut admettre ici un retour du temps sur lui-même, une

itération fondamentale" (*EDE* 153) ("One must admit here a return of time back on itself, a fundamental *iteration*"), wherein absolute consciousness produces time-consciousness by modifying *itself* in an avoidance of an infinite regress. For more on this, see Brough, "Emergence of an Absolute Consciousness": "Through the horizontal intentionality, the flow itself becomes 'apprehensible in the flowing' and both the apparent scandal of self-constitution and the specter of infinite regress are banished" (320). The modifications in question are "iterations" because they modify not only the "actual primal impression" but also "in succession, modifications of one another in the order in which they flow away," such that each "modification continuously generates ever new modification." However, by contrast with this continuous production, of which the "primal impression" is the "absolute beginning," the primal impression itself "is not produced" but is "*genesis spontanea;* it is primal generation." E. Husserl, *On the Phenomenology of the Consciousness of Internal Time (1893–1917),* based on Hua X, trans. J. B. Brough (Dordrecht: Kluwer, 1991), appendix 1, p. 106. Thus for Husserl, consciousness involves *both* continuous production and new impression, whereas for Levinas the "primal impression" is outside consciousness.

19. Cf. Husserl, *On the Phenomenology of the Consciousness of Internal Time,* appendix 1, p. 106.

20. Casey, "Levinas on Memory and the Trace," 241.

21. See B. Waldenfels, "Response and Responsibility in Levinas," and H. Miller, "Reply to Bernhard Waldenfels," in Peperzak, *Ethics as First Philosophy,* 39–58. Waldenfels charts the move in Levinas from the traditional notion of responsibility for something or somebody which can be imputed to a subject, to the "responsive ethics" of responsibility for the Other.

22. Cf. Husserl, *Phenomenology of the Consciousness of Internal Time,* § 31 and appendix 1. I thank Rudolf Bernet for drawing my attention to this feature of the *Urimpression.*

23. "The psyche, a uniqueness outside of concepts, is a seed of folly, already a psychosis" (*AE* 180/*OB* 142). In my view this language of psychosis is misleading, given the role of illeity as stand-in for the Law precluding a relation of fusion, and its relation to language.

24. Paradoxically, the escape from being demanded in Levinas's early text *De l'évasion,* originally published in 1935 in *Recherches Philosophiques* (reissued by Fata Morgana, Paris, 1982), will finally be achieved only through the inescapability of responsibility for the other person.

25. See also the discussion of "We will do and we will hear" in the talmudic reading "The Temptation of Temptation" in E. Levinas, *Quatre lectures talmudiques* (Paris: Minuit, 1968), 67–109; trans. A. Aronowicz, *Nine Talmudic Readings* (Indianapolis: Indiana University Press, 1990), 30–50; and Jill Robbins, *Prodigal Son/Elder Brother: Interpretation and Alterity in August-*

ine, Petrarch, Kafka, Levinas (Chicago: University of Chicago Press, 1991), chapter 4: "Alterity and the Judaic: Reading Levinas."

26. See E. Levinas, "Philosophy and the Idea of Infinity," in *EDE* 165–78/*CPP* 47–59. With Plato's "beyond being [*epekeina tes ousias*]," Descartes's proof of the existence of God in the Third Meditation is one of those few exceptions to Western philosophy's "destruction of transcendence" through the reduction of the Other to the Same: "The intentionality that animates the idea of infinity is not comparable with any other. . . . In thinking infinity the I *from the first thinks more than it thinks.* . . . The Infinite is the radically, absolutely other. The transcendence of infinity with respect to the ego that is separated from it and thinks it constitutes the first mark of its infinitude. The idea of infinity . . . has been *put* into us. It is not a reminiscence. It is experience in the sole radical sense of the term: a relationship with the exterior, with the other, without this exteriority being able to be integrated into the same" (*EDE* 172/*CPP* 45).

27. For Levinas on being-towards-death in Heidegger, see *TA* 58–64/*TO* 75–77.

28. Cf. Robbins, "Tracing Responsibility in Levinas's Ethical Thought," 177. For further discussion, see below.

29. On the gender of the *"Il,"* see J. Derrida, "At This Very Moment in This Work Here I Am," trans. R. Berezdivin, in *Re-Reading Levinas*, ed. R. Bernasconi and S. Critchley (Bloomington: Indiana University Press, 1981), 11–48. For discussions of the relation of illeity and the *il y a* see P. Davies, "A Linear Narrative? Blanchot with Heidegger in the Work of Levinas," in *Philosophers' Poets*, ed. D. Wood (London: Routledge, 1990), 37–69; J. Llewelyn, *Emmanuel Levinas: The Genealogy of Ethics* (London: Routledge, 1995), chapter 10; and Simon Critchley, *Very Little . . . Almost Nothing* (London: Routledge, 1997), 76–83. The question asked by Critchley is the same as mine: how may alterity be understood ethically? However, whereas he moves away from Levinas toward a discussion of the "facticity of dying" in Blanchot and Beckett, my approach is through the role of the Law; for a discussion of the Law in Blanchot, see my "The Trace of Trauma: Blindness, Testimony and the Gaze in Blanchot and Derrida," in *Maurice Blanchot: The Demand of Writing*, ed. Carolyn Bailey Gill (London: Routledge, 1996), 153–73. For the relationship of the *il y a*, illeity, and God, see also H. de Vries, "Adieu, à dieu, a-Dieu," in Peperzak, *Ethics as First Philosophy*, 218–19. De Vries reads the *il y a* as a necessary "privative" or non-sense, an "excluded third" in relation to the third person of illeity as a necessary condition of possibility of the ethical that also menaces it, and must do so if it is not to become "institution." The implication here that the *il y a* is in a relation to the Law of a "supplement" in Derrida's sense needs to be further developed if we are to avoid the clearly false view that the *il y a* is opposed

to or outside the Law. Perhaps the ultimate difficulty is that singularity, and thereby an unshakable responsibility, cannot be generated either by the Law (Kant) or by the traumatic relation to *autrui* alone, but requires also the relation of the Law to a non-personal alterity, of the *Il* to the *il y a*. The problem with the later Levinas is that he attempts to deal with this by ethicizing the *il y a*, which had previously stood for a non-ethical and un-negatable being from which escape was necessary, via a reworking of his earlier description of insomnia (see "De la conscience à la veille," *DVI* 34–61; and "God and Philosophy," *DVI* 94–127/*CPP* 153–73: "Insomnia—the wakefulness in awakening—is disturbed in the core of its formal or categorical *sameness* [égalité] by the *other*. . . . Insomnia is wakefulness, but a wakefulness without intentionality, dis-interested," 98–99/156), such that the *il y a* becomes vigilance and thereby a condition of passibility to the Other: "To support without compensation, the excessive or disheartening hubbub and encumberment of the *there is* is needed" (*AE* 209/*OB* 164).

30. Cf. the reading of Tractate *Shabbath* pp. 88a and 88b, "The Temptation of Temptation," in Levinas, *Quatre lectures talmudiques*, 91–92; trans. Aronowicz, *Nine Talmudic Readings*, 42. In this discussion the temporal structure of the Law is *nachträglich*, or traumatic. See J.-F. Lyotard, "Levinas's Logic," in Cohen, *Face to Face with Levinas*, 117–58: "According to Levinas, 'it' is not obligatory because 'it' is universal; 'it' is simply obligatory. Thus 'it' is to be done *before* 'it' is understood. In this way, the Lord requires of Israel not obedience but rather obligation towards Him, before He instructs the people as to what they will be obliged to do. In this way the domination of knowledge, that is, the infatuation with the enunciation, is interrupted" (152). My argument is that the disruption of the position of enunciation involves more than an interruption of the domination of knowledge, namely, the prior relation to the absolutely Other. See also Robbins, *Prodigal Son/Elder Brother*. I have discussed this talmudic reading in "Originality, Inspiration and the Passivity of the Subject: A Re-reading of Genius in Kant's *Third Critique*," in A. van den Braembussche, proceedings of the conference *The Kantian Turn: On Kant's Critique of Judgement and Its Influence on Contemporary Aesthetics* (Maastricht: Jan van Eyck Akademie, forthcoming).

31. Levinas, *Quatre lectures talmudiques*, 109; trans. Aronowicz, *Nine Talmudic Readings*, 50.

6

Ethics as First Philosophy and Religion

Jeffrey Bloechl

FOLLOWING THE DEFINITION established by Aristotle, ethics examines the relationship between our capacity to mark and repeat certain actions, which includes recognizing rules and giving them to oneself, and the passivity denoted in the fact that experiences and ideas impress themselves on us. The good life consists in managing this activity and passivity on the complex field of economic, social and political life. The primary occasion in which we feel this challenge is the encounter with someone in need, where a face alone is often enough to call forth a response visibly guided by prior education and experience. As many have noted, what seems to define this exceptional experience is the manner in which a call for help strikes the passerby before he can invoke the matrix which frames the response one elects to make. Passivity has gone ahead of activity, and cannot be reduced to it. The question of responsibility and thus the entire field of ethics is mobilized by the face of another human being. This basic observation reminds us that the appeal for help is not yet qualified by the dispositions of those who hear it, which in turn seems to invoke the thought that that appeal is *pure*. From this notion of a pure appeal, it is of course only a short—though perhaps not entirely evident—step to begin speaking of a responsibility which is *radical,* or originary. Responsibility as such would then designate the being of the individual singled out by a face or gaze which turns toward him from beyond all expectation.

The pure appeal and radical responsibility cannot be fitted within the limits of any concrete identity or situation. The ethics of this relation thus renounces the possibility of a finite object and, in turn, frees itself from all dependence on or mixture with other fields. But furthermore, having moved outside those other fields, it will then take the view that their accounts of human action, insofar as they are founded on basic definitions, have a contaminated definition of the appeal and a restricted definition of responsibility. Assuming the authority to pass judgment on all other disciplines, this ethics takes for itself the title "first philosophy."

An ethics of the pure appeal wishes not to be mistaken for an ethics which is founded. If there is an appeal which strikes me before I could even interpret it, then the idea that all human acts share a single foundation is itself embedded in the same matrix which that appeal is to mobilize. A founded ethics, in short, would then lie completely on the side of the response, and to call upon a foundation would be to give it to oneself. Such an ethics would therefore confine human action to the economy of competing desires, which alleges that every encounter can be explained solely in terms of differing projects of individual existence. In contrast, an ethics of the pure appeal considers ethics to begin precisely when, or rather because, something has escaped that economy.

I

The philosophy of Levinas presents us with a theory of attachment to the other person prior to any contact, encounter, or liaison. According to Levinas, my neighbor is the "first one on the scene" (*AE* 109/*OB* 87), looking at me and calling to me before any question of applying calculus or categories to determine his proximity. "He orders me from before being recognized." The very act of recognizing him is itself already a response to him. Recognition is already ordered by what it tries to capture in an image; to form an image of one's neighbor is already to respond to him. If the neighbor is truly the first one on the scene, not even the work of negation is enough to get free of Levinas's strictures: for me to negate every image I form of the other person is still to define him starting from myself, and so to retain our relation within a logic of identity and an anthropology of self-assertion. For Levinas, the relation with my neighbor is a "relation of kinship outside all biology, 'against all logic.' " My neighbor is "precisely *other*."

In order to understand how we may relate to this extraordinary otherness without immediately betraying it, it is first necessary to examine the conditions by which it is said to reveal itself. Why? Not simply because this otherness exceeds the reach of every concept, but also because all concepts have already been put in the wake of its experience and thought. The claim that my neighbor is the "first one on the scene" directs thinking not only to the extreme degree to which his otherness transcends me, but also to an understanding of myself which says that everything I am and do takes place after the fact of a relation with the Other. Defining this fact, Levinas always speaks the language of ethics and religion.[1] Community with my neighbor begins "in my obligation to him." This obligation, however, is not conscious, or rather, consciousness always arrives after the fact of the obligation. One is always already obliged. One starts from a debt so deep and so ravenous that it swallows the act of recognizing it. The relation with my neighbor would thus be a matter first and above all of a debt which is infinite.

Levinas's choice of the word "obligation" is of a single piece with his idea that my neighbor is the "first one on the scene." If my neighbor was already there before I caught sight of him, then on one hand he has a prior claim on the world I have been living from, while on the other hand I awaken to his proximity from the midst of a naive assumption that that world was simply there for me and me alone. The encounter with another person therefore involves not only a confrontation with a rival for the fruits of the earth but also a realization that my previous comportment had made no allowances for him. Levinas captures this drama with descriptions of a face which "traumatizes" me by removing every cause for self-assurance. The face of my neighbor expresses an otherness before and beyond the reach of every act starting from myself. In *Totality and Infinity*, this relation between a self-interested ego and a wholly ungraspable Other is described under the heading "Separation." Separation is the "ultimate structure" (*TeI* 53/*TI* 80).

At first sight, all of this would seem to imply a negative evaluation of the self-interested, self-absorbed ego, or what Levinas abbreviates as "the same." The isolated individual lives blindly for himself, as if the rightful and uncontested master over everything in his path. Yet this same self-absorption is indispensable for the introduction of an appeal to transcend that dark existence. After all, if the subject does not tend toward radical closure with itself, it remains open to Others with whom it might then appear to have something in common. Under such conditions, one could hardly speak of the revelation of an otherness which is absolute. In other words, in order for absolute exteriority to reveal itself as absolute exteriority, there must first be extreme interiority. If I am indeed deeply immersed in a world I make entirely my own, an otherness which reveals itself from beyond that world might well be said to defy all qualifications. The event of the "trauma" requires and then shatters the pretense of "the same." By awakening me to a separation presupposed in every act beginning from myself, the face thrusts on me the fact that my prior self-absorption, but also any future solicitude, has the fundamental character of responding. This is where Levinas's sense of pre-original obligation touches the more familiar moral sense of the word: the trauma which awakens me to the fact that I am always already responding leaves me no alternative but to somehow take up that fact more consciously, whether in the mode of care for the other person or in a more selfish retreat into my own concerns.

This word "trauma" is justified by the depth of the event it designates. The face which reports to me that my neighbor was there even before I came on the scene, and thus mutatis mutandis before I saw or heard him, does not merely weigh heavily on my conscience but puts the very workings of moral deliberation under pressure. To be traumatized by such a face is to be deprived of the time to evaluate what has befallen me and decide how to respond to it; it is to be singled out at a level deeper than that of the *Jemeinigkeit* formally present in every *Dasein* (*AE* 162/*OB* 126). Responsibility is a calling, then, but one which does not speak the language of affection, as is found in *Sein und Zeit* (§ 40). Unlike anxiety, which has an emotional tonality in which *Dasein* can identify itself,[2] the trauma which Levinas describes is so blunt and fleeting as to defy identification of any kind (one even hesitates to affirm that it *is*). According to Heidegger, anxious *Dasein* has fallen out of the everyday world back to a more fundamental "solipsism" which that world helps him to forget. According to Levinas, the subject confronted by his neighbor has been torn from naive solitude to the ethical relation forgotten in that solitude. Anxiety arises at the loss of an assured relation with the world. The face of the Other deprives us even of an assured identification with ourselves.

The assertion of an ethical relation prior to every form of solitude, and the accompanying idea that all solitude is in some way self-centered—Levinas sometimes says "narcissistic"—leaves the precise status of anxiety in doubt. Is anxiety, with its exclusive reference to the one whom it befalls, only a heightened experience of the solitude we are now to recognize as false? Or, admitting that Levinas's concept of "separation" designates only one possible definition of finitude, does anxiety, as the experience of groundlessness, testify to another such definition, another experience of it, and finally another ontology and another ethics than the one Levinas centers on pre-original obligation? Anxiety singularizes just as surely as does the face of my neighbor, but under different conditions and with different results. What place is there for the experience of anxiety in a philosophy which replaces the relation with Being by the relation with one's neighbor? Is the being who becomes anxious also a being who can be traumatized by a human face?

These questions touch directly on a fundamental claim in all of Levinas's original work: human being is characterized by a pursuit of self-satisfaction, self-interest, and power, which, however, continually betrays a more original lack of the foundation necessary to achieve them. According to Levinas, we tend naturally toward the assumption that who we are depends on what we make of ourselves, even though each successive act along that way continually depends on and so cannot master the freedom from which it has been committed. Sartre will have been right to define human striving as "useless passion," but wrong to have concluded his analysis there. For those of us pretending to live entirely from our own means, there is only exhaustion lying ahead, and not of the limited sort resolved simply by ceasing labor. Here it is a matter of losing the capacity to act in any way whatsoever, including the choice to turn from labor to repose. However, this is also not yet death, in which one passes from being to no longer being. To become exhausted in one's very existence is to arrive at its minimal condition; one is reduced to the "irremissibility of pure existing" (*TA* 26/*TO* 47), to the profound insomnia in which my gaze is no longer trained wearily on the blank night but, less than even this, becomes one with it, anonymous (*DE* 111/*EE* 66). Levinas calls this condition "horror," in which one is stripped bare before the elemental "there is." With this, Heideggerian anxiety is displaced from the heart of phenomenological anthropology, but under the following three conditions: first, Being is not experienced as absence of ground, as Heidegger asserts, but as overwhelming plenitude; second, it therefore does not withdraw or recede from us but approaches and threatens us; and third, this threat does not involve the possibility of severing us from Being—does not signal "the possibility of our impossibility" (*Sein und Zeit* § 53; cf. *TA* 92 n. 5/*TO* 70 n. 43)—but, to the contrary, confronts us with the impossibility of living solely from the premise that everything is to be approached in terms of individual possibility. The same intimacy with Being that permits us to be as beings also holds us at the brink of submergence back into Being without beings.

Here as everywhere, Levinas never ceases to appeal to the ontological difference between Being and beings, even while contesting Heidegger's account of its implications for *Dasein*. As Levinas conceives it, the existential significance of the ontological difference lies not in the idea that one is ultimately alone, but rather in the fact that that alleged solitude cannot found an adequate definition of human life. While it would indeed be possible to discern in the phenomenon of anxiety the basic conditions for an ethics of self-responsibility, that ethics could rival Levinas's ethics of pre-original obligation only at the price of committing its practitioners to a solitary existence marked for tragedy. If anxiety singularizes *Dasein* simply by throwing it back on its primordial relation to Being, which defies our urge for grounds and justification, then the account of human life contained in *Sein und Zeit* never breaches the field of ontology, where horror lurks. And this horror, one sees immediately, coincides with an absence of otherness, or "exteriority." Accordingly, the debate with Heidegger has been decisive in the emergence of ethics as first philosophy not only for giving Levinas the means to think being as act and human being as effort, but also for providing a perspective from which to criticize all of Western thought—through and through "egology"—for having promoted the sameness of the Same over the otherness of the Other (e.g., *EDE* 169/*CPP* 51). It is Levinas's acceptance and understanding of Heidegger's formulation of the ontological difference that justifies his insistence on approaching our relation to being as a primarily existential concern. It is his premise that that formulation is the crowning expression of Western thought[3] that justifies his move from dissatisfaction with Heidegger to a conclusion that first philosophy is not ontology *of any kind*, but ethics. After Heidegger and against Heidegger—against the entire tradition whose source is ancient Greece—Levinas considers our very being to be a matter of responsibility to the other person.

This existential reduction of ontology and, in turn, ethicization of existence is established only gradually, over the course of the twenty-five years between Levinas's early break with Heidegger, in "De l'E-vasion," and the appearance of *Totality and Infinity*, where Levinas's overt concern with the face of the other person and his conviction that Western philosophy cannot think it properly support a tendency to only summarize the path and the position claiming to supplant ontology with ethics. In *Otherwise Than Being*, which shifts focus back to the question of the subject, Levinas's remarks on being are, if anything, still more condensed, but also extremely straightforward. "Being," in the only sense that will interest Levinas, is to stand for the spontaneous self-interest captured in Spinoza's expression *conatus essendi* (*AE* 100/*OB* 79). Levinas translates this into the language of subjectivity: being is an innate tendency to identify first with oneself, which, however, and as experience teaches, must be ceaselessly renewed (one is never done with being oneself). In *Otherwise Than Being*, the word "being" always refers to a dynamic by which each of us "recurs" as a self (*AE* 132/*OB* 104). It is therefore in, or perhaps beneath, this word "recurrence" that one must seek the possibility of experiencing the face of the neighbor as a call to radical responsibility.

II

The originality of Levinas's conception of the subject lies here, as he refuses to conclude merely that the restlessness of being denotes an unconquerable lack of self-possession which each of must therefore accept as his own,[4] and tries instead to connect that restlessness to a positive intervention from outside. This move is not evident without a commitment to the radical priority of the other person: true, the fact that my identity recurs from moment to moment rather than enduring through time does indicate an openness in me which every act of self-identification would only seem to close, but that openness can be specifically ethical only if there is no space and no passage of time between it—between *me*—and my neighbor. The priority of my neighbor would thus entail an extreme contact, a friction of souls anterior even to the spatial contact of body upon body. The Other who comes between me and myself frustrates the *conatus essendi* from within; it makes of me a "reverse *conatus*" (*AE* 89/*OB* 70), so that my entire effort to be must be understood as a response to my neighbor's intervention from "the hither side" (*l'en-deça*) of being (cf. *AE* 182/*OB* 143: "restlessness for the other"). It is this anterior, "an-archic" openness to my neighbor that renders me susceptible to his call to radical responsibility. And it is to that an-archic level that the face, as traumatic appeal, penetrates.

Levinas's ethics, it thus appears, is centered on an appeal or, if one prefers, a trauma, which occurs in two times. Holding to the meta-phor of voice and command, one might say that the concrete appeal ascribed to the face of the neighbor presupposes a more originary appeal by which my ears may be considered already open (let us not say attuned) to hearing him. Emphasizing the violence with which this strikes me, one might also say that the traumatic appeal reaches what Levinas considers truly ethical depth only on the condition of a prior violence which has inflicted on me an originary "wound" (*AE* 106/*OB* 84) to my narcissism. It is important to bear in mind that this "first time" of the trauma is a transcendental condition, not a physical event: "The one affected by the other is an anarchic trauma, or an inspiration of the one by the other, and not a causality striking me-chanically" (*AE* 158/*OB* 123). The Other possesses—or, as Levinas prefers, "obsesses"—the Same from before being and time. Its pre-tenses notwithstanding, the sameness of the Same has never been insular or complete. The ethics of the trauma is to be an ethics of awakening.

This being the case, it convenes for us here to interrogate not the trauma as such (i.e., as an event), but rather the response one is to make to it. If the face of my neighbor opens me to a relation anterior to my relation with myself, and thus to a responsibility to him before and beyond everything I can orient to myself, how then am I to live by that insight? What will comprise a good response, a response that is at one and the same time for the other person and true to my (ethical) self? Levinas has already sketched the insight in a manner which leaves no doubt about the difficulty of the assignment: every-thing I am and do has already been anticipated by my neighbor, to whom everything is therefore first and foremost a response. I am not what I am, says Iago from the depth of his fealty to Othello. I am one-for-the-Other, says Levinas at the heart of *Otherwise Than Being*—infinitely so, and without possibility of either abdication or replacement.

It goes without saying that the only act completely adequate to this insight would be completely selfless. I am to strive for devotion to my neighbor in which my own concerns command attention and receive their dignity only through an overarching concern for his own. However, it also goes without saying that this is almost certainly impossible. Or rather, since Levinas has already identified being with individual action *and* defined individual action as narcissistic, it is almost certainly unthinkable. The possibility of a fully responsible act would seem excluded by a standing and, as we have seen, crucial conviction that human nature is simply incapable of it, or at best tormented by a scruple at odds with a more persistent selfish tendency.[5] If responsibility is to be taken up, if salvation is to come and the Good to be served, this will have to occur by an agency or at an initiative outside everything that falls under the definition of being as *conatus essendi*. Morality as a discipline which presupposes and governs an unruly freedom is thus a part of the problem Levinas sets out to overcome, as he makes clear in the initial pages of *Totality and Infinity* (*TeI* ix–xi/*TI* 21–23). Indeed, according to Levinas's own argument, the act in question will have to be so far from control by the individual will that it becomes difficult to see what sense it makes to refer to it as "good" at all, except by contrast with the darkness previously assigned to being. Goodness will occur in a sort of flash or sparkle disrupting a pervasive gloom, and then vanishing again. One thinks, at Levinas's own suggestion, of the monologue by Ikonnikov, in Vassili Grossmann's *Vie et destin*, where one finds, in the midst of hundreds of pages of black pessimism, the following remarkable account: Well into World War II, in a small Russian village already starved by the long winter and longer German occupation, a number of women were taken prisoner in retaliation for the death of two German soldiers. The women spent the night tortured by the fear that morning would bring their own deaths. Instead, it brought unexpected reprieve. As the women were freed, they were also asked to care for one of their German captors, now wounded. A horrendous scene ensued, as the sentiment of fear became lust for vengeance. Then something both beautiful and terrible happened. One among the women ran toward her former captor with the thought of strangling him. As she drew near, the man asked to drink. Suddenly and inexplicably, the woman's murderous rage fell away, and she gave the suffering stranger what little she had to offer.[6] Ikonnikov comments that neither the woman nor any who witnessed the scene could explain her actions, and concludes for himself that they were, properly speaking, "absurd," going wholly beyond what either the situation or duty called for. He also characterizes them by a "small goodness" (*une petite bonté*) which alone gives cause to hope that human destiny might lie elsewhere than cruelty and annihilation. Levinas takes up this expression, and speaks of the eternal gratuity of what escapes every system and ideology.

One can hardly deny that such events do occur. However, it is difficult to know quite how to understand them. Noting first that this is indeed, as Levinas seems bound to expect, a matter of single, perhaps isolated acts, and not the person and his character, one might propose the difficult ethical category of supererogation, in which the following conditions are present: first, the act is neither forbidden nor obligatory; second, it is morally good in both its intended consequences and its intrinsic value; third, it is done voluntarily, and for the sake of another person; and fourth, its omission is not wrong, and does not deserve either criticism or punishment.[7] This last point would, of course, have to be nuanced if supererogation is to be said of the "small goodness" in which Levinas sees a responsibility otherwise than being. Levinas has argued that the face of the neighbor awakens me to a responsibility which anticipates and defines everything I do. In other words, I am always already responding to another person who, however, precisely by remaining Other, nonetheless always asks for more. "The more I answer, the more I am responsible," we are told (*AE* 119/*OB* 93). In this sense, it is indeed wrong to omit an act of care for the other person, or even to limit the amount of care one gives. And yet, as beings, we also seem bound to commit precisely this offense. According to Levinas, we are subject to a command which can be violated only by falling short of what it asks, but this falling short is inherent to our being. From the perspective of supererogation, one will solve this riddle only with the strange concession that good acts which cannot be explained by character, duty, or circumstance are somehow inhuman.

Taking this word "inhuman" in the most positive sense, perhaps "small goodnesses" are then best understood as evidence of grace.

Here it would be necessary to distinguish between grace as a supplement of human nature designating the source of what Thomas Aquinas called "infused virtues" (faith, hope, and charity)[8] from Levinas's
clear aim beyond any irreducible entanglement with nature. As the
expression indicates, infused virtues are indwelling; they are inscribed in the soul. Levinas points to the source of goodness in an
openness anterior even to this; "grace" would then stand not for
something in me, even if put there from the outside, but rather for
the primordial fact that my interiority is wholly *for the Other*. If
"grace" is to appear in the lexicon of ethics as first philosophy, the
word will have to refer simply to an event expressing the an-archic
fact of "election" to unique responsibility for the neighbor, to a radical responsibility given eternally in advance.[9] This, in turn, means
that the trauma calls me (violently) back to a proper identity determined before and outside of being, so that the effort to take up the
responsibility depicted there can also be understood as an effort to
remain true to my self. However, this trueness to self can no longer
be understood as a process of developing latent human qualities or
fulfilling socially determined roles, but is instead a matter of un-
flinching adherence to the dictates of one's unique and irreducible
identity. Levinas's ethics of the Other is unexpectedly close to Heidegger in this much: it is, at least in part, an ethics of authenticity
and not, at least in the classical sense of the term, sincerity.[10]

This is both precious little to live by and, one might add, impossibly much. The face of my neighbor reveals to me that I am one-
for-the-Other, exposed to the Other before enclosed in myself. My
susceptibility to my neighbor's call to radical responsibility brings to
light an extreme passivity beneath all activity or power. This passivity, and it alone, defines me as unique. Open to the Other before
closed into myself, I am this responsibility, here and now, more than
and before I am anything else. There can be no identification, no
community, no *sensus communis*, which does not presuppose this
openness and, as Levinas never tires of observing, also covers it up.

This singularization, and this alone, would at last be unassailable.
Coming to me from wholly outside, and breaking me open to the
wholly outside, the face of the other person is the one event which
can anchor me in a way that does not require justification by my own
effort to be. Because the Other is closer to me than I am to myself,
his face does not remove the ground from beneath me without at

the same time putting me in contact with something infinitely more concrete, and immeasurably more certain (one could read Levinas's entire itinerary as a tortured search for this extreme certainty). Because the other person is therefore more than I could ever measure, his face also does not relieve me of everything most dear to me without at the same time bathing me in superabundance. The call to a responsibility anterior to being and possession is also the call to an identity which would finally be out of reach of either anxiety or melancholy (afflictions we are henceforth to consider as imposed by ontology). "Paradoxically," says Levinas, "it is qua *alienus*—foreigner and other (*étranger et autre*)—that one is not alienated" (*AE* 76/*OB* 59).

III

All of this, however, might seem only to expose what is in fact the most elemental form of self-interest: the pleasure one experiences in simply living, in simply continuing to be oneself.[11] After all, to tell me that the act which guided by my own will and determined by my own capacities to that degree falsifies the responsibility of being one-for-the-Other is to deprive me of the only tools available to me should I wish to come fully to my neighbor's aid. What will motivate the act that suspends individual initiative and intention? Here it is a matter of an ego which has lost possession of itself entirely, so that there can be no question of an end projected over and beyond the other person in its path. The same face which disarms the approaching narcissist seems also to awaken in him a more uncontrolled charge which it is difficult to connect with the language of investment or possession befitting ordinary pleasure. All of this is ruled out by a face which looks at me from beyond what Freud has led us to think of as the economy of tension and discharge. If, then, life goes on nonetheless, and indeed henceforth under the aegis of the Other, Levinas's account of this encounter obliges us to envision a somewhat different investment and a somewhat different pleasure than can be accommodated by an economic analysis. I would take pleasure in the one thing, ethical alterity, which cannot be the object of pleasure. I would, in short, *enjoy my responsibility*. What prevents the one-for-the-Other from this decline into perversion? What saves ethics as first philosophy from ending in this most violent and irresistible of possessions?

Far from having overlooked these questions, Levinas can be said to have pursued them through a number of successive levels. To begin with, it follows from the idea that the human face is hyperconcrete that there can be no confusion between the responsibility it commands and any pleasure we might experience in taking it up. At this level, Levinas might respond along the lines of Kant's Second *Critique*, and distinguish between the pleasure which sometimes coincides with good action and good action itself. Obedience to the law, Kant argued, follows a different logic than the self-interest to which, moreover, it is both prior and superior. This, however, has not yet addressed the possibility that there is a particular kind of pleasure awakened only by the command to responsibility. Perhaps there are cases where one takes possession of what must not be possessed precisely because it must not be possessed (and not merely because it stands in the way of something else). In *Pompes funèbres*, the sheer helplessness of Genet's friends and lovers awakens in him a monstrous hunger to betray them to the police, whereupon his own great suffering at their fate proves to him that he does love them deeply. As Genet himself well knew, the passion in this cycle of betrayal and self-affirmation presupposes and draws on his dependence on those whom he betrays, which is also to say that its destructive force consumes not only his friends and lovers but also Genet himself. For Genet, love of neighbor is expressed in use of neighbor and thus destruction of neighbor, which at bottom is also destruction of self. The face of the neighbor disarms everything standing in the way of a drive which aims finally at self-annihilation. The helplessness of the other person escorts Genet into a universe where pleasure inclines toward death, and where the charity of one-for-the-Other is immersed in the brutal surge of forces which love only themselves. What will Levinas make of these confessions? If being is defined by a self-interestedness which passes spontaneously over the responsibility Genet seems helpless not to abuse, then perversion of any kind must belong to the intransigence of our narcissism. Genet, Levinas might conclude, struggles with his narcissism *from within* his narcissism, perhaps even under the form of insisting on it. The exteriority of the other person is indeed seen and recognized—Genet leaves little doubt about it—but is then submitted to the selfish urges of a confused and immature will.

This conclusion highlights two important observations. On the one hand, Levinas has no trouble with the notion that the same point at which he detects the institution of radical responsibility can also adjourn to profound evil. On the other hand, both that responsibility and its extreme perversion seem to confront us at the height of self-awareness, when a neighbor's face singles us out as one-for-the-Other. Your face can awaken me to a responsibility beyond any meaning I may give to it, or it can awaken in me a morbid desire which consumes every investment I may make in this world, including in our relation. What distinguishes these two paths? Whereas perversion is an already operative form of referring everything to oneself, what Levinas sometimes calls the "metaphysical desire" for the Good (e.g., *TeI* 3–5/*TI* 33–35) points infinitely beyond being and possession.

At the same time, Levinas does not deny that this requires the individual under appeal to deliberately assent to what the Other asks. The importance of this foot still planted in being must not be underestimated: the good life is a matter of human effort, not the arbitrary actions of a deity. By the same stroke, however, that goodness is always already contaminated by being, and thus always already in need of a renewal of human effort. The psychological correlate of a command never fully satisfied is a conscience never fully at rest, and its ontological correlate is a world never fully redeemed. With a single gesture, Levinas's ethics turns away from both a supernatural God and all utopianism (*AE* 232/*OB* 184). Regarding each new moment, nothing is assured except that there is always more to do. The face of my neighbor breaks my hold on the world, calling me back to a root leading beneath and outside of it, so that our proximity is the site not only of responsibility to and for my neighbor, but also to and for the entire world—near and far, now and always. In my neighbor's gaze, the entire world calls out for help. In his face, it is not just this one other person who obsesses me, but all the other Others, too. This is more than an empirical complication: in the human face, I am commanded by all the Others at once (*AE* 204/*OB* 160).

Thus, although, as Levinas does not fail to state, the idea of a responsibility leading beyond being does threaten to deprive of us the bearings necessary to discern good from evil (*DVI* 115/*CPP* 166), his proposed remedy to that difficulty can be found already in place, where the I-Other relation of that responsibility is interwoven with a social and cultural dimension which we can expect to focus and guide the former. To be sure, my relation with my neighbor "gives meaning to my relations with all the others" (*AE* 202/*OB* 159), but the presence of those other Others, calling out to me with equal vigor, distracts me from an unqualified response to my neighbor, *and vice versa:* "The other and the third party, my neighbors, contemporaries of one another, put distance between me and the other and third party" (*AE* 200/*OB* 157). The call to responsibility is already a call to justice, to care for many Others at once. The competing appeals of my neighbor and the other Others literally give me pause: I must stop and reflect, think. And with this, the veritable birth of consciousness, my devotion to the absolute otherness revealing itself in my neighbor's face is already framed in language and phenomenality. True, that face will have exposed the innate pretentiousness of all words and appearances, but the fact that not one but many Others claim my responsibility forces me to use them nonetheless. Ethics cannot be first philosophy without also committing itself to inspiring a just and effective society. This means accepting that certain tools are indispensable for feeding and clothing the masses, while watching carefully for the way this leads inevitably back into patronization and then abuse. Revolution will be necessary from time to time. The ethics of the other person claims to also be the politics of that revolution.[12]

If, then, it is to be the practical demands of a responsibility to many Others at once which will save us from confusion and mishap, the apparent price will be permanent tension and ambiguity. Adjusted to account for multiple responsibilities, Levinas's ethics settles the good life on an unresolvable obsession. One cannot decide for the neighbor without deciding against the other Others, and one cannot decide for one of those other Others without deciding against that neighbor. Custom, laws, and habit no doubt help us to apportion our resources with a considerable degree of justice, but Levinas gives us no reason to suppose that they absolve us from the ethical censure arriving from all those faces at once. A responsibility divided among countless Others remains an insatiable responsibility; it remains a responsibility which promises only to return again and again without possibility of ending.

In a manner not unlike what befalls the brute effort to be, the task of caring for the Others would then seem prey to a kind of slow exhaustion which would lower us gradually from zeal to resoluteness and then desperation finally into an indifference at the brink of horror (*AE* 207–9/*OB* 163–64). The only thing that may save us from this danger—and Levinas himself seems not to have mentioned it—is the specific concretion of each call to responsibility. After all, when asked for help, one does not only think of the infinite responsibility which perhaps emerges there, but also attends to the particular needs of this person here and now. Faces rarely implore without also indicating what it is they need. Can it be that all that saves us from the same tragic consequences Levinas expects from fundamental ontology is a gaze turned humbly away from the otherness which transcends us and toward what ails the flesh and blood in which we meet it?

Still, this is not a possibility which Levinas can entertain without conceding limits to our responsibility and thus, by implication, qualifying the otherness of the Other. His argument tends therefore in the contrary direction, calling for a commitment to surrender any and all claim to anything strictly for ourselves. And from there, the "one" in one-for-the-Other can only be the center point of an obsession received from wholly outside but also turned ravenously inward. Responsibility is to occur in a constant and arduous turning of oneself inside out; the reversal of *conatus essendi* converts the inwardness of care of self into a ceaseless outpouring of gifts for the neighbor. This cannot occur by predetermined pace or in accordance with preestablished limits. Commitment to radical and infinite responsibility is without qualification. Nor, then, can this occur by degrees. Perhaps one does approach readiness for this commitment only slowly, but the decision itself is by definition stark and without reservation: one is not truly for-the-Other until one has resolved to wipe away every trace of being for-oneself.

Needless to say, Levinas's own argument militates strongly against the idea that one can actually reach this state of pure altruism by one's own efforts, much less sustain it. Since, then, if it arrives at all it would have to do so by surprise, befalling us or overtaking us, the real point of inquiry must be his conception of our attempt to commit to it and live by it. What would it mean to willingly submit all concern for oneself to concern for Others? What could be the motivation? And what would it be to get close? Let us note first that

Levinas's analysis of the call to justice assumes that the plurality of appeals moves us to a point of sufficient lucidity to discern the needs and rights of the Other who is one's neighbor, the needs and rights of the other Others, and one's own authentic identity as resource for them all. As brute event of singularization, this does not involve conquering one's self-serving inclinations but, to the contrary, receiving an image of oneself as one-for-the-Other(s). It is this image which must be recognized and accepted if one is to embark on what Levinas understands as the good life, the life approaching adequacy with being one-for-the-Other. Under normal circumstances, these are two different things: to receive an image and to accept it as the truth. Levinas conflates the two when he speaks of a unicity in the subject that would be anterior to its own identity with itself, and then invests the face of the Other, as trauma, with the power to exhume that unicity: the face of my neighbor singles me out without possibility of denial; my responsibility is irrecusable. One has not truly seen the face of the Other if one has not been traumatized by it, and one has not been traumatized if one has not understood immediately and unmistakably that one is one-for-the-Other. The face of the Other who is first on the scene, of the Other who is closer to me than I am to myself, leaves me no room to pause and consider, no room to observe and interpret what approaches, and no room to consider its likelihood or appeal. The moment I see it, its message is already true. Whatever desire it is that motivates me to follow this path awakens at this same moment, and without possibility of my having summoned it. *This is not a desire that can be attributed to the individual will, which is by definition egocentric.* In the philosophy of Levinas, moments of supreme commitment—or if one prefers, events of grace—erupt from beneath individual freedom, taking possession of the soul long enough to carry it briefly beyond the range of action oriented first to oneself. This would seem to mean that my actions are therefore most responsible (most for-the-Other) when they are least mine. But this would also seem to mean an end to all concern with focus, distinctions, or the specificity of just who it is that faces me here and now. How could there be such definition in a desire no longer in any way shaped or guided by the subject whom it possesses? Absolute desire for the Good—or, what amounts now to the same thing, desire for the absolute—belongs not at all to me and it cares not at all for my neighbor. And by this alone can it be considered truly free of the narcissistic web of being.

The possibility of an eruption of this absolute desire, a desire which would be untrammeled in its rush toward what Levinas leads us to think of as the Good, is provided for in advance by the notion of an attachment anterior even to the form in which one makes sense of it—an attachment in which, brought to our attention by the face of the Other, we are to recognize an anarchic interruption of our relation with ourselves. Something has always already insinuated itself, always already touched us and then slipped away without possibility of detection, and yet not without tearing us open and turning us inside out, not without having *wounded us* at a depth beyond healing (e.g., *AE* 93/*OB* 74). The passivity evident in this existential suffering is not only the site of my responsibility, as Levinas frequently asserts, but also the opening of being to the Good. The movement to embrace my responsibility inverts the tendency of being to associate with itself, bending it back toward the source of an interruption which that tendency presupposes. As Levinas's discussion of other Others seems to confirm, this cannot be a question of abandoning oneself straightforwardly to the insatiable need of one's neighbor. Instead, it is a matter of a commitment made by an individual already availed of a social and cultural identity to transcend every norm or guideline embedded there, in favor of an identity which, whether ideal or simply fictive, would know no such norms or guidelines.

The desire which this threatens to awaken is not a possibility which can be accounted for either by the concept of horror or by a concession that even radical responsibility is mediated by principles and norms, if also aimed beyond them. Here it is a matter neither of the ego's failure to evade being nor of any strategy by which it may temporarily succeed, but rather a desire opposed to both. *Opposed,* and not merely distinct: the desire to remove everything between me and the satisfaction of an exterior command is a desire to purge myself of everything comprising my identity as this person under appeal, here and now. Pursued to its limit, the discipline of self-denial can pass over into a desire for death.

Against this, it is tempting to suppose that the self-denial in question could never quite extinguish our effort to be because it would never cease to invoke it, so that even the most severe ethical asceticism would remain under the power of something ultimately narcissistic. This hypothesis might then find further support from Levinas's constant and sometimes explicit avoidance of the language of moral conversion and political utopianism, except that it says nothing to the fact that the body of the argument nonetheless compels us to act *as if* sainthood were the proper ideal. A nonstandard reading of Levinas might therefore defend a more pronounced dualism of desires in his work: one would either be for-oneself, even if only minimally, or else for-the-Other, but then only in those rarest of moments mentioned in the discussion of Grossmann's book. This second interpretation leaves open the question of how a powerful desire for an increasingly just life can spill over into the seemingly very different desire for death. What is the relationship between the desire inhabiting narcissism and the desire for death?

The only way to maintain a real difference between a desire for death and a narcissistic love of live, but without pretending that they have nothing in common, is to admit them as equally definitive forces within each of us. The only way to avoid severing what qualifies here as "grace" from human interaction—*the only way to maintain a hold on the idea that ethics has to do with more than the economy of self-interest*—is to suppose that "love of life" and "desire for death" stand for forces constantly at odds with one another, and that whatever balance makes life possible can sometimes break down, so that the release of unlimited force coincides with the disintegration of contours formerly marking individual identity.

In one important respect, this seems quite close to Levinas: life, as he himself teaches, is made up of endless tension. In quite another respect, however, the distance from him could hardly be greater: if being is effort-to-be, and if effort-to-be can be said of the person in whom one nonetheless also witnesses events of extraordinary selflessness, what one glimpses in those events will no longer be Spirit beyond being (cf. *AE* 5–6/*OB* 5), but simply forces no longer encumbered by it. Goodness will not transcend being but consume it. And ethics as first philosophy will indeed admit a religious horizon, but only to find religion contained within a materialist account of its phenomena.

The claim that one is responsible for one's neighbor before and outside one's responsibility for oneself depends on submitting the relation to being to the relation with the Good. This gesture installs ethics as first philosophy and opens the way to religion. In the philosophy of Levinas, this move is mediated decisively first by an acceptance of Heidegger's notion of ontological difference, but secondly by a reduction of the Heideggerian definition of being to act and effort. To Levinas, the analytic of *Dasein* thus appears as a description of solitary life still in need of completion by a move to the plurality of *Daseins* which this indicates. Levinas's own concept of "separation" is in part a concession that being is solitary and self-centered. However, it also refers to the relation which this can equally imply: the individual ego, as the "same," is in separated relation with the "other" person, one's neighbor. The asymmetry of this relation determines that, on one hand, the subject, as the Same, tends always to associate first with itself, while on the other hand precisely this tendency is to be considered a suppression of the proper nature of one's relation with the Other. One is always already responsible—radically responsible—and yet, in the more familiar sense, never responsible enough. One is ordered to one's neighbor before oneself, and also despite oneself. The only way to satisfy this pre-original ordering, and the only way to fulfill the notion of ethics as first philosophy, is to transcend being entirely. This possibility is not admitted by individual being or human nature, such as Levinas defines them. Ethics as first philosophy points toward and depends on events of grace. For ethics to elude fundamental ontology, something wholly Other must have interrupted the economy of self-interest.

This otherness is to be revealed to us in the face of a neighbor, which does not merely contest our narcissistic being, but breaks it open all the way to an anarchic assignment one-for-the-Other. Here "anarchy" must signify a relation not yet contaminated by being, one that is activated only by the human face. To submit to the appeal of that face is to put oneself in the service of a movement beyond being. That concrete appeal can therefore be said to stimulate a desire which, in its extreme form, tests the limits of life itself. The desire for goodness beyond being is an absolute desire, but also, and perhaps therefore, a desire for death. The real risk of ethics as first philosophy and religion is not, as Levinas seems to indicate, a misappropriation of the ethical appeal, but, to the contrary, a strange, uncontrolled willingness to go precisely where it leads. Ethics, one must therefore conclude, has as much to do with *limiting* a desire beyond being as it does with keeping that desire in view. And here, where Levinas has perhaps overemphasized the knot between ethics and religion, one feels compelled to insist on an equal knot with self-interest. Prudence would require managing both a desire for the Other and a desire which serves oneself, irreducibly and without end.

NOTES

1. It is of course questionable whether this is a *fact* at all, since, like Kant's equally strange "fact of reason," it must be considered prior to both the actions and the capacities of the mind which apprehends it.

2. Levinas has understood this from the beginning. In 1932 he proposed to translate the term in question, Heidegger's *Befindlichkeit* (*befindet sich*: to find oneself), as "disposition affective" ("Martin Heidegger et l'ontologie," *EDE* 68), a choice which has since found close agreement in Martineau's use of "affection" in his French translation of *Sein und Zeit*. In English translation, Macquarrie and Robinson employ the unfortunate "state-of-mind," whereas Stambaugh suggests "attunement" for both *Befindlichkeit* and *Stimmung,* or "mood." Heidegger himself uses the term *Befindlichkeit* for the first time in his 1924 conference on "The Concept of Time" (Tübingen: Niemeyer, 1989), in order to translate Augustine's Latin term *affectio.*

3. This of course presumes a great deal, but debating the point would require a lengthy discussion with Heidegger, or at least the Heidegger invoked here, before turning to Levinas. I therefore put the matter aside, noting only that Levinas himself recognizes occasional exceptions to this defining feature of Western thought.

4. For this position, cf. J.-P. Sartre, *Being and Nothingness: An Essay on Phenomenological Ontology,* trans. H. Barnes (New York: Philosophical Library, 1958), 198.

5. This mistrust of the possibility of agreement between human nature and what the Christian tradition has called grace displays what might be hazarded as a Protestant sympathy in Levinas's thinking.

6. V. Grossmann, *Vie et destin* (Paris: L'Age d'homme, 1980), 383–84. Cf. E. Levinas, "La proximité de l'autre," reprinted in *Altérité et transcendence* (Paris: Fata Morgana, 1995), 116–18.

7. My definition of supererogation adapts that of D. Heyd, *Supererogation: Its Status in Ethical Theory* (Cambridge: Cambridge University Press, 1982), 115.

8. Thomas Aquinas, *Summa Theologica,* I II q. 65 art. 2.

9. Cf. J.-L. Chrétien, "La dette et l'éléction," in *Emmanuel Levinas,* ed. C. Chalier and M. Abensour (Paris: L'Herne, 1991), 262–73.

10. For this distinction, see L. Trilling, *Sincerity and Authenticity* (Cambridge: Harvard University Press, 1971). *Otherwise Than Being* does ascribe a sincerity to everything we say to our neighbor, but denies that it is an "attribute" of that saying (*AE* 183/*OB* 143–44). One is always already sincere—always already open and giving—even while forgetting or resisting that very fact. Conversely, accepting the implications of this sincerity must take the form of accepting a responsibility that defines one's very selfhood.

11. I have in mind Spinoza's sense of *hilaritas,* in which all parts of mind and body are affected positively, resulting in a continuation of harmonious functioning which is in itself, without anything added, pleasurable. Cf. *Ethics* III, Prop. XI, note; and IV, Prop. XLII, proof. This reference to Spinoza is intended only as an anthropological benchmark for the analyses which follow. *Hilaritas* itself is not perverse, at least not in the familiar sense of the term, but rather one candidate for the ontological possibility of perversion.

12. Cf. E. Levinas, "De l'unicité," in *Entre Nous* (Paris: Grasset, 1991), 215–17; and *Autrement que savoir* (Paris: Osiris, 1986), 59–62.

II
The Question of God

7

The Bible Gives to Thought: Levinas on the Possibility and Proper Nature of Biblical Thinking

Roger Burggraeve

FAITH IS MATURE or fully developed only if it is reflective, that is, only if it involves a thinking interaction with the Scriptures which orient and inspire it. This is not only a crucial element in Levinas's conception of Judaism, but also says much about how Levinas relates to his own Judaism. I will say more about this in the first part of this essay, sketching his specifically *mitnagged* Jewish background. This, in turn, will explain much of why he argues for what can be called an intellectual lay Judaism.

The biographical information forms my point of departure for a second part, in which I will explore the manner in which Levinas's philosophical approach to Scripture can also inspire us. I will first show what it means for him to speak of a biblical thinking, or to speak of the Bible itself as a particular mode of thinking. This moves into some discussion of Levinas's reflections on an "internal Jewish identity," as distinct from a purely external identity. Such an internal identity calls for a surpassing of the limits imposed by a purely historical-literary conception of Scripture. It thus becomes necessary and possible to clarify the originality of that biblical thinking by studying the relation between Bible and Talmud. In a third part of this essay, I follow Levinas's thinking in an attempt to describe the specific spirituality involved in a thinking approach to Scripture. A fourth part situates Levinas's reflective-philosophical reading of Scripture as a "mediation" between Word and life. This permits me to state my own position with regard to some of these themes.

I. A PLEA FOR AN INTELLECTUAL LAY JUDAISM

In order to understand some of the background for Levinas's emphasis on a philosophical reading of Scripture, it will help to note some
biographical facts concerning his Jewish formation.

Jewish Mitnagged Background

Levinas was born in Kovno (present-day Kaunas), Lithuania, on Janu-
ary 12, 1906.[1] As capital of the province and an important cultural
center at the time, Kovno was one of the largest cities in Lithuania,
one of the three Baltic States on the northwest border of White Russia. Levinas came from a rather well-to-do family which had risen
through hard work and commerce. His father was the bookseller Je-
hiel Levinas, and his mother was Dvora Gurvitch.

From his early youth, Levinas was tutored in "modern" Hebrew
and, by extension, the Bible. This private study was carried on at a
continuous and intense pace, paralleling his middle and high school
education, until 1918. Not even the successive immigrations and constant meandering brought on by World War I put an end to it. The
adjective "modern," incidentally, does not signify a Hebrew which is
somehow different from the Hebrew of the Bible, but rather a conception of Hebrew as a modern language, a language freed from the
control of religious texts but without thereby diminishing the value
or dignity of studying biblical texts in Hebrew. In this same "modern" spirit, Levinas also received instruction in the Talmud (to be
understood as the historical whole of rabbinic commentary on and
interpretations of the Law of Moses), which he would later accent
as essential for Judaism. Levinas's original Jewish formation must
therefore be considered Jewish in general but not specifically talmudic.[2]

However, his background was indeed colored by the *mitnagged*
Judaism then abundant in the area. *Mitnagged* means, literally, "op-
ponent." The object of that opposition was Hassidism, a sort of pious
Judaism that emerged midway through the eighteenth century
among the often illiterate rural Jews of the Ukrainian provinces of
what was then Poland (Volhynia, Podolia, Galicia). The great impulse
came from Israel ben Eliezer (1700–1760), also called Baal Shem
Tov, which can mean "friendly Master of the Name (God)," "pos-

sessor of the good name," or "entrusted by the people." He taught that true religion does not necessarily consist in the study of Jewish texts, but rather in an unmediated, upright, and joyous love of God. The core of this living religiosity is *enthusiasm,* literally "to-be-in-God" (en-theos-eimi), such as Buber has also defined it in *Die Erzählungen der Chassidim.* Those who enthused others were called "tsaddikim," the just, or better, "those-found-to-be-just," or perhaps "those-found-good." Those who became enthused, the enthusiasts, were called "Hassidim," the pious, those who remained faithful to the covenant and who formed Hassidic communities under the leadership of the tsaddikim. This enthusiasm expressed itself concretely in direct participation in a pervasive experience of God's omnipresence, reached through intense prayer and in daily life itself, with all its tasks and requirements.

Hassidism met with sharp resistance, above all in Lithuania and White Russia. There ruled in those places a sober and intellectual Judaism, founded on the discipline of Talmud study. Resistance to Hassidism was driven first by Elijah ben Solomon (1720–97), also known as the Gaon of Vilnius (still the capital of Lithuania), and taken further by what became known as *mitnaggedim,* or "opponents." According to Levinas, ben Solomon was one of the last great geniuses of the Talmud. He was also the founder of the yeshiva, or "academy of higher Talmud study," where the Talmud was no longer read privately but in groups, under the guidance of an advanced teacher. In his Jewish writings, Levinas refers more often to Rabbi Chaim Voloziner (1789–1821), the favorite student of ben Solomon. Voloziner is even the subject of a separate and penetrating study which also throws important light on Levinas's own thinking: "A l'image de Dieu, d'après Rabbi Haim Voloziner" (1977).[3] In a somewhat later study, "Judaisme et kénose" (1985), he comes explicitly back to Voloziner, relating that in the whole of eastern Europe, Lithuania was the country and Vilnius the city where Judaism reached its spiritual peak.[4] The level of Talmud study was extreme, and there was also a complete Jewish way of life based on this study and even experienced *as* study. In Levinas's country of birth, the predominant Judaism was clearly intellectual.[5]

While there is no question that Levinas was influenced by this mitnagged Judaism, this occurred not so much through particular ideas as through a general underlying trend and spirituality. And while the mitnagged resistance to Hassidism tempered over the years, the two currents of Judaism have remained historically apart. This is evident not only from the use of two distinct prayer books and liturgies, but also the difference between, in Hassidism, an emphasis on emotion, inwardness, subjectivity, and the experience of God, and, in mitnaggedism, an emphasis on strictly applying a rationality of exteriority and objectivity to the study of the Talmud. Even without the sharp edges of earlier conflict, these differences were still real enough when Levinas was brought up in the Jewish world. It is above all this difference of accent in climate and tonality that would mark Levinas's Jewish identity. His mitnagged background brings into relief his almost visceral—some would also say exaggerated and obsessive—resistance to mystical enthusiasm and every form of religious awakening, with its recurring nostalgia for a consuming, emotional religious experience of intense inwardness and spirit. His first collection of essays on Judaism, *Difficile Liberté* (1963, enlarged in 1976), is a pregnant illustration of mitnagged rationality, from which Levinas interprets Judaism and pleads for an intellectual and philosophical approach to the "Jewish texts" which, in his view, give themselves to thinking—that is, they are already a particular form of thinking which emerges properly through their resistance to rigorous critical-reflective engagement.

Levinas's mitnagged Judaism influenced not only his interaction with Jewish texts and tradition but also, and equally, his philosophical work. His intellectual Judaism confronts the Western preference for the sort of thinking manifest in ancient Greece and renewed in the Enlightenment. Levinas's philosophy involves the reciprocal reinforcement of Jewish and Western intellectuality, based on what he calls an "allegiance to the intellectualism of reason."[6]

An Intellectual Approach to Jewish Texts

It was nevertheless not until 1947 that Levinas began to apply himself rigorously to the Talmud. This was under the guidance of the remarkable Chouchani, "renowned and inexorable master of exegesis and the Talmud,"[7] whom Levinas himself came to consider the summit of what mitnagged Judaism had to offer. Chouchani's approach to the Talmud was not pious but intellectual and inventive; it can be considered a major inspiration for Levinas's effort to translate his own basic Jewish and Hebrew experiences into the language of Western philosophy. The results of those efforts include, most evidently, his numerous Talmud lessons which, beginning in 1957, he gave almost annually to an assembly of French-speaking Jewish intellectuals in Paris. These have appeared in collections, including *Quatre lectures talmudiques* (1968), *Du sacré au saint: Cinq nouvelles lectures talmudiques* (1977), *L'au-delà du verset: Lectures et discours talmudiques* (1982), *A l'heure des nations* (1988), and *Nouvelles lectures talmudiques* (1995). Through the Talmud, which he understood as the work of *sages* and not priests, prophets, or theologians, Levinas came to see the Bible not primarily as a whole of revealed truths, but as a thinking which has as much claim to speak in philosophy as do the verses of the pre-Socratics, Homer, Trakl, or Hölderlin. Such a conception rests on the conviction, typical of the Talmud, that Scripture, as an expression of a culture which is human and not simply religious, can contain within itself a powerful rationality available to a tenacious thinking which can always penetrate it further.[8]

In 1946, Levinas became director of the École Normale Israélite Orientale in Paris, which trained teachers for elementary and grade schools in the Mediterranean region (including Tunisia and Morocco). In this function, which he retained until beginning his university career in 1961,[9] he promoted an ambitious and fully intellectual approach to the study of the scriptural sources of the Jewish tradition. In connection with his efforts to widen the École from an "École des maîtres" to an "École de cadres," Levinas also hoped to free Judaism from its culturally privatized and "clericalized" ghetto. In the years after World War II, he never ceased to argue for an intellectual lay Judaism, writing that "Judaism can survive only if it is recognized and handed down by its laity."[10] This intellectual lay Judaism would be possible only if Jewish texts, which the traditional orthodoxy had always entrusted to the ministers of the cultus, were freed from this frequently dogmatizing and apologetic monopoly and studied more widely anew. For the Jewish texts to "nourish souls, they must once again nourish brains."[11] They must become the tool of serious thought—not of historical-archaeological erudition, but of a tenacious and relentless thinking which can critically scrutinize and interrogate them until they yield new "instruction" and life-sustaining insights on humanity, society, and God. According to Levinas, this "Jewish thinking" is even the primary condition for the survival of Judaism.[12]

Only such a transhistorical conception of the Jewish texts would make possible an indispensable "Jewish intellectual elite" whose reflective approach to the essential Jewish texts would make them the true "masters" of Judaism. Levinas therefore also made frequent appearances at the Jewish formation centers in Paris, above all the École and the Centre Universitaire d'Études Juives, in an effort to bring the growing number of young, well-educated Jewish intellectuals together into a broad reflection group, or perhaps better, a current of thought. Not without some humor, he referred to this group as the "École de Paris," even though most of the interested participants came not from France but from more distant places like Oran and Obernai, Moscow, Kiev, and Tunis.[13] Here, too, he promoted the formation of a specifically Jewish intelligentsia united in a philosophical approach to the Jewish texts, above all the Talmud. His own contributions along this line resulted in many of his published talmudic lessons and readings.

II. SCRIPTURE AS THINKING

In order to explain what he envisioned with an intellectual lay Judaism, Levinas began from an account of believing Jewish identity. This involves a distinction between an extrinsic or outward identity and an intrinsic or inward identity.

From Extrinsic to Intrinsic Identity

One can of course find one's own religious identity chiefly or even exclusively in an extrinsic identification with, for instance, Judaism as a social unity recognizable in more or less specific duties, objective gestalts, official teaching on orthodoxy, forms of authority, traditions, institutions, organizations, a uniform division and classification of time, and so forth. While such an extrinsic identification certainly has a function and meaning, it also easily acquires a formal, external, and fideistic character. Such a traditionalism founds itself by conforming to or inserting itself into an objective order. Concretely, it finds expression in a specific religious practice. Identity would thus be a matter of insertion into a distinctive unity of establishments, structures, symbols, rituals, and language. However, this identification does not, for the most part, take on the appearance of a purely external, objective identity. To the contrary, it appears quite internal and subjective, as a "solemn" repetition of inherited gestures and the "devoted" cultivation of tradition.

Traditionalism and pietism cannot truly comprise an adequate rationality. Faith solely in the name of a tradition or in the name of a form of devotion is not a sufficient reason to exist. Naturally, one can try (and even succeed) to maintain one's own religion by means of a *pedagogy of exaltation,* which strives to provide subjects with an emotional support and to excite in them an enthusiasm in which they are willing to accept a number of truths, guidelines, and practices without any appeal to reason. But such a purely emotional self-identification has no real future, for even if the sentiments involved remain pure, they can only be maintained in the protected, greenhouse-like environment. In our culture of critical reflection, only those things which bear the mark of thinking can either long appeal or long endure. Likewise, in our "late modern" culture, which seems now to have overshot the Enlightenment ("modernity") thought of autonomy all the way to extreme individualism and subjectivism, and which moreover harbors a powerful allergy to "the totalization of reason" or the rationalizing pretension of a self-enclosed and universally binding explanation of all things, we must answer to the demand for a critically self-relativized rationality. Without this, we fall back into "premodern" irrationalism and conservative fundamentalism. And the emerging postmodern also forbids us an easy return to any simple or convenient religious self-consciousness. If it hopes to avoid being sidelined or ridiculed the moment it makes contact with the rest of the world, faith will always need to exercise the ascesis of critical rationality.[14]

The intrinsic religious identity rests on an intellectual and reflective appropriation of the confession of faith and the message bound up with it. Internal identity can (and must) of course express and establish itself in objective forms and social structures, but its source and point of departure lies elsewhere—namely, in a reflective approach to the Scriptures.

More than an Archaeological Fossil

Under the influence of the Enlightenment, this thinking approach to Scripture has become confused with a scientific study consisting mainly of historical and philological research. What have become the classical methods of historical-critical and literary exegesis are an abiding expression and realization of the modern turn of Western rationality. One wants to know the facts. One will therefore attempt to ascertain whether everything the Bible reports is indeed completely true. Did it occur as it is recorded, or are those stories really myth and riddle? One conducts research, seeks proof and verification. Who wrote which books, chapters, or verses of the Bible? When were they written? What was their historical, cultural, social, and political context? Is there archaeological evidence substantiating, for example, the Exodus story? What are the reliable sources for what the Bible recounts about David, Solomon, and the building of the temple?

Although such a conception of Scripture requires a great deal of penetrating insight and scientific competence, it is not, strictly speaking, a reflective approach to the text. For one thing, it can close itself up in its own method and approach to such a degree that it remains only a distant and unengaged study of Scripture. Levinas illustrates this possibility with a look at the "Wissenschaft des Judentums," an important phenomenon in modern western European Judaism.[15]

The "Wissenschaft des Judentums" came into existence during the nineteenth century in Germany, under the influence of Leopold Zunz. It was developed further by Heinrich Graetz, author of the monumental *Geschichte der Juden,* and Zacharias Frankel, founder of the so-called positive-historical school and of the journal *Monatsschrift für Geschichte und Wissenschaft des Judentums* (1851). This school stood in reaction to reformist Judaism and wished to preserve the essential, ritual, and national aspects of traditional Judaism. The movement was therefore called "conservative." Nevertheless, it did accept the results of historical research. In 1854 the Jewish Theological Seminary was founded in Breslau, with the intentions of forming conservative rabbis and furthering the historical study of Judaism.

This seminary and its students accounted for an enormous spread of historical scientific study of Judaism throughout central and western Europe. This influence continued to the eve of World War II (the *Monatsschrift* was disbanded in 1939), during which time most Jews considered it self-evident that its perspective—advocating a strongly, almost exclusively philological and historical-critical conception of texts—was practically the only scientific approach to Judaism. Concerning this, Levinas has said: "Fifty centuries were put on cue-cards: one immense Hebrew epigraph, written in bundles dedicated to hearing their historical witness, and this only in order to situate the point where their influences cross. What a cemetery! The graves of one hundred and fifty generations!"[16] Naturally, there can be no contesting the value of a philological-historical conception of texts, but this can only be propadeutic or preliminary. Still less do I wish to contest the possibility that the philologist-historian can be penetrated by a great tenderness for the moving folklore which these texts bear. And yet that sentiment is ambiguous, since it flows from his manner of thinking. On the basis of his historical-critical approach, he might unwillingly presuppose that the text before him is an old and dated document. The freedom from engagement which defines philological work insofar as it considers the text a historical document does not come without a high price. For the philologist-historian risks perpetuating the moment of his own conclusions. Only a reference to cue cards orients his research. He is like an archaeologist who discovers a tool from the Neolithic Age and guards against ever using it. He is enthused only at the historical value of his discovery, without any interest in its implications or promise. A text studied solely as a historical and philological document remains a bygone and dead thing for which, according to the ironic expression of Leopold Zunz, the practitioners of the "Wissenschaft des Judentums" have prepared a beautiful burial.[17]

Hence does one observe a remarkable double standard. On the one hand, we consider Socrates, Plato, Aristotle, Montaigne, or Goethe with a conviction that they remain disposed to serve as guides and models for our existence. They are considered sources of inspiration for giving meaning to our lives, and speak to us from the height of an eternal worth. In contrast, the biblical texts viewed from a historical-philological perspective appear only as "curiosa" or "speciosa" best kept in a museum or the basement of some theological library where they bear witness to a bygone culture, like that of the Aztecs in Mexico.[18]

To consider our biblical texts only as archaeological fossils is to deprive them of any capacity to support our efforts to give meaning to existence. A believing Jew schooled in the vaunted humanism of the West is not stimulated to take the Scriptures truly in hand. This is why the biblical texts must not be considered only as archaeological findings. They call for immeasurably more and better.

However necessary and useful a historical-philological and literary approach to the Bible may be, it is therefore also insufficient. It, too, must be transcended and taken up into a higher level. Even if we were to achieve final knowledge of all factual events recorded in the Bible and complete control over every text recording them, this still would not furnish us with sufficient insight to live by. Some people can fall so completely under the spell of this historical-literary approach that they never really leave it. But in order to truly grow, it is necessary to take some distance from this "science" and approach the Bible with the great existential questions of our existence. This points not to an *anti*-historical or *anti*-philological approach to Scripture, but rather one which is *trans*-historical and *trans*-philological.

The Bible As "Founding" Word

As beings in search of meaning, we encounter biblical texts as the source of orientation and foundation for our existential, historical, and cultural perspectives. In this way, the Bible can become a Word to live by. This experience of the Bible shows, in other words, how it can be a modality of human existence. One does the Bible a disservice by reducing it to a source of information or an implement—a means to study basic facts or historical events and figures—as if it is a "handbook" one can literally pick up like a telephone or hammer and then put down again after finishing with it. Our relation to the Bible can never be purely instrumental or functional. One is wrong to interpret the Bible as something *Zuhandenes* (Heidegger), that is, something that merely offers itself to hands already on their way to concrete tasks.

This is why the Talmud teaches that not only certain actions, people, or events are impure, such as one reads in the Bible, but also the hands themselves. Our hands are always busy making us the master of everything within our reach. There is nothing more active, brutal, and restless than the hand which touches everything and brings everything close in order to possess or use it.[19] A respectful relation to the Bible thus avoids treating it as if it is simply there to be used.

An adult approach to the Bible culminates in relating oneself to it as "founding Word," as a word whose inner truth founds and supports my very existence. Such a founding Word is more than edifying or pious; it puts me in relation to what grounds my existence, gives breadth and depth to it, guides it and holds it open.[20]

III. THE BIBLE AS THINKING

According to Levinas, in order for the "founding" Word to truly become a Word to live by, it must first become a Word to learn from. An existential engagement with Scripture can never be achieved in the blind obedience which suspends critical judgment from reading and reflection. One can look into the mirror of God's Word only with clear and open eyes. Scripture can appear human only if one looks at it *as a human,* which is to say, as a thinking being. This is why an existentially engaged relation to the Bible must be mediated by reflective consideration which presupposes but also goes beyond historical-philological and literary analysis. In order to truly understand the life-giving meaning and proper bearing of Scripture, immediate sensibility and spontaneous intuition are not enough; one has need of keen attention which thinks, thinks again, and thinks through.

This thinking approach to Scripture belongs specifically to the adult or mature way of looking into the scriptural mirror. The Bible is a Word which gives rise to thinking and in which our entire existence can live so that we come to the truth. Far from a simplistic or unreflective obedience, this involves a conscious confrontation with the message inhabiting Scripture, giving rise to thinking. Biblical texts call for the reflective resources of thinking readers so that the enduring insights and values contained there can continue to nourish souls. We must turn to the Scriptures not so much for plausibility as for instruction, basic and directive insights about human beings, society, and the meaning of life. Just as a purely philological and historical-critical approach to Plato, Montaigne, or Goethe will never suffice to truly learn from them, so too must we go beyond that approach when studying Moses and the Prophets.

Even when one has become convinced that the biblical texts speak as truly and meaningfully about human life today as do any other texts, it is still necessary to always study them anew, to reread them and think through them again from a contemporary perspective. This is not out of apologetic defense, but in order to make them communicable by deepening them critically. It is not the case that what the Bible says is true because it is in the Bible, but rather that it is in the Bible because it is true. To think through the Bible again and again means to bring it back to the level of discussion precisely in order to call its intrinsic truth-value into service for us here today. A thorough, reflective investigation which gauges the basic metaphysical, anthropological, and ethical insights to be found in Scripture translates them into "living truths," or better, "truths that give life." In this way, the particular thinking already at work in a text can come fully to life again.[21] This is also the way to rescue the Scriptures from a secular existence in which they are confined to a book—thus to a "thing" alien from life—so that the great and living voice of their "founding message" can be heard again.[22]

   In line with Levinas, we might also designate this reflective, philosophical conception of how to read Scripture as the "reading of the Bible without images." To read the Bible in the way one reads a picture book or a comic strip is to give an imaginary or anecdotal meaning to texts and stories by which we then populate our imaginary world in all its curiosity with "strong stories" and "exact facts." Such a reading pays no attention to the meaning suggested in those texts and stories, meaning which greatly exceeds their purely historical truth. To reduce the Bible to some sort of cartoon strip, full of rich imagery and fascinating stories, would be to take no account of the numerous interpretations and whole culture of thought which exist thanks to the text and around the text, and which is always in reflective redefinition and renewal. The reading of the Bible as a "religious picture book" is superficial and thoughtless; in the end, it mummifies the life-giving text. It passes shamelessly over the spiritual life of a tradition which is not at all a simple repetition of biblical texts but, to the contrary, a reflective commentary and deepening that ceaselessly gives rise to thinking.[23]

Biblical Thinking Is an Original Thinking

Only such an approach can lead one to discover how the biblical texts can make an original and important contribution to culture and the "spiritual life." Until now, I have simply presupposed this irreducible and powerfully life-giving identity. It is time to bring it explicitly to light.

Even if Scripture is recognized to be the bearer of enduring insights and values concerning humanity and the world, one can still try, out of a sort of intellectual shame, to reduce those insights and values to general humanistic ideals. However, then they lose both their attraction and their relevance. One can then forgive the believing intellectual formed in our Western culture for a lack of interest in the study of such unruly texts, since all of the insights to be found there would then be available in Western humanism (whose source is Athens)—not to mention more easily. In order to realize the very particular and indispensable contribution of biblical texts (whose source is Jerusalem), one must take them as one's starting point in the conviction that they are not leftovers of a completely bygone time but bearers of a living culture crucial for reaching a truly human and meaningful existence. Hence do the Scriptures deserve to be addressed at the same level of reflection as the other great texts of Western culture. In order for the original and enduring—or better, always new and irreducible—meaning of biblical texts to nourish souls, they must first appeal to our minds.[24]

In this connection, a look at Levinas's view of the relation between the Bible and the Talmud (Jewish commentary on Scripture) can be clarifying.[25] For the most part, Christians understand the Bible to be something broad or general, since it forms the point of intersection with the Jewish confession as well as, partly, that of Islam. In contrast, then, the Talmud is considered more narrow, since it belongs particularly and specifically to Judaism. The Jewish tradition, however, views this comparison from precisely the reverse angle. The Bible, also called the Torah,[26] with its specific revelation-content, which speaks specifically to Israel, is considered more particular, whereas the Talmud expresses biblical thinking on a generally human level. The Talmud transcends the particular "incidents" or events of the history of Israel, and it generalizes them by explicating their intrinsic meaning and human value. The talmudic commentators were not theologians or prophets but rather sages who put forth every manner of discussion in their commentaries.[27] They focused on meanings which appeared in a discourse frequently dressed in a religious, ceremonial, or theological language, seeking to explain and communicate them without either denying or minimizing their proper content. Indeed, this content, as portrayed in texts, formed for these commentators the source of their particular sort of thinking, via all sorts of commentary and discussion. The Talmud and rabbinic literature display a centuries-long tension concerned with not violating the letter of the biblical text while taking that text as a basic fact. This literature is thus inspired not by the interiority of the human "soul" but the exteriority of the "verse." Accordingly, they were constantly occupied with the task of distilling from the historical and religious passages of the Bible a thinkable truth for the human soul. They did not predetermine the Bible as the bearer of a code or as a dogmatic tract; they did not consider Scripture as a collection of citations available to theologians, or as a recipe book which spiritual writers can draw on to illustrate their incitements. Their style of reflection exhibits a broadly and deeply developed world of thought which one is to enter only gradually and with patience (just as is the case with entry into the Greek world), with the help of basic study and discipline, both methodological and systematic, as well as a keen sense of the fundamental questions and thematic—and all of this with the temerity of a thinking and investigating spirit.[28] In other words, a talmudic spirit always approaches the texts of the Bible and the tradition as the evidence and source of a specific way of thinking which is taken completely seriously only by pursuing one's own thinking through and beyond.

When one takes the Bible itself as one's point of departure for further reflection and penetration, one comes not so much to one or another vision as to an irreducible form of thinking with its own originality. And to relate to this thinking reflectively, to read the Bible reflectively, is first to listen honestly to the text itself. It is to avoid immediately rejecting its suggestions, and instead to accept them without prejudice, from a philosophical standpoint. One then asks whether their meaning and implications can be justified rationally by what we already find in ourselves. Such a reading always seeks, in other words, the "objective and communicable credibility" of the text. Such a conception rests consciously on the conviction that biblical texts, as the expression of a human and not only religious culture, do contain a rationality and thus can become accessible to thought, or rather is already thought. In short, Scripture contains completely original and irreducible insights which, via a philosophical standpoint, can be made generally available to human souls.

In our time, texts from Scripture are quickly cast aside on the ground of their place within a particular faith-confession. The text is rejected before and without having been read, thus before and without having been listened to for the echo of a thinking at least as radical and founding as the thinking to be heard, for example, in the fragments of the pre-Socratics. There are situations where a biblical text, even when restricted to the role of illustration or suggestions, nonetheless lets loose an idea that takes on its own life and, even within the philosophical texts written within the Greek tradition, can and must come to power—and not merely because that idea belongs to the Bible, but rather because of the degree to which we recognize ourselves through it and can think through it.[29]

IV. BIBLICAL THINKING AS SPIRITUALITY

According to Levinas, this reflective approach to the Scriptures comes with a specific spirituality, namely, that of "strict application." In order to clarify this spirituality, he compares and contrasts it with the so-called spirituality of the "emergent source" (*la source qui jaillit;* literally, the source which gushes forth), which strives after an immediate and emotional-intuitive contact with the truth of Scripture.

The Spirituality of the Emergent Source

The spirituality of the emergent source is bound closely to "religious enthusiasm," which involves the possibility of contact via an inner feeling, or affection. The word *enthusiasm* has its root in the Greek word *entheos*, which means "to have a god in oneself, to be possessed by a god, or taken up into a god." Driven by a sort of "spiritual" hunger for depth-experience, one strives to overcome the limits of one's own ego and enter into direct contact with the Other, entering into or losing oneself in the divine. It is here that some speak—wrongly—of "mystical union": one is drawn to the divine mystery like a moth toward fire. One seeks a direct and pure unity with the divine; one seeks an intimate, soothing, sweet, and all-encompassing proximity with, or better, *in* divine presence. As a model for describing this union, one turns quite naturally toward the experience of romantic love. The passion and feeling of love stimulates a desire to experience complete immersion, totally fulfilling unity. The relation

between myself and the Other, my beloved, must become "commu-
nion," duality in unity, so that the pain of separate existence and the
experience of always being Other can be taken up and overcome.
The desire for ecstatic elevation into the divine is analogous to this,
for it, too, involves a clouding of limits and distinctions. In seeking
participation in the divine, one hopes to enter into the sacred womb
of the divine. The core of this "religious enthusiasm" is thus the experience of a merciful embrace which befalls us as pure gift, or rather
literally comes over us and takes us up so that we live in and through
its grace.[30]

An important quality of "religious enthusiasm" is of course that of
feeling, as is suggested immediately by the more everyday sense of
the word *enthusiasm.*[31] Feeling, it turns out here, is not only the quality but also the medium along which one tries to achieve participation
in the divine. This implies a specific interpretation of feeling: feeling
as inner emotion, or affection. This places an accent not on the object-pole of the feeling—in other words, the immediate and lived
contact with a concrete reality—but rather, and even exclusively, on
the subject-pole, on attachment to oneself as the lived experience of
oneself.

Through feeling, one falls back into oneself, into an inwardness in
which there is a deep experience of intimacy with oneself which is
not emptiness but, to the contrary, richness. In this sense, feeling is
essentially resistant to every attempt to reduce the ego to a function,
element, or category defined within an overarching totality or objective system (such as, for instance, the impersonal dialectic of history,
the economic and sociopolitical system, etc.). Rather than immersing
one in an all-encompassing, exterior whole, feeling affirms and deep-
ens the subject's irreducible self-experience. As immediate contact
with the concrete (Other), feeling also characterizes the manner in
which one falls back in oneself and concentrates on oneself. Through
this movement of self-coinciding and interiorization, the subject is
one with its own experiencing and living of life. Feeling is thus above
all an "inward-movement" to the immanence of inwardness and intimacy with oneself. We can therefore designate feeling as an ongoing
dynamic of "intro-version," back into oneself (*vers soi*).[32]

The inward dynamic of feeling is also bound to a metaphysical
significance.[33] The fall back into subjectivity which occurs in feeling
can lead deeper than the subject itself, to a depth beneath interiority,

or on "this side" (*en-deçà*) of it. This possibility flows directly from the essence of feeling as movement inward. A feeling can take me back not only into intimacy with my deepest self, but beyond that, or beneath it, to a "sub-terranean" ground which supports and inspires everything. Such feeling thus calls me back to the roots of my very self. It opens the subject to the possibility of reaching the un-grounded depths of its experience of itself. Immanence is then the avenue to transcendence, to going beyond myself, thanks to and via my self-affection to and in the wholly Other, which, as "wholly Un-grounded," is also and at the same time closer to me than I am to myself (*intimior intimo meo,* to cite Augustine). By way of contrast with "transascendance," which reaches beyond (*au-delà*) the subject, via the object-pole of feeling—beyond the "other" of concrete reality, toward the wholly Other—we might call this a "transdescendence" reaching back into the very depths of the subject itself.

Proponents of religious enthusiasm have begun not from philo-sophical-critical reflection but from the pursuit of existential experi-ence; not coincidentally, and perhaps involuntarily, they conclude at precisely this point, where the limits of subjectivity seem to open directly on the wholly Other. They place emphasis above all on the subjective dimension of affection, which leads them inevitably into an unnuanced and one-sided subjectivism. In inner emotion, they seek above all, or perhaps even exclusively, a lived experience of intense inwardness and "spirit" that conveys a sense of direct partici-pation in divine reality. In other words, they do not seek this partici-pation along the path of presence in the world, where one is busy with things, ethical responsibility, and creation; to the contrary, all of this is considered a detour. They choose rather a shorter way, a short-cut inward via the fall back into oneself which occurs in affection, which is to go so far as to let go of that inwardness and thus get beyond the violence of simple closure. They seek an intense experi-ence of being grafted onto, or rather *into,* divine reality, which stands neither outside nor over against us, but can be discovered and experi-enced in our depths as the core of our very selfhood. Through this religious enthusiasm, one's own inner feeling for oneself, one's self-affection, becomes the source of spirituality, truth, value, and mean-ing—in short, of spiritual life—and is no longer simply an exterior reality. The "master" is no longer found outside, but inside, no longer in the heights but the depths. In religious enthusiasm, there is no longer any separation, but an inseparable and direct "in-dwelling" of the divine in the subjective, and vice versa.

This religious enthusiasm is also paired immediately with the specific spirituality already designated as the spirituality of the "emergent source."[34] The "spiritual" life is then presented as an inner source lying in the depths of the subject and from which religious experiences immediately well up in intuitive feeling. These experiences bring such a glow and fervency that the subject might come not only to goodness but also to his or her "true self." It is no wonder that such a position looks with suspicion on another spirituality which places emphasis on ethics and rationality. Such a cool and detached spirituality would be far too abstract and unsuited to nourish the development of "spiritual" or "inner" life. It would be far too lacking in forms and images to dramatize the "soul" of the spiritual adventure. According to the tendency of religious enthusiasm, we must restore the dignity of the specific forms and language of religious experiences which cannot be reduced to ethical expression. In the final analysis, religious experience would then be a matter of an emotional bond with the deepest Ground of Reality, which is to say with the deepest ground of my self.

However, it is necessary to submit this spirituality of an emergent feeling of God to serious reconsideration. Does it not appeal to a highly subjective and uncontrolled rush of forces and passions? Does it not also express an infantile desire to return to the womb, where every imperfect solution to the calamity of separation is resolved? In short, is it not the narcissistic projection of an unfulfilled wish?

The Spirituality of Strict Application

A very different sort of spirituality, one focusing on the object-pole of feeling, is that of strict application. It begins not from the subject and its inner experience, but from the "object," the "Other" that comes over us from "elsewhere." This does not involve an immediate, inner feeling but a process of study in which one is confronted with what is other than oneself. We do not discover this "otherness" but find it. We can therefore call this confrontation an experience in the strict sense of the word: we meet with something that we have not found in ourselves and could not possibly have found there. We strike against something that resists and breaks through the project of supporting and pursuing our own preferences, expectations, and interpretive schemes. Precisely for this reason, the "meeting" with the Other is often disappointing with respect to what we had expected or with respect to the desires we had harbored. It brings something radically new, unexpected, and therefore painful into our existence, and in that way dispossesses us and places us in question. This is also why we often feel a temptation to flee from the confrontation with the Other. We would rather not go there or remain there. We would rather be left undisturbed in our identity and stability, and would rather abide in the security of the "same."

In order to give real content and meaning to this "exteriority" which we thus encounter, one needs to apply oneself, and this requires time. Those who quickly—as if receiving an immediate welling-up—define and relate the Other to themselves will never truly discover the content which this Other "reveals." It must be humbly and scrupulously, with receptiveness and patience, that we encroach on the Other, so that through our respectful and devoted listening, but also thorough and penetrating thinking and meditation, its "mystery" can slowly reveal itself without either betraying itself or abasing itself before shameless eyes. We can call this listening real "learning."

In contrast with the spirituality of the emergent source, which nourishes itself on immediate intuition and sensitivity, we can think of this approach to the Other as the "spirituality of strict application." It applies itself in tireless "study" to the Other testified in the revelation tradition, which has been precipitated by the biblical texts (the Latin *studere* means "to apply oneself, to make an effort toward something").

Since the biblical tradition does not come from the inner disturbance of the subject but presents itself as an unambiguous alterity preceding the subject itself—"signaled," moreover, by the wholly Other which has given itself to experience and is known through a long history—one must attach and apply oneself explicitly to this pregivenness. We can characterize this application as a strict application because it is dedicated to something that comes from outside: the Word of Scripture. This Word does not easily surrender its secret. To enter into this "mystery" is, already at first sight, certainly not a light and simple exercise, but to the contrary asks for hard work, demanding much time and all the resources of one's thinking. This perhaps explains why this spirituality is less attractive or "fascinating." In place of a source, it is better here to speak of a struggle, a battle fought with open visor, raising argument against argument, slowly developing a stubborn, unconquerable idea. In contrast with the intuition that illumines and upraises the heart with a surprising freshness, here there is the labor of questions and research which takes up each successive answer with greater fruitfulness, and begins again. The Word demands to be conquered: far from a gentle, refreshing spring to drink from, it is a hard nut which can be cracked only with the most rigorous attention.[35]

This makes it clear that learning and study play a crucial role in the development of a mature faith, or what Levinas calls a "religion of adults." Such a religion does not permit itself to be seduced by and enclosed in the first moment of a charming but still hazy discovery; it transcends and consolidates this first discovery by deepening it rigorously, but without wishing to immediately achieve—here and now—new insights or world-shaking results. One cannot be a mature believer in a purely emotional or almost instinctive way. One can be unbelieving without knowing it. Or, stronger still: if there is no thinking, then there is also no faith. One must want to be religious with one's whole heart, but one must not *only* desire, as if driven by some naive élan, or spontaneous rush of heart, or any surprising tide of the heavenly Spirit. Being a believer consciously, or a conscious believer, is possible only if one also applies oneself to Scripture. And this application must be more than a simple reading, more than pious credence or hasty "edifying reading." It must be the ascesis of patient and thorough study which seeks critically not only for understanding but also and above all to discover and develop a vision which can support spiritual life. To apply oneself in this way is to constantly reread and reappropriate the revelation from which and by which the human adventure can be judged and receive meaning. This returns me to Levinas's plea for a reflective faith and the intellectual lay Judaism we have seen in this analysis.

A Mysticism of Disenchantment

All of this must not lead to the conclusion that such an intellectual application to Scripture would be a spiritless exercise, without intensity or passion. To the contrary, it is possible only if one devotes oneself to it "with heart and soul." One is so buoyed up by Scripture that one applies oneself to it with growing enthusiasm. Note immediately the double movement of spiritual passion, or enthusiasm: on the one hand, one is completely fulfilled by the text; on the other hand, one is completely present to the text—"von der Sache ganz erfüllt" ("completely filled by the thing") and "ganz in der Sache gegenwartig" ("wholly present in the thing"), to speak with Hegel.[36] This implies a particular form of experience, and even of mystical enthusiasm. An intellectual application that thinks steadily through, which critically tests, investigates, and rethinks, is a form of rationality which is itself a specific sort of experience and feeling. This would be the sweetness of the nut that one tastes after having finally cracked it. The enthusiastic application of reason to the text (active enthusiasm) also awakens enthusiasm (passive enthusiasm). Here, reason and experience are no longer opposed, but one: as applied to the Other in and of Scripture, rationality itself is experience and emotion, and vice versa. At the same time, this also transcends the classic opposition between the lucid soberness of reason and the hot-blooded enthusiasm of feeling. In the spirituality of strict application, the two go together.

This does not do away with the paradox of "transportment" flowing from a reflective approach to Scripture. Notwithstanding all the enthusiasm of the approach itself, this "transportment" presents itself as a "mysticism of disenchantment" (*dégrisement*).[37] During the hard work of applying oneself in heart and mind, we are always moved—and hurt—by the "bewildering new insights" that make the foundations of our daily existence tremble and from which we therefore all too gladly flee. In this respect, the study of texts and tradition is not always free of ambiguity. We all know only too well how some people make this sort of timely and yet untimely appeal to traditions or "sacred texts," wisdom, or formative experiences in order to defend an already calcified way of life and thinking. They would rather remain smug in their self-assured position than permit themselves to be put in question by the Other and, like Abraham, go in search of something new in a foreign land. The moment a reflective approach to Scripture appears to involve having their established insights and convictions put in question—the moment it challenges "the same"— they find all manner of reasons and rationalizations to avoid applying themselves in that way. But those of us who find the (mad?) courage to see this disenchantment all the way through are rewarded with new horizons which in turn fulfill spiritual desire in new ways. In this sense, this disenchantment can be considered a specific but no less mystical path to enthusiasm.

The paradoxical enthusiasm of "lucid passion" and "sweet disenchantment" can be illustrated by the following story:

> The Talmud tells of Rabbi Raba, a man who passed all his time immersed in the study of the Torah. While doing so, he was observed to run his fingers so hard over the sole of his foot that blood ran from it. This was certainly no edifying sight: why did this scholar of Scripture not meditate turned peacefully inward? At the very least, he could signify his rapt attention by running his hand through his beard. Still, Raba's gesture can be seen in retrospect as appropriate: the act of kneading his fingers into his foot until it bled expressed the seriousness of his struggle with the biblical text. He had likewise to run his fingers over the Word until blood sprang from it, until it yielded the life it harbors. By rubbing his foot until it bled, Rabbi Raba not only gave plastic expression to a passionate commitment to the rational engagement of Scripture, but also incarnated and experienced this approach himself!

Approach to Scripture As Creative Remembering

A concrete reading which wishes to come to the heart of the text precisely out of respect for the message which one knows lies hidden there is possible only through a sort of violence done to the words. Only in this way can one unlock the original message buried under layers of later conventions and distortions. It stands to reason that meaningful words covered in such layers of use and convention, once they have been brought back across history to the light of day, already possess and deliver considerable "food for thought" which the inexhaustible richness of Scripture helped discover. Through repeated and almost intrusive digging, the layers which bury and falsify, leading us to misunderstand and confuse, must be gradually removed from the Word.

We might designate this approach to the text as "creative remembering." Remembering a tradition or a text is much more concretely active than simply calling up the past again. To remember a tradition creatively is not only to preserve or protect a text, but also to open it up so that its original grounding experience can once again be a source for thinking and living. The tradition registered in and through memory is delivered by remembering over from the domain of concrete implements (the text) to the domain of insight and meaning-giving.

From all of this it may be seen how the spirituality of strict application bears witness to God's transcendence, and much less ambiguously than does the spirituality of the emergent source. By wrestling with Scripture in its objective expression, the subject remains in a lively awareness of God's exteriority and "holiness" (*heilig* or *sanctus:* originates from *sancire:* "to split, or separate"). Through the discipline of faithful adherence to that which does not spring from the depths of one's own inner experience but which comes over me and addresses me, I experience a presence that lies outside the limits of inner, "spiritual" life. This presence remains inaccessible to the very thoughts that lay hold of it. God remains outside precisely because God is God. But through applying myself strictly to Scripture, I can come wondrously near this wholly transcendent God. Levinas even goes so far as to say that this approach to Scripture, this thinking study, can lead to an intimacy with God as great as that of prayer.[38]

V. NEITHER THE FIRST WORD NOR THE LAST

These remarks on the spirituality of strict application make it finally possible to situate a reflective-philosophical reading of Scripture. As "mediator" between Word and life, such a reading has neither the first word nor the last.

Inspired Wisdom

First of all, the reflective-philosophical reading does not have the first word. It does not begin from itself but rests on the "pre-given" resources of tradition flowing from Scripture. As the "other" in which reason confronts itself, Scripture is itself a fact of experience so that the approach reason makes to the text is a lived experience in the true sense of the word. In this sense, we can speak here of an "inspired rationality" out of which develops and unfolds a rational force not simply based on itself but bound to the heteronomous origin of the

Word. This is an obedient rationality, holding itself open to what comes from "elsewhere."

This reminds us of artistic inspiration. In authentic artistic activity, artists often have a sense of not being the author of their own work. The artistic activity can be experienced as a "calling," a being called and animated by an inspiration which one does not create but discovers. Artistic inspiration involves the consciousness of a radically alien intervention in human activity and self-determination, the experience of a subterranean "en-spirit-ment" which not only comes from elsewhere but is also much greater and deeper than my limited ego and its meager capacities. This, then, is the experience of "possession" by an extraordinary power. One can also speak of "enthusiasm" here, referring to a sense of being stricken to the very marrow by something Other. Artists do not resist this "infiltration," but surrender themselves to it completely, grateful for the great gift of inspiration befalling them or taking them up into itself.[39] However, this heteronomous activity does not at all take away the artist's creative activity and role. To the contrary, inspiration awakens in us the impulse to create. It is the work of the artist to manage and work this impulse out, which requires artists to respect (and in a sense master) the specific laws and conditions of their craft and technique in order to indeed bring that inspiration to expression. Inspiration overwhelms artists without doing violence to them. This denotes a heteronomy which is the source of autonomy.

This can also be said, although in a different sense, of the reflective approach to Scripture. Insofar as it is inspired, it has a heteronomous origin, but as a human activity it is nonetheless the work of a person and takes place according to the particular laws governing rationality. As heteronomous source of a reflective approach to the text, Scripture does not exclude the autonomous capacities of rationality, but in fact calls them to develop their proper fulfillment—and with enthusiasm. Scripture itself is not without thought, but rather a specific form of thinking: it literally "gives" to thinking. Just as inspiration does not rule out the artistic activity and craft of the artist, but to the contrary supports it and makes it possible, so Scripture—as "way of thinking"—does not rule thinking out, but challenges it—thus displaying a degree of faith in its capacities—to give its best to the effort of making the message of the text available in and through thought.

A Pure Enthusiasm

Inspired wisdom also does not have the last word. The reflective approach to Scripture, however uplifting and enthusing it may be, does not occur simply for itself. Just as it is not its own origin, it is also not its own aim or end, but stands in service of biblically inspired, meaningful life and action.

This means that it is also far from undermining or putting on trial the existential engagement of the believing self. To the contrary, a reflective approach to Scripture seeks to nourish, support, and guide such an engagement, and in that way resist or compensate for the one-sidedness of the so-called "postmodern" spirit of the times. The human being points above and beyond itself toward a "sense" that cannot be reduced to that person. Persons truly realize their humanity only if they allows themselves to be claimed by this "sense," thus transcending themselves.

Of course, not every surrender or action is responsible, not every engagement is meaningful, and not every involvement or attachment is good. By thinking along with Levinas, I have tried to protect the purity of such an involvement with Scripture. But we must not be blind to the distortion of surrender, action, or engagement which can rapidly occur when emotions win out over a truth which is discerned rationally: what follows then is an irrational circuit of attachment to attachment, action upon action, and enthusiasm at enthusiasm.[40] Those who abandon themselves to such a course ask too much of themselves—passing over both the ground and content of what they abandon themselves to—and act as if communicative force is to be found only in the enthusiasm and emotions around the message (and not in the message itself).

Ultimately, such people give the impression of a lack of faith in the intrinsic truth of what they experience, at least considering that they seem to need to appeal to emotional and demagogic means to convince those around them. Such persons must by necessity busy themselves with the "attractiveness" and "expressivity" of the object of their attention so that they quickly risk becoming over-extended and exhausted, with the result that they must step back. But there is also no happy end awaiting those to whom such witness is addressed: they are so continually driven and beleaguered by the fantastic, or rather fanatic, enthusiasm of their neighbor's witness that they are eventually without the freedom and space to choose for themselves whether to accept the call to join them.

A reflective approach to Scripture seeks to protect and promote precisely this inner freedom, grounded in rational insight. A faith which is experienced heart and soul in personal engagement can become established and grow to maturity and depth only if it consciously resists all cheap consumption and the rapid diversion of interest toward only what sparkles with newness rather than what is simply true—that is, toward what possesses its own meaning in itself and thus stands in the way of an existence truly moved by thinking. Faith is a free and in that sense properly human act which does not rest on any other order, and neither responds to nor exercises any emotional violence, ideological compulsion, or manipulation.

Permeating Life

This reflective, philosophical approach to Scripture cannot, in its turn, become an end point. No less so than the historical-literary approach to Scripture, the reflective-philosophical approach runs the risk of becoming an "objective and detached study" in which we apply our understanding apart from the insights by which Scripture can yield instructions to live by. One can misuse the reflective approach to Scripture and avoid confronting one's own life with the message to be found in Scripture. But one can just as easily open oneself to the help it offers in a "truth that sets us free." But this requires one to directly—eye to eye—confront the kernel of the text which reflection has laid bare. Everything therefore depends on which conscious choice one finally makes.

CONCLUSION: SOURCE OF THOUGHT AND LIFE

What Levinas says about intellectual lay Judaism is, in my view, largely applicable to the related concern of better realizing a Christian way of life. There can be no mature Christian faith without a thinking relation to Scripture, which is evident from the rich tradition of hermeneutics in Christian reflection. This does not mean that the reflective approach to Scripture is thus the beginning and the end. Thinking from and about the Bible follows and responds to a source for thinking which is at once an experience and a tradition: Scripture. And it is also followed by the response of the believer which is born by the enthusiasm of lucid insight. Engaged believers surrender themselves precisely in order to make their faith true and to experience it in that way. In this sense, what transpires here is a reflection and a meaning-giving which is only relative but which nonetheless has indispensable worth. "From beneath," the reflective approach to Scripture is already open to a heteronomous source of meaning; "from above," it is also already open to a transcendent aim. It makes possible a mature and free answer to the Word. At the same time, this is also a bearing witness to God, to the wholly Other which is also the marvelous Proximity in the Scripture to which we apply our thinking.

NOTES

1. According to the Julian calendar then still in use in czarist Russia, the date was December 30, 1905.

2. E. Levinas, "Entretiens," in F. Poirié, *Emmanuel Levinas: Qui êtes-vous?* (Lyon: La Manufacture, 1987), 67.

3. E. Levinas, *L'au-delà du verset: Lectures et discours talmudiques* (Paris: Minuit, 1982), 182–200.

4. E. Levinas, *A l'heure des nations: Lectures talmudiques, essais, et entretiens* (Paris: Minuit, 1988), 138–51.

5. Levinas, "Entretiens," 64.

6. *TeI* xvii/*TI* 29.

7. E. Levinas, *Difficile Liberté: Essais sur le judaisme* (Paris: Albin Michel, 1976), 373.

8. Ibid., 352.

9. Levinas, "Entretiens," 87.

10. Levinas, *Difficile Liberté*, 274.

11. Ibid., 299.

12. Ibid., 330–31.

13. E. Levinas, *Quatre lectures talmudiques* (Paris: Minuit, 1968), 23.

14. Levinas, *Difficile Liberté*, 342–44.

15. Ibid., 304.

16. Ibid., 300.

17. E. Levinas, "L'Ecole Normale Israélite Orientale," *L'Alliance Israélite Universelle* 145 (October 1963): 18.

18. Levinas, *Difficile Liberté*, 305.

19. Levinas, *A l'heure des nations,* 32–33.

20. E. Levinas, *Ethique et Infini: Dialogues avec Philippe Nemo* (Paris: Fayard, 1982), 17–19.

21. Levinas, *A l'heure des nations,* 71.

22. Levinas, *Ethique et Infini,* 125–26.

23. E. Levinas, "Lire le Bible sans images," *Esprit* 6 (1990): 120.

24. Th. De Boer, *De God van de filosofen en de God van Pascal* (The Hague: Meinema, 1989), 147ff.

25. See Levinas, *Quatre lectures talmudiques,* 10: "The Talmud is the translation of the oral heritage of Israel. It regulates the daily and ritual life as well as the thinking—the interpretation of Scripture included—of those Jews avowing Judaism" (trans. J. Bloechl).

26. Cf. Levinas, *L'au-delà du verset,* 165 n. 2: "The written Torah is the name for the forty-eight books of the Jewish biblical canon. In the more restricted sense, the Torah is from Moses: the Pentateuch. In the widest sense of the word, the Torah is the whole of the Bible and the Talmud with their commentaries and even including the collections and homiletic texts of the *Haggadah*" (trans. J. Bloechl).

27. Cf. ibid., 175: "The Talmud is comprised of discussions between learned rabbis which took place between the first century before the common era and the sixth century afterward. Historically, these discussions are played out by extension from the most ancient traditions and they mirror a process in which the center of Jewish spirituality in the Temple is replaced by centers of study, thus from the ordained ministry to study. These discussions and lessons concern above all the portion of Revelation bearing prescriptions: rites, morality, the law, but in their own way also the form of parables about the whole spiritual universe of humankind: about philosophy and religion" (trans. J. Bloechl).

28. Levinas, *Difficile Liberté,* 314.

29. Levinas, "Entretiens," 110–11.

30. Cf. *TeI* 12, 18, 23, 186, 279/*TI* 41–42, 47, 52, 212, 278–79; *Difficile Liberté,* 22, 28, 43, 44, 65, 78, 139, 142, 177, 190–91, 243; *EDE* 172; and E. Levinas, "La pensée de Martin Buber et le judaïsme contemporain," in *Martin Buber: L'homme et le philosophe* (Brussels: Editions de l'Institut de Sociologie de l'Université Libre de Bruxelles, 1968), 49–50.

31. Among those who have argued for a revaluation of this sense of "feeling" is Levinas's friend the prominent existentialist Jean Wahl. Cf. J. Wahl, *Existence humaine et transcendence* (Neuchâtel, 1944), 28–30, 34–38; see Levinas's intervention in the discussion recorded in J. Wahl, *Petite histoire de l'existentialisme* (Paris: Ed. Club Maintenant, 1947), 81–89; E. Levinas, "Jean Wahl et le sentiment," in *Noms propres* (Paris: Fata Morgana, 1976), 141–47; and E. Levinas, "Jean Wahl: Sans avoir ni être," in *Jean Wahl et Gabriel Marcel,* ed. J. Hersch (Paris: Beauchesne, 1976), 13–31.

32. Wahl, *Existence humaine et transcendance*, 30–34.

33. Ibid., 34–38. Cf. also Levinas, "Jean Wahl: Sans avoir ni être," 13–31.

34. Levinas, *Difficile Liberté*, 47–48.

35. Ibid., 17, 42–45, 155–56, 164, 167–68, 238, 246.

36. G. W. F. Hegel, *Vorlesungen über Aesthetik* (Berlin, 1955), 297.

37. E. Levinas, *De Dieu qui vient à l'idée* (Paris: Vrin, 1982), 57.

38. Levinas, *L'au-delà du verset*, 109.

39. Cf. E. Levinas, *Sur Maurice Blanchot* (Montpellier: Fata Morgana, 1975), 29–30.

40. Levinas, *Difficile Liberté*, 197–98.

8

The Significance of Levinas's Work for Christian Thought

Adriaan T. Peperzak

IT IS A FACT which gives one pause for consideration that in Holland, Belgium, France, the United States, Italy, and South America the work of Emmanuel Levinas has found its greatest readership among Christian philosophers and theologians. Although this work is supported by a long Jewish tradition—even in its strictly philosophical elements—it has impressed many Christians by its orientation, which, despite its great originality, seems familiar to them.

Levinas's work rings with the voice of a master, not only in the sense of a teacher who translates a common heritage, but also in the sense of a critic who poses questions of conscience and who exposes the pseudo-answers and dishonest modes of conduct to which we are inclined. When we enter into his writings, they force us to a discussion through which our own thought and action can be renewed.

Turning for a moment to my title, I must note that it cannot concern a presentation of the (complete) meaning of this work for all varieties or the entire field of Christian thought. Such a task would be far too great for me, and possibly for every philosopher or theologian. Who could boast of having a total knowledge of Levinasian thought at one's disposal, or venture to say that one can grasp the entirety of Christian thinking "in one's own words" and thoughts? Therefore, in the following I will only consider *some* of the significance of Levinas's work within my own limited understanding of Christian life and thought. In doing so, I will attempt both to heed the voice of a master and to link that voice with an interpretation of Christianity which I hope is not erroneous, though it is certainly fragmentary.

Before beginning, however, I would like to address a few remarks to the expression "Christian thought." As the first Christian writings already show, there are not only many variants of a Christian interpretation of nature, the world, and history, but also different levels upon which one may speak of "thought." Not every thought expressed by a Christian is "Christian," and not every Christian is "a thinker," but every authentic Christian at the least practices a naive and implicit type of Christian-oriented thinking. One might possibly even consider dogmatic proclamations a type of thought, but here I will primarily concentrate on naive religious convictions and on a pair of theological and philosophical reflections in which Christianity has expressed itself—albeit incompletely, and possibly in a somewhat biased form. In this connection, I will refer mainly to the non-technical essays in which Levinas has expressed his understanding of Christianity while taking a certain distance from it.

It is then not my intention to systematically compare Levinas's chief ideas with the theses of a Christian dogmatic and moral theology; rather, I will attempt to contribute something to answering the following questions: Why is Levinas's work so important for contemporary Christians, and how can it become fruitful for them? Levinas's critique of totality may be read as an invitation to criticize the idea that Christian faith can be presented as a doctrinal system. The wish to gather the evangelical message into a theological encyclopedia or *summa* understands itself as an attempt to represent truth by identifying it in the theses and syntheses of a surveyable whole. The panorama of a complete dogmatics is a glorification of the onto-theological ego, which through knowledge has secured itself against the shocking character of the unexpected. The critique of egological totalitarianism can be carried out in strictly philosophical critique of the universal reduction of all otherness to the Same. Still, the magnificent tautologies that result from this reduction can also appear too rich. The wealth they represent symbolizes a different spirit than the spirit of poverty which the Prophets and the Beatitudes extol.

Systematic syntheses, handbooks, and comprehensive professions of faith may have a catechetical and didactic use, and they may even be indispensable, but they are certainly secondary. Living tradition is a continuous awakening to authenticity, through continually new interpretations which always critically test, purify, and deepen what has already been said and interpreted. Handbooks and *summae* belong to levels of administration which have expanded greatly since the churches began to organize the Kingdom of God in accord with the political models of profane society. The theoretical systematization of Christian belief, the organization of Christian practice through a quasi-juridical codex, the subjugation of fraternal life and discourse under the structure of a quasi-political and disciplinary regime in which the power of monarchic, aristocratic, or democratic authorities is exercised—all of this gives evidence of the same spirit as the totalizing tendencies of Western science, technology, and philosophy. Is this spirit typically Greek? Greco-Roman? European? Is it the spirit of modern planning and technology? Or does it betray a universal human tendency toward domination and monopolization?

It is time that we Catholics and Protestants understand and practice a critical but fraternal discussion with one another and with our older brothers the Jews, as an essential element of our effort toward better self-understanding and the construction of our own religious community. In the hope that such a discussion will be more successful, I will now risk some questions and thoughts which have come to me in reading Levinas's works, forcing me into a search which is not only intellectual but also existential.

GOD

Although it is the most difficult and dangerous, I would like to begin with the question of God. In proceeding this way, I do not mean to suggest that the philosophy of Levinas is only a philosophy of religion. Some commentators have remarked that Levinas has the great merit of having enriched phenomenology through an ethics and philosophy of religion, but that is only a very small—and not the most important—part of the truth. The statement is even false when taken to mean that one could separate ethics and the philosophy of religion from the remainder of philosophy. The Levinasian philosophy is a *prima philosophia*, a "first philosophy" which is at least as radical or fundamental as the dialectic of Plato, the logic of Hegel, or the Heideggerian ontology. Not only is it unthinkable that thought of God and thought of the Good could stand alone, they also unavoidably change all other thoughts which one might have. But one cannot radically thematize the basic questions of philosophy—such as What is thinking? or What is the significance of life, desire, and thought?—if one abstains from ethical and religious terminology and conceptuality. As the defenders of the ontological argument knew—though it is true that they have not always formulated it well—the question of the infinite is posed from the beginning. The modern idea that one can separate "is" from "ought" and the finite from the infinite, thus making finite being the theme of an ontology before having to address the question of the Good, "values," gods, and God, testified to an absolute autonomy which viewed the relation to the Other, and therefore morality and religion as well, as secondary and subordinate phenomena.

If we now attempt to speak about God, we must first come to an understanding among ourselves not about *the* meaning of the word "God"—because, after all, this question is much too difficult for human beings—but rather about some meanings which "God" cannot have in philosophy and theology.

We have the many excellent exegetes of the last hundred years to thank for the fact that we can again understand epic, mythic, and poetic narratives about God as they are meant, and not as scientific, philosophical, or theological theories of the construction of the universe. But we are still tempted sometimes to grasp the Kingdom of God as a second, ideal, or utopian world somehow behind, before, or after our finite, guilty, and sorrowful world. Behind, before, or after this mortal life, the real life would be taking place in an eternal realm untouched by misery or sin. An adult, modern person can no longer believe in a world behind the world. Such a belief has supposedly never been the case for adults, because it would degrade God's Kingdom to an improved version of the finite and mortal world, in which God would be the ruler of a paradise.[1]

Modern man has attempted to take on the role of an absolute ruler. The scientific and technological planning of the world seems to aim at a universal domination through the human will. Because the typically modern form of atheism seems now to be foundering, we live once more in danger of an infantilism which gladly subjects itself to parties, ideologies, myths, leaders, and pseudo-religious doctrines. The monotheism of the great religions presupposes a wakeful and mature individual who has rejected all gods, including a thaumaturgical Most High—atheistic in this particular sense, then—and who stands alone in the world. Such a one cannot count on a radical improvement in the world or the abolition of wickedness and evil; one does not find comfort in the promise of a "life after death," but rather awaits one's own death and the death of others as a fate that no one can love or approve of. One thus stands helpless and without understanding when confronted by suffering, especially the suffering which can be understood neither as the consequence of one's own crime nor as sacrifice for others. Salvation or redemption cannot mean that the good life presently missing will be given afterwards, in a second and similar, though better, time and world. Prayer becomes conditional when we no longer know what is good for us and what we may expect from the Good. What we desire the most is a meaning that does not pale as soon as we have reached it.

SALVATION AND LAW

Levinas has often intimated that in the desire for personal salvation there also lies hidden a great deal of narcissism. A radical distinction separates the satisfaction of vital, aesthetic, theoretical, and "religious" needs from the absolute sense of desire for that which an individual is radically destined or called to. Only this sense can deliver us the from the disgust of self-enjoyment. This is the sense of my unchosen responsibility for the life and salvation of the Other. While I am chosen as "for the Other"—prior to any possible choice of my own—it is possible for me to live for an existence "after my death," thus for an existence that belongs not to me, but rather to the Other. As substitute, hostage, or victim, I am already dead inasmuch as a radical "being-for-the-Other" implies that my life no longer belongs to me and in this sense is no longer my own.[2] Although as an independent and free will I must take the world into possession and enjoy it, I have always already sacrificed and lost this property in that I have received the Other in my house and given over my own for the Other.

The fundamental law through which my humanity is constituted and the *normative* tenets without which a *descriptive* definition of my existence is impossible form a philosophical interpretation of the Mosaic law and the prophetic texts among the *Ebed Jahweh*. If Christians consider the man Jesus to be the perfection (*plerōma*) of the law, they believe that his life for the others can be understood as exemplary obedience to the law of self-sacrifice, and that his death is the extreme consequence of that obedience. To be taken hostage or delivered over to the Other is an orientation that rejects hedonism. All suffering is a test, as it presses us to accept the authentic script of our destiny and to give shape to it through forms of giving. The subjectivity which accepts its passivity refutes the ideal of appropriation through a poverty which the Bible terms "blessed." This poverty is a passion that not only Jesus but also innumerable Jews and non-Jews have suffered and died from. How was it possible that the executioners of this passion were very often Christians who held important positions in their church? Is there a residue of paganism in the "Christian" interpretation and continuation of the biblical tradition? Can it explain the anti-Semitism so often and so unfortunately present in the Christian tradition?

MYSTICISM AND LOVE

Enthusiasm, magical metamorphoses, "mystical" fusion, participation in the truth, and ruling magical forces are all typical forms of non-monotheistic religiosity endangered by the pure sobriety of the prophetic testimony and inspiration of ethical responsibility.[3] Does Christianity contain similar seeds, or do these belong, if and when they appear, to its falsification?

Through his critique of mysticism and sacramentality, Levinas calls us to a radical purification of our religious practice and conviction. If it is true that—as Paul says—all power and authority are subjugated to the servant of God, who has sacrificed his life for all, then magic is at an end. The celebration of the sacraments then cannot be represented as a form of magical overwhelming. The eucharistic remembrance of the central event of Christ's passion may contain no trace of irresponsible and infantile thaumaturgy. The responsibility of each of us touched, taught, and inspired by the celebrated event can in no way be weakened, replaced, or violated by the influence of a higher will. Every hope for a secret mechanism of the allotment of grace *ex opere operato* is to be rejected. The core of the sacramental prayer consists in gratitude for a life which successfully embodies ultimate meaning, and in the hope that we may also live and die for others in like manner. But this prayer does not rule out the thought— one should rather say that it rules it in—that this form of life and death must be *given* to us. "Everything is grace," not only the creation which has constituted us—before every possible acceptation—as independent, always obligated subjects, but also the justice that is realized through our responsibility. The heteronomy of the law which always orients us develops into a second heteronomy—or into a second phase of the same radical heteronomy: the grace of the law-*abiding* loyalty to our original passivity. The free conduct in which we follow the call inscribed in our conscience, the human good through which God reveals his way, presupposes the inspiration of the Spirit that motivated creation. The meaning of creation reveals itself in the inspiration which makes us servants and friends of the Spirit.

Is the thought of human autonomy, without which a religion for adults is unthinkable, not destroyed by the thought that grace not only determines our central task but also grants us the very capacity to be good? Does a Christian theology of grace, like Christian mysticism and the belief in a hypostatic union of God and man, exhibit a primitive and magical conception of the work of God and religion? The criterion on which Levinas always insists holds that every religious relation in which one forgets one's fellow is inauthentic. In a discussion with some Christian philosophers and theologians on the concept of "revelation,"[4] his key references included not only Jeremiah 22:16 ("He did justice to the poor and unhappy, and that benefitted him. This is surely what is called to know me, says the Eternal") but also Matthew 25 (25:40: "And the King will answer, 'Truly I say to you: What you did to one of the least of my brethren, you did to me' "; and 25:45: "Truly, I say to you, what you did not to the least of these, you did not to me") and the first letter of John, in which we read, among other things: "If someone says that he loves God, but hates his brother, he is a liar. For he cannot love God, whom he has not seen, if he does not love his brother, whom he has seen" (1 John 4:20); "Whoever does not love abides in death. . . . If one has this world's good, and sees his brother in need, yet closes his heart from him, how does the love of God abide in him?" (1 John 3:14–17); and "No one has ever seen God; if we love one another, God abides in us, and his love is perfected in us. By this we know that we abide in him, and he in us, because he has given us of his own Spirit" (1 John 4:8–9, 12–13).

The inseparability of God's love of us, our love of God, and the love of each person for the other is so constantly and strongly proclaimed in the books of the New Testament that we Christians must be fully in agreement with Levinas on this point at least. However, there remain some questions and doubts concerning the meaning we should attribute to the mystical union of humans with God. Can we understand and defend the notion that the Christian conception of the mystical is radically distinct from magical enthusiasm, and that it does not contradict the prophetic reading of responsibility for one's neighbor, but rather demands and presupposes it, possibly even coincides with it?

The mystical moment of the Christian religion shows itself in the writings of the great mystics who have come forth in all periods of Christian history. They have assumed no independent authority in relation to Christian life and practice, but have emphatically experienced and brought to expression what was believed in the churches concerning the possibility of an intimacy between God and people.

At times, it is said that the mystics have experienced God and union with him. But that is an inaccurate and misleading expression. The presence of God which they write about—they write considerably more about God's absence,[5] incidentally—is in their own words not a presence of God "as He is," "since the condition of this life does not admit of that."[6] God does not allow himself to be seen (cf. 1 John 4:20, as cited above); the vision of God kills; it demands the self-sacrifice of an entire life in the service of the transcendent, an obedience that gives away and consumes. God is near when the mystics ponder his actions and desire union with him, whose hiddenness does not diminish but grows.[7] The acts of God through which Christians know themselves to be carried, the creation by which they are called to servitude, the passing by of God in Jewish and Christian history, the practical and theoretical unfolding of life from God and for one's neighbor—gratitude is the appropriate answer to these acts, a gratitude which knows of itself that it is a gift. "Gratitude for giving thanks" (*rendre grâce de rendre grâce*), to owe one's very thankfulness to the initiative of an Other, is the opposite of an attempt to consider oneself the origin.[8] The mystic experiences the essentially veiled presence of God as the tension between the past of a having-passed and a coming which is continually deferred (always still to come). But "desire for his presence"—does this not sound like a sublimated need, a kind of hunger which should be satisfied by God as the highest good? If that were mystical desire, the ultimate meaning of life would lie in a highest autarchy or self-sufficiency. Does not such a hedonism destroy the absolute demands of the moral task constituting our lives?

What is the content of the presence which mystics yearn for? What is this aim of the love through which the saints characterize God? When we have understood the texts from Jeremiah, Matthew, and John cited a moment ago, we can also understand the answer which John of the Cross offers for these questions: to say that the love of God is a desire for his presence means that love desires *yet more love* (*está clamando por más amor*).[9] The "fulfillment" or completion for which love yearns is a greater love. Love wants no stilling of its hunger, but rather a radicalization of itself. The "perfect grace which I desire"—which Moses expresses with the words (Exodus 33:13) "Show me your Face, so that I may know you and find the perfect grace in your sight, which I desire"—is understood by John of the Cross as "the perfect love of God's glory."[10] John knows that not even Moses could see the face of God, since no soul in this weak life can bear the enjoyment of seeing the face of God.[11] Love itself is the healing and health of the soul,[12] for which it gladly gives its life, because "the soul lives where it loves more than there where it gives life."[13] The soul remains ill so long as its love is not perfect, that is, so long as it is not unified with the presence and figure (*presencia y figura*) of the beloved and so is "reshaped" or "transfigured."[14] This unification and transfiguration is in no way a submerging of the independent subject into an ocean of divine energy and feeling, but a completely different sort of transformation. In praying that God may "take possession" of it,[15] the soul expresses its desire that the "sketch" (*cierto dibujo*) of love which it has become through radical passivity be transformed into an actual figure of perfect love. This happens, John says, when in grace, that is to say through the Spirit, the soul shows the *figura*—the form and the appearance of the one who is the definitive word of God, or, drawing on another metaphor, the Son of God, or again, using a third metaphor, the splendor of God's glory.[16] The suffering of love (*dolencia de amor*) which is commented on in the text cited here, far from expressing a narcissistic nostalgia for the mother's lap, is the pain that lies in not being-for-the-Other in a perfect mode. Authentic suffering consists in the imperfection of love (*falta de amor*). It shows that the soul has a lack of love—though not a complete lack—since it is only through the love it does have that it can discover what it lacks.[17]

DEATH

Unity with God is reached as a likeness with the Son, that is to say, through uniformity with the perfect example of the Good. This correspondence can be characterized by the words Levinas cites from Jeremiah. Since the goodness or love of one's neighbor includes giving one's own life and therefore one's own death for the Other, it can be clarified through the Christian metaphors in which the cross has become the central image. The God of whom it is said that he is *semper major,* greater than every reality in which he can be thought, reveals himself as *semper minor:* in the hiddenness of a man who was put to death because he did not flee the choice to serve, but became completely one with it.

In our history, we have been confronted with the terrible fact that Christians, whose election implies the suffering and death of Christ—a suffering and death which they are to fulfill—have again and again imposed suffering and death on the Jews. How is it possible that we have not recognized the Passion in the persecuted of God's people, and why is it so difficult for Jews to recognize the same passion in the man Jesus?

The encounter with Christ is an encounter with the poor, leprous, foreign, or marginal. The presence of Christ is, as the presence of God, indirect and essentially hidden. The presence of one's neighbor is at the same time both the memory of the Lord's passing by and an anticipation of his coming. Between the events we memorialize and the ever-deferred coming, Christ does not reveal himself through appearances—he is no phenomenon of our experiential world—but through representatives in the form of the needy. The poor come to us "in the name of the Lord." Christ therefore comes from the distance as an exception which disturbs the order of the powers and authorities. The recognition of this presence presupposes that one understands the Spirit. It presupposes that one at least exercises an initial obedience.

RESURRECTION AND FORGIVENESS

There are at least two other aspects of Christian belief which can awaken doubt regarding its purity: the resurrection and the forgiveness of sins.

Is not the image of the resurrection an un-biblical and even anti-biblical version of the apotheoses by which Greeks and Romans have deified the most beloved of their heroes? Such deifications were only possible because their gods were human, all too human. The Christian who celebrates the death of Christ testifies to the indestructible meaningfulness and the posthumous fruitfulness of a life that has exhausted itself in obedience. The Christian overcoming of death does not lie in the promise of a second, utopian, or paradisal life; it does not refer to a repetition of life on a happier plane; rather, it announces the possibility of perfect intimacy with the spirit of God, a spirit that is love. In the death of the righteous, the spirit of the Torah has revealed itself to be invincible. The peace which the resurrected preaches to his disciples and the blessedness of the Sermon on the Mount are not forms of gratification but a "consolation": in finding the authentic meaning of life, one will be completely united with the task to which one has been called. And yet, perfect obedience to the law of love seems to be beyond our capacity.

How can one really and truly live for all others? When Christians speak of the forgiveness of sin, do they not awaken the suspicion that they take neither human crime nor the divine commandments seriously? Do we not say that the passion of Christ has expunged sins, repaying them on our behalf? Do we not trust that God's mercy clothes us in a justice given from on high? We represent salvation as the participation in a drama performed for us and with us. Do we do so in order to free ourselves from the hard demands of the law, the responsibilities of love and justly deserved punishments? Do we then prefer the pathos of tragedy to the prosaic and boring everydayness of a morality which is continually unsatisfied?

I hope we are all convinced that intimacy with God can never mean that the law of love can be abolished in the Kingdom of God. There is no place in heaven for the criminal. On the other hand, we are also convinced that life and hope have the same duration. As stated, Christian hope is always hope for a greater and deeper capacity for love, and never a hope for a mixing of love with injustice, or

God with the devil. Sometimes hope for greater love can mean hope for a *beginning* of love, for a conversion from the habits of sin. Deliverance through a turn to the law of justice and the practice of being-for-the-Other is both possible and necessary for every egoist—consequently for all people. That turn presupposes grace, however; it presupposes the spirit of the Good which is older than us. Grace reveals itself as mercy, which, along with conscience, gives us the ability to act. The law through which we are obligated to each other is not contrary or contradictory to grace, as if one had to choose between the two as between two primary relations or alliances. When we say that grace in itself takes up the law, that cannot mean that love relativizes or degrades the law—its own law!—to a provisional status. The sense of the law is love. It is the spirit through which God educates human beings.

AUTONOMY AND HETERONOMY

The heteronomous orientation of original passivity affirms and strengthens the autonomy of a subject who is at home in the world and enjoys life. Autonomy and heteronomy go together, once love of life develops through a conversion of spontaneous egoism into hospitality and gratitude. Gratitude and hope do not primarily concern the enjoyment of life, but rather the possibility and the capacity for hospitality, sufferance, service and hope, and gratitude itself. Patristic and medieval theologians have employed Greek categories in their attempt to think the unity of autonomy and heteronomy and the inseparable distinctness of God and humans. Revelation was understood as a word about being, and was interpreted with the help of concepts such as "participation" and "analogy." Wishing to expand on the central place of the will, late medieval and modern theologians have favored other categories, and interpreted revelation above all in juridical metaphors. Judgments, decisions, decrees, laws, rewards and punishments, and convictions and defenses all placed the language of religious ontology into the shadows and were accompanied by a critique of the Greek influences through which the biblical message was supposedly polluted. Was this critique a return to a truly Judaic understanding of the biblical tradition? Do the Greek elements within Christian theology permit a defense as *logoi spermati-*

koi of Christianity? Or must we begin by freeing ourselves of all Greek influence, including all ontology, in order that we might hear the pure voice of the one God, who kills or subdues all gods?

The Levinasian critique of ontology is certainly not a plea for the eradication of the Greek components of our culture. Levinas has frequently pointed to the greatness of the Greek conception of rationality, metaphysics, science, and politics. Judaism does not aim at a destruction of Greek, Roman, German, or any other culture. Indeed, it is essentially universalistic. Does not the Judaic people stand for the whole of humanity? Modern individuals cannot sever their Greek roots. Those who nonetheless attempt to do so fall into ridiculous caricatures of Greek thinking. But it is clear that the spirit of Christianity is not Greek. Is it Judaic? Are we children, brothers and sisters, or distant relatives of Israel? All of the Jews standing at the beginning of Christian history—Jesus, Jacob, Peter, John, Paul— attempted to renew the heritage of Israel. Through their interpretation of the Mosaic and prophetic traditions, they wished to cleanly set them forth, while also deepening and radicalizing them. The new message of which they spoke was contained in the Pentateuch. The law of love is, as they knew, just as old as the revelation through which God assembled his people. The perfection, the *plerōma*, of the old law was the development of the very content of this law.

It is a tragedy of Judaism and of Christianity that they so quickly separated from one another. What was meant as a Judaic return to the source became an extra-Judaic, often even an anti-Judaic movement of hellenized Asians, Africans, Romans, Germans, and so on. Since the break between the Jews who rejected Jesus and those who acknowledged him as the greatest of all prophets, the two families have never ceased searching in the Bible for traces and instructions of God. Currents of interpretation divided for two thousand years—on one side the long history of talmudic and post-talmudic commentaries and discussions, on the other side the New Testament and the multiplicity of Christian theologies—have presented the faith of Abraham in a broken form which contradicts the universalistic claim of Judaism and the desire of Christianity to gather all Jews and Gentiles to itself. Was it necessary for Paul and his followers to leave the synagogue to devote themselves to the Gentiles? Was there then a fault of impatience, or was the failure of the dialogue a necessary detour toward the universalism which still lies in the future? Through that division, Christians have lost a part of their heritage, precisely that part of the talmudic and later Jewish developments that went unnoticed or misunderstood by Christians. No Christian church may say that it fully understands the Bible as long as it has not patiently opened itself to the long wisdom of the Jewish interpreters. But then we cannot fully understand either the *plerōma* of the law and ourselves so long as we ourselves have not worked through the questions that separate us from our Jewish brothers and sisters. Perhaps the Spirit of God reveals itself now, in the as yet still modest efforts of a halting discussion about our profound affinities.

If we seize the chance today to study seriously a contemporary witness of the tradition of Israel, it is primarily a modest effort to better understand both the others and ourselves, thereby contributing in some small way to hastening the coming of the one and universal God.

NOTES

A prior version of this text was written for a colloquium with and on Emmanuel Levinas which took place in Aachen and Simpelveld from May 31 through June 2, 1982. The exploratory nature of this essay has meant limiting the number of explicit references to Levinas's work. Many implicit references point to *Difficile Liberté: Essais sur le judaïsme* (Paris: Albin Michel, 1963 and enlarged in 1976). For more extensive discussion and analyses, I refer the reader to my books *To the Other: An Introduction to the Philosophy of Emmanuel Levinas* (West Lafayette, Ind.: Purdue University Press, 1993) and *Beyond: The Philosophy of Emmanuel Levinas* (Evanston: Northwestern University Press, 1997).

1. "The Kingdom of heaven is ethical," says Levinas, but without neglecting to remind the reader one last time, only a page later, of his resistance to *foundationalism,* anthropocentrism, and utopianism. Cf. *AE* 231–32/ *OB* 183–84.

2. The idea that I am not for-myself, as Sartre thought, but for-the-Other lies at the heart of *Otherwise Than Being or Beyond Essence,* especially chapter 4, "Substitution." It is, however, anticipated to a considerable extent by what *Totality and Infinity* I.B. calls the structure of "separation."

3. For a definitive statement of Levinas's position on these matters, and for clear evidence that the word "participation" refers not to Plato but Lévy-Bruhl, see his essay "Lévy-Bruhl et la philosophie contemporaine" (1957),

republished in E. Levinas, *Entre Nous: Essais sur le penser-à-l'autre* (Paris: Grasset, 1991), 53–67.

4. Cf. Levinas's intervention in the discussion recorded in *La Révélation* (Bruxelles: Publications des Fac. Saint-Louis, 1977), 224–25. The discussion itself was preceded by Levinas's contribution: "La révélation dans la tradition juive," 55–77, an important essay since re-published in E. Levinas, *L'au-delà du verset: Lectures et discours talmudiques* (Paris: Minuit, 1982); trans. S. Hand, "Revelation in the Jewish Tradition," in *The Levinas Reader* (Oxford: Blackwell, 1989).

5. The following citations are all taken from the commentary of John of the Cross in his *Cántico Espiritual*, Version B. (*Editor's note:* the difference between Version A and Version B is not unimportant for this discussion: in Version B, Fray John adds to Version A a stanza—number 11—beginning with the words, "Reveal your presence . . ." In the following notes, Peperzak's Spanish citations are repeated immediately in English, as taken from *The Collected Works of St. John of the Cross*, trans. K. Kavanaugh, O.C.D., and O. Rodriguez, O.C.D. [Washington, D.C.: Institute of Carmelite Studies, 1979]. I have occasionally modified the translations slightly.)

6. *Canción* 11a, n. 3: "todas (estas presencias espirituales) son encubiertas, porque no se muestra Dios en ellas como es, porque no lo sufre la condición de esta vida" (p. 449: "all are hidden, for in them God does not reveal Himself as He is, since the conditions of this life do not allow such a manifestation").

7. Ibid., n. 4: "sintió estar alli un inmenso ser encubierto, del cual le communica Dios ciertos visos entreoscuros de su divina hermosura. . . . en deseo de aquello que siente encubierto allí en aquella presencia. . . . con deseo de engolfarse en aquel sumo bien que siente presente y encubierto, porque, aunque está encubierto, muy notablemente siente el bien y deleite que allí hay" (p. 449: "the soul feels an immense hidden being is there from which God communicates to her some semi-clear glimpses of His divine beauty. . . . desire for what she feels hidden there in that presence. . . . longing to be engulfed in that supreme good she feels present and hidden, for although it is hidden she has a noticeable experience of the good and delight present there").

8. Levinas himself knots this sense of religious debt (*dette*), thus a pre-originary initiative as the source of identity, and the reversion of self-possession into gift, all in *AE* 195–207/*OB* 153–162.

9. *Canción* 11a, n. 10 (pp. 451–52 passim).

10. Ibid., n. 5: "la gracia complida que deseo, lo cual es llegar al perfecto amor de la gloria de Dios" (p. 450: "the full grace which I desire [Exodus 33:12–13], that is, to reach the perfect love of the glory of God").

11. Ibid., n. 5: "es tanta la hermosura de mi cara y el deleite de la vista

de mi ser, que no la podrá sufrir tu alma en esa suerte de vida tan flaca" (p. 450: "such is the beauty of My face and the delight derived from the sight of my being, that your soul will be unable to withstand it in a life as weak as this"). Levinas refers frequently to the immediately subsequent passage from Exodus, in which Moses must remain in a cleft in the rocks as God "passes by." Cf., e.g., *EDE* 202/*TrO* 359.

12. Ibid., n. 11: "la salud del alma es el amor de Dios" (p. 452: "love of God is the soul's health").

13. Ibid., n. 10: "porque más vive el alma adonde ama que donde anima, y así tiene en poco esta vida temporal" (p. 452: "for the soul lives where it loves more than where it gives life, and thus has but little esteem for this temporal life").

14. Ibid., n. 12: "el amor nunca llega a estar perfecto hasta que emparejan tan en uno los amantes, que se transfiguran el uno en el otro, y entonces está el amor todo sano" (pp. 452–53: "love never reaches perfection until the lovers are so united that one is transfigured in the other, and then the love is in full health").

15. Ibid., n. 2: "Deseando, pues, el alma verse poseída ya de este gran Dios . . ." (p. 448: "The soul, desiring to be possessed by this immense God . . .").

16. Ibid., n. 12 (references occur on p. 453).

17. Ibid., n. 14 (p. 453). This turn from what is felt as an affliction—as the incapacity to be wholly one-for-the-Other—into the expression of a deeper grace, thus a turn from inadequacy to a certain dignity, is expressed similarly where Levinas refers to our anarchic responsibility to and for the Other as the condition of being "sick with love" (Song of Songs 6:8). Cf. *AE* 181 n/*OB* 198 n. 5.

9

Commanded Love and Divine Transcendence in Levinas and Kierkegaard

Merold Westphal

LEVINAS'S ESSAY "God and Philosophy" is contemporaneous with *Otherwise Than Being or Beyond Essence* and develops theological implications of the argument left largely unthematized in what we might call the *magnum opus* of Levinas II.[1] Levinas sets the God of the Bible over against "the philosophical discourse of the West" and its interpretation of rationality; and he taunts "rational theology" for accepting "vassalage" to philosophy's claim to be "the amplitude of an all-encompassing structure or of an ultimate comprehension" which "compels every other discourse to justify itself before philosophy" (*GP* 153–54). We are reminded of Heidegger's critique of onto-theology.

In an earlier essay, Levinas had evoked that critique by speaking of "the notion of God, which a thought called faith succeeds in getting expressed and introduces into philosophical discourse" (*CPP* 62). In onto-theology, or in Heidegger's account of it, "the deity can come into philosophy only insofar as philosophy, of its own accord and by its own nature, requires and determines that and how the deity enters into it."[2] For theology to seek the imprimatur (censorship?) of onto-theologically constituted metaphysics would be to sell its soul and its birthright simultaneously. For the "god of philosophy" is religiously useless. "Man can neither pray nor sacrifice to this god. Before the *causa sui,* man can neither fall to his knees in awe nor can he play music and dance before this god."[3]

The scenario sketched by Levinas in which it is *faith* that introduces the notion of God into philosophy suggests the interruption of the latter's complacent hegemony by a double alterity. First, faith is presented as a thought, challenging the notion that philosophy has a monopoly on meaning and intelligibility. Second, the God who is introduced into philosophical discourse by this interloping outsider has come to the party uninvited. This God is not at the beck and call of philosophy's project of *episteme* or *Wissenschaft* in accord with the *principium reddendae rationis.* So it is not surprising that throughout the essay, this God (along with the human face we always find between ourselves and deity) is presented as a disturbance to philosophical thought, even the "absolute disturbance" of "an absolute alterity" (*CPP* 64). This God is the philosopher's stone, to be sure, but "a stone of stumbling, and a rock of offense" (Isaiah 8:14, 1 Peter 2:8, King James Version), rather than the keystone or the cornerstone of the temple of Being as Presence.

But (to return to "God and Philosophy"), while the taunt that rational theology stands in vassalage to philosophy again evokes Heidegger's critique, it does not merely echo it. In the first place, the problem with rational theology is not its *Seinsvergessenheit.* "If the intellectual understanding of the biblical God, theology, does not reach to the level of philosophical thought, that is not because it thinks of God as *a being* without first explicating the 'being of this being,' but because in thematizing God it brings God into the course of being. But, in the most unlikely way . . . the God of the Bible signifies the beyond being, transcendence" (*GP* 154). The issue is transcendence, not the ontological difference.[4]

Second, rational theology tries to take divine transcendence into account "with adverbs of height applied to the verb being; God is said to exist eminently or par excellence." For Heidegger, to speak of God as the Highest Being is the first step toward onto-theology. But Levinas asks, "And does not the modality which this adverb . . . expresses modify the verbal meaning of the verb to be to the point of excluding it from the thinkable as something inapprehendable, excluding it from the *esse* showing itself, that is, showing itself meaningfully in a theme?" (*GP* 154; cf. 159). In other words, does not the metaphor of height deconstruct the ontological totality rather than constitute it onto-theologically?

What is the ontological totality that needs to be deconstructed if transcendence is to prevail over immanence, if the Other is to avoid reduction to the Same, if the God of the Bible is to escape the vassal-

age that rational theology accepts? In this essay, Levinas describes it
in terms of four themes against which he wages a sustained polemic:
(1) being as manifestation, (2) meaning as thematization, (3) the present as the time when being becomes manifest as thematized meaning, and (4) transcendental subjectivity or the I think as both the
agent and location of this event (*Ereignis*?).

(1) *Being as manifestation.* Levinas speaks of "the coincidence of
being with appearance in which, for Western philosophy, meaning or
rationality lie[s]" (*GP* 161). Philosophy derives its cultural hegemony
from "the strict coinciding of thought, in which philosophy resides,
and the idea of reality in which this thought thinks. For thought, this
coinciding means not having to think beyond what belongs to 'being's
move' ['*geste d'être*']. . . . For the being of reality, this coinciding
means: to illuminate thought and the conceived by showing itself. . . .
Rationality has to be understood as the incessant emergence of
thought from the energy of 'being's move,' or its manifestation, and
reason has to be understood out of this rationality" (*GP* 153–54).[5] In
other words, "meaning is equivalent to the manifestation of being,
and manifestation equivalent to being's *esse*" (*GP* 173), or more
briefly, "being *is* manifestation" (*GP* 155).

(2) *Meaning as thematization.* The meaning that arises from the
manifestation of being (subjective and objective genitive) is not just
any old meaning. It is thematized content. For Western philosophy,
"meaning or intelligibility coincides with the manifestation of being,
as if the very doings of being led to clarity, in the form of intelligibility, and then became an intentional thematization in an experience.
Pressing toward or waiting for it, all the potentialities of experience
are derived from or susceptible to such thematization. Thematic exposition concludes the business of being or truth" (*GP* 155). Where
"being" and "truth" are placed in apposition, "spirit is taken to be
coextensive with knowing" (*GP* 155) and theory is primary.

(3) *Presence.* But thematization is representation, and representation ties meaning to the present. "As rational speech, philosophy is
taken to move from evidence to evidence, directed to what is seen,
to what shows itself, thus directed to the present. The term *present*
suggests both the idea of a privileged position in the temporal series
and the idea of manifestation" (*CPP* 61). Nothing can remain hidden;
everything must be brought to presence, "which is the time of the
Same" (*GP* 154).

The Same? How so? Perhaps the point is best put in Aristotelian language. Knowledge is the immaterial reception of the form in the intellect, which means that the form in the intellect and the form in the thing are identical—not numerically, of course, but the one is the perfect image of the other. Like Heidegger before him and Derrida after him, though in different ways, Levinas seeks to undermine the infatuation with presence that undergirds the notion of philosophy as the mirror of nature and the corresponding requirement that everything, even God, be squeezed into the Procrustean bed of correspondence and adequation.

(4) *The I think.* References to "the now" are always token reflexive, and it is the I think to which they are relative. "Transcendental subjectivity is the figure of this presence; no significance precedes that which I give to myself" (*GP* 157). We should not assume that Levinas is adopting transcendental idealism. In addition to the Kantian language of the I think he uses the Cartesian, realistic language of the *cogito*, and the Husserlian language of intentionality, which is ambiguous on this matter. The argument is meant to apply just as fully to realisms that speak of the intellect as to idealisms that speak of the transcendental unity of apperception. We can return to Aristotle. The claim that "no signification precedes that which I give to myself" does not mean that, empirically speaking, the form of the hundred-year-old oak tree was not in the tree before it was in my intellect. It means that since I can re-present the tree by bringing that form to presence, nothing about this meaning is essentially prior (transcendent) to my thinking. Being as essence and intellect as representation are contemporaneous, honeymooning, as it were, in an eternal now.[6]

Levinas does not deny that there is a dimension of human experience to which these notions are appropriate; what he denies is the totalizing claim that this is the whole story, or, if not the whole story, the most basic story. As early as 1951 he embarks on the "reckless undertaking" not just of asking "Is Ontology Fundamental?" but of making it a rhetorical question with a negative answer;[7] in 1965 he defines the Other as enigma in terms of "this way of manifesting himself without manifesting himself" (*CPP* 66) and the Infinite as "not a cognition but an approach, a neighboring with what signifies itself without revealing itself" (*CPP* 73); and in 1984, "Transcendence and Intelligibility" signify not two mutually exclusive domains but an intelligibility of transcendence "Otherwise than According to Knowledge."[8]

So we should not be surprised to find "God and Philosophy" insisting on an intelligibility and rationality that transcend the immanence of ontology, where (re)presentational thought and being are identical twins. "The intelligibility of transcendence is not something ontological. . . . But the break between philosophical intelligibility and the beyond being . . . does not exclude God from signifyingness" (GP 172). Indeed, we can ask

> whether the meaning that is equivalent to the *esse* of being, that is, the meaning of philosophy, is not already a restriction of meaning. Is it not already a derivative or a drafting of meaning? . . . We must ask if beyond the intelligibility and rationalism of identity, consciousness, the present, and being—beyond the intelligibility of immanence—the signifyingness, rationality, and rationalism of transcendence are not understood. Over and beyond being does not a meaning whose priority, translated into ontological language, would have to be called *antecedent* to being, show itself? (GP 154–55)[9]

This makes it clear why Levinas cannot find a dime's worth of difference between rational theology (which we can understand as the attempt to establish the existence and nature of God by rational argument independent of specific religious experiences or divine revelation) and those theologies that appeal precisely to religious experience or revelation (GP 158–59, 168, 171). To him, they are three variants on the vassalage of God-talk to the discourse of immanence. Since being is manifestation, God must shine forth. God is real only to the degree that God shows himself to human understanding, whether this be by reason, experience, or revelation.[10]

We can also see now why Levinas wishes to distinguish his critique of onto-theology not only, as we have already seen, from Heidegger's, but also from those of Pascal and Pseudo-Dionysius.[11] He makes it clear that in going beyond being he does not intend to relapse "into speaking of opinion or faith. In fact, in staying or wanting to be outside of reason, faith and opinion speak the language of being. Nothing is less opposed to ontology than opinion and faith" (GP 155). He explicitly identifies Pascal's contrast between the God of Abraham, Isaac, and Jacob and the God of the philosophers with this relapse. He assumes—mistakenly, I believe—that Pascal locates religious faith within the framework of Plato's divided line, on which *pistis* (faith, belief) is the second level up from the bottom and still a mode of *doxa* (opinion), the bottom "half" that falls short of *dianoia, noesis,* and *episteme.* So construed, Pascal would belong not only to ontology but also, more specifically, to rational theology, when, "for the benefit of religion, it reserves a domain from the authority of philosophy . . . [which] will have been recognized to be philosophically unverifiable" (*GP* 153). Levinas sees in a recent book which denies that "God" is a concept at all a continuation of Pascal's refusal "to accept the transcendence of the God of Abraham, Isaac, and Jacob among the concepts without which there would be no thought. What the Bible puts above all comprehension would have not yet reached the threshold of intelligibility!" (*GP* 154).[12]

Pseudo-Dionysius is quite willing to place the God of the Bible above all comprehension, and, indeed, explicitly beyond being. For like Levinas, he sees such a strict correlation between human thought and being that it would be irreligious not to find God otherwise than being or beyond essence.[13] But when Levinas writes that "the transcendence of God cannot be stated or conceived in terms of being, the element of philosophy, *behind which philosophy sees only night*" (*GP* 172, my emphasis), he suggests that negative theology is other to philosophy only on the latter's terms.[14] What Pascal and Pseudo-Dionysius have in common, on Levinas's reading, is that while they refuse to constrict faith within the bounds of ontology, they accept philosophy's claim to have a monopoly on meaning. Rather than posit a rationality of transcendence, they leave faith outside the pale of intelligibility. But then, whether they say it is found below or above the privileged realm of evidence and presence is of little import.

If the break with the onto-theological mode of ontological immanence is not made by the appeal to religious experience or divine revelation, where is it to be found? This question generates no suspense. We know Levinas finds it in the experience of responsibility for the Other.[15] Put in terms of language, the (rhetorical) question is: "can discourse signify otherwise than by signifying a theme?" (*GP* 159). This question also generates no suspense. We know, for example, from an earlier talmudic study, that for Levinas "speech, in its original essence, is a commitment to a third party on behalf of our neighbor: the act *par excellence*, the institution of society. The original function of speech consists not in designating an object in order to communicate with the other in a game with no consequences but in assuming toward someone a responsibility on behalf of someone else. . . . Responsibility would be the essence of language."[16]

But language is ethically constituted when we are addressed as well as when we speak. "The epiphany of the face is wholly language" (*CPP* 55), and "The face is a living presence; it is expression. . . . The face speaks. The manifestation of the face is already discourse" (*TI* 66, cf. 193). The saying which the face is can be without words. "The enigma extends as far as the phenomenon that bears the trace of the *saying* which has already withdrawn from the *said*" (*CPP* 69).

It is this last theme that Levinas picks up in "God and Philosophy." Part of what the nakedness of the neighbor's face signifies is that it does not always have access to forums where its empirical voice can be heard. It must "be heard like cries not voiced or thematized, already addressed to God. There the resonance of silence—*Geläut der Stille*—certainly sounds. . . . My responsibility . . . is the hearing or understanding of this cry" (*GP* 167–68).

The use of the phrase *Geläut der Stille* is intended to distance Levinas even further from Heidegger. It is the latter who first uses this phrase to signify a silence at the origin of language. But, in the first place, it is language that speaks and not the neighbor. "The peal of stillness is not anything human."[17] Second, Heidegger's interest in this silence belongs to the project of linking language more closely to the thinking of Being. For him, *"The essential being of language is Saying as Showing."*[18] This showing that is heard in silence is prior to language as signs, but in Levinasian perspective it is just another version of being as manifestation.

The very different saying that Levinas wants us to hear in the silence interrupts the language of manifestation, thematization, and representation. "Language understood in this [ethical] way loses its superfluous and strange function of doubling up thought and being. Saying as testimony precedes all the said. Saying, before setting forth a said, is already the testimony of this responsibility [for the neighbor]—and even the saying of a said, as an approach to the other, is a responsibility for him" (*GP* 170).[19]

In the language of speech act theory, constative, assertive, indicative speech acts belong to immanence. It is commanding, ordering, imperative speech acts that awaken to transcendence. What awakens is not just a demand (*GP* 161), but "a demand that no obedience is equal to, no obedience puts to sleep" (156). Perhaps that is why the image of being awakened is the mildest way for Levinas to speak about the "disturbance" (156, 158; also a favorite term in "Phenomenon and Enigma") which ontological complacency undergoes. It is a "devastating" (162–64), "jolting" (159), "breaking up" (159–61, 173) of consciousness as governed by the I think, which is "interrupted" (160) by an "exposedness" (157) to the Other that can only be described as a "trauma" (161, 163, 166, 173). This awakening is the moral equivalent of reveille at boot camp.

And God is the drill sergeant! In order for transcendence not to be absorbed in immanence,

> it is necessary that the desirable or God remain separated in the desire; as desirable it is near but different: holy. This can only be if the desirable orders me to what is the non-desirable, the undesirable par excellence—the other. The reference to the other is an awakening, an awakening to proximity, and this is a responsibility for the neighbor. . . . We have designated this way for the Infinite, or for God, to refer, from the heart of its very desirability, to the non-desirable proximity of others, by the term "illeity." . . . Through this reversal the desirable escapes desire. The goodness of the Good—the Good which never sleeps or nods [Psalm 121:4]—inclines the movement it calls forth, to turn it from the Good and orient it toward the other, and only thus toward the Good; through this separation or holiness it remains a third person, the *he* in the depth of the you. He is good in just this eminent sense: He does not fill me up with goods, but compels me to goodness, which is better than goods received. (*GP* 164–65)[20]

This sounds very much like the biblical God who commands "You shall love your neighbor as yourself." And Levinas, invoking the classical distinction between eros and agape, makes it clear that it is neighbor love he has in mind. "Love is only possible through the idea of the Infinite . . . which devastates and awakens" (*GP* 164). Suggesting that any love which arises from the lover's need is an attempt to reduce the Other to the Same, to make the Other part of me as the object of my enjoyment, Levinas boldly says no to Plato's Diotima. "The celestial and the vulgar Venus are sisters." Both are "concupiscence in Pascal's sense of the term, an assuming and an investing by the *I*" (*GP* 164). But there is a "love without Eros" (*GP* 165) precisely when I rise and shine to the rude awakening by the God who deflects my love for Infinite Goodness "to the non-desirable proximity of others" and thus "compels me to goodness" (*GP* 165).[21] This is the overcoming of onto-theology, for "in this strange mission that orders the approach to the other, God is drawn out of objectivity, presence, and being. . . . His absolute remoteness, his transcendence, turns into my responsibility—non-erotic par excellence—for the other" (*GP* 165).

At the outset of "God and Philosophy," Levinas promised to oppose the God of the Bible to the God of the philosophers and of rational theology, in this case the Beautiful Itself of erotic Platonism. He has done so by contrasting the transcendence of the God who commands neighbor love to the immanence of the God who is the obscure object of indigent, needy desire. As "the desirable escapes desire" (*GP* 165) in this way, divine transcendence is defined not in cosmological terms but in ethical terms. God is "high and lofty" (Isaiah 6:1) not by being outside the world but by resisting my project of making the whole of being, including God, into satisfaction of my needs, means to my ends.[22]

So it is a bit surprising that Levinas returns to "Philosophy and the Idea of Infinity" (1957) and develops much of his argument in relation to Descartes's Third Meditation, since Descartes's God is not famous for commanding neighbor love. Actually, it is not Descartes's God that interests Levinas so much as the idea of God as infinite, an idea whose innateness means not simply that it is a priori but that it has been put into us. This is a *Sinngebung* of which the I think is not the subject. Levinas calls this a passivity to be sharply distinguished from the receptivity of knowing which, as "an assembling of a dispersed given in the simultaneity of presence, in immanence" (*GP* 166), "assumes what affects it" (*GP* 172; cf. 160, 163).

If we think of Aristotle here rather than Kant, we will realize that cognitivity is a passivity not just of sense but also of intellect. The active intellect is active indeed in getting the form of the thing into the intellect; but this is not the immaterial hijacking of the form, nor even the immaterial transplanting of the form, but the immaterial reception of the form. The intellect did not create the form, and it is not free to edit it. It must take it as it finds it; what is more, it must strenuously discipline itself so as to be truly receptive and not the author of distortion and error.

In his critique of understanding, Hegel identifies this receptivity as surrender. "Instead of entering into the immanent content of the

thing, [the Understanding] is forever surveying the whole and standing above the particular existence of which it is speaking. . . . Scientific cognition [philosophy as system], on the contrary, demands
surrender [*sich übergeben*] to the life of the object, or what amounts
to the same thing, confronting and expressing *its* inner necessity."[23]

Similarly, Heidegger, speaking of the natural and humanistic sci-
ences in distinction from metaphysics, refers to the "submissive attitude [*Dienststellung*] taken up by scientific theory" such that "the
distinction of science lies in the fact that . . . it and it alone explicitly
allows the object itself the first and last word. In this objectivity of
questioning, definition and proof there is a certain limited [N.B.] sub-
mission [*Unterwerfung*] to what-is, so that this may reveal itself."[24]
Later on, Heidegger will portray the thinking that is "releasement
[*Gelassenheit*] toward things and openness to the mystery" as "a kind
of passivity" in which there is present "higher acting [that] is yet no
activity" and is thus "beyond the distinction between activity and
passivity."[25]

Levinas has no quarrel with these analyses. He only insists that
they belong entirely to the rationality of immanence. The traumatic
passivity of the command to love the undesirable is of a wholly different order. The primacy of ethics over ontology is Kantian only to a
point;[26] for here it means not the autonomy of the rational will but
the heteronomy of the will taken hostage, for "to be one's brother's
keeper is to be his hostage" (*GP* 168).

But it is precisely this ethical dimension that is not present in
Descartes's notion of Infinity as prior to the *cogito*. Levinas develops
the notion that the idea of God is "put into" us into a conception of
creation that opens into his an-archic notion of time and the trace. To
be created means to be subject to an idea that is essentially prior to
me,[27] which exceeds every horizon of my thought and cannot be gathered into the present of my I think (*GP* 161; cf. *OB* 122). But nothing
in Descartes suggests that creation signifies a demand or a call to be
obeyed; and when Levinas adds that ethical dimension, it looks a bit
like a transplanted organ in danger of being rejected by the Cartesian
immune system (*GP* 161; *OB* 110, 113).

Would Levinas not have done better to appeal to Augustine and
Kierkegaard, for whom commanded neighbor love does not need to
be added onto the idea of a God who disturbs the ontological sleep
of Plato and Hegel, respectively, but belongs to that idea essentially?

To be sure, their notions of God are "contaminated" by biblical faith in ways that those of Plato and Descartes are not. So they cannot support the deconstruction of Western philosophy from within in quite the same way in which Levinas hopes Plato's *epekeina tes ousias* and Descartes's idea of God as the idea of Infinity will be able to (*TI* 48–52, 102–3). But Levinas acknowledges that it is only "the *formal* design" of Descartes's analysis that is of use to him (*CPP* 53), and we have just seen that the omitted content is precisely the ethical demand that is absolutely central to Levinas's project.

The same can be said in regard to Plato, as can be seen from Levinas's assimilation of the celestial and vulgar Venuses to one another and to philosophy's immanence. Yes, Plato's Good is otherwise than being and beyond essence. But it is also the Beautiful that attracts without diverting desire to the undesirable. Plato and Descartes can disturb the soul's sleep and the *cogito*'s complacency, but they are not the rude awakening that is needed really to overcome ontology and establish "ethics as first philosophy."[28]

For Augustine as for Levinas, divine transcendence is a more radical enemy of human tranquillity.[29] In both cases, we encounter it as a disturbing wake-up call. *Wachtet auf, ruft uns die Stimme.*[30] Since both are exploring the meaningfulness of the transcendence of the biblical God, it is fitting that the awakening motif is itself a biblical one. In Isaiah 52:1, for example, the prophet announces the impending deliverance from captivity with these words: "Awake, awake, put on your strength, O Zion! Put on your beautiful garments, O Jerusalem, the holy city." Eschatological expectation is the typical context for wake-up calls in the New Testament as well. Thus the tragicomic sequence in which we find Jesus urging his disciples to wakeful readiness (Matthew 24:42),[31] repeating this admonition in the parable of the wise and the foolish bridesmaids or virgins (Matthew 25:1–13), and, at a more immediate and mundane level, urging them to stay awake with him in Gethsemane. Whereupon they fall asleep, not once, but twice (Matthew 26:36–46). Eschatological calls to awaken or to stay awake are also found in Romans 13:11, Ephesians 5:14, 1 Thessalonians 5:1–6, and Revelation 3:2–3.[32] Two of these show up in Augustine's *Confessions.*

Augustine's intellectual conversion takes place in Book VII. But since he is not the onto-theologian he is sometimes taken to be, it is not enough that his theoretical questions are answered to his full satisfaction. Beyond the question of truth is the question of the way. "The way—the Savior himself—pleased me, but I was still reluctant to enter its narrowness" (VIII, 1).[33] This reluctance turns out to be "the iron bondage of my own will," which allowed lust to become habit. Three metaphors describe this bondage: a chain, a weight (perhaps the ball at the end of the chain), and the lethargy and drowsiness of sleep. Deliverance from this slavery to his old ways begins "when you called me: *Awake, thou that sleepest, and arise from the dead, and Christ shall give thee light*" (VIII, 5).[34]

Although Augustine repeats that he is convinced of the truth of the Christian faith, he can "find nothing to say except lazy words spoken half asleep: 'A minute,' 'just a minute,' 'just a little time longer.' But there was no limit to the minutes, and the little time longer went a long way" (VIII, 5). Eventually, however, in the famous garden scene where the child's voice repeats the words "Take it and read it," Augustine is awakened. Remembering the conversion of Antony, he picks up the Bible and reads, "*Not in rioting and drunkenness, not in chambering and wantonness, not in strife and envying: but put ye on the Lord Jesus Christ, and make not provision for the flesh in concupiscence*" (VIII, 12).

Augustine quotes only the portion that was decisive for him, Romans 13:13–14. He tells us that he read no further, but not that he did not begin reading earlier. Even if he read only the verses he quotes, the words served as a wake-up call from God, which makes the two previous verses most interesting. "Besides this, you know what time it is, how it is now the moment for you to wake from sleep. For salvation is nearer to us now than when we became believers; the night is far gone, the day is near. Let us then lay aside the works of darkness and put on the armor of light" (Romans 13:11–12). The traumas of awakening for Augustine were neither an intellectual paradigm shift nor the discovery of a cognitive breakdown or dead end. They were the teleological suspension of indicative discourse in imperative discourse. He went from being the subject to being the suspect, from *cogito* to culprit.[35]

If we back up to the previous paragraph in Romans 13 (vv. 8–10), we find a brief discourse on commanded love including the reminders (1) that we owe love to one another, (2) that "Love your neighbor as yourself" is a summary of the commandments against adultery, murder, theft, and so forth, and thus (3) that "love is the fulfilling of the law." Even if he read this portion of the text, Augustine does not mention it. For as he himself understands, his besetting sin is not indifference to others but a twofold lust expressed in an illicit sexual relation and in a career oriented toward fame and fortune rather than service (VIII, 1 and 6). That is why he zeroes in on that passage about the flesh and its concupiscence; or perhaps, why it zeroes in on him.

But Augustine knows that the God who jolted him out of the key elements of his private and public life is the God of Moses in Leviticus, the God of Jesus in Matthew, and the God of Paul a paragraph earlier in Romans—the God who commands neighbor love. So when he says to God, "Blessed is the man who loves you," we have the celestial Venus; and when he adds, "who loves his friend in you," we have either the vulgar or the celestial Venus, depending on how "Platonic" the friendship is; but when he adds "and his enemy because of you" (IV, 9), we see that our desire has been deflected to the undesirable by the one who "compels me to goodness" (*GP* 165). This is not Venus but the Yahweh of Leviticus 19:18 to whom Jesus appeals when he includes "You shall love your neighbor as yourself" in his summary of the whole law (Matthew 22:34–40),[36] and when he rejects the interpretation of this that says, "You shall love your neighbor and hate your enemy," insisting rather, "Love your enemies and pray for those who persecute you, so that you may be children of your Father in heaven." To exclude enemies from the category of neighbors is to imitate, not the perfection of the heavenly Father, but tax collectors and Gentiles, who serve the vulgar Venus by restricting their love to those they find desirable (Matthew 5:43–48).

Like Levinas and Augustine, Kierkegaard understands divine transcendence in terms of commanded love. The first half of *Works of Love* includes six meditations on that theme. Three are directly on the command "You shall love your neighbor as yourself," and three others are on related texts: "Love is the fulfillment of the law" (Romans 13:10); "But the sum of the commandments is love out of a pure heart and out of a good conscience and out of a sincere faith" (1 Timothy 1:5); and "Owe no one anything, except to love one another" (Romans 13:8).[37] The other two essays affirm that God is the source and origin of love and that love of God is inseparable from love of neighbor. "If anyone says, 'I love God' and hates his brother, he is a liar; for how can he who does not love his brother, whom he has seen, love God, whom he has not seen?" (1 John 4:20).

Although he works exclusively from New Testament texts, Kierke-gaard knows that commanded love first appears in Judaism.[38] If he regularly identifies it as Christian love, it is because his target is Christendom, whose paganism he seeks to expose.[39] He draws a sus-tained contrast between commanded love and celebrated love, which turns out to be a variation on the contrast between agape and eros. Recognizing the distinction between the vulgar and celestial Ven-uses, Kierkegaard presents two species of celebrated love, erotic love in the narrow, sexual sense, and friendship. Since he lumps these together, it is clear that the problem with celebrated love is not sen-suality but selfishness (WL 52).[40]

The argument that erotic love and friendship are forms of self-love revolves around the preferential and spontaneous character of these relations. The beloved and the friend are selected from among the others, preferred above the others. There is something essentially exclusionary about both forms of love (WL 52). To be preferred, the beloved and the friend must be attractive *to me*. They must satisfy *my* drives and inclinations (WL 44, 49–52, 56). Sexual attraction is just one mode of this relation. Kierkegaard notes that cultural affinity, for example, is another (WL 60). It is because *my* drives and inclina-tions, whether vulgar or celestial, are the basis of the preferential, exclusionary relationship that both modes of celebrated love can be called spontaneous. I am the origin of both relationships; both loves reach out from my erotic or educated nature toward that which pleases me.

Levinas might say that erotic love and friendship are the reduction of the Other to the Same.[41] Kierkegaard would understand immedi-ately, for he tells us that " 'the neighbor' is what thinkers call 'the other,' that by which the selfishness in self-love is to be tested" (WL 21). Commanded love of neighbor is the end to preference. In order to be my neighbor you need not be attractive to me sexually, cultur-ally, or in any other way; indeed, you may be more than a little repul-sive. Like Augustine, Kierkegaard notes that the enemy is also the neighbor, and points to the radical equality that the command intro-duces, since there is no basis to exclude anyone.[42] The love that is deflected by the command to the undesirable is no longer spontane-ous. Its basis is nothing within me but rather a divine authority that is thoroughly heteronomous (WL 96–97). Not only does the com-mand come from outside me; it is there prior to any act on my part.

In relation to God I begin with an infinite debt. Thus, like Levinas, Kierkegaard links the notion of creation to that of an obligation that precedes the I think (*WL* 102, 115; cf. 69).[43]

The depth of the affinity between Kierkegaard and Levinas can be seen if we push the analysis a radical step further. A feature of "God and Philosophy" that clearly marks it as belonging to Levinas II has barely been mentioned to this point. In speaking about the obligation I bear toward the Other, Levinas uses the images of substitution, accusation, hostage, and expiation (*GP* 164–71). Along with the notions of obsession and persecution, these are central to the argument of the central chapter of *Otherwise Than Being*, "Substitution."[44] Of the many important themes expressed by this cluster of ideas, one is especially significant in the present context. It is the answer they give to the question, What does the face of the Other say? Which Said (*Dit*) comes closest to catching the meaning of its *Geläut der Stille*?

In *Totality and Infinity*, the answer given by Levinas I is simple enough: "You shall not commit murder" (*TI* 199, 216, 262, 303). In other writings, this gets translated as "You shall not usurp my place in the sun"[45] and as "You shall not let me die alone."[46] This latter formulation goes dramatically beyond anything to be found in liberal natural rights theory (where rights tend to reduce to the right to be left alone).[47] But in explicating substitution and the notions that cluster around it, Levinas goes even further. In the trauma of substitution I am taken hostage for the Other and find myself responsible for "the misfortunes *and faults* of a neighbor . . . [this responsibility] is something completely astonishing, a responsibility that even extends to the obligation to answer *for another's freedom, to be responsible for his responsibility*" (*GP* 166–67, my emphasis; cf. *CPP* 123). Substitution means expiation, responsibility "for the other—for his distress *and his freedom*" (*GP* 169, my emphasis). Right after the dedication of *Otherwise Than Being* to the victims of the Holocaust, Levinas gives us a page of quotations, the first of which is Ezekiel 3:20. When a righteous man goes bad, "he shall die: because you did not warn him, he shall die for his sin, and the righteous deeds which he has done shall not be remembered, *but his blood will I require at your hand*" (my emphasis). The gloss on this text, again in terms of substitution and being taken hostage, tells us that we stand "accused of *what the others do* or suffer, or responsible for *what they do* or suffer" (*OB* 112, my emphasis).

This is not paternalism, which says (1) I have superior wisdom in relation to the Other and (2) the Other has a duty to be guided by my wisdom. The Levinasian text knows nothing of superior wisdom, nor of a duty the Other has to submit to my guidance. It knows only my responsibility for the Other's use or misuse of his or her freedom. It is not my job to make the Other just like me, but to help the Other to become good.

Perhaps not everyone will agree with Levinas on this point, but Kierkegaard does. His formulation of this awesome responsibility, however, is quite specific. I am commanded to love my neighbor, but "truly to love another person is to help that person to love God" (*WL* 130; cf. 107, 120–21). It is at this point, where perhaps the greatest kinship between Levinas and Kierkegaard is to be found, that we find ourselves face-to-face with their sharpest divergence. Kierkegaard insists that God is always the middle term in my relation to the neighbor (*WL* 58, 67, 107, 119–21, 142). While we could conceivably use this language to express the Levinasian notion that it is God who deflects desire toward the undesirable, Levinas is more in the habit of placing the neighbor between me and God.

This is not just a question of imagery. Kierkegaard writes, "Ultimately, love for God is the decisive factor; from this originates love for the neighbor." For this reason, the commandment "commands loving God above all else, and *then* loving the neighbor" (*WL* 57–58, my emphasis). Love for God comes first (*WL* 108, 112–13), and Kierkegaard is eloquent about the beauty and importance of this prior rendez-vous that takes place in hidden inwardness (*WL* 3–10).[48]

Levinas is very skittish about any private relation to God prior to my relation to my neighbor.[49] One reason is that he fears that religion in such a mode can encourage indifference to my neighbor or even legitimize oppression of my neighbor. But this can hardly be an objection against Kierkegaard, who includes an essay on 1 John 4:20 on the impossibility of loving God without loving the neighbor, and who presents the God who is to be loved first precisely as the God who tells me I must love my neighbor. "Shut your door and pray to God— because God is surely the highest . . . when you open the door that you shut in order to pray to God and go out the very first person you meet is the neighbor whom you *shall* love" (*WL* 51).

But perhaps another reason why Levinas will not allow love of God to be prior to love of neighbor comes to light in "God and Philoso-

phy." The God who deflects desire toward "the non-desirable proximity of others" does so as the Good that "inclines the movement it
calls forth, to turn it from the Good and orient it toward the other,
and only thus toward the Good" (*GP* 165). Kierkegaard will agree
with, nay insist on, this "only thus." It is only as loving our neighbor
that we can also love God; but Levinas is not comfortable with this
"also." He introduces the term "illeity" for the God who is "the *he* in
the depth of the you. He is good in just this eminent sense; He does
not fill me up with goods, but compels me to goodness, which is
better than goods received" (*GP* 165).

   This sounds like a theology of law without grace. But there is a
prior and deeper issue. Is this a theology without God? If God is only
"the *he* in the depth of the you," does this mean that God is not a
distinct personal being but rather the depth dimension of the human
person? Does Levinas persuasively redefine "God" to mean simply
the trans-empirical moral significance of the neighbor?[50] Levinas
writes, "[God] is neither an object *nor an interlocutor*. His absolute
remoteness, his transcendence, turns into my responsibility—non-
erotic par excellence—for the other. And this analysis implies that
God is not simply the 'first other,' the 'other par excellence,' or the
'absolutely other,' but other than the other . . . transcendent to the
point of absence, to the point of a possible confusion with the stirring
of the *there is*" (*GP* 165–66, first emphasis added).[51] The reason for
this possible confusion is clear. By refusing to let this "he" be another
"you," Levinas makes it all but impossible to distinguish "him" from
some "it." It seems that "he" is only apparently a personal pronoun,
or that its personal character is entirely derivative from the human
"you" behind which it stands.

   By contrast, Kierkegaard's God is unambiguously personal, an interlocutor who could never be confused with the *there is,* who is
other than the human Other precisely by being the "first other," the
"other par excellence," or the "absolutely other." Thus at the outset
of *Works of Love* we encounter the following prayer: "How could one
speak properly about love if *you* were forgotten, *you* God of love,
source of all love in heaven and on earth; *you* who spared nothing
but in love gave everything; *you* who are love, so that one who loves
is what he is only by being in *you*" (*WL* 5, my emphasis).

   We cannot ask philosophy to resolve this difference, for both Levinas and Kierkegaard are engaged in the task of interrupting the domi-

nant discourse of Western philosophy with reference to the biblical God, of awakening the complacency of immanence with the trauma of transcendence. It could be argued, however, that Kierkegaard's is the more genuinely biblical God. Neither when the issue is posed in terms of law and grace nor when it is posed in terms of whether God is a distinct, personal interlocutor should it be thought that the issue concerns the differences between Judaism and Christianity. For the argument would be that the God of the Jewish Bible and not just of the New Testament is (1) a God of grace as well as of law and (2) a personal being who speaks and to whom we speak (and only as such the ground of the moral significance of the neighbor). The question, at least for Jews and Christians, is whether to stick with the biblical portrayals of God as a fully personal interlocutor or to allow oneself to be pulled toward something less personal than the God of Abraham, Isaac, and Jacob. By whom? For what "reason"?

Beyond these philosophical and theological issues, there is a psychological dimension to the (apparent) disagreement. Speaking of love's hidden life with God, Kierkegaard writes, "Just as the quiet lake originates deep down in hidden springs no eye has seen, so also does a person's love originate even more deeply in God's love. If there were no gushing spring at the bottom, if God were not love, then there would be neither the little lake nor a human being's love. Just as the quiet lake originates darkly in the deep spring, so a human being's love originates mysteriously in God's love" (*WL* 9–10). In other words, "We love because he first loved us" (1 John 4:19).

The psychological point is clear enough. As both Levinas and Kierkegaard emphasize, neighbor love runs counter to our natural self-love. Taken seriously, the command to practice it is truly traumatic. How, if at all, is it possible, even imperfectly? Our psychological knowledge, both formal and informal, gives a clear answer. Only by being loved do we develop the capacity to love. Kierkegaard gives us a moral transcription of God as *mysterium tremendum et fascinans.* God is *mysterium* by remaining hidden even within the piety of hidden inwardness, *tremendum* by commanding the subordination of self-love to neighbor love, and *fascinans* by being the forgiving love that gives us both our own sense of worth and our capacity to love others. Levinas's God is the *mysterium tremendum;* but where is the *fascinans* in the Good that gives no goods but only compels to goodness? When the command to love is unaccompanied by the love that enables obedience to the command, is this not a recipe for despair and even cynicism?

Of course, the need for Kierkegaard's kind of God does not guarantee the reality of such a God. The world may be as Sartre portrays it, a godless world in which love can never be more than the demand to be loved. But Kierkegaard's analysis gives us a powerful rationale for hoping rather than fearing that there is a truly personal God, one who first loves and then commands love. If philosophy, as disinterested, pure reason, had brought to clear and distinct presence either the unreality of such a God or the unwarranted nature of belief in such a God, we might feel obliged simply to disregard hope in a kind of epistemic Stoicism. But both Levinas and Kierkegaard (and a host of others) have given us compelling reasons not to accept this self-portrait of philosophy (sometimes called Modernity).

But is it not dangerous to let reason be guided by hope? Yes indeed. The danger is that reason will either find God conveniently unreal or will find a convenient God, one who is all *fascinans* and no *tremendum* (and who usually ceases to be *mysterium* in the process). That is what Kierkegaard saw in the God of Hegel and the God of Christendom. But he tries his best to rescue the biblical God both from philosophy and from the middle class, and it is not just Climacus in the *Concluding Unscientific Postscript* but Kierkegaard throughout the entire authorship who is devoted to making the life of faith more difficult, not easier. And beyond Kierkegaard, both Augustine and Levinas stand ready to provide insights that can be helpful in guarding against a piety of convenience.

One of the insights we can gain from all three is that in the final analysis it is not a matter of insight, as if we eliminate the danger simply by understanding it. Just as, for Kierkegaard, love is always the works of love, so here faith is the work of faith. There is no reason why it should be easier to love God than to love the neighbor. "But all things excellent are as difficult as they are rare."[52]

NOTES

1. The French originals were published in 1975 and 1974, respectively, but "God and Philosophy" was given as a lecture at Catholic, Jewish, and Protestant institutions during 1973 and 1974. Henceforth cited as GP, refer-

ring to the Lingis translation, as found in *CPP*. Translations of the essay
also appear in *Emmanuel Levinas: Basic Philosophical Writings*, ed. A. T.
Peperzak, S. Critchley, and R. Bernasconi (Bloomington: Indiana University
Press, 1996); *The Levinas Reader*, ed. S. Hand (Oxford: Basil Blackwell,
1989); and *GCM*.

2. M. Heidegger, *Identity and Difference*, trans. J. Stambaugh (New
York: Harper and Row, 1969), 56.

3. Ibid., 72.

4. In *The Essence of Reasons*, trans. T. Malick (Evanston: Northwestern
University Press, 1969), Heidegger reduces these two issues to one. Transcendence is simply *Dasein*'s move beyond beings to Being.

5. On p. 162, Levinas describes this coinciding in the language of adequation, derived from both medieval realism and Husserlian phenomenology. John Llewelyn writes that for Levinas, "atheism is defined as the
restriction of thinking to intentional representation where the thinking and
what is represented may in principle be mutually adequate." *Emmanuel
Levinas: The Genealogy of Ethics* (New York: Routledge, 1995), 160.

6. In the *Concluding Unscientific Postscript*, Kierkegaard's Climacus insists that all claims to the identity of thought and being are premature for
those who exist in time and that the system betrays its absurdity by pretending to see everything *sub specie aeternitatis*.

7. E. Levinas, "Is Ontology Fundamental?" in Peperzak, Critchley, and
Bernasconi, *Emmanuel Levinas*, 2.

8. E. Levinas, "Transcendence and Intelligibility," ibid., 154.

9. And, if antecedent to being, also prior to the transcendental subjectivity to which being shows itself. Levinas's language here evokes Heidegger's
talk in *Being and Time* about knowing as a founded mode of being-in-the-
world (§ 13) and about assertion as a derivative mode of interpretation (§
33). But Levinas is headed in a different direction and will seek to decenter
the present in terms of an ur-past rather than an ultra-future.

10. What Levinas's argument suppresses is the fact that, for example,
Aquinas's rational theology, Rudolf Otto's appeal to religious experience,
and Karl Barth's theology of revelation all insist that in God's self-showing
God remains hidden. All three deny the adequacy of our knowledge of God,
in the philosophical sense of the term, though not, of course, its adequacy
for religious purposes. On religious experience, cf. E. Levinas, "Ethics as
First Philosophy," in Hand, *The Levinas Reader*, 77.

11. I retain Heidegger's term "onto-theology" because it seems to me
that only the less interesting part of his critique revolves around the ontological difference; the heart of the matter is a critique of calculative-representa-
tional thinking under the rule of the principle of sufficient reason, or so I
argue in "Overcoming Onto-theology" (in *God, the Gift, and Postmodern-*

ism, ed. J. D. Caputo and M. Scanlon [Bloomington: Indiana University Press, 1999]). Heidegger's project of overcoming metaphysics and Levinas's project of overcoming ontology are deeply akin in their rejection of the primacy of theoretical intentionality.

12. In his critique of Levinas's critique of thematization, Theo de Boer seems to accept at face value the assimilation of Pascal to Plato. "Theology and Philosophy of Religion According to Levinas," in *Ethics as First Philosophy,* ed. Adriaan T. Peperzak (New York: Routledge, 1995); see especially p. 168 in relation to p. 162. It should be noted that Levinas does not completely distance himself from Pascal. Although he does not mention the heart, he describes his own move beyond ontology as a move "among reasons that 'reason' does not know, and which have not begun in philosophy" (*GP* 172).

13. See *Pseudo-Dionysius: The Complete Works,* trans. C. Luibheid (New York: Paulist Press, 1987), 49–50, 53, 135, 138, 263.

14. There is no explicit reference to Pseudo-Dionysius or negative theology here, but the implication is quite direct in the light of Pseudo-Dionysius's description of what lies beyond being as "the truly mysterious darkness of unknowing" (ibid., 137).

15. This is why, although he distances himself from Heidegger, Pascal, and Pseudo-Dionysius, Levinas associates himself with Kant, whom he sees as freeing ethics from ontology (*OB* 129).

16. E. Levinas, *Nine Talmudic Readings,* trans. A. Aronowicz (Bloomington: Indiana University Press, 1990), 21.

17. M. Heidegger, "Language," in *Poetry, Language, Thought,* trans. A. Hofstadter (New York: Harper and Row, 1871), 207. Cf. "The Nature of Language," in *On the Way to Language,* trans. P. Herz and J. Stambaugh (New York: Harper and Row, 1971), 108. Robert Bernasconi discusses this theme in *The Question of Language in Heidegger's History of Being* (Atlantic Highlands, N.J.: Humanities Press, 1985). When Heidegger says "*die Sprache spricht,*" there is an obvious, if surprising, affinity with structuralism, and Levinas is saying no to both.

18. Heidegger, "The Way to Language," in *On the Way to Language,* 123.

19. On the doubling of thought and being, see *CPP* 69–70. On the notion of testimony, see E. Levinas, "Truth of Disclosure and Truth of Testimony," in Peperzak, Critchley, and Bernasconi, *Emmanuel Levinas.*

20. For Levinas's distinction between the sacred and the holy, see "Desacralization and Disenchantment," in *Nine Talmudic Readings.* On proximity, see "Language and Proximity" in *CPP.*

21. Cf. *OB* 122–23: "The Good assigns the subject . . . to approach the other, the neighbor. This is an assignation to a non-erotic proximity, to a

desire of the non-desirable, to a desire of the stranger in the neighbor. It is outside of concupiscence."

22. Isaiah recognizes this and responds to the divine epiphany, not with awe before the sublime but with guilt before the holy. Only after seraphic cleansing and absolution—"your guilt has departed and your sin is blotted out" (6:6)—is Isaiah able to respond "Here am I" (6:8; *me voici*).

23. G. W. F. Hegel, *Phenomenology of Spirit*, trans. A. V. Miller (Oxford: Clarendon Press, 1977), 32. This is, incidentally, as realistic a formula as one could want. Hegel describes scientific surrender as "absorbed in its object" and "immersed in the material."

24. M. Heidegger, "What Is Metaphysics?" in *Existentialism from Dostoevsky to Sartre*, rev. ed., ed. W. Kaufmann (New York: New American Library, 1975), 243.

25. M. Heidegger, *Discourse on Thinking*, trans. J. M. Anderson and E. H. Freund (New York: Harper and Row, 1966), 54–61.

26. See note 15 above.

27. See the paragraph concluding with note 6 above.

28. The phrase quoted here is both the title of an important essay in which Levinas summarizes much of his thinking and the title of a book of essays on the importance of Levinas for philosophy, literature, and religion. See notes 10 and 12 above.

29. In his 1921 lectures on Augustine and Neoplatonism, Heidegger stresses, over against the Neoplatonic elements in the *Confessions,* the emphasis on the strenuous difficulty of the life of faith. See M. Heidegger, *Gesamtausgabe,* Bd. 60, *Phänomenologie des Religiösen Lebens* (Frankfurt a.M.: Klostermann, 1995). For context and analysis, see J. D. Caputo, "Toward a Postmodern Theology of the Cross: Augustine, Heidegger, Derrida," in *Postmodern Philosophy and Christian Thought,* ed. M. Westphal (Bloomington: Indiana University Press, 1999), and my "Heidegger's 'Theologische' Jugendschriften," *Research in Phenomenology* 27 (1997): 247–61.

30. Bach's cantata BWV 140.

31. For an expanded version of this text, see Mark 13:32–37.

32. For Heidegger's commentary on the passage in 1 Thessalonians, see his 1920–21 lectures, *Einleitung in die Phänomenologie der Religion,* in *Gesamtausgabe,* Bd. 60, pp. 102–5.

33. Quotations from Augustine will be by book and chapter from *The Confessions of St. Augustine,* trans. R. Warner (New York: New American Library, 1963).

34. The biblical quotation is from Ephesians 5:14. Some scholars think this is an early Christian hymn based on Isaiah 60:1: "Arise, shine; for your light has come, and the glory of the Lord has risen upon you."

35. Heidegger accordingly sharply distinguishes Augustinian from Cartesian self-certainty. *Gesamtausgabe,* Bd. 60, pp. 298–99.

36. Cf. Romans 13:8–10, Galatians 5:14, and James 2:8.

37. N.B.: In the two texts from Romans, Kierkegaard thematizes the paragraph just prior to the one that triggered Augustine's conversion.

38. S. Kierkegaard, *Works of Love*, trans. H. V. Hong and E. H. Hong (Princeton: Princeton University Press, 1995), 24. Cited henceforth as *WL*.

39. *WL* 47–50, 59, 109, 120, 128, 146, 198–201.

40. Cf. S. Kierkegaard, *Either/Or*, trans. H. V. Hong and E. H. Hong (Princeton: Princeton University Press, 1987), 2:49, 91.

41. Levinas's analysis of enjoyment is pertinent here. See *TI* 122–51; *OB* 61–74.

42. *WL* 19, 58, 60, 68–74, 81. On the theme of equality in Kierkegaard's writings, see G. Outka, "Equality and the Fate of Theism in Modern Culture," *Journal of Religion* 67 (July 1987): 275–88; and Outka, "Equality and Individuality: Thoughts on Two Themes in Kierkegaard," *Journal of Religious Ethics* 10 (Fall 1982): 171–203. My own discussion of this theme in *Postscript* is found in *Becoming a Self: A Reading of Kierkegaard's "Concluding Unscientific Postscript"* (West Lafayette, Ind.: Purdue University Press, 1996).

43. Kierkegaard also suggests a philosophy of language in which constative, assertive, indicative speech acts lose their privilege before the divine command. "The divine authority of the Gospel does not speak to one person about another . . . no, when the Gospel speaks, it speaks to the single individual. It does not speak *about* us human beings, you and me, but speaks *to* us human beings" (*WL* 14).

44. This chapter was first presented as a lecture in 1967. The notions of substitution and hostage are already found in talmudic studies from 1964 and 1966. See Levinas, *Nine Talmudic Readings*, 49, 85, 87.

45. Cf., e.g., "Dialogue with Emmanuel Levinas" and "Bad Conscience and the Inexorable," in *Face to Face with Levinas*, ed. R. A. Cohen (Albany: SUNY, 1986), 24 and 38, respectively; "Emmanuel Levinas," in *French Philosophers in Conversation*, ed. R. Mortley (London: Routledge, 1991), 19; and "Ethics as First Philosophy," in Hand, *The Levinas Reader*, 82.

46. Cf. "Dialogue with Emmanuel Levinas," 24; "Bad Conscience and the Inexorable," 38; "Emmanuel Levinas," 15; and "Beyond Intentionality," in *Philosophy in France Today*, ed. A. Montefiore (Cambridge: Cambridge University Press, 1983), 112.

47. For an attempt to take rights theory beyond this limitation, see H. Shue, *Basic Rights: Subsistence, Affluence, and U.S. Foreign Policy* (Princeton: Princeton University Press, 1980).

48. There is a double hiddenness. My God relation is not a public event. It takes place behind closed doors even if I am among others in a house of worship. And God remains hidden from any brazen and presumptuous

inquisitiveness that would seek to see God (*WL* 9–10). Most emphatically, the priority of the God relation is not the return of the primacy of theory, knowledge, and the I think.

49. I have discussed this skittishness in "Levinas' Teleological Suspension of the Religious," in Peperzak, *Ethics as First Philosophy.*

50. John Llewelyn gives just such a reading of Levinas in *Emmanuel Levinas: The Genealogy of Ethics,* chapter 12. For my discussion of this issue in the context of "Phenomenon and Enigma," see "The Transparent Shadow: Kierkegaard and Levinas in Dialogue," in *Kierkegaard in Post/Modernity,* ed. M. Matustik and M. Westphal (Bloomington: Indiana University Press, 1995).

51. On the *there is* (*il y a*), cf. *EE* 57–85, *TI* 190–91, *OB* 162–65, and E. Levinas, *Difficult Freedom: Essays on Judaism,* trans. S. Hand (Baltimore: Johns Hopkins University Press, 1991), 292..

52. This is the final sentence of Spinoza's *Ethics.*

10

The Voice without Name: Homage to Levinas

Jean-Luc Marion

THE FACE AND THE FAÇADE

AMONG THE MANY radical innovations that Emmanuel Levinas has introduced into phenomenology, or imposed on it, there is one which seems most important: that of the appeal. In effect, the appeal has achieved the rank of a concept, or more precisely, to speak the language of the early Husserl, it is a founding phenomenological act (and thus is itself not founded). This imposition became virtually inevitable as soon as Levinas had accomplished two prior revolutions. First was a reversal of centrifugal intentionality, which moves from the ego to the object, into a counter-intentionality moving back toward the ego. Next was a replacement of the existing object with a face which is the origin of this counter-intentionality, and which thus, strictly speaking, does not have to exist. Henceforth, among and outside the swarming mass of phenomena on which is exercised my intentionality, constituting them as objects, there can also be distinguished counter-phenomena: the face, or faces. *Counter-phenomena,* because their appearing consists less in giving themselves to be seen directly, or countenanced—what Levinas elsewhere captures with the word "façade" (*TeI* 167/*TI* 192)—than in imposing on my own gaze the weight of a glory irreducible to intentional objectivity. And thus, such phenomena—faces—do not merely offer this or that particular spectacle among others, but break into the middle of the field of visibility accessible and originating from my gaze, with what is inaccessible or invisible as such, bright flashes from a luminous source, dazzling me, fixing my gaze, throwing it back on itself. "Responsibility for the Other—going against intentionality and the will which intentionality does not succeed in dissimulating—signifies not the disclosure of a given and its reception, but the exposition of me to the Other, prior to all decision"—and, we would add, prior to all vision (*AE* 180/*OB* 141). Such a reversal of intentionality and phenomenality, passing from the object which is visible and aimed at to the face which aims and is thus non-visible, radically alters the entire horizon of phenomenological analysis, as we have all indeed noticed. In that much, we have all become Levinasians, and definitively.

However, this conclusion raises a considerable difficulty: if the face does not properly give itself to be seen in the same sense as does an object or a being, how does it come to me, or reach me at all? If one concedes, whether hypothetically or according to the thesis proposed by Heidegger in section 7 of *Sein und Zeit,* that the concept of "phenomenon" is understood as "that which shows itself,"[1] is it still possible for the face to pretend to the plenary rank of phenomenon? Without a doubt, or at least perhaps, if one undertakes to clarify, going beyond Heidegger—which is to say against him—precisely how a phenomenon can show *itself,* how it can make itself a phenomenon (or phenomenalize itself) not only as such or as itself, but also and above all from itself. What *self* can a phenomenon make use of (and serve) in such a manner that it is able to show *itself*? This *self* cannot yet bear on any subjectivity, nor on the least ipseity or "mineness" (*Jemeinigkeit*), since for Heidegger all of these concern ordinary phenomena and not *Dasein.* This *self* could do so still less for Levinas, since for him the phenomenon par excellence which it is a matter here of justifying is precisely not that of one's own subjectivity (this ipseity of the type characterized by "mineness"), but that of an Other of which one can be assured of only a single phenomenal trait, namely, that it transgresses, suspends, in short defeats, (my) "mineness." The *self* according to which the phenomenon shows *itself* (in general or that of the Other) thus remains, as such, enigmatic or indeterminate. How, then, to think the mode in which it can show *itself*? We propose, by way of radical hypothesis, that the *self* of the *self-showing* can be legitimated with phenomenological rigor only insofar as it is found returned to the *self* of a *self-giving.* In other words, no phenomenon can show itself in itself and from itself unless it first gives itself in itself and from itself: it is this givenness— *donation*[2]—which assures the original self, and which permits "showingness" (*monstration*). *Self*-giving permits *self*-showing. The question of how the face shows itself is thus a matter of determining how it gives itself. For not all phenomena are given in the same mode.

THE APPEAL

The mode of givenness of the face is determined by Levinas without ambiguity—it gives itself in the mode of the appeal: "It is precisely in this call to my responsibility by the face which assigns me, which commands me, which calls to me; it is in this placing into question that the Other is my neighbor." Or: "In the appeal which addresses me in the face of the Other, I grasp in an immediate fashion the graces of love: spirituality, the lived experience of authentic humanity."[3] Formally, one might say that phenomenality thus passes from vision to speech, or from a vision which sees, produced by the ego, to speech which is heard, which is to say, received by the ego. One should not underestimate the importance of this turn, since the intervention of hearing in the place and instead of vision breaks with the metaphysical primacy of the gaze, of the *intuitus* which regards presence only because it maintains, or guards a present (*qui ne régarde la présence que parce qu'il y garde un présent*). But one should also not underestimate the difficulty which this involves, for the appeal neither shows something nor directly shows itself, but only indicates that from which it originates and to which it testifies: the face remains non-visible, in retreat. To receive the face implies not so much to see it as to undergo the impact or feel the shock of its arrival. The *I*, placed in the accusative by the assault of counter-intentionality, does not discover the face as a new phenomenon which is as accessible and thus identifiable as all the others, but simply discovers itself as affected, touched, and shaken by it. Hence, the face does not befall me without identifying itself through its own specific form of manifestation. It gives itself, perhaps, but precisely what does it show that I can identify? Does it show *itself* otherwise than itself? This difficulty can be summarized as follows: how can one assign an identity to the origin of the appeal such that one can specify which face is involved each time, but without thereby reducing it to a visible phenomenon in the mode of a spectacle? Can the impact exerted by the appeal and the shock in which it occurs—thus attaining its specificity with regard to common, visible phenomena—preserve this extreme abstraction even while also permitting itself to be identified as such, that is to say even in giving, along with itself, that by which the appeal is accomplished? Does the appeal say only the pure Saying of the appeal, or does it also achieve and allow to appear an inevitable Said, the Said which says—or rather, who says—the identity of the one who appeals (*ce qui appelle*)? One must guard against folding this question back on the better-known opposition between the Saying and the Said, since in a certain sense the latter awaits and depends on the intelligibility of the former; for if "no Said equals the sincerity of the Saying," can this sincerity, which "is not reducible to anything ontic, or anything ontological," still accomplish itself—say itself, show itself, and even give itself (*AE* 183/*OB* 143–44)? Is this still a matter of phenomenality, or must one already renounce seeing what this is, in order to escape the vision which sees only a visible spectacle? What does it mean for me to become "someone who, *in the absence of anyone else*, is called to be someone, and cannot slip away from this call" (*AE* 68/*OB* 53, my emphasis)? Must one then admit that I am called by nothing, by no Other? Certainly not, since it is rather that the Other comes to me without being anything at all. But then, in order to call me, must the Other leave its identity—as definitively inaccessible—in suspense? It seems, in fact, that Levinas has not only admitted an ambiguity but knowingly emphasized it. For the face which appeals can be assigned equally to the Other or to God, thus avowing the indecision of its origin as well as the necessity of questioning both identity and individuation. To evoke "the wonder of the I claimed *by God* in the face of the neighbor" (*DVI* 265) amounts to suggesting that the claim which refers to the face—to that of the Other—effectively goes back to God, in the fashion of some strange ethical occasionalism in which the effective cause (God) recovers and would always precede a simply occasional cause (the other person), so that one can escape this murderous challenge only by admitting either that the appeal does not coincide with the face, or else that responsibility remains originally dual. But do these solutions not in fact dissolve the very thing they were to protect? Similarly, how to understand the following sequence: "What is called the *word of God*—does it not come to me in the demand which addresses me and claims me, and . . . tears through the form of generality under which alone the individual who resembles me appears to me and shows himself, in order thus to occur as the face of *the other person*?" Who (or what) calls—God and his word, or the Other and his or her face? As clarifying and magnificent as it is, does not the emergence of the theme of the *à-Dieu* nonetheless hypostatize this ambiguity to the point of rendering it exemplary and insurmountable? "The *à-Dieu* is not a process of being: in the appeal, I am referred to *the other person* through whom it signifies, to the neighbor for whom I have to fear."[4] What does it mean that the appeal can and must refer me to an Other (*autre*) as well as to its agent, the other person who, however, it does not make act toward me? Does the appeal come from the other person, or does it refer me to the Other only from an other than the other person—no doubt God?

ANONYMITY

Confronted by this ambiguity, we are disposed to only two attitudes. One can renounce the phenomenological innovation of the appeal, and conclude that since it does not show us anything which is, it does not show itself and thus does not give itself. Or, following an injunction which Levinas himself stated once, as if in passing, one would have to concede that "the formal structure of interpellation has to be developed" (*TeI* 41/*TI* 69). We will attempt to follow this second path. This means recognizing, hypothetically, the indetermination of the appeal, its anonymity in principle. And in fact, this anonymity had already been established by Heidegger. At first he does so positively, in the context of the existential analytic of *Dasein*, where the call of conscience occurs in saying nothing and only in saying nothing has its proper impact on *Dasein*, thus reconducting it to its authentic mode of being: "*What* does the conscience call [what speaks in the mode of appeal, *Was* ruft?] to him to whom it appeals [*dem Angerufenen*]? Taken strictly, nothing. The call asserts nothing, gives no information about world-events, has nothing to tell. Least of all does it try to set going a 'soliloquy' in the Self to which it has appealed. 'Nothing' gets called *to* [*zu*-gerufen] this Self, but it has been *summoned* [*aufgerufen*] to itself—that is, to its ownmost potentiality-for-Being."[5] Here, not only does the call not decide between God and the other person, assigning *Dasein* only to itself, but it functions precisely to close transcendence into itself, extinguishing every external claim, disqualifying it as a pure and simple fall back into an inauthentic mode of being. This understanding of the appeal reveals just how far its anonymity can (and here must) go: beyond every identifiable origin, but above all beyond all assignable exteriority. The appeal works, and can only work on nothing other than the ipseity of the self, which it does not fissure but in fact requires.

One thus understands better why Heidegger would later take up this anonymity again, but negatively and polemically. To be sure, he does mention an appeal which calls to an other than *Dasein,* in the occurrence, the appeal of the Father: "The Christian sees the humanity of man, the *humanitas* of *homo,* in contradistinction to *Deitas.* He is the man of the history of redemption who, as a 'child of God,' hears and accepts the call of the Father [*den Anspruch des Vaters*] in Christ." But this appeal, identifiable and identified, remains secondary (ontical) and superficial (non-ontological). It must therefore grant priority to another call, the call of Being—*Anspruch des Seins.*[6] This advance substitution of being for the other person or God—for the *à-Dieu*—as the origin of the appeal elicits at least two remarks. Note first how it confirms the anonymity of the appeal: the same event which, in the same form, affects and defeats the autonomous ipseity of the *I* can also move the entire length of the spectrum of possible expressions, including the gap between the finite and the infinite, and between the non-ontological and the ontological. One thus sees clearly that the appeal admits no fixed identity, and that it calls from wherever it wills, like the Spirit which blows from wherever it wills. The working of the appeal is such as to imply that its origin remains fluid, always wandering; one cannot begin from the shock of the appeal and trace it back to some univocally identifiable source. Anyone can do it—anyone can make the appeal. This brings us to a second remark which, moreover, contradicts the first: the fluidity of the appeal remains masked by Heidegger, since he assigns it—without justification—to Being and only Being. Heidegger marks the anonymity of the appeal with a disqualification of Being's competitors (the other person, God, the *à-Dieu*, etc.), but he also immediately masks this gesture to the profit of one of its faces, or rather to the profit of the non-face which offers Being. When, in a recent work, I pointed out this ambiguity, some critics believed or wanted to believe that I attempted to reverse the Heideggerian position: in place of privileging the call of Being, I thus would have—imitating the ambiguous gesture of Levinas in favor of the appeal *à-Dieu*—privileged the appeal of God. However, it was evidently not a matter there of such a simplistic reversal, but rather of reestablishing—or in fact of conquering—the appeal as such, with no other specification than the pure exertion of its simple and sufficient anonymity: "In the end, what seems more essential than this (reduction by) claim is finally the reduction of every claim to the pure form of the appeal."[7] The pure form of the appeal: this formula indicates that in order to deploy itself as that which lays a claim on me, it is necessary only that its impact on me places me in the accusative and in fact the dative, receiving thus what gives itself, but without posing preliminary conditions for identifying what gives itself—without presuming that it is a matter of being, the other person, the *à-Dieu*, or the Father. Receiving the appeal does not require breaking through anonymity, but rather confronting its voice without name. In the end, that which Heidegger designates in passing as a "voice without sound—*lautlose Stimme*"[8]—must be received as what Claudel refers to as "this unknown speech whose work and pressure I feel in myself."[9]

Plainly, this thesis is susceptible to one general objection, seemingly of great weight since it has been raised so often: does my summons by the appeal, even admitting that it is accomplished only in my response—thus following a word from Levinas: "the appeal is understood in the response"[10]—suppose some instance or agency which performs it, some first or final pole which makes the claim and whose initiative tears, by silence or by sound, into what comes after the "subject," a subject which we henceforth refer to as devoted (*l'adonné*), as this one who responds to the gift (*le don*) of the appeal? In short, it would be necessary that the devoted always devotes itself to . . . And thus, one must inevitably ask: who or what summons, invokes, or surprises the devoted? This question develops into a suspicion about the identity of what could exert the claim: God (by revelation), the other person (by obligation), being (by the event), life (by auto-affection), and so forth. Does not this simple and abstract description of the appeal in general dissimulate, and moreover sometimes quite badly, one of these instances—in this case, the first: God—a nostalgia in the entire enterprise, censured to be sure, but all the better to liberate it? Is it not the case, according to this hypothesis, that the appeal and the response, such that they bring givenness to its term, in fact aim purely and simply at restoring a quasi-metaphysical system (*dispositif*)? Such a transcendent principle, finally, a principle which is in other words self-founded, would give rise to a subjectivity which is derived and yet always privileged, since it would remain in charge of a common phenomenality.

Let us consider this point. We maintain that it belongs essentially and by principle to the appeal that it give itself, but without giving its name. Several arguments permit us to establish this claim. First, the appeal comes from a saturated phenomenon,[11] or what we might also think of here as a paradox; now the paradox can be declined into four perfectly distinct types—event, idol, flesh, and icon—and yet each of them can accomplish the same and unique type of appeal. Thus, the description of the appeal as such does not depend on the specification of this or that paradox. Consequently, one could not, beginning from an appeal, directly return to this or that type of paradox, and still less to identify its name there. At any rate, this indifference of the appeal to the type of saturated phenomenon which provokes it finds additional confirmation in the possibility of a paradox of paradoxes—revelation—in which are concentrated all such types: here, the appeal—if perchance it is indeed borne out, for phenomenology can only describe its possibility, not establish it as a fact—would bear no single name because it would assume them all. Its anonymity would be reinforced by the very excess of the paradox, which would require an infinite denomination; thus, no appeal would offer a name *less* than that which occurs in a phenomenon of revelation. The name par excellence of God, such as it is revealed to Moses, attests precisely to the impertinence of every essential or descriptive name, reducing itself to an empty tautology—"I am who am"—which opens the way to an endless litany of names. And the voice which reveals, reveals exactly because it remains without voice, or more exactly because it remains without Name. The Name gives itself only in saying itself without any name, thus and always, according to Denys, "*anonumon kai polyonumon*,"[12] or according to Levinas, "The word God is still absent from the phrase in which God is for the first time involved in words. It does not all state 'I believe in God.' To bear witness to God is precisely not to state this extraordinary word, as if glory could be lodged in a theme and posited as a thesis, or become being's essence" (*AE* 190/*OB* 149). Thus, far from having to fear that such an appeal leads surreptitiously to the nomination of a transcendent *numen* and a—misgotten—turn toward "theology," one must conclude that, to the contrary, every phenomenon of revelation (in its possibility) and above all a Revelation (in its actuality) would imply the radical anonymity of that which appeals. This, then, is an anonymity in accordance with the paradox which appeals.

The second argument for the anonymity of the appeal is drawn from the definition of the gift in general, at least as understood according to givenness: the gift appears as such precisely when it is recovered in the reduction, and one of the figures of this reduced gift is realized exactly by placing the one who gives between parentheses—as with the inheritance received from a deceased either misunderstood or unknown, the one who gives while ignorant of both oneself and what one gives (artist, lover, actor, player, politician, etc.), the gods who give "without envy" or calculation, or the settlement of a debt always already there, incommensurable and disequilibrated (as in life received, and perhaps death to give).[13] If the gift can—indeed, if it must—give itself without identifying the one who gives, *a fortiori,* the appeal can and must accomplish itself without needing or giving its name. The reduced gift, the gift which has been legitimated phenomenologically, deploys itself according to an immanent and intrinsic givenness, which does not at all require one who gives, nor even its identity. It is worth repeating that such an appeal bears the contingency of the pure given (including the determinations of arrival, accomplished fact, and incident) all the more in that it emerges without a known, identified, and named donator. Hence, from the reduced gift emerges the anonymous gift of the appeal.

THE RESPONDENT

A third argument in favor of establishing an appeal which gives itself without name, moreover, one which justifies the first two, is drawn from the very articulation of the appeal and the response. Phenomenologically, the appeal must remain anonymous because it never functions to name itself but only appeals to the respondent to respond, and thus to excite in the respondent his or her ultimate function. For only the appeal makes the respondent, and without having to presuppose it or, still less, make itself known to him or her. Before the appeal, there is in effect not yet any listener, no witness, no devotee who could always already hear the name of the appeal; the sole and primary function of the appeal is to convoke such a witness and not at all to say itself in saying its name—an enterprise which would be not merely in vain but, in all rigor, impossible. And if it is ever necessary to give a name to the appeal, this would be the office of neither the appeal itself nor the one who gives, but the response, or the one who receives: the response recognizes that which the appeal gives to it, and thus identifies it itself. Consequently, one might eventually return across the declared gift in order to be able to name the appeal for the first time. The appeal calls for the response, always itself: it thus receives its eventual name only from that response, which however gives it afterwards. Only the "Here I am!" of the response can raise the appeal to the level of a "You are there!," thus attributing a name to it. This rule is verified in, for instance, the political appeal (the event): that which raises it remains, at the very moment in which it does so, abstract—which is to say almost completely unknown: "I appeared to myself, alone and deprived of everything";[14] but those who take this appeal upon themselves (thus, its devoted recipients) name it strictly in the measure that they name themselves—"Republicans," "Bonapartists," "Leninists," "Gaullists," and so forth. Accordingly, in their response they give a full name to what or who appeals. But inversely, for those who have not heard at all, or who, having heard, have not at all wished to hear, the absence of a response maintains the anonymity of the appeal. This is also true of the loving appeal (the icon): when she appears, a woman—entering into public visibility—in her charm (even if only mediocre) exerts (or attempts to exert) an appeal; however, even if everyone does see it (or could see it), not everyone responds to it in the same way, not all consider her equally appealing. Some gazes slip over and past her without seeing her, without envisaging her, without giving a name to her face. Here again, the anonymity of the appeal can be said to result from a default of response. And yet, if one of the onlookers does take the appeal of that woman's face upon himself—if their gazes truly meet—such that "it was like an apparition" to him, the response will confer a unique name (and perhaps a surname) to the appeal, because the devoted will permit himself to be governed entirely by what he will receive: "She was seated, in the middle of the bench, all alone; or at least he did not distinguish anyone else, with his dazzled eyes."[15] The same could be said when one hears a painting or sees a melody (the idol), is befallen by feelings of anxiety, joy, or suffering (the flesh)—in short, of all paradoxes in which the appeal is named according to the measure of the devoted, which is to say in the response. This same process can also serve as the guiding thread leading into phenomenality: that which is given (the appeal) in a first moment does not yet show itself, thus remaining anonymous. It shows itself only if the devoted converts it into a phenomenon (in the response), at which point it takes on visibility and perhaps receives a name. It has an anonymity, then, awaiting and depending on the response.

The anonymity of who or what appeals therefore does not weaken the concept of the appeal, but in fact confirms it: since *I* recognize *myself* claimed and "interlocated" (*interloqué*)[16] before all consciousness of my subjectivity—which, moreover, results precisely from this—all knowledge of the identity of the one who appeals will be added after the fact of the claim, and thus will never precede it as if already presupposed by it. At the origin is accomplished the claim, not the consciousness of this claim by the "interlocated," and still less the knowledge by which one can identify who or what appeals. At any rate, the surprise, thus the loss of knowledge, prohibits the "interlocated" from understanding and knowing the claim as a determined and designated object. To discover *myself* claimed, or convoked, would be wholly without rigor if the surprise did not deprive me of myself—at least for a time, and sometimes definitively—in the instant of convocation by what and who exerts the appeal. Reciprocally, if I knew from the beginning that it is being, the other person, God, or life which convokes me, I would escape in advance the complete status of the devoted, since, after all, this would spare me all surprise. Knowing in advance (or at least immediately) with whom or what I am involved through this word I have heard, I would also know (what) or respond (to whom) from the posteriority of a constitution, or within the equality of a dialogue, but without the "interlocated" passivity of a surprise. In short, I would make recourse to an *I*, which delivers itself from the status of a *me*. Anonymity thus belongs strictly to the conditions for the possibility of the appeal because it is what defines the appeal's unconditioned poverty: in accordance with the principle of insufficient reason, the appeal does not have to be known in order to be recognized, and need not identify itself in order to exert itself. This poverty alone is capable of truly wounding the "subject," exiling it from all authenticity, so that it is truly devoted. Strictly speaking, an appeal which would say its name would no longer appeal, but instead present the one who appeals, delivering it back to the simple visibility of an occupant of the world, stifling the voice with the evidence of a spectacle.[17] An appeal truly resonates only in those voices which, to the contrary, show absolutely nothing, not even the image excited by a sonorous vibration; the appeal truly sounds, in other words, in "the soundless trumpets which everyone hears."[18]

THE APPEAL WITHOUT NAME: THE FATHER

The appeal without name attests to itself, strangely enough, in the situation which at first sight seems most plainly an exception to it: paternity. Since a father gives a proper name to his offspring, it seems evident to suppose that he calls them and that this call always bears a name: his own. Yet this description remains inadequate to the things themselves, for it approaches them from neither the father's real point of view nor from that of his offspring, but from a perspective which is phenomenologically unjustifiable—that of a third person inexplicably disposing information proper to each of the two poles, which, as such, nevertheless remain irreducible. If, to the contrary, one applies oneself to a description from the real perspective of one of the two poles taken separately, the situation is transformed completely. The father calls his child, gives the child a name, his own; his appeal thus has a name and consists in giving a name. This much is in keeping with common appearance. However, it still remains to understand why he thus gives a name. One might respond that this is evident, since after all the child does not yet have one and so remains anonymous. But in that case, how and by what right does the father give his name to a child without a name and thus, strictly speaking, offering no indication that the child is indeed of this father? One will respond again that this is evident from the fact that the father knows from intimate experience that this child is born of his efforts, of his own wife, in his own house, and in his presence. As excellent as they are, these reasons nonetheless suffer from a weakness which is well known: by definition, and in fact by temporal delay, by the initial delay between conception and birth, biological paternity is without an immediate and direct proof, and thus always uncertain (not to mention the fact that through technical advances it will become more and more so in the near future). Every child is naturally born of his or her mother, whereas strictly speaking he or she is born of an unknown father. The father only finds the child, which is to say that he only receives the child eventually. Likewise, it has been admitted since time immemorial that the sole proof of paternity resides in the juridical recognition of the child by the father. Paternity is accomplished symbolically, and thus neither first of all nor ever biologically. One becomes a father—in every case, and not only legal adoption—by recognizing and claiming as one's own a child both discovered and natural. Adoption remains the normative figure of paternity. At this point, the question becomes: what can motivate a father to recognize a child who does not bear his name, since that child is as yet without any name whatsoever? Why not behave as do some animal species, and indeed some allegedly developed sectors of society, and deny one's fatherhood, leaving the child without a paternal name? Here it will be asserted, and not without reason, that this marks a point where powerful ethical forces intervene (responsibility, fidelity, altruism, the shaping of a destiny, etc.), yet one might just as well ask how these forces can become constraining motives for a personal and voluntary decision, since sometimes they are not enough. In the final account, there is only one correct response to this question: the father is defined as a father from or according to the appeal to recognize his paternity, which is exerted on him by the infant (and the whole context surrounding the child's birth). The infant calls silently to the father to give the child his name—the father's name, the name which the child does not have, which is and yet which will never be the child's own. The infant thus exerts an anonymous appeal on the father, so that when the father recognizes himself as father, when he reaches the point of recognizing the child as his own, the point of giving the child his name, he is—in naming—about to render a response to an appeal. The name given to the infant is nothing other than the father's response to an appeal without name. The anonymity of the appeal (and of the infant) neither contradicts nor stands in the way of paternity, but constitutes the field and the stakes of its possibility. The father will thus give birth to his own paternity in the measure that he will respond to the anonymous appeal of the infant with a nominative response. This nomination is deployed henceforth according to a history: first the father gives his own name (patronymic), but also a Christian name, both of which are therefore borrowed; next he will give a real identity, through speech and language, but also community, religion, culture, worldview, and so forth. Without ever ceasing to give the child a real name through the indefinite succession of his responses, the father will nonetheless never extinguish the anonymity of the initial appeal. To the contrary, everything he does can only underscore it, since all of these identities will be swallowed into the gulf of the original absence of name, and without filling it up. In the end, the child "will take leave of his father and mother," exceeding every given name and response in order to finally confront his or her own anonymity alone. At that moment, the child will become an adult— someone who knows one's anonymity and must give it a name oneself. From the father's point of view, the child therefore gives him- or herself as an anonymous appeal and always remains so.

THE APPEAL WITHOUT NAME: THE CHILD

At the same time, it also customary to say that the child names his or her father, and all the more easily so since the child bears the father's name as his or her own; if the child is named like the father and as the father names the child, then the father can be said to exert an appeal gifted with a name—one which calls the child to and through a name. This much is in keeping with general appearances. It remains, however, to understand it. For if the father is without any biological certitude of his paternity, then the child is also without any immediate and direct proof of his son- or daughtership. The child must accept it on the father's faith and following the symbolic argument of recognition by him. What actually transpires in the child's adoption of the father's name wagers first on the father's adoption of the child. The child thus bears—like a heavy burden or a pressing yoke—a name which is not his or her own. This name, and the other names which complete it, come to the child as a fact always already accomplished for and without him or her, which is to say against the child. For it is proper to the proper name that it is improper: it alienates. How does this improper name exert itself? First of all, as an appeal. In naming me like my father, the name returns me to him, like an obsessive paradigm; it matters little whether I love him or hate him, admire him or pity him, since in any case I can identify myself only by referring myself to him. Before me, more inside me than is myself, this name names me by calling me to him. My historicity declares itself to the degree that, by acceptance or refusal, acquisition or loss, I add responses to this unique appeal of the name. And yet, this name which makes that appeal remains strangely anonymous. To begin with, it does not tell me who I am, since it belongs first to another, my father: in this sense, its anonymity is a direct result of the alienation that it imposes on me. Next, it also does not tell me who my father is: far from identifying him, it dissimulates him and even erects an unknown father: everything that I know of my father I have learned from his stories, his confessions, and his lies, as well as frequently from narratives supplied by others—in short, I have learned about him by encountering his name, and then deconstructing it or corroborating it whenever he does not speak, whenever he leaves something unsaid. The name of the father masks his identity, substituting itself incessantly for empirical individuality. This name does not merely show me nothing, but conceals. One may therefore say of this appeal by which I am named, that it is anonymous, or better, antonymous. A father gives himself to a child as an appeal which does not even say his name, but rather says only a name—and the otherness of the name (*un nom autre*).

One could without difficulty recognize this anonymity of the voice that appeals in other situations taking up what we improperly call intersubjectivity, but also still more so in situations dealing with painting, flesh, or the event (the other types of paradox). We will not insist on this here, instead leaving it to others to complete such analyses with the appropriate examples. Here, it is important rather to emphasize that the anonymity of the appeal opens a historicity of response. Or, invoking a statement from Levinas, "Paternity is produced as an innumerable future" (*TeI* 256/*TI* 279). In effect, since the appeal no more assures the nomination of its identity than that which gives itself shows itself by itself, the response could never—even if multiplied indefinitely—do justice to the anonymity of the appeal. The response can always be suspected—can always suspect itself—of having identified the appeal badly or only partially, of not having accomplished its injunction perfectly, of not having exploited every possibility. The appeal excites the response, but never appeases it. Each advance remains a commencement, and the response is never done with recommencing (like desire). Only it begins to say that which silences the appeal, but it can never say this all the way to the end. Thus is opened its historicity. The appeal gives, or rather constitutes of itself, the given, but it still does not show itself: one can therefore consider it the mark of a limit, a destiny (*un destin*)—a message which remains unseen and a voice which breaks. The response that the devoted gives, and in which his or her selfhood is fully received, attempts to make that limit which gives itself without showing itself show itself, after all. But, since by definition the givenness of the self does not manifest itself, it is in fact masked, regardless of whether it dissimulates itself or shows itself, and to the point that that givenness is reserved from appearing. Hence must it be said that the response never knows if and to what extent it can make what gives itself also show itself. The response can no more annul its originary delay behind the appeal than what shows itself can pretend to exhaust what gives itself. The response is thus always in need of completing. The historicity of the response is opened here, with this ceaseless delay thus always still to be completed—with a delay by which it is temporalized radically, beginning from an already given which is not yet shown, beginning, thus, from the past. If difference differs according to appeal and response, and not primarily temporality, it could be that temporalization no longer occurs through the present (as in metaphysics) or the future (as in Heidegger's existential analytic), but well and truly through the past: according to the anonymity of an appeal which the response never ceases to rename. For the response which comes after the appeal comes back to it insofar as it confers on it a name in order to, in the end, show that which gave it in the first place: every response surges in the present returning toward a past appeal, in order to receive a givenness which is always already accomplished. And yet, since this turn back toward originary givenness can only show what it shows, but never demonstrate that this exhausts everything already there, the response remains by principle in deficit, a step behind. It ceaselessly readjusts itself, just behind the appeal; relapsed from the given, it thus lets surge the lapse of delay, a delayed time—the time of the delay (*un temps de retard—le temps du retard*). And this time of the delay does not cease to reproduce itself in the measure that the response returns toward the appeal, repeating and persisting in responding to it in a mode which is always differing and thus with an adequation which always differs. The future (*Zukunft*) arrives to the present (*Ankunft*) beginning from the information (*Auskunft*)—at each moment insufficient—that the response delivers about the appeal. Repetition (resumption of the search) of the appeal by the response, replacing (into play and light) what gives itself without name by what shows itself—in short, recalling the appeal—engages a historicity and disengages a temporality. The history of the devoted is comprised of the series—uninterrupted but, ultimately, suspended—of its responses. And the devoted dies the moment it can no longer respond, can no longer give one more name to the appeal without name.

One will thus conclude first that it belongs to the very sense of the appeal that it remain essentially anonymous, and not by default but excess—the excess of an alterity over what it alters, and this because it precedes it. However, this anonymity does not at all entail an indistinctness or equivalence among appeals, but rather indicates simply that their identities are decided only in the concretion of hearing and thus responding to them respectively, with *respectively* signifying that the turn to the appeal, which is also a return to it, fixes it for the first time as such. But there is more: the appeal, originally anonymous, identified through and in the response, announces itself as a gift and must be received as such. Its phenomenality can be reduced neither to that of an object nor to that of a being, but is precisely that of givenness. Levinas attests that the other person, as appeal, establishes the possibility of a phenomenology of givenness: "Transcendence is not a vision of the Other, but an original givenness" (*TeI* 149/*TI* 174). It remains to be determined whether this transcendence offers the only givenness, or if other immanence could add to it, thus deploying a phenomenology of givenness in general. But the appearance of this very question we owe to Levinas.

NOTES

This essay is the text of a paper given at the Sorbonne in Paris in 1996, and is previously unpublished in any language. However, it expands analyses that have since appeared in my *Etant donné: Essai d'une phénoménologie de la donation* (Paris: P.U.F., 1997), especially 367ff. and 408ff. (*Translator's note:* Marion's original subtitle was "Homage—à partir—de Lévinas," with that "à partir" inviting a sense of both building on and taking leave of. As will become clear, this reference to the difficult status of indebtedness is central to the concerns of the essay as a whole.)

1. M. Heidegger, *Sein und Zeit,* 10th ed. (Freiburg i.B.: Niemayer, 1963), 29; trans. J. Macquarrie and E. Robinson, *Being and Time* (London: SCM Press, 1962), 51.

2. *Translator's note:* It is a matter here of Husserl's *Gegebenheit,* translated in English as "givenness" and in French as "donation," a term which however is also present with a similar meaning in English. Since the more standard "givenness" displays an affinity with "gift" parallel and equal to that of Marion's "donation" and "le don," I have stayed with it, though at the cost of some trouble with such related terms as "donateur" (one who gives) and "adonné" (devoted), all of which remain in the same semantic line in French.

3. E. Levinas, "Notes sur le sense," in *DVI* 245, and "Entretien avec Roger Pol-Droit," in *Les Imprévus de l'histoire,* ed. P. Hayat (Montpellier: Fata Morgana, 1994), 204.

4. E. Levinas, "La conscience non-intentionelle," in *Entre Nous: Essais sur le penser-à-l'autre* (Paris: Grasset, 1991), 150 (my emphasis).

5. Heidegger, *Sein und Zeit,* 273/318.

6. M. Heidegger, "Brief über den 'Humanismus,' " in *Gesamtausgabe,* Bd. 9, pp. 319 and 307; trans. *Basic Writings* (New York: Harper and Row, 1977), 200. See also "Nachwort zu 'Was ist Metaphysik?' " in *Gesamtausgabe,* Bd. 9, pp. 307 and 311; trans. *Existentialism from Dostoevski to Sartre,* ed. W. Kaufmann (New York: Penguin, 1975), 261 and 264.

7. J.-L. Marion, *Réduction et donation: Recherches sur Husserl, Heidegger et la phénoménologie* (Paris: P.U.F., 1989), 296.

8. Heidegger, "Nachwort zu 'Was ist Metaphysik?' " 309/263.

9. P. Claudel, *La jeune fille Violaine* (2nd version), in *Théâtre,* t.1, ed. J. Madule (Paris: Pléiade, 1956), 573.

10. *AE* 190/*OB* 149. See also J.-L. Chrétien, *L'appel et la réponse* (Paris: Minuit, 1992), 42: "Every radical thought of the appeal implies that the appeal is understood only in the response."

11. For an extended development of this concept, see my provisional essay "Le phénomène saturé," in *Phénoménologie et théologie,* ed. J.-F. Courtine (Paris: Criterion, 1992), 79–127; trans. T. A. Carlson, "The Saturated Phenomenon," in *Philosophy Today,* Spring 1996, 103–24.

12. Denys, *Divine Names,* I, 6, P.G. 3, 596 a-b.

13. See my "Esquisse d'un concept phénoménologique du don," in *Filosofia della rivelazione,* ed. M. M. Olivetti (Biblioteca dell' Rome: "Archivio di Fiolosofia," 1994), 75–94.

14. C. de Gaulle, *Mémoires de la guerre,* I, 2, t.1 (Paris: Gallimard, 1954), 67.

15. G. Flaubert, *L'éducation sentimentale*, I, 1, *Oeuvres complètes* (Paris: Editions B. Masson, 1964), t.2, p. 9.

16. *Translator's note:* The word means "dumbstruck" or perhaps, in the light of the foregoing, "bedazzled." Marion has given separation to this concept of subjectivity in "L'Interloqué," in *Who Comes After the Subject?*, ed. E. Cadava, P. Connor, and J.-L. Nancy (New York: Routledge, 1991), 236–45.

17. Cf. Heidegger, *Sein und Zeit*, 275/319: "The indefiniteness and undefinability proper to the caller is not just nothing, but a *positive* characteristic. It makes known to us that the caller surges solely in its calling to . . . , which is *heard only as such,* and without any coaxing" (translation altered). We also adopt a passage from Chrétien, *L'appel et la réponse*, 60: "This being called is first, and this affection precedes any determination of the identity of that which calls me. To suppose that this identity can be assigned will occur only through a posterior interrogation. Initially, being called leaves open all possibilities for the nature of the one who calls." This holds not only for the "Platonic appeal . . . neutral and impersonal par excellence" (ibid., 27), but all appeals whatsoever.

18. P. Claudel, *L'annonce faite à Marie* (1st version) I, 1, in *Théâtre*, ed. J. Madaule and J. Petit (Paris: Pléiade, 1965), 32.

11

The Price of Being Dispossessed: Levinas's God and Freud's Trauma

Rudi Visker

THE WORD "dispossession" is not mine. It comes from Levinas.[1] It is not merely a word among all those others which his thought has bestowed on us, but is its central word, the one word which it cannot give to us, not even if it would wish to do so, for it is a word that his thought does not possess and in a certain sense fails to give to itself. Every thought is busy with such a word, a word around which it circles endlessly without ever finding a place there, without ever setting its foot on the ground and taking hold of the very thing it seeks. But without this failure there would be no thinking; thinking would not search, it would not speak and it would not write, should it indeed lay hold of that thing, grounding itself in a word in which everything is said and which makes all other words superfluous. There is only "room for thought" because it harbors something unthought from which it wishes to protect itself. By joining words together, thinking hopes to form a sort of chain to lay around that "something," a chain by which to somehow hold it in place. But however strenuous that attempt, it never quite succeeds at this, and the greater the thought the greater its vulnerability. No work of thought is ever without a weak link somewhere in the chain, one which is imperceptible for the thinker who wrought it, less secure than the others, a link in which that "something" which defies this thought takes up its abode. Not that this "something" will remain there, for it is too mobile and too cunning for that. It knows that it would betray itself by burrowing in a single place alone, and so it digs tunnels to other words and always comes up, mole-like, where it is least expected. Hence is

thinking not merely vulnerable, but helpless, and this is a helplessness which defies all attempts to come to its aid. For it does not help
to refer thinking to the word in which it is grounded: what conclusion
could it draw from that? Any word which it would choose to set its
foot on in order to establish itself, to give itself a foundation, would
immediately forsake that effort, becoming in its turn merely another
word which thinking sinks through. Every thinking is thus alone,
without recourse to help arriving from the outside. It knows that it
must go its own way and above all that this will mean it must always
remain in motion, always seeking new words to say the same thing.
Or better: although it "knows" that no word can quell the gnawing
going on beneath it, this knowledge does not exempt it from its task
to bring together enough words in the right manner, for there is no
other way for thought to protect itself from that unbearable noise.
Perhaps thinking speaks or writes not so much to hear itself, but only
to make itself heard well enough to drown out this noise which has
already wormed its way back into what it has just been writing or
saying. And perhaps most of all, what drives thinkers and makes them
rely on a language that they "know" they cannot trust is this anxiety
at being left alone with those words on which their thinking had
relied—to see them crumble away, riddled by the holes that their
thinking had been unable to stop up.

Hence, perhaps, the confusion of the one who comes after this
thinking and who can see those holes which the author not only could
not see but needed not to see. For good writing—and Levinas wrote
well—is writing in which the holes that inevitably appear also disappear so quickly that the writer does not get to see them. But a good
reader cannot afford to be blinded in that way which for the author
is a grace. A good reading must try to follow the author all the way
until seeing what the author saw and wanted us to see. But the reader
must also always look over the author's shoulder, for if one does not
see the holes from which the author tries to escape, then one will fail
to understand the price of that thinking, and thus will overlook its
true value. Readers must allow themselves to be led to the grounding
word of the thinking which they try to penetrate, but they must also
always hear the manner in which that thinking falls through that
word. It is this hearing that distinguishes the reader from the author:
for a reader to be who one truly is, he or she must hear something

that the other was not permitted to hear—precisely in order to be who one would be.

Undoubtedly, it is this *asymmetry* which makes philosophy such an endless task, and so disorienting an enterprise. To be sure, there is the canon, there are the great texts of the tradition. But how to relate to them, if we wish to avoid merely repeating them, and if this wish inevitably means that, in one way or another, we cannot escape having, like Oedipus, "one eye too many," which makes us see what those great texts could not see? And to see what those texts could not see is not to see or to think better than they did. For there seems to be a sort of doom hanging over this kind of vision: in making us become aware of the price of that other thought, thus becoming able to "appreciate" it, it seems fated to shift us to another position where we cannot pay that same price ourselves. Not because we are unwilling, but because we simply cannot: one does not take possession of thought, one is possessed by it. The price of seeing a thought is to become lost before it. This may sound somewhat dramatic, but it nonetheless seems better to bring it out in the open than to act as if thinking is a free commodity of which anyone can partake without taking away from the others. It is not only a mistake, but *pure hubris* to ask of a reader that he or she make the work of someone else accessible. What a reading really comes to is permitting others to see beyond the first understanding one has of a work, to what in it remains *in*accessible and, once that has been understood, to why we can no longer presume we are justified in taking its side.

One is thus served notice: there comes here not a philosopher but a bookkeeper—someone who brandishes evidence of unpaid accounts, laden with the unpleasant task of cautiously reminding a thinker's followers that they may have overextended themselves when buying into that thinker's work. Thinking is solitary, and it is not a reader's task to violate that solitude. To the contrary, it is this above all that one must protect. Hence my title and my program: to bring out the price of being dispossessed is not just to show how that very word dispossesses Levinas himself, how his thinking disintegrates when directly confronted with it, but also how the greatness of that thinking somehow dispossesses us. And in order to bring this into view, I begin with a reading which is undisturbed by that asymmetry which inhabits and defines philosophy—a reading which belongs to no one in particular, but which somehow remains in

circulation, and which I call the "official version" of Levinas. But
how to counter this reading which knows of no "dispossession," least
of all of itself, and which strolls happily along, filling in or stopping
up those essential holes in Levinas's text, treating them as if they
were ordinary mole-holes, and as if philosophy would ideally be as
flat as an English lawn? For surely to merely indicate these holes to
the reader would be but another way of making certain that the
reader does not stumble. And a mistaken way at that, for these holes
are everywhere and nowhere, as I will try to show—by tightening
the sail in which Levinas's thoughts have been caught, until it is so
tight that only the most innocent reader will not pause before taking
the next step. Still, since we do have to take a next step, always and
now, let me begin with a brutal statement which, however, will qualify itself as our reading progresses: the "holes" come from God.
"God" is the name for the plot of dispossession made possible by the
structure of Levinas's thinking, but which at the same time under-
mines and limits it. God is the mole which that thinking has tried to
live with.

I. A DISCOMFORT THAT LIBERATES?

For the moment, the most important thing to be said of that God is
that nothing can be said *about* him. God is not an object of speech.
He is the object of no speech whatsoever, thus including theo-*logy*
(*AE* 148/*OB* 196 n. 19), not even when it is negative (*AE* 14/*OB* 12).
God is not a theme. He does not permit himself to be thematized,
not because there could be no Saying which would determine him
exhaustively, not because every said—every predicate—would fall
short of him, but because that very Saying (*le Dire*), every saying,
already testifies in its structure to what Levinas calls "the first word."
And that first word—which appears, not by chance, last in the text
which I cite here—"is" God. It says nothing, except "the saying itself." But this changes everything: "if the first saying says this saying,
here the saying and the said cannot equal one another. . . . Someone
has escaped the themes" (*EDE* 236/*CPP* 126). It is that difference
between the Saying and that which is Said, between the "someone"
who says and the "something" that he or she says or that is said about
him or her, that Levinas points to in dropping the word "God." *Drops*

it: both in the sense of "renouncing" all use of a word and in the contrary sense of suddenly and unexpectedly but not without precautions, engaging a word that—precisely because it "falls"—cannot abide unnoticed. For Levinas never begins with God. He not only wants to break with onto-theology, as did Heidegger, but also refuses to introduce that word into his philosophy in the name of one or another religion—even if it would be Jewish: "How to be sure that the Word one takes up is indeed the Word of God? One must go in search of the original experience. Philosophy—or phenomenology—is necessary to hear His voice."[2] Nevertheless, this must not be taken to mean that Levinas has succumbed to what he himself calls "the temptation and the illusion which would consist in finding again by philosophy the empirical data of the positive religions" (*EDE* 190/ *TrO* 348). The original experience which he strikes up against with his phenomenology is one which puts it—and with it, all philosophy—in its place, a place alongside all of the existing religions. For the experience in question is a "heteronomous experience" (*EDE* 190/*TrO* 348), and Levinas wishes to show, against the philosophical tradition, that such an experience is not a contradiction in terms but, to the contrary, points to a movement of transcendence reaching us "like a bridgehead 'of the other shore' " and without which "the simple coexistence of philosophy and religion in souls and even in civilizations is but an inadmissible weakness of the mind" (*EDE* 190/*TrO* 348).

Hence an ambitious program which, as is well known, is bold enough to jump over Heidegger: "to hear a God not contaminated by being is a human possibility no less important and no less precarious than to bring Being out of the oblivion in which it is said to have fallen in metaphysics and in onto-theology" (*AE* x/*OB* xlii). An onto-theological conception of God would therefore be problematic not so much because it confuses Being with God—with the "highest being"—but also and above all because it confuses God with Being, thereby contaminating and denying God.[3] It would therefore be necessary to "destroy," in its turn, even Heidegger's "destruction" of metaphysics, and to distrust the thoughtfulness of "thoughtful thinking," if one is to understand what it means that there is a withdrawal which *in no way* cooperates with manifestation, and thus differs from the sort of withdrawal of Being that the later Heidegger pointed to. But this is not the place to engage this struggle—about which, how-

ever, it would be precipitous to conclude, as some have done, that it
merely rests on a misunderstanding.[4] Let it suffice here to observe
that Levinas's ethics cannot be an ethics of *Gelassenheit* in which I
would "let" the Other "be" the Other, would let him or her appear
qua Other, as the Other that he or she "is." For the prime concern of
this ethics is not how I affect the Other, but how the Other affects
me. And that is anything but reassuring: the Other divides me, "de-
nucleates" and beleaguers me, does not leave me alone but instead
obsesses me and persecutes me, takes me hostage and traumatizes
me, brings me to hate myself, to abdicate my place at the center of
my own concerns, to give everything up, to give nothing more to
myself, and thus to hemorrhage ceaselessly; the Other burns him- or
herself into my skin, and penetrates me[5]—in short: the Other does
virtually everything to me, except "let me be."

Still—and Levinas cannot repeat it enough—all of this happens
"without alienation" (*AE* 143, 146/*OB* 112, 114–15, among many
other references of this sort). The Other does not enslave but liberates, awakens, disillusions, purifies, and elevates.[6] One cannot but
conclude: the Other brings me a trauma which heals. Even if the
Other "paralyzes" me (e.g., *TeI* 145/*TI* 145; *AE* 133/*OB* 104), he or
she gives the precise movement that I needed—paralyzing my paral-
ysis and so pulling down the walls which had hindered my movement
(e.g., *AE* 227/*OB* 180). The Other's face taps a source in me henceforth not to be closed; it inflicts a wound in me which purifies with
its continual flow of blood: the Other does not permit me to be alone,
but leaves me no choice than to come out of my shell (for he or she
smokes me out of every hiding place, every *refugium*), to step outside,
to bare myself and stand in a nakedness which, as Levinas likes to
say, is still more naked than that of my bare skin, for it inverts my
skin, turns it inside out, so that I become an outside without an inside
(*envers sans endroit*) that no longer has any secrets, no longer any
interiority, leaving me completely open, empty, without possibility
of holding anything within myself and thus without possibility of
holding anything *for* myself. One must not forget that it is precisely
these extraordinarily violent expressions that Levinas will take up in
order to explain what he means by "proximity," the nearness of the
neighbor which, perhaps because we have coupled it so long with
love, has taken on the connotation of a sweetness "human, all too
human": "The proximity of the other is the immediate opening up

for the other of the immediacy of enjoyment—it is the immediacy of taste, the 'materializing of matter,' altered (*altérée*) by the immediacy of contact" (*AE* 94/*OB* 74).

Not only altered, but also excited, awakened, stimulated as when one becomes thirsty:[7] for the "matter" in question here is my own, which the Other's face brings to life, sowing in it the "restlessness" (*AE* 32/*OB* 25) by which it is something more than dead material, or more than material driven from within and adapting to its own form. The Other "inspires" my matter, "literally" inflating it (*AE* 160/*OB* 124), so that its form becomes too small, forcing outside, since the inside—interiority—has become oppressive, stifling. *Angustia,* says Levinas: anxiety in and through the oppressive proximity of the Other, through which I feel "ill at ease in my own skin" (*AE* 137/*OB* 108), like matter in its form, but "already tight," as in a "Nessus tunic" (*AE* 137/*OB* 108)—skin which betrays me and burns me, because it leaves me exposed to the Other who disturbs me. Yet this is a disturbance which liberates me, for it "materializes" my matter to a point where it "is more material than all matter" (*AE* 137/*OB* 108) and undergoes a change that I myself can neither enact nor resist: instead of binding me to myself (materiality of care for myself—a self that I am never rid of and which I—in what I do, and in where I am—continually stumble over as if over a doppelgänger, for even my solitude is something I share with myself),[8] matter is now "the very locus of the for-the-other" (*le lieu même du pour-l'autre; AE* 97/*OB* 77), and I move from my natural place. My place is not nature—the Other does not bring me down, does not call me back to my nature, as for Sartre, but raises me up, calls me up out of nature. Hence the unrest which I feel: the gaze of the Other rests on me not as on inert matter, but is accomplished in a "turgescence,"[9] a swelling of bodily tension. And hence do I blush. . . . But why from shame, as the official version of Levinas would have it? And what has all of this to do with God and with saying?

We have digressed, but not unintentionally. We are not lost, but in fact have come to a critical point, a point to which, sooner or later and in one or another manner, every reader of Levinas must eventually come. A point which we have staged didactically in order not to forget a problem that is difficult to dispel. Nevertheless, we will keep with the agreed-upon procedure. We have marked a point which we later shall have cause to reexamine. But for the moment, let us follow the strings of the official version. The melody is well known: they play (with) the face and the form.

II. THE PROXIMITY OF THE OTHER

It is the face of the Other that makes me uneasy and—what, according to the "official version," amounts to the same thing—before which I am ashamed. And this would not be the case if in the face I did not "hear the word of God,"[10] and if the Other would not stand "closer to God" (*EDE* 174/*CPP* 56) than I do. But again, this is not an argument which begins from God. Levinas is describing human relations, and he thinks that at a certain moment those descriptions make words like "God" or "creation" necessary (again) (cf. *CPP* 100). Let us follow him further, for the analysis of the preceding section had almost reached this very point.

A simple example of the otherwise abstract-sounding "materialization of matter" is close at hand. In an important sense, a person receives his or her hand from the Other. The hand stops being an organ for grasping things when it comes upon the Other: this particular sort of touch is of a different nature than any other, and it gives the hand another structure than does the feeling of grasping things. Such a grasping is a taking of possession, it is already property: "in stroking an animal already the hide hardens in the skin" (*EDE* 228/*CPP* 118)—the tiger is already a fur coat and the pig already a sofa. Things offer themselves to the grasp without imposing themselves. They have a form which makes them recognizable and therefore familiar. They do not call us or our hands into question, and they allow us to remain in a practical or theoretical mode. In short, precisely because they appear, have a beginning and end, and thus a form which defines them, they are already referred to us: "The illuminated object is something one encounters, but from the very fact that it is illuminated one encounters it as if it came to us" (*TA* 47/*TO* 64), and hence we can, whether literally or not, also take hold of it. To make things our own, to reduce their otherness to sameness, to "totalize" them, is not the same thing as to abolish their otherness, not the same thing as to "over run" them, as Heidegger said of technology. One can let nature be nature, one can "build, think, and dwell" and still let things be or appear without having them lose their role and disturb us, as does the hand of a dead man. A hand turned cold is an anomaly because it permits itself to be felt as a thing, and the cry with which one pulls back one's own hand upon suddenly realizing that what one feels is not coursing with life, as expected, but still and dead—that cry punishes the hand, or exorcises it in order to prevent it from receding to the pre-human. The skin of the Other does not offer itself to us like leather to be used, but *unsettles* our hand so that it no longer knows quite what to do. It is through *this* disturbance that it can open and, like the hand of a child—of which it is said, not for nothing, that it is quickly filled—learn to stroke rather than strike. But even without touching the Other, his or her proximity ensures that I know no pause with my hands, and that they are already not my own when I fly at his or her throat and slit it with them.[11] And yet the Other also brings my hands to rest: I can extend my hand and thereby, says Levinas, open myself fully, disarm myself, give myself to the Other naked. Symbolic handshake: whatever the effort it costs, it is not for nothing perceived as self-overcoming and therefore a step toward peace—"for it is not certain that war was at the beginning" (*AE* 151/*OB* 118).

First there was the proximity of Saying. These are the same thing: Saying is proximity. Not through *what* it says, but through *that* it says. In the proximity of the Other, one cannot be silent. One cannot not speak—as with the stranger sitting nearby in a waiting room: one first of all speaks in order to break the silence. An unbearable silence that is not, as one sometimes hears contended, unnatural but precisely the menace of the violence of nature, menace of regression. Even if one says nothing, one must restrain oneself in order not to say something; one must keep busy, occupy oneself, as when, in that same waiting room, one reaches for a nearby magazine. And if this gesture of self-protection somehow always fails to make us feel comfortable, it is not because one feels threatened and limited in one's freedom, as Sartre thinks, but rather because under the gaze of that other person, one feels this freedom brought to life and yet also guilty of allowing it to die by keeping silent. The words that stick on our tongue die there, and leave us with a bad aftertaste—but this is the taste of a spoiled freedom, the taste of the placenta wherein the child suffocates. For a human being, says Levinas, is not someone who wants to speak. We cannot do otherwise. And Levinas asks himself why: "What then came to wound the subject, so that he should expose his thoughts or himself in his saying?" (*AE* 106/*OB* 84, translation corrected). Why indeed are our thoughts not kept to ourselves? Why does keeping silent cost us so much effort? And why is this always understood—for instance, by Heidegger—as a *Verschwiegenheit* (*Sein und Zeit* § 34) which is "telling" and thus also speaks? Is this not already an acknowledgment and a recognition of the "bleeding wound of saying" (*AE* 192/*OB* 151) which "cannot heal" (*AE* 162/*OB* 126), and which the Other, through his or her sheer proximity and without even touching us, has opened?

Before it says something, the saying says and it says itself; it says something first of all in order to say itself, to "express itself," to declare itself as one declares one's love, out of a certain unease: hence not because one has *decided* to do so, but simply because one cannot do otherwise—it must come out—than allow oneself to be drawn out through the opening which one did not open oneself. This proximity is not like that of things—not contiguity—but obsession, a besiegement stronger than the walls of Jericho. I must contain myself so as not to give way before this trumpet which is not even a weapon. "Sick with love," reads Levinas in the Song of Songs (*AE* 181 n/*OB* 198 n. 5), "impossibility of being silent" (*AE* 182/*OB* 143).

This impossibility is all the more incomprehensible than the impossibility of keeping one's feelings of love to oneself, for it is a matter of a saying which begins to stir in myself and wants to get out in the proximity of an Other who is not special to me, an Other whom Levinas calls the "undesirable par excellence" (*DVI* 113/*CPP* 164; *AE* 157/*OB* 123), a stranger to whom I attach no importance—someone who is as "untelling" as can be. But then, from where comes my unrest, that wave which propels me outward? Levinas answers: from the very structure of the trauma. It is worth pausing before this answer, for although to my knowledge the official version never mentions it, this matter of the trauma, this is nonetheless a point that can help it to avoid unnecessary detours in the path leading to the standard and familiar story of the face and the form.

III. RESPONSIBILITY IS MISPLACED

Otherwise Than Being would not be the book it is without its persistent preoccupation with the trauma (*traumatisme*) which I incur through the proximity of the Other. And yet, as I already mentioned, there is something counter-intuitive about this trauma. For equally persistent is Levinas's claim that it does not alienate me, but purifies and elevates me. Instead of limiting my freedom—as is the case in pathology—Levinas's trauma establishes it, or "invests" it. But how can a trauma, something which escapes my freedom, thus something of which I am not the subject but to which I am subjected—how can this liberate me? How can I be healed by a shock that uproots me, knocks me loose, tears me away from my every anchoring? Why should such a shock be "sobering," or "awaken" me? What could I gain from a complete loss of interiority? How could the "nothing private" by which Levinas characterizes the proximity of the Other (*AE* 176, 184/*OB* 138, 144), how could being lain bare before the Other be anything but sheer terror—is it not precisely in totalitarianism that every form of privacy falls away? Or yet again: why would penetration by the Other—"the-one-penetrated-by-the-Other" (*AE* 64/*OB* 49)—be anything but brutal violence? How, then, are they not rape and trauma in the most common sense of those words?

Before rejecting as either meaningless or against all intuition the notion of a trauma without alienation, one must first understand what a trauma is and in what sense Levinas uses that word. Indeed, it is difficult to avoid the impression that it is either a failure or an unwillingness to take this word for what it is (and perhaps more unwillingness than failure, for the misunderstanding is so convenient that it cannot be innocent) that lies behind all those misinterpretations of Levinas's ethics which either reduce it (and often without noticing) to a thaumaturgy which miraculously heals us of contact with the Other or the Other's appeal, or which discards it for having failed to bring to the problem of the subject and the Other more than a mere reversal where the Other is to constitute me rather than me the Other (alter ego). In both cases, Levinas's philosophy has been narrowed to an ethics which is no longer comprehensible, and that incomprehensibility is then used as an excuse either to embrace that ethics—in which case responsibility would be "practical" and for that reason incomprehensible, or, to invoke a favorite term of late, "undecidable"—or else to dismiss it, in which case the excessiveness of such a responsibility would be considered merely the consequence of philosophical deficiency: the asymmetry which Levinas recognizes in the Other would be too asymmetric and his or her transcendence too absolute. And all of this would be the price of a philosophy which—as Derrida recently suggested—is ultimately unable to maintain a distinction between the infinite otherness of God and that of the other person. The problem with this ethics would thus be that it is "already religion."[12]

This may be true. But if it is, then it represents a problem which Levinas's ethics engages frontally, and not, as Derrida suggests, one which escapes it. For the central insight of that ethics is that everything in ethics turns around affects which cannot be described without that description falling short. Discomfort, shame, self-accusation, and the contrition rising in me simply through a sense of the proximity of the Other—these are not affects like all others. I can feel angry because someone has insulted me, but I feel shame and discomfort *without any reason.* Why should I feel embarrassed before an Other whom I do not know and whom I have nothing to do with? I have *no reason* to be afraid of him; he keeps his distance over there, and I know where I am going. I have done nothing wrong, and so have the law on my side. And still there is something about the Other's gaze which does not leave me indifferent—for a moment I hesitate, I slow my pace, as if I have lost sight of my destination: "Whence comes to me this shock when I pass, indifferent, under the gaze of the Other?" (*EDE* 193/*TrO* 350). Surely, nothing has happened there. The Other has not asked me a single thing!

The Other calls to me in spite of him- or herself. The Other's proximity alone suffices. There is no need of beseechment or imploring hands. Whether or not the Other actually turns toward me, I am turned toward the Other. Responsibility, says Levinas in a constantly recurring formula, is an answer *without a question* (e.g., AE 191/*OB* 150). This formula also characterizes what *Otherwise Than Being* calls "saying"—for saying and responsibility go together, both involve being ordered-to or opened-to the Other without any decision to open *oneself.* But to think that since it is not we who are behind this opening, it must be the Other who opens us, is to misunderstand what is at stake here. After all, why would the Other open us? Surely, it is too simple to think that we speak because we are first spoken to, and although one cannot deny the subtlety of those who would have language address us before we address one another in it, this model, too, starts with a first address (a *Zu-sage* which is still a *sagen*) to which we must pay heed for us to speak properly and "enter" into the *Spielraum* which unfolds for us. But Levinas's idea of a "response without a question" seems to suggest that there is no such "entering." Somehow, both saying and responsibility never quite "take place." They are *literally* misplaced, out of joint, pointing to an anachronism which cannot be resolved, synchronized, serialized, or situated, for example, in the chain of cause and effect, without nullifying the "plot" or "intrigue" in which they show up. What *Otherwise Than Being* repeatedly calls the "intrigue"[13] of saying or responsibility stands or falls with this anachronism which represents an absurdity within the order of being. For how could there "be" something like "a sound that would be audible only in its echo" (*AE* 134/*OB* 106), "an indebtedness before any loan" (*AE* 143/*OB* 111), and "an accusation preceding the fault" (*AE* 144/*OB* 113)? How can one be responsible without having any part in it? How can one be involved where one was not involved? Is it not mistaken to hold someone responsible for the mistakes of the Other? Or for the misuse that that Other has made of his or her own responsibility? And yet, parents are not only answerable for their children, but feel themselves responsible, even long after the children have grown up and begun to stand on their own. And yet, not just by law but even in accordance with popular sentiment, secretaries of state must resign their posts for mistakes made under their administration. And yet we are reproached—indeed, we reproach ourselves—for not having intervened in things gone wrong which we had nothing to do with, and which we did not even know about while they happened. And yet it is not without embarrassment that we open our lunchboxes when seated between two people we do not know—again in a waiting room, or perhaps at the train station—even if there is nothing to indicate they are hungry. Is it a mistake to say that bread is made to be shared?

Such affects are not mistaken. It is only that they are out of place within the order they disturb. And that order does not understand them because they come from somewhere else. Not that they are from another order. Rather, they come from something that cannot or will not be of any order, something which does not permit itself to be understood because "it has left before having come" (*EDE* 210/*CPP* 68), thus something that breaks with the order of consciousness which can only know, re-cognize, and admit what has first been rendered familiar and knowable. This is an order, then, which cannot accept something which escapes the grasp of the present and places the primacy of the present in question. And which therefore cannot but understand responsibility as an engagement, a *self-engaging* answer to a need which presents itself, which thus announces itself and over which one can in all freedom make a judgment on how to act, if at all—and after one has investigated it *from all sides* and then weighed the pluses and minuses of each choice.

One understands why Levinas has resisted calling the face of the Other a *phenomenon,* why he refers to it as too great for its form, and why he places so much emphasis on the fact that "the Other who manifests himself in a face, as it were breaks through his own plastic essence," that the Other "divests himself" of that form, of that face which, however, "has nonetheless already made him manifest" (*CPP* 56, translation corrected). For this silent manifestation is more and other than "appearance"; it has rather something of a demonstration that lays hold of us purely and simply by passing us by, and without even asking anything of us. Though there is nothing to see, we are intrigued. Or better: this intrigue, the fact that we feel uneasy, that we are embarrassed or ashamed, has nothing to do with what there is to see of or from the Other. And it is precisely there that our discomfort is to be found: we are seized by something that we ourselves can in no way grasp or lay hold of. We are "out of order," out of our usual rhythm—*dispossessed*—without knowing why.

This "without why" is not that of the rose that blooms and which we must learn to simply let bloom. It places our own bloom in question, and there is nothing in it to learn. Whether the Other is young or old, whether his or her face is faded or withered—*"peau à rides,"* skin with wrinkles (*AE* 112, 118/*OB* 88, 93)—and however "mad" it may appear,[14] my shame seems to establish my responsibility for the fact that the Other receives no water, that his or her skin is dry and shriveled already before I could have cared for it. I always come too late to this responsibility, it is older than my capacity and my freedom, and it has a structure which permits me never to truly learn from the experience—the next time is never better—because it holds me in the web of an intrigue that is precisely intriguing because it turns around a past which has never been present. An intrigue which Levinas calls "religious" (*AE* 188/*OB* 147) and which cannot be understood except by relating to an Other who Levinas says comes in the "trace of God."

IV. AFFECTS WITHOUT CONTEXT

Why does the Other come in the trace of God? What does it mean that in the Other's face *I* hear "the word of God," "the word that points to my debt and my duty before the Other"?[15] In order to understand what brings Levinas to these formulations, one has to bear in mind the extreme unlikeliness of what they are trying to describe. For how can a face which withdraws from its own form, a face that breaks that form open, that breaks through it, eclipsing the light in which, as we have seen, the world and everything in it are familiar to me—how can such a formless face, despite the falling away of that familiarity, in its being-not-referred-to-me, in its ab-soluteness, still touch "something" in me? Why is the effect of what is thus absolutely alien and non-familiar not what one might expect it to be? Why should I feel guilt rather than, for example, panic? Why are discomfort and shame the same thing for Levinas? Why is my disintegration specifically ethical? And why, then, is it totally different from the disintegration that overwhelms me and makes itself *my master* when *the* absolute Other that Levinas calls the *il y a* emerges, and which is characterized precisely by opening me to the *apeiron* (cf. *TeI* 132/*TI* 159)—the monstrous and formless which, for example, some science fiction and horror films try to capture in an image? An image of the formless which, fortunately, is still not without form and thus still reassuring, while only invoking a fright which we can no longer imagine. But why does the ab-soluteness of the Other who completely withdraws from his or her own form, and whose alterity Levinas insists has nothing to do with the form of his or her visage— which is, of course, recognizably human—why does this Other not directly instill the same sort of fright in me? Why am I not "crushed" (*TA* 65, 77/*TO* 85, 91) or "burned" (*TeI* 49/*TI* 77) by the Other's transcendence, which refuses capture in the forms by which it would become immanent to me? If by withdrawing from his or her form and thereby upsetting the order in which things are given to me—but without imposing themselves on me (*DE* 73–74/*EE* 47)—if in this way the Other, despite him- or herself, through being other than his or her "form," becomes *intrusive*, or "obsessing," then why am I not petrified by the Other, or why do I not run away in panic, as occurs when in *horror* I am overtaken by an absolute otherness which I can in no way situate or comprehend? The answer can only be: because the otherness of the Other is not absolute in that sense. Not only because the Other is a trace of God, but moreover because I, too, am a trace of God.[16] But I only know that—and without my being able to appropriate that knowing, for that "knowing" is ethics—through the Other.

Were it only a response to the situation in which it emerges, my discomfort would not be shame but panic. For in retrospect, there does seem to be something special about that situation, and we were thus too quick to suppose that there was nothing in it which could clarify the kind of affect involved here. For even if the Other leaves us "in peace," he or she is still an Other, and this alterity which is without form could at best explain our discomfort. *But it cannot explain the specific feeling of shame.* That our discomfort is an *ethical* discomfort, and that Levinas can define it by responsibility, cannot be explained by the falling away of "forms." A discomfort which is shame, a suffocation (*angustia*) which is more than anxiety at nothingness, presupposes something more. It presupposes another scene. It presupposes what Freud would call the first time of the trauma—but then a time which overturns the normal course of time in everyday life: that of a past which not only never has been present, but never will be. This is why this past asserts itself through an *affect.*

Contrition, discomfort, and shame are affects without context. They emerge from nowhere, out of nothing, and can in no way be clarified by the context in which they assert themselves. That context, as it were, breaks open because there is something in those affects which is out of accord, something which does not tally or fit. Something other breaks through. Something which has not been worked out and which could not have been worked out otherwise, says Freud, who then goes in search of what that could have been.[17] And he discovers something interesting: the adult Emma, who has come to him now because she has not dared to enter a clothing store alone since an episode at age twelve, when she fled a store in panic after seeing two salesmen laughing—at her clothes, she now thinks—displays a phobia which cannot be explained solely on the basis of that situation as such. For as a woman, Emma now dresses quite differently than she did as a twelve-year-old, and even the company of a child seems to be enough for her to feel at ease while shopping for clothes. Freud discovers that there has been something operating behind the scenes since the beginning of Emma's puberty and which still limits her freedom, an other, hidden scene which works its way through into the second scene (at age twelve) and whose meaning comes to light only now—but without Emma being able to grasp it—coming over her as affect, taking hold of her as she enters any clothing shop unaccompanied. That first scene occurred in another shop, which the eight-year-old Emma entered to buy candy. The shopkeeper, a grocer, had touched her genitals through her clothes, grinning while he did so. And the little Emma returned again to the shop—Freud makes note of this, but the *Project* pursues it no further—perhaps not only because she wanted more candy, and it happened again, after which she never returned. Perhaps that touching had *intrigued* her, and that was why she went back, just as we all retrace our steps when intrigued by something. But nothing came of it, nothing that she could do something with, like with candy, and Emma grew up, forgot the first incident, and got on with her life until a phobia for clothing shops began to unravel it. And then there was—fortunately—Freud, who associated the salesmen's laughter with the grocer's grin, and brought the clothing of the adult and twelve-year-old together with that of the child, and saw in all of that a *hysteron proteron hysterikon,* along with a complicated scheme which shows that without the little Emma's noticing it—*à l'insu,* Levinas would say—a force had entered her psychic apparatus in such a way that the apparatus could not operate since it simply was not put together for it. What occurred in that first scene could not be represented, "bound," neutralized, or worked out by it. It was thus in fact nothing, and yet it had somehow impressed itself on Emma, but without leaving her with an impression of that impression. She would only notice later, when she reached an age at which a woman knows what to do when someone touches her. But the salesmen did *not* touch her, but only laughed, and the striking thing about that laughter was that it quite literally struck hard enough to make her lose self-control, bringing her "out of her mind." For that laughter, says Freud, awakened the (unconscious) memories of the other, first shop, which in turn exposed her to what *"she could not have experienced then,* a release of sexuality, which asserted itself in anxiety" (*E* 354/*Origins* 411). And Freud concludes that "here we come upon an instance of a memory awakening an affect *which is not awakened by the [remembered] event itself,* because in the meantime the change to puberty has made possible another understanding of what is remembered" (*E* 356/*Origins* 413).

As if the grocer's hand had impressed a small scar in Emma's skin but without that skin itself feeling it (she did indeed feel that she was touched, but not that she was scarred), and which only later, as that skin grew, became legible. Or actually not. For this writing came too soon. In a certain sense, it was too big for Emma's small skin, and thus not only mutilated it, but also distorted itself so that it could no longer be read by the time the salesmen looked and laughed at Emma. She was exposed to something which at that time she could not read (which is, according to Freud's notion of a "delay in puberty," normal), and now still less (and that is another matter). But this explanation seems not in keeping with what Freud says. For Freud, everything seems to center around "memory traces which can be *understood* only upon the appearance of one's own sexual perception" (*E* 356/*Origins* 413)—or almost everything, for all adolescents have such memory traces and yet not all become hysterical. The scene with the salesmen provided the more sexually "mature" Emma with a context through which her psychic apparatus could, via association, "read," interpret, and understand the first scene as something sexual. But that same process of association also led her to misread the second scene: she thought that the salesmen were laughing at her clothes, while for her own part finding one of them attractive (as she later remembered)—a combination that called up the offense in the grocery store, so that the new situation involves a sense of danger completely disproportionate to the event itself ("they want to touch me again"), with the result that Emma runs away in "some kind of fright" (*E* 353/*Origins* 410). Now that she finally reads the first scene, this scene, "understood at last," makes her misread the second: the laughter of the salesmen becomes a grin which promises no good, which is terror itself, and she flees. As if the impression of that first scar was so great that it still impresses itself now—or rather, only now—in all other signs and, being itself deformed, deforms them too, so that the very sight of it *petrifies* Emma—even though she has reached the age in which a laugh, however erotic it may be, need not be threatening, and in which she herself is adult enough to ignore someone grinning with an ulterior motive, or else simply put him in his place.

Emma's trauma thus has to do with a trace that wipes out all other traces, infiltrating everywhere. Through that trace, the laughter of the salesmen is *suddenly transformed* into grinning, it "signifies" something other than it "signifies," it becomes a leer which cannot signify anything because it comes too close and does not keep the distance necessary for a signifier to give way to signification. Such laughter is no longer laughter at all but the convulsion of a deformed face, as Levinas would say, leering at her and petrifying her just as does the *il y a* which emerges as all familiar forms fall away, leaving nothing to protect us from the power of suction thus coming into existence. This, Levinas might add, shows us what happens when the face does not "precede eros."[18] For Emma, eros is from the beginning disturbance, "ambiguous" and unreliable—in short, terror, and thus not the "experience" of a face that is taken in by its blush and instead of breaking through its form descends into it, or drops into it so that the form trembles, glows, loses its control, or breaks in the manner of lovers' eyes, when sexual pleasure takes them into their own flesh and into the flesh of the Other, a flesh that begins to take possession of their faces, allowing them to descend stealthily from their sublime height, and to flirt with incarnation while delivering themselves to the "vertigo" of a pleasure which, even at the very limit of the impersonal, still does not swallow up the personal (*TeI* 242/*TI* 264). Eros: supreme vulnerability of a face that finds itself released from the need to be a face, a face which trusts itself to become "weighted down with a skin" (*AE* 107/*OB* 85; *TeI* 242/*TI* 264) as divers carry weights they can later throw away. None of this, however, was possible for Emma, who seemed to carry a weight in her that she could not throw away, a heaviness whose power she began to feel only later, as it threatened to crush her from the inside out, operating like a black hole which sucks everything else into it, skewing the poles of the field in which, for a healthy woman of her age, she should have felt attracted and attractive, and without experiencing that feeling as a threat. Emma's trauma lies in that interval by which all future seductive smiles have become welded to a past grin that, in refusing to pass, makes all (sexual-erotic) laughter meaningless to her, an interval into which the entire field of erotics and seduction has disappeared, just as suddenly and just as inexplicably as ships sink in the Bermuda Triangle.

This comparison might seem far-fetched, but as we will see, it is in fact both apt and to the point. It must help us to see not only the similarities but also the differences between, on the one hand, Freud's manner of thinking the structure of the trauma within the framework of a metapsychology still modeled on physical science, and, on the other, Levinas's at first sight rather strange attempt to free it from such a framework and make it the cornerstone of a metaphysics which has the—to our ears today—strange pretense to put psychoanalysis in its place. Not to refute or reject it, but to establish itself without it. For the trace with which Levinas is concerned is not only "better" (*AE* 70/*OB* 54) but also "otherwise"—it belongs in an "otherwise than being" which, instead of worrying about some disturbance within the order of consciousness, as Freud did, remains sovereign and prior to it.

V. A SHOCK WITHOUT AFFECT

In Freud's discussion of a trauma, he makes a distinction between two "times" which, however, do not simply follow each other as such. While the real course of events does move from the scene in the grocery store (when Emma is eight) to the scene in the clothing store (when she is twelve), the temporality of the trauma is somewhat different. There, things happen in a certain sense in the reverse order: the first scene, which in itself had nothing traumatic about it, becomes traumatogenic only "afterwards" (*après coup, nachträglich*), that is to say, through the second scene. It is therefore not the case that the first scene is simply the "cause" and the second its "effect." To stay with this terminology, one would have to say that the cause becomes "richer," or changes, through the effect that it causes. The effect works "thus" upon the cause, thereby "awakening" an affect that, as we have seen, could not have been awakened "through the remembered event itself," an affect that was not there so long as the "cause" was still without an effect. But then how can this affect be there once there is an effect? What sort of "memory trace" is this that changes once it is "activated"? And what is the nature of that change? Is it nothing more than an actualization of slumbering potential?

When Emma fled the clothing store in panic, it was because she felt assaulted, and because *she did not have time* (an expression we will find again in Levinas) to "meet" that assault. She was unprepared for it, says Freud, because it came from an unexpected corner: for it is not in her case a perception "but a memory-trace which unexpectedly releases unpleasure" (*E* 358/*Origins* 416). The surprise is, as

Levinas would say, "complete" (*AE* 126, 189/*OB* 99, 148: *absolument surpris*), for the assault comes not from outside (in itself, the scene in the clothing store has nothing threatening about it), but from "inside." Moreover, this is an inside of which Emma was completely unaware, an "inside" which does not coincide with the "inside" of her psychic apparatus, for it had entered that apparatus without being spoiled by it. Borrowing a word from Lacan, we might refer to this inside which remains "outside" the inside of an intimacy which has no knowledge and thus no understanding of it, as *ex-timacy*.[19] This ex-timacy makes the ordinary inside of intimacy vulnerable from inside out: it acts somewhat like a traitor within the walls, opening the gates at the most unexpected moment, allowing the seemingly innocent passerby to slip inside and arm himself with the weapons— the "energy"—to begin sowing terror. This is what *overcomes* Emma when the grin appears as more than a harmless memory trace, more ex-timate than the intimacy of her ordinary memories, forming an alliance with the laughter and thus attacking her, so to speak, on two fronts at once, so that she no longer knew how to react. The assault is everywhere and nowhere, no longer localizable: it comes from neither outside nor (the ordinary) inside, but from an outside in the inside or an inside in the outside.

What is confusing and debilitating about that assault is not only that Emma—literally—cannot "place" it, but also that—again, literally—it leaves her no "time." Something that had seemed past now suddenly seems not at all past; something returns, a bit like in *The Return of the Living Dead*. Not entirely so, however, for that which returns was not yet as it is now. It returns, but having changed. The memory trace in question there suddenly appears to be something other than the impression of a present now past. And it is through this that the actual present—the laughter in the clothing store—also seems to be different from the present we are all familiar with. For this present refuses to pass, it intrudes, becomes *intrusive* and silences Emma, *persecutes*[20] her all the way into the future which is already forced under the "sign" of what to avoid. What Freud calls *Nachträglichkeit*, or afterwardsness, seems to bring with it a sort of implosion of the ecstases of time—time lacks the strength to unfold, and as it thus becomes one-dimensional it is no longer an "element," becoming flat and at the same time heavy, leaving Emma unable to breathe, smothering her in the manner of damp laundry which is not aired properly.[21]

What is oppressive in the trauma, the angst (*angustia*) that it awakens, is thus that the a priori forms of sensibility are suspended, put out of order. In this way, Emma is taken hostage by *the* Other-in-oneself. And regardless of how one twists or turns it, this Other "is." One can call it the unconscious (which, as one knows, has neither place nor time), but the unconscious, too, "is." It cannot be clarified or explained by the expression "otherwise than being," which Levinas wishes to join to the trauma. *Taken strictly*, one also cannot use any of the terms which one is nevertheless tempted to reach for when, based on I know not what optimism, one appeals to psychoanalysis in order to contest metaphysics. For before we associate this strange trace about which we have already heard Freud speak with the trace discussed by Levinas—a trace that differs from all other traces, the trace of a "God" who has passed without ever having been present, thus the trace of an "absolute past" which has never been present[22]—we would do well to look carefully once again at what happened to Emma.

More happened in the grocery store than Emma herself realized. But that "more" announced itself only later, in connection with the second scene. And still, it must in some way have already "been" there. Freud is aware of the difficulty this involves, and he rejects, after some explanation and not without reason, the term "unconscious affect"—after all, what sort of affect can go entirely unnoticed? An unconscious affect, he says, can in the strict sense signify at most that there has been a "potential beginning" (*eine Ansatzmöglichkeit*) of affect-formation which somehow could not "develop" (*entfalten; Ubw* 137/*SE* 178). Freud adds that this is due to (secondary) repression, which leads to all sorts of problems that I must leave aside here. I thus admit that I twist Freud slightly—more than slightly, some would say—in the direction of Lyotard, referring now to the first "time" of the trauma as a "*shock* without affect."[23] The fact that there is no affect is not the problem; this means only that at the moment of the shock itself one feels no affect. The problem is with the *shock*, a term which suggests that little Emma's psychic apparatus received a stimulus to work through (the entire scene in the grocery store) which, however, it did not entirely do (and "not entirely" is something other than "entirely not"). Some of that stimulus escaped her apparatus (the *intriguing* sensation in her genitals, and the grin which accompanied it). However, the excessive "remainder" of stimulation which could not be worked out does not let go of that apparatus and smuggles itself inside. It is the intrusion of that unworked surplus which justifies the expression "*shock* without affect." Or, in Freud's language, a language I twist, though not without reason: though the remainder does not form an unconscious affect,[24] there has indeed been something like a "potential beginning" to affect- formation— but it alone remains. Remember: Emma was "intrigued" (Levinas's term!) and went back to the shop, it happened a second time, we may assume, and only then did she stay away. And we know that there is nothing to indicate that the first scene itself was already laden with negative affects. In any case, considered in itself, it was not trauma- tizing. The intriguing feeling that motivated a second visit to the store seems after that to disappear. Even if she was touched again, there was nothing special about this touch; Emma had first thought it something unusual, but this seemed not to be the case. It was a touch and nothing more. With what had initially intrigued her, she found out she could do nothing—it did not admit representation, not even affect-representation. And it therefore disappeared—literally, it did not re-present itself.

The entire scene in the grocery store involved no more than a memory trace in which the being-touched and the grin were only one moment among others. Yet without her noticing, Emma was, as we have already seen, "scarred" by it; the un-worked-out "quantity" of excitation had entered her psychic apparatus. There was a shock that Emma did not feel and that she would feel only later, in the meantime spreading as a sort of "affective cloud" (thus, not an affect per se), an "energy" of which it must be said that her psychic appara- tus not so much *did* not know what to do with it as *could* not know, since it had not even registered that energy. It did not become an affect, but it nonetheless continued to exert itself, "as a thermal con- dition of the system which, because it was not determined, could not be worked out."[25] But this changes with the second scene, in which, as Lyotard says, an "affect without shock" is released: nothing special happens, and yet Emma panics. The "sound" of the shock without affect becomes audible only in its echo[26]—in an affect without shock. The second time thus does not so much follow the first as it goes before it. The first time reverberates in the second, which forms the context in which a sound hitherto inaudible can finally be heard. Or, in terms of the energy metaphor, the energy which at first was not registered now suddenly announces itself and allows itself to be worked out or transposed into the affect which overwhelms Emma. In the language of Freud's *Project,* one could say that the (as it were) innocent memory trace of the first scene was linked to a gas bubble of unused, unregistered energy. Through the salesmen's laughter in the second scene, that "link" and thus that "trace" begin to vibrate (Freud speaks of "association"), so that that gas bubble is released and comes rapidly to the surface. And then there seems to occur something similar to what, according to the most recent theories, also occurs in the Bermuda Triangle: through the release of gases from the ocean floor (!), mixing then with seawater, the relative weight of the water decreases, sinking the ships which had been built to float on normal water. The gas bubble comes to the edge of the psychic apparatus, and makes it so porous that Emma's ego no longer has time to meet the present perception (laughter) and react to the danger which could be bound up with it. The laughter escaped *attention* because it was immediately too close to the retina, attracted as it is by that dark grin which now casts aside its earlier silence and lets itself be heard. Everything snaps shut, and henceforth Emma knows only that she must avoid entering clothing shops. She must sacrifice—quite literally—part of her "time" and part of her "place" if her life is to have time and place. The price of this trauma is a phobia that literally *dis-possesses* Emma: in order to maintain at least some control over the danger lurking "in" her, she projects it outside ("clothing shops are to be avoided!"), but this requires her to accept the formation of an "enclave" (*Ubw* 143/SE 184) in that "outside" which belongs to the sphere of unconscious influence. And that is, as Freud soberly remarks, a "great sacrifice of personal freedom" (*Ubw* 143/SE 184).

For Levinas, this *tremendum* which determines Emma's life would not be very different from what he describes elsewhere as the *fascinosum.*[27] What psychoanalysis describes is an ex-stasis toward the inside, but not therefore any less possessing. The figuration in which angst is bound up—Freud's "phobic outer structure (*phobische Vorbau*)" (*Ubw* 143/SE 184)—is at the same time the forecourt where the gods are born. And where, as Levinas would add, humanity is debased and enslaved: for—like Emma—it will have to bring sacrifices to keep its peace and tranquillity, in an attempt to bring the gods which are unreliable (and which Lacan therefore locates in "the real")[28] into the symbolic order, in the hope that they will answer and that a covenant may exist.[29] Vain hope, says Levinas, hope that is nothing but vanity and hopeless hope since it aims at the *"bad infinite"* (*TeI* 132/*TI* 159) of an outside to which the subject is attached, but without being separated from it. Endless spiral of ever bloodier sacrifices,[30] or sacred spell which lets time tick away at the gate of a Law which never answers[31]—there is no difference between the heteronomy of a *transdescendence* which either renders us immobile or forces us to ceaselessly repeat the same rigid gestures, and binds the subject with the very bonds by which it tries to protect itself from it. What is absent from such a "transcendence" is the goodness of a Good which is *transascendent* because "the distance it expresses, unlike all distances, enters into the *way of existing*" of the being involved there (*TeI* 5/*TI* 35, emphasis in source).[32] Which is "only" to say that this being is responsible. For responsibility is an impossibility-of-disappearing in which the subject thus abides: here, too, there is infinity (for responsibility is without end), but then with a good liberating the subject, rather than depleting it. Indeed, the Good animates and inspires the subject, and without the subject's bending or breaking under its breath, but holding itself up. By singularizing me into an irreplaceable I, the responsibility which is thus "irrecusable" (*AE* 139/*OB* 109) distinguishes itself from the "impossibility-to-disappear" in which there lies the terror of the *il y a*. The *il y a* paralyzes: it sucks the subject into it, it obsesses it and ensnares it, it compels the subject to bear witness to its own naked depersonalization, but without permitting it the distance necessary to escape from it. In the *il y a*, something comes too close, so that, as in the case of Emma, everything falls shut. Angst, oppression, a feeling of suffocation: these are the final affects which for a subject left without any escape announces its impossibility-to-disappear in its very disappearance. The terror of the *il y a* is the announcement of a still greater terror: the imminence of a "being without beings," an existence without existents in which the existent that I am will disappear but without its nothingness offering me any peace. It is this menace which, according to Levinas, stands central in psychoanalysis: the menace of an unreliable "primary process" always ready to submit the "secondary process" to itself. The unconscious: a "thinking that thinks otherwise,"[33] a being without consciousness, but still a being. One understands why Levinas turns his back on psychoanalysis: not because he did not wish to acknowledge it, but to the contrary precisely because he had indeed recognized it. The place of psychoanalysis—this is the place of the *il y a*.

It is this same *il y a* that the metaphysics of Levinas discerns and engages in culture: it is to be put to work—as negativity yes, but one which will have to work!—in an ethics in which, as we already know, and just as in Freud, everything turns around an affect that "leaves us no time," that "intrudes" on us, "dis-possesses" us. But unlike in Freud, this affect does not suffocate and overpower us, does not alienate and enslave us. If it oppresses us, then it is an oppression which liberates. And hence is the place of that affect an other trauma, a trauma that heals. A good trauma, then, for this is the trauma of a Good that leaves us "no time" (*CPP* 98) to refuse it or choose for it, but which, as Levinas always adds, is good precisely because it "redeems" (*rachète*) the "violence of (that) un-freedom" (*AE* 158–59/ *OB* 123). This un-freedom is thus that of a trauma which, in contrast to the one Freud describes, liberates. Not because it comes from the Other—for why wouldn't the Other enslave me, as Sartre thought?—but because here, too, an other scene breaks through. This other scene is that of creation.

VI. *EX NIHILO,* AN OTHER SCENE

At first sight, the God that Levinas wishes us to hear "on the hither side of being" somewhat resembles the man in the grocery store who could not keep his hands off Emma. God too does something to us the meaning of which comes to light only later, after the fact. And here too without our being able to understand that meaning "afterwards," or make it our own. All of the gravity belonging to Levinas's philosophy of creation, as well as the reason why he calls it *ex nihilo,* lie in this *après coup,* in this "posteriority of the anterior" (*TeI* 25/*TI* 54): "The cause of being is thought or known by its effect *as though* it were posterior to its effect. One speaks lightly of the possibility of this 'as though' which is taken to indicate an illusion. But this illusion is not unfounded: it constitutes a positive event" (*TeI* 25/*TI* 54).

Levinas calls this positive event "separation": creation of an independent being which can ignore its own creatureliness. Creation is *ex nihilo* because it breaks with the chain of cause and effect, and creates a being which need not feel the imprint of the creator, a being which thus can be atheistic—not in the sense of denial or rejection, but as a "having no knowledge of" (*TeI* 29–30/*TI* 58; *AE* 133/*OB* 105). Between cause and effect, there is a hiatus by which the cause frees itself from its effect and thus also sets that effect free. The absoluteness of God—for Levinas is concerned here with God—lies in the humility with which God withdraws, not wishing to intrude on or prove himself to the one he has created. This God holds his breath in order to make himself smaller, opening up space beside him, but he also exhales carefully so as to counteract the suction from his inhaling, and above all to preserve the distance between himself and his creation.[34] This God "passes by" without leaving anything but a sign or a trace (in the sense of an impression),[35] wipes away all traces that could lead back to him, and weaves them into an "intrigue" which cannot be dissolved by speaking his name or calling out to him.[36]

This intrigue "which connects to what detaches itself absolutely" (*AE* 188/*OB* 147) is of course that of "proximity" and "responsibility." Inexplicable proximity, drive to go outside of myself, directing myself to someone who offers me no motivation, no inducement to approach him or her, someone who, as we have seen, is "uninteresting." "Saying" of a responsibility that begins without there having been a question or an announcement: "The Infinite orders me to the 'neighbor' as a face, without being exposed to me. . . . The order has not been the cause of my response, nor even a question that would have preceded it in a dialogue . . . [it is an] order that I find only in my response itself" (*AE* 191/*OB* 150). That response is—literally—extraordinary, motivated by nothing in the actual context in which it is given. And therefore, says Levinas, it points beyond itself to another context which, however, must not be taken as a mere alternative. The relation to God is found only in my relation to my neighbor—which does not mean that God is invisible or inaccessible (*absconditissimus*)—*but instead that God is accessible in ethics* (cf. *TeI* 51/*TI* 78), which in turn means that for Levinas ethics is not so much a "correlate of the religious," but "the element in which religious transcendence can have meaning."[37] One sees why Levinas thinks that his description of human relations reaches a point where words like "God" and "creation" are necessary. For human relations do not answer to our expectations, and they withdraw from the descriptions one finds in someone like Sartre. As soon as one feels not only uneasy but morally ashamed, the analyses of Sartre fall silent.[38] As soon as shame is more than the loss of my freedom (shame according to Sartre), as soon as it accuses itself of that freedom and goes against it by giving something up for someone else, it is already an affect that escapes its context and in which it displays the trace "of a passage which never became present, possibly nothingness. *But the surplus over pure nothingness,* an infinitesimal difference, is in my non-indifference to the neighbor, where I am obedient *as though* to an order addressed to me" (*AE* 116/*OB* 91).

Levinas's whole effort is to draw the philosophical consequences of this *as if:* I behave as if I have been commanded, and yet there is no one who spoke. Do I hear voices then? No, says Levinas, but it is the voice of God which I hear "in the face of my neighbor." *God himself, I do not hear.* God only lets himself be heard in an affect which is not directed to him. Anachoresis of a transcendence which "owes it to itself" to interrupt itself even before it is heard (*AE* 194/ *OB* 152). The voice of God is nowhere other than in the relation between me and the Other: *creatio ex nihilo* means that the God who could have constructed the entire violin was, so to speak, pleased to "make" of me a sounding board which releases the sound it was built to release only at the moment that my neighbor passes by and, without realizing it, provides the strings on which that sound can be heard, but "only afterwards."

Creation is thus for Levinas the first moment of the trauma. But it is a moment which is no moment at all, and which, as distinct from what Freud calls the first scene, can in no way be situated in the temporal order which it disturbs. Which is why God is not quite like the man in the grocery store, and why the scene of creation ultimately cannot be compared with Freud's "memory trace," in which there comes to life an affect that, in a sense—but only in a sense—did not previously exist. Creation is not the past of an energy which remained unnoticed but was there nonetheless; it is an absolute past that escapes every present and origin, thereby anchoring metaphysics in ethics. Metaphysical movement—transascendence—"is" only in the ethical affection which itself "is" not, since it falls outside of being and therefore dis-inter-ests. This interruption of inter-esse, of the *conatus* that binds us to being, is not purely negative. It presents itself as an affect of non-indifference—of non-disinterest—which cannot be clarified by its context in being. It is "otherwise-than-being," the *epekeina* of the Good that breaks through in this affect, thus preventing metaphysics from becoming onto-theology, or religion from becoming theology, in which a "pious thought hastily deduces the existence of God" (*AE* 119/*OB* 93). The existence of God must not be proven or denied, for revelation does not bear proof: it "is accomplished by the one that receives it" (*AE* 199/*OB* 156), and is thus no more and no less than "the echo of a sound that would precede the resonance of this sound" (*AE* 141/*OB* 111). And therefore is it ab-solute past but also ab-solute future. The God who has always already passed by is always still to come. This metaphysics supports this ethics, and the ethics supports the metaphysics: both rest on a principle (a beginning which "is" not a beginning) of dispossession that Levinas calls "God": "Dieu ne prend jamais corps [God never takes on a body]."[39]

One thus has hands only because one can never get one's hands on God. Through this non-absorption—through the resistance of the infinity which does not show itself in or through immanence—God "is" the "first word." Other than all others. God "is" the hiatus between face and form, between Saying and Said. Of the Other. But also of me. For God "is" the misery that the Other ("stripped of its very form, a face is frozen in its nudity")[40] did not wish and the affection that leaves me no peace. The misery of the Other leaves me no peace, the one affection infects the others and God "is" the system without system of that Contagion, the Plague that is no Plague. According to Levinas.

—According to Levinas! But where are the "holes" sighted at the beginning? Where are the holes? Did you not promise to stretch the fabric of the official reading so much that it would now simply tear apart on its own?

—Yes, but I have not said that it would happen immediately. Or without exertion. I mean: the fabric of a great thought tears only when one has run over it long enough. Only if one runs back and forth across it. For example, because one is intrigued. And I cannot imagine that this thinking does not intrigue you. It seems the very essence of coherence. But does that coherence convince you? Are you converted to this thinking now that it has shown you its inner architectonic and its outer defense walls, how they were designed to protect in advance against all the objections—and let us be frank: there have not been that many—later raised in an attempt to embarrass it? It is to this dissociation between seeing that coherence and being convinced by it that I wanted to call attention, and to which I pointed already when I stated that the task of reading is to go beyond a first grasp, to an un-grasping which attends to the solitude of a thinking. This solitude is uncomfortable, which is perhaps why people are so often converted, and why it is so gladly agreed that philosophy is a dialogue. But the dialogue lives from a silence which it cannot make communal and which is not communal. It is due to this silence that the "holes" of the Other are not merely gaps which I can fill in. I did not want to drown out the silence here with my own arguments, for that would be to locate those holes of which it is said that they are everywhere. I wished only to let this silence be heard, in the hope that it will cause discomfort—*for only if it does that* can one understand that in this discomfort, which is not shame and without which philosophy would not be the kind of practice that it is, lies hidden the beginning of what philosophy could *and should* object to Levinas.

NOTES

1. My first sentence alludes to the title of an earlier piece on Levinas, entitled "Dis-possessed: How to Remain Silent 'After Levinas,'" *Man and World* 29 (1996): 19–46.

2. E. Levinas, *Altérité et transcendence* (Paris: Fata Morgana, 1995), 177.

3. E. Levinas, *Dieu, la Mort, et le Temps* (Paris: Grasset, 1993), 137, 143.

4. I have made a start along this line in a forthcoming article: "Zum-Buch-sein (I). Heidegger, het boek en iemand anders."

5. One need only open *Totality and Infinity* or *Otherwise Than Being* to come upon one or more of these expressions. Jan de Greef has written, already some time ago, a very interesting article on Levinas's almost compulsive recourse to "military" and "pathological metaphors": "L'affectivité chez Lévinas," in *Figures de la Finitude: Etudes d'Anthropologie Philosophique*, ed. G. Florival (Paris/Louvain-la-Neuve: Peeters, 1988), 53–65 (conference given in 1984).

6. All of these are words used by Levinas himself. This also goes for all of the following appraisals and metaphors.

7. This last notion is also contained in the French *altérer*.

8. On this notion of "materiality," cf. *TA* 36–38/*TO* 55–57 and *DE* 139ff./*EE* 82ff.

9. E. Levinas, "Transcendence et Hauteur," in *Liberté et commandement* (Paris: Fata Morgana, 1994), 66.

10. Levinas, *Altérité et transcendence*, 114.

11. Whereas in proximity I bear myself in my own hands—the Saying that says only itself and nothing else says "here I am" and offers them to the Other—here I no longer have myself, so to speak, fully in hand. It is rather that my hands have me, or that I have become my hands. The tension between "having hands" and "being hands" has disappeared.

12. Cf. J. Derrida, "Donner la mort," in *L'éthique du don: Jacques Derrida et la pensée du don. Colloque de Royaumont décembre 1990*, ed. J. M. Rabaté and M. Wetzel (Paris: Métaille-Transition, 1992), 81. Elsewhere I have tried to show how Levinas would consider such remarks to have missed his problematic *completely*—and not only because the distinction between the otherness of God and that of one's neighbor is, in fact, central to it. See my "Anti-Racism's First Word: How Not to Inherit Derrida's Legacy from Levinas," to appear.

13. Together with "trauma," this is one of the central and recurrent concepts in *Otherwise Than Being*.

14. Cf., e.g., *AE* 180/*OB* 142: "The psyche, a uniqueness outside of concepts, is a seed of folly, already a psychosis. It is not an ego, but me under assignation." Countless such passages are to be found in Levinas's work.

15. Levinas's own clarification of my previous citation. See " 'Wat men van zichzelf eist, eist men van een heilige': Een gesprek met Emmanuel Levinas," in J. Goud, *God als Raadsel: Peilingen in het spoor van Levinas* (Kampen/Kapellen: Kok, 1992), 145.

16. The remainder of my investigation is directed to clarifying the difference between these two "traces." The fact that for Levinas I, too, am a trace of God is confirmed beyond any doubt at *TeI* 78/*TI* 104: "Creation leaves to the creature a trace of dependence, but it is an unparalleled dependence."

17. For what follows, see S. Freud, "Entwurf einer Psychologie" (1895), in his *Aus den Anfängen der Psychoanalyse: Briefe an Wilhelm Fliess, Abhandlungen und Notizen aus den Jahren 1887–1902* (Frankfurt a.M.: S. Fischer Verlag, 1962). English translation by J. Strachey in *The Origins of Psychoanalysis: Letters to Wilhelm Fliess* (New York: Basic Books, 1954). Henceforth cited as *E* and *Origins*. The translation has occasionally been modified slightly. All italics in passages cited are mine.

18. The analysis of eros appearing in *Totality and Infinity* comes in a

section bearing the general title "Au delà du Visage" (*TeI* 232ff./*TI* 251ff.), which signifies a priority Levinas continues to uphold later (e.g., *AE* 113 n. 27/*OB* 192 n. 27).

19. The term itself comes from J.-A. Miller, "Extimité," in *Lacanian Theory of Discourse: Subject, Structure, and Society*, ed. M. Brasher et al. (New York/London: Routledge, 1994), 74–87.

20. I intentionally use the words with which Levinas describes "proximity" in *Otherwise Than Being*.

21. In "Das Unbewusste" (1915), Freud explains that the affect of angst is an inversion of another affect which is denied the possibility of manifesting itself, due to an unconscious repression of the representation bearing it. The affect which "gets no air" becomes, as it were, toxic, just as an organism does when forced to hold its breath ("its heart cannot breathe"). It is through this poisoning that the affect becomes angst. In S. Freud, *Psychologie des Unbewussten: Studienausgabe Band III* (Frankfurt a.M.: S. Fischer Verlag, 1975), 141. English translation by J. Strachey et al. in *The Standard Edition of the Complete Psychological Works* (London: Hogarth Press, 1954–73), vol. 14. Henceforth cited as *Ubw* and *SE*.

22. On this notion of a "trace" differing from all other traces, conceived out of Levinas's unwillingness to envision the impression of a past presence, cf. E. Levinas, "La trace de l'autre," in *EDE* 187–202/*TrO* 345–59.

23. In what follows, I am inspired by the brilliant first part of J.-F. Lyotard, *Heidegger and the Jews* (Minneapolis: University of Minnesota Press, 1990), above all pp. 11–35.

24. On this point, I depart from Lyotard. Cf. ibid., pp. 15–16, where he refers twice and without reservation to "unconscious affects" in Freud, *Ubw* 136–38/*SE* 177–79, and where, as we have seen, something else is in fact asserted.

25. Lyotard, *Heidegger and the Jews*, 15–16.

26. As one will recall, Levinas also uses this image of a sound audible only in its echo (cf. *AE* 134/*OB* 106 and my commentary in section III above).

27. For example, every time *Totality and Infinity* goes on the offensive against "gods without faces" (e.g., *TeI* 115, 132, 134/*TI* 142, 158, 160).

28. J. Lacan, *Les quatre concepts fondamentaux de la psychanalyse (Séminaire XI)* (Paris: Seuil, 1973), 45.

29. J. Lacan, *L'angoisse: Séminaire 1962–1963* (unpublished manuscript), session on June 5, 1963, and passim.

30. Lacan, *Les quatres concepts fondamentaux de la psychanalyse*, 247 ("les dieux obscurs").

31. On this problematic of a Law that withdraws from the relation, but precisely in this way imprisons, cf. J. Derrida, "Préjuges—devant la loi," in *La faculté de juger: Colloque de Cérisy 1982* (Paris: Minuit, 1985).

32. Too often, it is forgotten that already at the beginning of *Totality and Infinity* Levinas says that "transcendence . . . is necessarily a transascendence" (*TeI* 5/*TI* 35), and that he never retracts this. *Every* critique which, remaining in line with Derrida's "Violence and Metaphysics," brings the notion of "*the* other in the same" into confrontation with the distinction, crucial to *Totality and Infinity* and *Otherwise Than Being*, between "le même et l'autre," *will thus first have to explain whether and how that "other" still leaves room for there to be a self*—in other words, whether the transdescendence of "the other in the same" is still indeed a transcendence.

33. This expression comes from Rudolf Bernet, "Inconscient et conscience: Sur la nature de la pulsion, du désir, de la représentation et de l'affect," in *Création et événement: Autour de Jean Ladrière*, ed. G. Florival and J. Greisch, Colloque de Cérisy 1995, Louvain (Paris: Editions de l'Institut Supérieur de Philosophie de Louvain-la-Neuve/Editions Peeters, 1996), 145–64.

34. Through the rhythm of this inhaling and exhaling, there comes into being an "intersubjective space," a "curvature" (*TeI* 267/*TI* 291) which prevents it from becoming pure dispersion or pure fusion. What Sam Ijsseling once called the "explosion of the transcendental" is countered here by the thought—inspired by Lurianic Kabbalah—that "the limitation of the creative Infinite, and multiplicity—are compatible with the perfection of Infinity" (*TeI* 77/*TI* 104). *Bonum et dispersum convertuntur.*

35. Cf. note 22 above.

36. Cf., e.g., *AE* 190/*OB* 149: " 'Here I am' (*me voici*), in the name of God, without referring myself directly to his presence. 'Here I am,' that and just that! The word God is still absent from the phrase in which God is involved in words for the first time. It does not at all state 'I believe in God.' To bear witness to God is precisely not to state this extraordinary word."

37. E. Levinas, *Nouvelles lectures talmudiques* (Paris: Minuit, 1996), 30.

38. J.-P. Sartre, *L'être et le néant: Essai d'ontologie phénoménologie* (Paris: Gallimard, 1943), 265ff. However, I have shown elsewhere that the discussion between Levinas and Sartre must be conducted at a much deeper level than this, and that there are good reasons not to follow Levinas too quickly in his critique of Sartre, a critique which, in spite of all else, in fact shares more with Sartre than one might suspect. See "A Sartrean in Disguise? Levinas on Racism," to appear in *Levinas: The Face of the Other: The Fifteenth Annual Symposium of the Simon Silverman Phenomenology Center* (Pittsburgh: Duquesne University Press, 1998).

39. Levinas, *Altérite et transcendence*, 172.

40. See my attempt to turn this citation (*CPP* 96, translation altered) against Levinas, in "Dis-possessed," especially pp. 34ff.; and my subsequent attempt to clarify what was at stake in that first attempt: "The Core of My Opposition to Levinas," *Ethical Perspectives* 4 (1997): 154–70.

12

Adieu—sans Dieu: Derrida and Levinas

John D. Caputo

IN THE SEMITIC WORLD of desert wanderers, nothing is more important than hospitality. Hospitality is the fundamental condition of survival, an unconditional necessity of life. The duty owed the wanderer and the stranger is holy and inviolable, and without it the world of wanderers would perish by its own hand. To provide a place of respite and refuge, to offer bread and water, even to take food out of one's own mouth in order to share it with the stranger, in short, to make welcome, that is the law of the land, indeed, that is the law of God (Are these the same law? Is it the one law because it is the other?). The traveler who appears at our door is marked by God, who has signed the face of the stranger and placed him or her under divine protection. The one who receives the stranger receives God and bears the mark of "the God who loves the stranger."

In Derrida's view—and to understand this we would have to understand more carefully what he has written about *khora*—we are all more or less to be found in this Semitic or archi-Semitic condition. For him, we are all Semites, or archi-Semites, more or less uprooted or displaced, dispersed or disseminated, lost or astray. We are all radically *nomadic,* desert wanderers, without a home, *"destinerrant,"* Derrida says, wandering in a *khora,* radically "an-khoral." That is why hospitality is so central to Derrida's thought, and why his interests today are so much centered on the "crimes against hospitality that are endured by the wayfarers and hostages of our times, day after day incarcerated or expelled, from concentration camps to retention camps, from border to border, near to us or far" (A 132).[1] Hospitality is the virtue of a Semite, what is required in a world of wanderers, of exiles and displaced persons. This is true for Derrida not only in the metonymic sense which besets us all, even the most well housed and well heeled, but also and especially in the literal, political sense. In *Adieu: à Emmanuel Levinas,* a very beautiful book written in loving memory of Levinas, written *to* (*à*) Levinas, exiles and refugees wander constantly across the surface of the text, periodically showing up at the door, illegal immigrants in need of help—the defenseless scapegoats of the right wing in France and the United States—their solicitous faces pressed against the window.

> By way of certain discrete but transparent allusions, Levinas oriented our view toward what is happening today, in Israel as well as in Europe and France, in Africa, in America, in Asia, since at least the first world war and since what Hannah Arendt called *The Decline of the Nation-State:* everywhere that refugees of any kind, immigrants with or without citizenship, exiles or displaced persons, with or without papers, from the heart of Nazi Europe to the former Yugoslavia, from the Middle East to Rwanda, from Zaire to California, from St. Bernard Church in the thirteenth arrondissement in Paris, Cambodians, Armenians, Palestinians, Algerians and so many others summon socio- and geo-political space to a mutation—a legal and political mutation, but first of all, if this distinction still retains its pertinence, an ethical conversion. (A 131; cf. 118, 175–76)

These exiled and displaced people, who lack the wherewithal to lay down their heads, are the constant concern and preoccupation of this book, and more than ever, with each passing year, of Derrida's work in general, of what is called, for better or for worse, "deconstruction." It is as if the voices of the dispossessed and displaced are constantly to be heard in the background of Derrida's book, like people speaking during a lecture, exchanging greetings, bidding farewell. We keep hearing the quiet murmur of their *"bonjour," "bienvenue, oui, bienvenue,"* and *"adieu,"* even as the text, trying not to be distracted, proceeds to analyze what they are saying, subjecting these words of welcome and departure to a meticulous philosophical scrutiny. In a world of wanderers, the words exchanged between travelers are among the most important words in the language, words not of elemental "power," as in virile Heideggerian bravado, but of elemental holiness. Such holy words command respect and draw the attention of the sages; they are the first subject of philosophy, the subject of first philosophy.

HOW CAN DERRIDA SAY *ADIEU*?

Adieu is such a word, an archi-Semitic or Franco-archi-Semitic word. *Adieu* resounds with God's own name. One could hardly imagine a word that would be more a word of God, a word to God. *Adieu:* (I commend you) to God, God be with you. This word, a beautiful prayer embedded in ordinary language, is very precious for Levinas, for whom everything is turned to God, *ad deum* (in what Derrida calls Christian Latin French). As scandalous as it may seem to Derrida's secularizing, Nietzscheanizing admirers, *adieu* is also very precious to Derrida, for whom it is also a prayer and even a kind of French poem (A 205), even though Derrida "rightly passes for an atheist," as he says in *Circonfession.*[2] "*Adieu*" is the title of Derrida's book, of the first essay of the book, and the word he addresses to Levinas in the graveside eulogy, when he bid adieu to Levinas, on December 27, 1995, in the Pantin Cemetery, all of which ends very poignantly, "Adieu, Emmanuel."

But how can Derrida say *adieu*? How can he mean it? What does he mean? How can this be a word of elemental importance and commanding holiness for Derrida? How can he, who rightly passes for an atheist, rightly commend Emmanuel to God? Are we to believe that Derrida prays, that he keeps a secret prie-dieu sheltered from the eyes of the world, that he is a man of prayers and tears? Surely "*adieu*" is just an expression for him, a convention, a matter of semantics, a way to bid farewell in French, especially to a dearly departed friend and sage, whatever it might mean, *ad literam*? How does Derrida dare to say *adieu* after saying "*je passe à juste titre pour athée*" ("I pass rightly for an atheist")? How can Derrida say "*adieu*"—*sans Dieu*?

Let us listen to Derrida listening to Levinas saying *adieu*. A-Dieu, *ad deum*, to God, who is infinite, *à l'infini*, since the idea of God, according to Descartes and a long tradition, is the idea of the Infinite. The *à* in *à-Dieu* represents a turn toward God, not a turn taken by an auto-turning, autonomous self, but a being-already-turned to God, long before the conscious self takes one turn or another. Here I am always already turned to God. By God. I am promised to God long before I would, by my own intentional act, seek or aspire for God. I am delivered over to God from time immemorial, in a way that no preposition, even this *à* to which we here have recourse, can "translate." No preposition can express my being pre-positioned to and by God, my prepossession by God. No preposition can plumb the depths of the devotion by which I am always already vowed to God (*DVI* 250; *A* 179). This preposition *à* signifies a being taken possession of and being prepossessed by God, taken over by the Infinite which is designated and proposed by it. Before the subject can turn to God, it finds itself already turned, so that when, in prayer and devotion, the subject turns to God, that turn comes as a response to a prior address by God who has already called us. We are turned to God in advance of every conscious act or free choice, before being, before presence, already vowed and promised to God, in the excess of a desire called "to-God," *ad deum, ad infinitum.* The *à-Dieu* is the very diachrony of time, the disproportion of the finite and the Infinite, the very being-vowed before any conscious act, which is "devoted to God" (*DVI* 12; *A* 180–81; cf. *TO* 114–20).[3]

For Levinas, the *à* in *adieu, à-Dieu,* is trying to translate a primordial devotion as old as hospitality itself, as old as biblical hospitality, and older still, as old as time out of mind. That is why, Derrida says, "it is not unusual that at the moment of saying in what the *à-Dieu* consists, Levinas evokes God's love of the stranger. God will be first of all, as it is said, 'he who loves the stranger' " (*DVI* 250; *A* 180). God makes his face shine upon the face of the stranger; the stranger stands in the shelter and shade of God's loving care. The self is always already turned to God who has in turn turned the self to the stranger, deflected it in a certain way, ordered and commanded the self to the stranger, who bears God's trace and seal. Being turned to the Other means a devotion to God which responds without desire for reciprocity, in a love without eros, in a relation without correlation and reciprocity, like the non-reciprocity, the interruption of symmetry and commensurability of death itself.

A-Dieu, to-God, to-the-Infinite, to-the-*tout autre,* who is a positive infinity, an infinite yes, *oui,* to say yes to what separates itself, to welcome and greet what separates itself, whose departure is not different from its coming, this "deference" is the breath of the *à-Dieu* (*A* 113). But how can we imagine Derrida being already turned *to* God, by God, if Derrida rightly passes for an atheist? By whom is he turned, and to whom? To whom is he praying?

How can there be an *adieu sans Dieu*?

TRANSLATING *ADIEU*

I have pointed out the multiple immigrations and illegal immigrants, the strangers slipping across the frontiers of foreign lands under the cover of dark to be found in Derrida's *Adieu: à Emmanuel Levinas*. For just that reason, this book is also deeply concerned with "transla- tion," which is an elemental demand of hospitality, requiring us to adopt a new idiom, to speak in a new tongue that can be understood by the stranger—by the *goyim,* the Gentiles (unlike St. Thomas's famous treatise, Derrida's *Adieu* is a kind of *summa "pro" gentiles*). All along, we are being prepared by Derrida's *Adieu: à Emmanuel Levinas* for a translation of *adieu,* not only in the sense of trying to get it out of Christian Latin French, and not only in the sense of getting it out of its biblical tongue into a more universal, open-ended idiom, but more radically still, where it is not a question of any sort of semantic transfer at all. *Adieu* is concerned with what Derrida calls "an event of translation," the event "of *another translation,* of another thought of translation" (A 205), which will constitute a more radical mutation and transformation.

No regular reader of Derrida will be surprised to find that there are several processes of translation going on in this text at the same time.

(1) To begin with, there is the question of how to translate *adieu* into English. If we advert to an ancient protocol, no longer observed, that regulates the use of "farewell" and "welcome," we see that *stricto sensu* it is impossible to say *"adieu"* to the departed. Strictly speaking, according to the *Oxford English Dictionary,* and I know of nothing stricter than that, *adieu* should not be translated as "fare- well," because *adieu* is not directed to the wayfarer, to the one who is leaving, but to the one who remains behind. *Adieu,* to-God, does not mean "farewell," or "go with God," but rather "I commend you to God," like the English "good-bye," "God be with you," which would in fact be a better translation. *Adieu* was originally said by the one *departing* to the one *left behind,* while "farewell" was addressed to the *wayfarer,* to the one departing, by those left behind.

> *The one remaining behind:* "Farewell, fare thee well, go with God, have
>   a safe journey, wherever your travels may take you."
> *The traveler:* "Adieu, I commend you *to God,* to God's loving care while

I am gone, God be with you for as long as I am gone. May God's presence fill you in my absence."

To be sure, nowadays we have become very lax about such fine points, here as in so many other things.

So you see how difficult it would be, *stricto sensu*, to say *adieu* to Levinas, quite apart from the question of atheism. If death is a journey (from which no one has returned), it is a journey that the *Other* takes. If it is suggested that it is a journey for which I too have a reservation, then I protest, with Johannes Climacus, "not I, not now." Death is the journey taken by the Other, while we, the living, remain behind, in life. So, if we are the ones left behind by the departed, then we should bid "farewell" to him who is departing. "Fare thee well, Emmanuel, wherever you are going," wherever all the departed, *tout autre*, are going. If the proper protocol is to be observed, then at the hour of death, the one who is *dying* should bid *adieu* to those who remain behind, "God be with you after I am gone." After death, at the graveside or in a later testimonial volume, such an *adieu* would be very difficult, perhaps impossible, or even *the* impossible, for this *adieu* would be at best a ghostly word, the word of a *revenant* back to us from the grave, from the other side, the side of the wholly Other. Strictly speaking, then, to say *adieu* to the departed would require a kind of Copernican revolution in our thinking about death, in which we would imagine the deceased as staying behind, in some invisible realm, while we take leave of him into the visible. "Adieu, Emmanuel," we would say as we slip from his side, while he would bid us "farewell" as we depart, as we take our leave from death. That would be hard to imagine, even for Kant, who was much practiced in such Copernican turns and reversals.

(2) On a second level, there is a continuous translating and intermingling of "deconstruction" and "first philosophy," so that we are often not quite sure whose voice we are hearing, Jacques's or Emmanuel's, whether ethics is here being cast in a deconstructive form, or deconstruction is being given an ethical force, or whether, as Derrida likes to say, it is never a question of choosing between these possibilities.

(3) Meanwhile, on another and very important level, we see that Levinas himself is caught up in a very difficult project of trying to *translate the Torah*, of letting the Torah cross the borders marked by

Mount Sinai, opening the gates of Jerusalem, which is defined by the Torah, to all the "nations." The nations look on this intimate relation of Israel and Yahweh and do not understand the language they whisper to each other, and so this intimate relation, in which each is jealous of the other's affections, must be open to the nations, to the third ones, so that translation is a requirement of justice for the other Others. To be sure, Levinas wants to share the Torah like a gift with the *goyim*, to translate the Torah into Greek (which is a universal language for him), since if the Torah makes sense it must also speak in Greek, at least in an odd sort of hybrid Jewgreek, or perhaps a Franco-Jewgreek, *s'il y en a*, which makes plain the universal, human message of the Torah.

(4) But above all else, Derrida keeps posing a central and pressing question to Levinas, of how to *translate his ethics of the Other into a politics*, how to transport the ethics of hospitality into a politics of hospitality? How to let the beautiful ethical motifs of Levinas's ethics slip across its ethical borders into a political deed? This translation would represent a paradoxical leap, like raising the dagger over Isaac's outstretched limbs (cf. A 201, 204), a very risky business indeed. After all, how can a nation-state, a civil society, which is concerned above all with a strong national defense and national security, make itself a hostage of the Other? How do we translate and transport our hope in messianic peace into the "peace process," in, say, Northern Ireland or the Middle East? Must not the ethics of substitution—of giving everything to the Other, our jobs and our schools, even the bread out of our mouth, the ethics of being accused, responsible, obsessed, and a hostage of the Other—must that not be strictly confined within the borders of the privacy of ethical life? Is not substitution for the Other a virtue strictly to be maintained within the limits of ethics alone? How can a nation-state practice an absolute, unconditional hospitality to the Other? Is not national hospitality always subject to conditions, to immigration laws? But then would such a conditional hospitality still be hospitality (any more than "conditional love" would still be love)? Would it not be a disaster to let hospitality out of its ethical confines? "Thou shall not kill," sayeth the Lord, and that is the sum of the Torah. True enough, but it is also necessary to raise an army to defend oneself and discourage aggression against one's place in the sun. What is the way from the heavenly Jerusalem to the earthly one? Is there one? The storm of this paradox

thunders over the pages of *Adieu*. How to translate ethics into politics, to translate the *"viens, oui, oui"* of the ethics of the *tout autre* into a politics of deportees and immigrants? How to allow the free passage of refugees, of illegal immigrants and all of those "without papers," through porous national frontiers? The politics of *Adieu* is one of transporting, translating, bearing across the borders the immigrants and outcasts, the displaced, deported and persecuted. For the God who loves the stranger makes his face to shine upon just these very people.

In the end, for Derrida, *"adieu,"* a central word in the vocabulary of hospitality, is to be *translated into hospitality*. *"Adieu"* is another Derridean prayer, which he prays with all his heart, hidden away in his secret prie-dieu, his eyes filled with tears, in his ankhoral religion, his religion without religion:

> Come, yes, yes, welcome to the coming of the other, *à l'invention de l'autre,* yes, in the name of the God who loves the stranger, yes, to the God who makes himself present in the welcome extended to the stranger. Yes to the Other, yes, come, welcome to the coming of the wholly other, yes—amen to the coming of the yes. *Viens, oui, oui.*

Adieu is the subject of a very *radical* translation indeed, one that does not consist in a semantic transfer at all but requires the deed itself, a translation, shall we say, not in truth but in deed, or if in truth, then in the Augustinian sense of *facere veritatem*, doing and making truth indeed, not of discoursing about it. We do not "understand" the word *adieu* by thinking something but by *doing* something. In this translation, the borders between ethics and politics become as porous as possible, passing freely between each other and intermingling with each other, like immigrants who are no longer blocked by border police. In the process, Derrida—with the help of a certain death of God in Levinas—also blurs the lines between theism and atheism, between theology and a-theology, *Dieu* and *sans Dieu, Dieu* and *a-Dieu* (as in a-morphic), and this precisely in the name of the God who loves the stranger. That is because, as we shall see, *the name of God can and must be translated into hospitality,* something which the beautiful French word *adieu,* this Franco-Semitic poem and prayer, embodies *ad literam*. Otherwise, the name of God is a tinkling cymbal and sounding brass. Derrida is not out to erase or wipe away the name of God—God forbid!—but to translate it, and by translating it to keep it safe, *sauf le nom.* That, in the end, is how it is possible for Derrida to say *à-Dieu* while rightly passing for an atheist, to say *adieu—sans Dieu,* like the German mystic who prayed that God rid him of God, while himself passing rightly for a Dominican friar.

FROM HOST TO HOSTAGE
THE ETHICS OF HOSPITALITY

To demonstrate this proposal in detail, let us begin with Derrida's reading of Levinasian ethics as an extended commentary on the notion of hospitality, as a vast and sweeping hymn to hospitality, a term which, while discussed extensively of late by Derrida,[4] Levinas himself does not frequently use. *Totality and Infinity* represents for Derrida "an immense treatise *on hospitality,* which is attested to less by the actual occurrences of this word than by the lexical chains that form around the word *l'accueil,* welcome. 'The face is always given to a welcome and the welcome only welcomes the face'" (A 49). What is the relation to the Other in *Totality and Infinity,* to the face of the Other, to *l'infini,* if not one of an unconditional hospitality, a welcoming (*accueillir*) by the Same of the Other (*TeI* 276/*TI* 299)? Hospitality is "yes to the other," but this yes is a second yes ("*oui, oui*"), coming as it does in response to the first yes, which is the Other him- or herself. The Other is not a no, not the one who I am not, but a yes, a "positive" infinity constituting an infinite yes which elicits our affirmation and desire (yes). "It is not I, it is the other that can say *yes,*" writes Levinas (*TeI* 66/*TI* 93). Derrida comments: "To have welcomed this *yes* of the other, to greet this infinite one in separation, in other words in its holiness, this is the experience of the *à-Dieu*" (A 51–53, 110–11 n. 5). To say yes to this yes, to pronounce this second yes, *oui, oui,* that is hospitality. Accordingly, the I always comes second, and when a seemingly autonomous agent acts, far from being something decisionistic, it acts in response to the Other, so that what passes for autonomy is really heteronomy, and answering a call is for all the world not acting on one's own (A 52–54; *PdA* 86–88/*PoF* 68–69). Hospitality means to maintain an "open door" to the Other, to keep one's door ajar—the very opposite of today's "gated communities," which for Derrida is what a community always is—ready for the coming of the Other, ready to run the risk of receiving more than one can contain, like a city open to the approach of the enemy (A 100 n. 1). Such risky hospitality puts the self at risk, like Penelope, who, while waiting to welcome Ulysses home, had a guest too many. Penelope's risk raises the question of how to safeguard the self and the home (A 58–59 n. 2), and hence of how hospitality would be possible for the safekeepers of "national security," who keep guard over the national homeland.

Derrida quickly—instantly—recognizes the claims of the third one (*le tiers*) as having *already* been inscribed in the face of the Other, *already* part of that epiphany. The immediacy of the relation to the Other is immediately interrupted by the third (A 66). If I welcome the Other into my home, the third cannot be left out in the cold by my welcoming. *As soon as I open my door to the Other,* the third one is always already there, *also* knocking. I am, we two are, already seen by the third one even as I am regarded by the Other. In the face of the Other the faces of the other Others are also inscribed, lest this relationship to the Other become a private affair, exclusive and exclusionary, just between "us," which is the essence of inhospitality and closed doors. The Levinasian notion of justice, in which the scarcity of our resources forces us to calculate and allocate among all the other Others, is very central to Derrida, whose sights are set on finding a way to open the doors of ethics to politics. The third one menaces the purity of the ethical twosome, imposing the demands of a justice for all, inscribing politics on the very face of ethics. To put an even more pointed tip on it, my covenant with the Other is always already menaced by the Others (*goyim*). My "originary word of honor," my "oath" (*jurer*) to the Other, is always already threatened by the perjury, the abjury, the injury of turning to the third. Whence the Job-like lament of the just man, "What do I have to do with justice?," which puts such impossible demands upon me, which puts me in a position where I cannot tell the difference between fidelity and betrayal, melding the ethical together with all that betrays it— synchrony, totality, the political order (A 68–69).

In *Totality and Infinity,* the welcome (*accueil*) of the Other takes the form of a welcoming into one's home, into the gathering-recollectedness (*recueillement*) of the home, which is itself constituted by the more primary welcome extended by the feminine. The home is a refuge, an asylum from the world into which the masculine subject retreats. A man is *made* at home in the very home which is supposed to be his own, his castle. That means a man is both a guest and a host in his home, in the double sense of the French *hôte*, a hospitable host of the Other while also a guest of a more primordial welcome. That baldly androcentric account of the home reflects a theocentrism, for the earth over which man rules is also a home into which humankind has been invited as a guest of the more primordial divine hospitality. That theocentrism, Derrida claims, in turn opens up a way to overturn Levinas's androcentrism, a way of turning the *pre*-ethical hospitality of the feminine into something ethical par excellence. For there is now an analogy between God and the woman, each of whom extends to man a more primordial hospitality, making the proprietor himself a guest in his own home. Woman then is the figure of "welcoming par excellence," of a welcoming before welcoming, of the divine hospitality. Derrida would thus try "another reading" (A 82) of Levinas's androcentrism, which would turn it into a "feminist manifesto" by defining absolute hospitality in terms of the feminine (not empirical women).[5] Hence instead of being pre-ethical in the sense of not yet ethical, the feminine becomes the very pre-ethical origin of ethics, the absolutely originary, pre-originary, and nothing less (A 83).

When we turn to *Otherwise Than Being*, Derrida singles out a striking shift of tone from the language of host and hospitality—"The subject is a host" (*TeI* 276/*TI* 299)—to the language of hostage—"A subject is a hostage [*otage*]" (*AE* 142/*OB* 112). *Hôte* (host/guest) and *otage* (hostage) are related, for a hostage is a "guest" received or surrendered in substitutive pledge, as a substitute for another, a token at the disposition of the sovereign, a captive whose way is blocked (*obsidatus*) (A 105). In the new, more radical language of "substitution" in *Otherwise Than Being*, I am persecuted without having done anything, accused and obsessed, which has the effect of dislodging all the more ruthlessly and shockingly the primacy of intentionality. The effect of the epiphany of the Other is not to raise the question but to put me in question. The subject finds him- or herself contested, interpellated, "sued" (*mise en cause*), accused without blame, under accusation by everyone—in short, a hostage (A 103–5). The host become hostage begins to look more and more like Penelope, and there is an unnerving link, both semantic and etymological, between hostility and hospitality.

Clearly, the calming and tranquilizing language of hospitality, which always assumes I am the master of the house in which I welcome the Other, is here pressed to its limits, pressed forward to what Derrida calls an "absolute visitation," one that is absolutely unexpected and absolutely uninvited, like an unexpected messianic coming (A 115). For insofar as I invite, prepare, and call for the coming of the Other, insofar as *l'invention de l'autre* takes place within the horizon of expectation, where I set down in advance who is to come, when, and under what conditions, where there is a carefully prepared guest list of who is welcome and who is not to be admitted, then that is not the coming of the Other but the coming of the Same—"An order where there is no absolute surprise, the order of what I shall call the invention of the same."[6] In an absolute visitation, the Good chooses me before I welcome it (*AE* 158/*OB* 123), has always already passed by, like the Ancient of Days, in a time before memory, bending my capacity for welcoming to it; elective assignation is prior to any welcome, not only more originary but more violent and traumatizing (A 109). My conscious act of welcome is always too late, coming only after the Other has always already come. Here hospitality is pressed beyond itself, to a hospitality beyond or perhaps "without" hospitality.

That brings us to the political question, to the possibility of absolute visitation in the political order, to the visitation of the ethical upon politics, a question which has become all the more difficult, indeed impossibly difficult.

TRANSLATING THE TORAH: FROM SINAI TO *VISAGE*

The theme of a 1996 conference honoring the first anniversary of Levinas's death was "Visage and Sinai," reflecting the two sides, the two faces, of Levinas's work: *visage,* first philosophy or ethics, the law of the face; and *Sinai,* Judaism, the Jewish law, Torah. These two, which of course spell Athens and Jerusalem all over again, are to be conjoined, the face *and* Sinai, not disjoined, and so we are invited to see how the two communicate with each other. For Derrida, as we shall see, the *oeuvre* of Levinas can be understood as a work of *translating* Sinai into *visage,* so that *visage,* the phenomenology or meta-phenomenology of *visage,* is the way that Levinas has found to render the Torah into a universal language, producing a new revised standard Levinasian version, which lets the Torah make its way into the nations and gain a hearing among the *goyim*. Derrida's meticulous and beautiful analysis turns on a reference Levinas makes in *In the Time of the Nations* to what Levinas calls the Torah before Sinai. In a section entitled "The Nations and the Messianic Time," commenting on a rabbinic teaching according to which "the nations are determined to take part in the Messianic age," Levinas asks:

> Has not the history of the nations already been in a sense that glorification of the Eternal in Israel, a participation in the history of Israel, which can be assessed by the degree to which their national solidarity is open to the other, the stranger? *A recognition of the Torah before Sinai?* (*BtV* 97; my emphasis)

Upon this text Derrida comments:

> Let us risk a first *translation:* would there be a recognition of the law *before* the event, and hence *outside* the localizable event, before the singular, dated, situated taking place of the gift of the Torah to the people? Would there be a *recognition* of it? Would it have been possible and thinkable? Before all revelation? A recognition of the Torah before Sinai by the peoples or the nations for which the name, the place, the event *Sinai* would not signify anything? Or nothing of what they signify for Israel or for what the language of Israel names? In short, by the third? (A 119, first emphasis added)

Is there a law before or beyond or outside the datable event of Sinai, a gift of a law beyond the gifts that Israel enjoys, a recognition of this law before or after or without the Sinai revelation? Can the intimacy of the one-to-one relation between God and Israel, can the jealousy and exclusivity of this famous twosome, be interrupted by the third? By the other Others, *les autres Autres,* who do not speak the language in which God and Israel communicate in private, who therefore require a *translation*? Translation is always a requirement imposed by the third, the other Others, who do not share the exclusive language of the two. Translation is required for the *goyim* who do not speak the language in which God and Israel exchange promises with each other. Translation is a requirement of justice, lest the relation between the Same and the wholly Other be exclusionary. Can the Torah, the revelation at Sinai, be translated? Can there be a *messianic* law beyond the *messianism* that is organized around Sinai? Is there a messianic time for *all* the nations, including the *goyim*?

In speaking of a people for whom the word *Sinai* does not mean anything, Derrida adds, Levinas is not putting the unique election of Israel into question but simply facing up to the test of hospitality— of "hospitality beyond all revelation" (*A* 119). Do not the demands of hospitality impose this work of translation upon Israel? Would not Israel otherwise be very inhospitable, clearly falling short of the rabbinic measure, according to which a nation should be judged by "the degree to which their national solidarity is open to the other, the stranger"? Clearly, this question of translation for Derrida is likewise through and through a *political* question in which the politics of Israel, what is today called Israel, and the borderlands of "Sinai" are under messianic scrutiny. Without weakening the election of Israel, Levinas searches for "a universal message for which it [Israel] has responsibility before or independently of the place and the event of the gift of the law: human universality, humanitarian hospitality extricated from a singularity of event which would become then empirical." There is a lesson here for Israel itself, for the modern state which has been given, or has taken, this biblical name, for its ethics, and perhaps finally for "its messianic politics of hospitality" (*A* 120).

This universal message, Levinas says, is one of "fraternity, humanity"—like Kant and the Western tradition in general, Levinas equates humanity with brothers—"hospitality," which together, according to Derrida, "determine an experience of the Torah and of messianic time even *before* or outside of Sinai—even for those who do not pretend 'to the title bearer or messenger of the Torah' " (*A* 121; *ITN* 97). We have to do here with a "messianic that we may call a structural or a priori messianicity," not absolutely ahistorical, to be sure, but "proper to a historicity without particular and empirically determinable incarnation. Without (*sans*) revelation or without being dated by a given revelation." That *sans* is important, for it loosens the link of the Torah to the determinate here and now of Sinai, to the particular event of a particular people, Sinai. Levinas does not break with the very idea of "election," which is important to him, but only with the idea of an election confined to a certain people (*A* 128). To which Derrida adds, "the hypothesis that I thus risk here"—the distinction between a structural messianic and a particular messianism linked to a given revelation—"is evidently not Levinas' "—that is, because it is Derrida's translation—"but it seeks to advance in his direction—perhaps in order still to meet him. 'In the heart of a chiasm'; as he said one day" (A 121–22). Levinas is looking for a way to translate the universal "human message borne by Judaism" (*ITN* 97), for a rendering of the Torah that opens upon universal humanity; Derrida is translating this translation, translating Levinas, who has already translated the Torah, into the distinction between the structural messianic and the concrete messianisms.[7]

The messianic order is defined by hospitality. As Levinas writes: "One belongs to the Messianic order when one has been able to admit others among one's own. That a people should admit those who come and settle among them—even though they are foreigners with their way of speaking, their smell—that a people should give them *akhsaniah* [accommodations], such as a place at the inn, the wherewithal to breathe and to live—is a song to the glory of the God of Israel" (*ITN* 98). A series of translations: hospitality is Jewish, the essence of the Torah, but it is also universally human; hospitality is humanitarianism itself, but it is not merely human, for it is also divine. "Welcome is the word for the divine decision" (A 132). The Jewish and the non-Jewish, the divine and the human, reach across and touch each other.

Clearly, what Levinas says has a political bearing or translatability; he is not in search of something non-political, but of another politics (A 144). He is always, albeit usually quite discreetly, commenting upon what is happening today, in Israel and Algeria, France and the United States, wherever there are refugees and immigrants, those who seek political asylum, with or without citizenship, who call for a change, an ethical conversion, for a more hospitable social and geopolitical space (A 131). This ethics of hospitality must certainly translate into politics, must have a bearing (*ferre, latus*), must be borne across (*translatus*) the borders of ethics and politics. Indeed, for Derrida, the ethics of hospitality has a political bearing, as regards the Palestinians and the modern state that today bears the name of Israel, that Levinas would find unbearable. The question of the state is couched by Levinas in terms of the relation between the state of Caesar and the state of David. This is a distinction, but not the opposition that Levinas says one finds in Christianity, which thereby exposed itself to the risk of a state religion (*BtV* 177). As if, Derrida adds in pointed apposition, there is no risk of a state religion and the suppression of the civil rights of nonbelievers in Islam or in present-day Israel (A 138). He must confess, says Derrida, that he does not always subscribe to Levinas's analysis of the real situation of the modern state of Israel (A 144): for example, that it stands alone, without a friend in all the world, "surrounded by enemies" (*BtV* 194)—with the sole exception, of course, of the most massive military power history has ever seen. How can one subscribe to Levinas's analysis of history today, in the face of the colonial "implantations," the justification of torture, and everything that has so badly corrupted the "peace process" (A 148)?

The state itself, left to itself, is a tyrant for Levinas, a pagan idol, a Hegelian totality, unless and until it is interrupted by the messianic, which should then both inhabit and transcend it. What Levinas calls a "messianic politics" is always "beyond the state in the state," *au-delà de l'État dans l'État,* transcendence in immanence, a state within a state, a messianic state within the purely political state.[8] Just as in deconstruction justice, which is beyond the law, must be always embodied in the law, lest the law be a tyrant and justice ineffectual, so for Levinas the purely political state, without a messianic impulse, will be less than it is, less than a state, a tyrant and not a state. In accord with the deepest tendencies of deconstruction, then, the state as it is described by Levinas contains what it cannot contain: a messianic element, a call for prophetic justice, in virtue of which it is self-interrupting, auto-deconstructing. Indeed, it is here, in connection with the peace for which we all aspire, that Derrida first uses the word *deconstruction:* the aim of politics is peace, but peace is not a purely political concept (for such a peace would always be based on war, on the "balance of power"), but a messianic and prophetic concept. Peace is a concept that exceeds or overflows itself—and here we meet the first occurrence of the word *deconstruction—* "deconstructing itself," interrupting the political order with messianic transcendence (A 146). Peace is neither purely political nor purely apolitical. The affirmation of hospitality opens politics beyond itself, constituting a politics which is always already non-politics (*BtV* 191). Politics comes "after," in the second place, because the primordial injunction does not belong to a purely political order, but to an ethical, prophetic, messianic order, which is prior, first (A 148–49). The state of Israel is thereby held to a high, a messianic ideal: over and beyond providing a place of refuge for the Jews, it must incarnate the prophetic ideal and the idea of messianic peace. This is an impossible demand, what Derrida would call *the* impossible itself, but which Anwar Sadat helped make possible to his everlasting credit (*BtV* 194–95). It is also a demand which Israel cannot evade.

But what is peace? Better, since peace is really a relationship, "what does it mean 'to be in peace with'—someone else, a group, a state, a nation, oneself as an other?" (*A* 152). For one can only be in peace with the Other, for peace, like hospitality, is the welcome one extends to the Other. Peace requires separation; one is not precisely at peace with the Same. Peace is not fusion but presupposes pluralism, the radical separation, of the Same and the Other. Peace is not the unity of community, the coherence of the elements of a plurality (*TeI* 283/*TI* 306) or a totality, but welcoming the Other, which means affirming the Other in his or her alterity. Peace is for the living and is not confined to cemeteries. Here Levinas is referring to a satirical anecdote with which Kant began *Perpetual Peace,* according to which a Dutch innkeeper—one who offers hospitality, a refuge and rest to the wayfarer—hung out a sign saying "Perpetual Peace," *"Ewiger Friede,"* *requies perpetua, requiescat in pace,* R.I.P. On the contrary, peace is between the living. Peace is the welcome of the face of the Other, and as such the opposite of death, proceeding from the prohibition of murder, which is the essence of the Torah. Still, in Kant, genuine and perpetual peace is a system of contracts between nation-states which provide for peace while at the same time severely restricting the rights of refugees and immigrants. But for Derrida the demand of peace is for a hospitality without reserve, a gift of unconditional hospitality, and that requires "an other international law, an other politics of borders, an other politics of the humanitarian, indeed a humanitarian engagement which is held *effectively* beyond the interests of the nation-states" (*A* 176).

A POLITICS OF THE REFUGE

"Let us return to Jerusalem," says Derrida. But which one? To the heavenly one? To the biblical one? To the modern city which still bears that ancient name, which is a scene of strife and war? Or to the *idea* of Jerusalem, the messianic idea, which is the idea of messianic peace? It is just the undecidability among these Jerusalems, the negotiations of this undecidability and this intersection of war and peace, that interests Derrida. "We are there, in the earthly Jerusalem, between war and peace, in that war that one calls on all sides without believing it, without making ourselves believe it, the 'peace process' " (A 183). Derrida takes his lead from Levinas's text "Cities of Refuge," in *Beyond the Verse*, in which Levinas insists that the earthly Jerusalem must be established, that a city of earthly peace— let us call this the horizontal dimension, says Levinas—in order to accomplish a heavenly Jerusalem, a religious salvation, or vertical dimension. "No vertical dimension without a horizontal dimension," Levinas says (*BtV* 38). The approach to the gates of Jerusalem, for Levinas, is through the cities of refuge. In Numbers 35:9, the Lord commanded Moses to establish "cities of refuge" where those who are guilty not of murder but of unintentional manslaughter may take flight, establishing thus a refuge for them from the "blood-avenger," that is, the appointed executioner in murder cases, who might catch up with them before there is time for a proper trial. To be sure, Levinas says, there is a fine line between voluntary and involuntary killing, and so we should reach a point of infinite responsibility, where we are responsible even for our lapses and our lack of watchfulness. For after all, "the Torah is justice, a complete justice (*justice intégralé*) which goes beyond the ambiguous situations of the cities of refuge. A complete justice . . . absolute vigilance . . . Jerusalem will be defined by this Torah" (*BtV* 46).

Jerusalem must embody integral justice in a city of laws, even as the cities of refuge require sharpening their conscience to infinity. Beyond the state in the state. The promise of a Jerusalem defined by the Torah must be inscribed in the earthly Jerusalem. No vertical dimension, no heavenly peace, without a horizontal dimension, without an earthly peace, which means without the law. No justice without law. The cities of refuge are civilized institutions and political structures which protect subjective innocence and forgive objective guilt. That is "better" (*meilleur*) than barbarism, Levinas says, better than the law of the jungle, where men eat one another alive, even though it is not yet the law of God (*BtV* 51–52). The political order is situated between God and barbarism, between the heavenly city and the jungle. It is better than the latter, not as good as the former, not good but not as bad, a "makeshift" (*pis aller*), a make-do that we cannot do without. Justice here, like peace, is hypocritical, an uneasy peace, based on self-interest and conflict. "But what is promised in Jerusalem is a humanity of the Torah," a new humanity beyond the contradictions of politics (*BtV* 52). That means that the longing for Zion must not degenerate into a new nationalism or particularism, nor become simply a search for a place of refuge. Zionism must mean the hope of a fully human society, which is to be found not in pious thoughts and eyes cast heavenward, but here and now, in Jerusalem, in the city which today bears the name, and which also must embody the ideal of messianic peace. Jerusalem is unique, but it is also universal.[9]

But how do we cross this border? How do we make our way from this ethics of messianic hospitality into politics? How do we translate this *hope* in unconditional peace into the *actuality* of the "peace process" in Jerusalem today? How do we inscribe the heavenly Jerusalem in the earthly? How do we draw a politics, which is better than barbarism, from ethics? About this Levinas is usually silent, and when he does speak, it is not as helpful as one would hope. Israel's claim to the Holy Land, he says, is not nationalism but Zionism and arises from the grandeur of a religious project. Israel's claim to the Holy Land is not a national *conatus essendi* by which it fiercely clings to its place in the Middle Eastern sun (we are going to commit suicide just to please international opinion, Netanyahu has said,[10] that is to say, we will not allow ourselves to be a hostage for the Other). On the Israeli side, a religious project; on the Palestinian side, nationalism. "To the expression 'Palestinian nationalism,'" Derrida comments, "there will never correspond that of 'Israeli nationalism'" (A 196 n. 1), as if the Palestinians, as if Christians do not read the same Bible and invoke the same father, Abraham. What then should the justice due the third one look like? What should the law in the cities of refuge be? How to arrange political affairs? What is the "better" law?

Levinas's silence comes to us from an abyss, Derrida says (A 197), whose borders we are able to trace. Levinas is silent, not about the *formal necessity* of a relation between ethics and politics—that is a border that must be crossed; the "better" law is needed, the law is better than barbarism—but about the *actual content* of such a law. Derrida reads Levinas's silence benignly, not as elusiveness or evasion on Levinas's part, but as the respect Levinas shows for the singularity of the concrete situation, which is never formalizable, programmable, which is heterogeneous to calculation and science, requiring in each situation a unique analysis. Levinas's silence marks the "moment" of decision; the "abyss" of silence is the interval (*en-tretemps*) of decision that "de-tracks" time, knocks it "out of joint," a moment of anachrony and *contretemps* (A 200). In the moment of decision, the time is out of joint and we find ourselves in an impossible situation, caught up at one and the same time by the infinite demands of justice, that is, by what the unique situation demands of us, and the generality of the law, caught like father Abraham himself between the face of God and the face of Isaac, between the face of the wholly Other and all the other faces. The ethico-political moment of decision is opened up in the gaping interval, the disjointedness or out-of-jointedness, between "thou shalt not kill," which is the sum of the Torah and of messianic peace, and the necessity to raise an army and to patrol one's borders, in short, occasionally, under certain circumstances, once in awhile, to kill the Other. Thou shalt not kill, thou shalt always make thyself a hostage and substitute for the Other—except occasionally, when sometimes it is necessary to kill the Other. In the space between these impossible choices, we do what is "better," which means what is less bad.

Levinas's silence about programmable schemata, about the map that marks the way between two heterogeneous orders of ethics and politics, describes the discontinuity of an *entretemps* which provides the necessary moment of "indecision"—Derrida would ordinarily say "undecidability" here—in which a decision is taken. For the moment of non-response and undecidability is the condition of possibility of a responsible decision. Only in that silence can one give one's "word of honor," can one give the gift of one's unconditional word: "Without the silence, without the hiatus, which is not the absence of rules, but *the necessity of a leap in the instant of the ethical, legal or political decision,* we would have only to let knowledge reel off a program of action. Nothing would be more totalitarian and conducive to responsibility" (A 201, my emphasis). Let us make this the occasion to note in passing that here, as elsewhere, Derrida mediates between Levinas and Kierkegaard; that is what deconstruction is.

The discontinuity discernible here gives Derrida a break, opens up room to maneuver, allowing him simultaneously to subscribe to "everything that Levinas tells us about messianic peace or messianic hospitality, about the *au-delà* of politics in politics" (A 201), without necessarily sharing all his political opinions about the earthly Jerusalem, in particular, his claim that Zionism is not nationalism but something grander and more universal, which is exactly what every nationalism wants to claim for itself. It is always difficult *in fact* to steer the idea of "election" clear of nationalism, and that is what Levinas always wanted, but *in fact* did not always succeed at.[11]

The abyss between ethics and politics is not a defect but an opening (A 46–47), the space in which we can keep a certain loving distance from Levinas. Our love of Levinas does not prevent, but even requires, a certain contradiction of him. Even in the midst of this *dire adieu* we must recall that *le dire* is self-interrupting, self-correcting, self-contradicting, which is its very inspiration and respiration. Indeed, this abyss or hiatus is precisely what allows Derrida to distinguish a structural messianic from the concrete messianisms, which are inevitably lured by nationalism, particularism, exclusivism, by rigorous immigration laws and a love of excommunication to protect the community. That is why we must above all cling to what Levinas says about the *recognition* of a Torah *before* Sinai, for the face comes before Sinai, which is a proper name which one loves to appropriate. Sinai and at the same time the face, which is before Sinai. Sinai must come to embody the Contra-Diction itself, the self-interruption and—shall I say it? Derrida does not—the *self-deconstruction* of itself, in order both to announce the face and then to withdraw in the face of the face of the third one who *also* demands justice.

The third one does not speak Hebrew, is not privy to the intimacies exchanged between Yahweh and Israel, and so requires a translation, which is a basic requirement of justice and hospitality. The proper name *Sinai* should fill us with "fear and trembling" (A 204)— Derrida is citing a certain Johannes who loved *silentium* and father Abraham—for it demands *translation* into *visage*. The Torah comes from heaven; it comes crashing into the world, upsetting the "ontology of the world," the *conatus essendi*, with the scandal of its demand for a care for the stranger (*ITN* 61). Like the face of the Other, in which is inscribed the face of the third, so that the face is at once singular and plural, Sinai too must be singular and plural, itself and translatable everywhere else. *Visages*, a singular plural whose plural ending we cannot hear, is "a poem which in its turn rings in harmony with (*accorder*) another French language," still unheard, a language for the Other, the third one who does not speak our language, the stranger, the other of man, other than man, like a proper name un-translatable outside French.

The word *à-Dieu* is another French poem which likewise rings in harmony with another language. *Adieu* is accorded to the face, when we say good-bye. *A-Dieu, ad deum, à l'infini*, does not mean an encounter with infinite life, for in the face of the Other, infinitely exposed, vulnerable and mortal, we must also meet up with death, which is also infinite. Everything that Levinas has to say, from beginning to end, can be read as a meditation on death and an attempt to overturn the dominant line on death from Plato through Hegel to Heidegger, in which death returns a profit, constitutes a good investment for the self, a way the soul, the slave, or authentic *Dasein* may become itself. We say *adieu*—I commend you to God—at the hour of death of the Other who, defenseless before death, addresses an infinite appeal to me, an infinite word, a word of God. The death of the Other belongs neither to the order of being (as a transition to another mode of being) nor to the order of non-being (as being-towards-nothingness), but to the order of glory, Levinas says, in which an infinite appeal rises up beyond being and nothingness (A 207–8).[12] Rather than an angst before my own death, I fear—without limit—for the Other. The vulnerability of the Other, time, and growing old—that is the power to say *adieu* to the world.

TRANSLATING DECONSTRUCTION

Until a moment ago I had not said a thing about deconstruction and how ethics and deconstruction keep getting translated into each other in this text. *"Déconstruction"*—a word that surely does not capture everything that is going on in Derrida's work these days, which only captures a moment in its messianic moment, its affirmation of the impossible justice to come—is only mentioned twice in *Adieu*, but it will repay our patience to pay visits to both sites.

The first time, Derrida is speaking of Levinas's use of the concept of peace. Levinas "suggests" in *Beyond the Verse* that "peace is a concept which overflows the purely political" (195). Peace does not repudiate the political, the "purely political," but exceeds it. Peace is in part something political, but in another part peace exceeds politics, overflows a certain concept of the political. The concept of peace thus exceeds itself, overflows its borders, interrupts or, as Derrida says, *deconstructs* itself (A 145–46).[13] The Levinasian concept of peace is auto-deconstructing. A purely political peace (the law) can and must be deconstructible, to borrow a construction from "The Force of Law,"[14] but this always in the name of peace, which is not deconstructible (justice). Insofar as the political order forms an "*au-delà dans*"—a *beyond* politics *in* politics, *beyond* the state and *in* the state—a political interiorization of something transcendent to politics, namely, of peace or justice, of an ethical or messianic justice, it takes a form which can be deconstructed. The political order contains something that it cannot contain. Then, in parentheses, Derrida adds a more general observation. Let us note, he says, "each time this self-interruption is produced . . . each time this self-delimitation which is also an excess or transcendence of itself is produced, a process of deconstruction is under way" (A 146). Each time the law is interrupted in the name of justice, each time the concrete messianisms are interrupted in the name of the messianic, each time political peace is interrupted in the name of messianic peace, then a process of deconstruction is under way. That is a way to translate Levinas into deconstruction, to see deconstruction as a translation of Levinas.

The second occurrence of the verb *déconstruit* is found in Derrida's discussion of the unconditional quality of the welcome, *l'accueil*, in Levinas. Derrida is discussing Levinas's view that the Other must be welcomed "independently of its qualities," ontological predicates, marks of presence or prestige, or living, non-phantomic qualities. The face of the Other must be welcomed directly and immediately, urgently, without waiting or conditioning it upon a review of the Other's qualities and qualifications, passing them under the review of the self. We must run the disquieting—*unheimlich*—risk of hospitality which is offered to a kind of ghost, a person without qualities, a guest/ghost, a *Geist/Gast*. There would be no hospitality, then, without the disquieting risk of spectrality. "But the spectrality is not nothing; it exceeds, and then deconstructs all the ontological oppositions, being and nothing, life and death—and it gives. It is able to give, to order (*ordonner*), to forgive (*pardonner*); it is also able not to do it, as God beyond being. God without being, God not contaminated with being, is that not the most rigorous definition of the face, or of the *Tout Autre*? But is it not an apprehension as spectral as it is spiritual?" (A 193). The visible face of the Other, handsome or repulsive, dignified or ignoble, is deconstructed in the name of the Other's invisible dignity. The worldly worth and qualities of the Other are deconstructed in the name of their worldly, undeconstructible worthiness. Whether the Other is much or little, being or nothing, the face of the Other is marked by the withdrawal of this invisible God beyond being, without or uncontaminated by being. This holy ghost or specter of deconstruction deconstructs the visible, deconstructible qualities or qualifications of the Other. You do not have to qualify for a gift. You do not have to earn it. That is why it is a gift. The Other does not have to qualify, merit, or earn the welcome of hospitality. Otherwise we are just giving the Other his or her due.

In sum, two translations of Levinas into deconstruction, two border crossings of ethics into deconstruction, or perhaps the other way around: (1) political peace is deconstructible in the name of messianic peace, which is not deconstructible; (2) the visible face of the Other is deconstructible in the name of the invisible *visage*, which is not deconstructible.

ADIEU SANS DIEU

Let us now return to our guiding question, "How can Derrida dare to say *adieu*? How can there be an *adieu—sans Dieu*?"

In the view of deconstruction that I am defending here, deconstruction stands on the side of the God who loves the stranger, sharing God's loving concern for the Other, responding to the sign that God has placed on the face of the stranger. The God of deconstruction, *s'il y en a*, the *Dieu* of the deconstructive *adieu*, is through and through Semitic, that is, a God who commands hospitality for the Other. Deconstruction is the affirmation of the Other, a *viens, oui, oui* to *l'invention de l'autre*. That means—here comes the political translation, assuming that all this is not thoroughly political from the start—responsibility for and to the vulnerability of the stranger. Being always already turned to God, *à Dieu*, means being turned to the face of homeless, migrant bodies bearing all their life's belongings on their back, exiled, displaced people, persons "without papers" who have no standing before the law, who speak a foreign tongue, who lived in a land where it is impossible to live and who are not permitted to live where life is possible, nomadic people who have no place to lay their head. Derrida takes his stand *with* the God who loves the stranger, commending the stranger *to* God, *ad deum, à Dieu.* To God's command. But how can Derrida, who rightly passes for an atheist, who does not believe *in* God, bear witness *to* God, *à Dieu,* respond to God's commands, take his stand *with* God? He never enters into the uprightness and direction of what Kierkegaard called the one-to-one relation with God, but remains content with oblique and indirect relationships. How does Derrida dare say *à-Dieu,* if he does not believe in God, has no theology, and even dallies with the death of God?

Derrida's daring view, I would say, is very close to another, no less daring move on Levinas's part. Derrida is very close to a certain death of God, which is not only Nietzschean but, quite strikingly, both Nietzschean *and Levinasian.* There is a certain bidding adieu to God, *adieu à Dieu,* if I may say so, to be found at the end of *Otherwise Than Being,* a God with respect to whom Levinas, too, rightly passes for an atheist. In the final paragraph of *Otherwise Than Being,* Levinas says that this work is written "after the death of a certain god inhabiting the world behind the scenes" (*AE* 233/*OB* 185). However much Levinas would dissociate himself from Nietzsche's interpretation of "bad conscience," he does not hesitate to associate himself with the Nietzschean inversion of Platonism, and so indeed with Nietzsche's critique of the Platonic-Christian tradition, of Platonism and its "popular" version, Christianity. *Il n'y a pas d'arrière monde:* there is no hinterworld, no *Hinterwelt,* no second world hidden behind the first one. Hence there is no idea of the sweetness of an afterlife to bathe the wounds of mortal strife, no "eternal life" or "eternal reward" to pay us back for the expenditures we have made on behalf of the Other in Levinas. Indeed, Levinas would have every reason to agree with Nietzsche's critique of Christianity's "stroke of genius," which Derrida mentions at the end of *The Gift of Death,* which sees the Crucifixion as the amortization of an infinite debt which merits all eternal happiness. Levinas attacked Platonism from the start. *Time and the Other* is a sustained critique of Sartrean freedom and *Dasein's Seinskönnen,* to be sure, but it is no less a critique of the world of Plato, of his "world of light" which is a "world without time" (*TA* 88/*TO* 93). In Levinas's early language, time is not "a fallen form of Being" but "its very event" (*son événement même*) (*TA* 88/*TO* 92). Hence when Levinas mentions immortality, he treats it as analogous to insomnia, speaks of "this immortality from which one cannot escape" (*TA* 27/*TO* 48), and refers to the impossibility of death and even of the "horror of immortality" (*DE* 103/*EE* 63). One does not vanquish death by way of eternal life—Platonism and Christianity—but rather by way of the relation with the Other (*TA* 73/*TO* 81–82) and fecundity (*TA* 85–89/*TO* 90–94; *TeI* 244–47/*TI* 267–69). One does not transcend being by way of infinite being. For Levinas, being-in-the-world is all (but not all in all, which would be too totalizing; there is always an *au-delà-dans* in any *être dans le monde*).

There is no invisible world hidden behind the visible one, if that implies two worlds, one material and the other immaterial—as it does in Christian Platonism. *L'invisible* does not mean immaterial being but the trace. God passes us by, he says, has always already passed us by, by bypassing the visible and present in such a way as to have left his trace on the face of the stranger. From the point of view of knowledge, this is always an "ambiguous" operation, for the trace is *not* the residue of a presence, not a visible mark that can be traced back to originary presence and so made the basis of a demonstration (which means "showing") of the existence or being of God. The trace is not a diminished presence that leads us back to full presence; rather, the trace is always, structurally, withdrawn (*retrait*) (*AE* 14–15/*OB* 12). After the death of the Christian-Platonic God inhabiting an immaterial *Hinterwelt*, "the hostage discovers the trace . . . of what, always already past, always '*il*,' does not enter into any present," which "marks with its seal" the face of the stranger. God leaves his seal on the face of the stranger as he withdraws from the world (*AE* 233/*OB* 185), like a ripple of water that betrays a recent disturbance.

The relationship to God has to do with the social relation, he says, and God's epiphany takes place in the face of the stranger. "A God invisible," he says, "means not only a God unimaginable, but a God accessible in justice" (*TeI* 51/*TI* 78). Theology, which means the thematization, the thematic explicitation, of a content, *le dit*, "God," a massive semantic event, has no content; its concepts are empty, like Kantian concepts without intuitions, apart from the ethical relationship which founds them. Everything about the relationship to God that "cannot be led back to an interhuman relation" (*TeI* 52/*TI* 79) is a myth. Ethics funds theology the way perception funds theoretical constructs in phenomenology. Such concepts are empty, meaningless, vacuous except insofar as they can be led back, *remaner, reducere,* to the relation to the neighbor. Everything else is a fabrication of an overactive spatial imagination that requires demythologizing. No *Aufklärer* could have said it better.

For Levinas, God is neither a visible being in this world nor the invisible inhabitant of another, higher, immaterial world. God does not belong to any order of *being,* either this world's or the next's, or of *knowledge,* at all. It is hardly an exaggeration to say that we may speak of Levinas's God in much the way Derrida speaks of the gift of justice: God, if there is one, *Dieu, s'il y en a.* I commend you to God, if there is one, *à Dieu, s'il y en a.* God belongs to the order of ethics, to an ethical order (*ordo*), *as* the ethical order (*ordinans, ordonner*), to the order of the order which orders me to the stranger and the stranger to me. God is not a being or first principle, of the first order or the second, visible or invisible, material or immaterial, physical or spiritual, but, otherwise than being and knowledge, the *ordo ordinans* which orders me to the stranger. Levinas's God is perhaps best thought of as a certain holy "ought," not *der heilige Geist* but *das heilige Sollen,* forged from a covenant between Kant and Torah. From the point of view of immaterial being and another world, of a transcendent being and an afterlife, Levinas, like Derrida, rightly passes for an atheist.

L'invisible and *l'infini* are *ethical* categories for Levinas, not ontological or epistemological ones. God's holiness and separation, God's alterity and transcendence, are not that of a *substantia separata* or *substantia spiritualis,* but the seat of an ethical call which orders me to the stranger. As such, the name of God can only be uttered in the context of an ethical action. *Stricto sensu,* I would do as well not to say "God" at all, because God is nothing said, and as soon as I thematize God I create a disturbance in the ethical order and take leave of the order in which God is at work, in which God orders me. To stay related to God, to maintain a link with God, I should bid adieu to God, *adieu à Dieu,* and welcome the stranger. For it is only by loving and welcoming the stranger, by responding *in the name of* the God who loves the stranger, that God can be God. I pray to God to rid me of God. God can be God only if my relationship to God is oblique while my relationship to the neighbor is direct. God is God only if I am speaking to the stranger, only when I *use* the name of God as opposed to mentioning it, only when I *do* the name of God, *facere veritatum,* as when I say *"adieu"* to the Other. That means that the name of God must be *translated into hospitality,* but this translation takes place in an entirely pragmatic order, not a semantic one. The translation is radical, beyond any semantic transfer, beyond any aligning of meanings in different semantic fields, beyond being and knowledge, because it is a translation into witnessing, into action, into deeds, a translation not in truth but in deed, and if in truth then in the Augustinian sense of *facere veritatem.* The name of God belongs to the sphere of *dire* not of *dit,* of *dire adieu,* of *dire bonjour* and *adieu,* not to a discourse on or about God. God is structurally absent from theology, has already passed by by the time theology sets up shop.

According to Levinas, the glory of God rises up, beyond phenomenality, when, flushed out with no place to hide, "extradited" from my refuge, I say, beyond being, *me voici,* responding to the order which orders me to the stranger. The glory of the Infinite rises up in my responsibility and anarchic substitution. I do not thereby demonstrate the existence or verify my belief in the Infinite—as if this had to do with being or knowledge—but I "bear witness to it." "It is by the voice of the witness that the glory of the Infinite is glorified" (*AE* 186/*OB* 146). The *me voici* bears witness not to something that it knows or represents, not to anything that is or appears or is thematized, but to what commands me. But this command finds words only in the one who is commanded, sounds forth only in my saying, my *me voici*—for there is no other being, visible or invisible, to utter it. There is thus a curious autonomy in this heteronomy, for my saying is the very way the Infinite passes by, my words are the only way it is given utterance, and my obedience the only way the order is known. That means that I am in a certain way the author of the law that I obey, the author of what I have received.

There is accordingly a curious atheism in Levinas's theism, a curious religious atheism in his ethical theism (since ethics, which *is* hospitality and *à-Dieu,* cannot be a-theistic), a curious *sans Dieu* in his *adieu.* For all the world—for all that is visible, existent, and knowable—I am acting on my own, like an autonomous agent, without mention or thought of God, *sans Dieu,* and I might as well be an atheist. For all the world, I pass for an atheist. There is no need to say or to think God, who orders me to the stranger, or to affirm one's belief in God, or to have a theology ready for inspection if the Inquisitors come knocking at my door. Indeed, the very moment that God is in any way thematized or made an object of belief, the movement of the command, of witnessing, is interrupted. It is necessary to rid ourselves of God in order to witness to God. It is all the same whether one speaks *in the name of* God, or commends someone *to* God, or does not so much as mention God at all. That is why Levinas says:

> "Here I am, in the name of God," without (*sans*) referring myself directly to his presence. "Here I am," just that (*tout court*). The word God is still absent from the phrase in which God is for the first time involved in words. It does not at all state "I believe in God." To bear witness to God is precisely not to state this extraordinary word. . . . As a sign given to the other of this very signification, the "here I am" signifies me in the name of God, at the service of the human beings who regard me. . . . Witness is humility and admission, it is kerygma and prayer, glorification and recognition. (*AE* 190/*OB* 149)

The one translates into the other, with or without (*sans*) referring to God. There is a living, working translatability, a pragmatic equivalence, between *me voici, au nom de Dieu* and *me voici, tout court* which opens up the possibility of a witness to God, and even of prayer, *without* referring to God, from which the word *God* is absent. *Me voici, tout court—sans Dieu.* In short: *adieu—sans Dieu.* To God without God, *Dieu sans l'être.* As soon as I say *me voici* God is at work, God is witnessed, and I am answering *in* the name of God, in the name of all that that name names, whether or not I use this extraordinary name, whether or not I rightly pass for an atheist. As soon as I respond to the provocation of the stranger, the invocation of God has taken place. God is at work in this witnessing, has always already passed by, although for all the world the one who obeys rightly passes for an atheist. Witnessing does not supply evidence for that to which it bears witness, does not make its being or appearance more probable, and cannot be summoned as an argument for the existence of God. Indeed, God is God, and we bear witness to God only if we rid ourselves of God, which was the prayer of Meister Eckhart, although Levinas is not a negative theologian. For God is God only when God is at work ordering me to the Other, in the deep recess of *illeity* prior to all presence and thematization.

The word *God* is too much, too big and bombastic for ethics; it crowds ethics out, draws too much attention to itself, interrupting and suffocating ethics. Of this word *God*, God as something "said," Levinas says that it "is an overwhelming semantic event that subdues the subversion worked by illeity," by turning it from the order of command to the order of something meant, and this subversion is at work "at this very moment," as we speak and use the name *God* (*AE* 193/*OB* 151), as we move about in the semantic field. The semantics overwhelms the pragmatics and blocks the translation, which is not semantic. The whole meaning, the living meaning, of this term is nothing semantic, for it lies in the witness which is given to it, a meaning that is not translated but betrayed as soon as "God" is said and thematized in theology, whether that be in a positive theology or even in the most negative of negative theologies. Witnessing is not theology, either positive or negative, but service to the neighbor who regards me. As Johannes Climacus might have said, witnessing is not a thought but a deed. Becoming a Christian, Climacus said, is not a *what* but a *how*. Just so, *adieu, à-Dieu*, and let us say that the name of God in general for Levinas and Derrida is not a *what* but a *how*. Just so with prayers and tears; they too are a matter of the *how*, not the *what*, so that one could spend all one's days in prayers and tears while rightly passing for an atheist.

We are tempted to identify the bond of our relation to this illeity—this God without being, or God without being called God—as religion, Levinas says (*AE* 188/*OB* 147), and in *Totality and Infinity* that is what he called it (*TeI* 10/*TI* 40). Perhaps it is best called what Derrida calls a "religion without (*sans*) religion," which would fit very nicely with an *adieu sans Dieu*. We can certainly call it ethics. From a robustly religious point of view, one would say that Levinas has reduced religion to ethics, thinned it out into a purely ethical event, which is what Merold Westphal has called an "ethical suspension of religion." To speak non-reductively, Levinas has *translated* religion into ethics, translated the name of God as wholly Other into a wholly ethical name, a name whose whole signification is service to the neighbor and the stranger who regard me.

Now, as we have said, a parallel translation has been going on in deconstruction, which is all about messianic peace, so that the two have begun to converge upon and be translated into each other. Even as for Levinas, religion, *me voici, au nom de Dieu*, translates into ethics, *me voici, tout court*, so for Derrida, for whom deconstruction is justice, messianic peace, and hospitality, deconstruction undergoes a parallel translation into ethics, and therefore into the name of God, into a working equivalence with speaking *in* the name of God. *Me voici, au nom de Dieu* and *me voici, tout court:* these translate into the same thing, into hospitality, which is their common meaning, whether or not one rightly passes for an atheist. *Me voici, au nom de Dieu*, that is all the meaning the word *God* has for Levinas; *me voici, tout court*, that is all the meaning of God that deconstruction needs. God is mixed with words even—indeed precisely—when the name of God is used but not mentioned, when it is a performative not a constative, even or precisely when the name of God is absent from the phrase.[15]

Thus an odd sort of *sans Dieu* disturbs the Levinasian-Derridean *à-Dieu*. An odd convergence of two atheisms inhabits their archi-Semitic hospitality. There is, thus, an unnerving undecidability between theism and atheism, theology and a-theology, *Dieu* and *sans Dieu*, *Dieu* and *à-Dieu*, where the *à* has now become a privative *a*, as in *amorphe*. The first atheism is that of Derrida, who rightly passes for an atheist, who does not by the most conventional standards "believe in God," for whom God translates *without remainder* into service to the neighbor; we find the Other in Levinas, who is an atheist about "God," the thematic, mentioned, thetic, said God, the *theos* of theology. The God of Levinas and the undeconstructible in Derrida both translate into service to the stranger, into hospitality. In this complex *mis en abyme* of translations, the name of God is finally translated into hospitality.

For Derrida, the undecidability between theology and atheology, theism and atheism, *Dieu* and *sans Dieu* or *à-Dieu* (in the privative sense), transpires in the desert, in the *khora*, in the indeterminate spacing in which all the nominal unities, the temporary unities of meaning around which we organize our works and days, are inscribed. Whenever we attempt to seize the *what*, to swear an oath by the *what*, to enforce the *what* with institutional power, to threaten the Other in the name of the *what*, the sands of undecidability shift and the graven images and fragile structures of the *what* crumble under our touch. The standard and conventional difference between *theos* and *atheos*, theology and atheology, between those who rightly pass for atheists and those who do not, between the "infidels" and the "believers," is such stuff as war is made of, of which the war over the holy city of Jerusalem may be taken as paradigmatic. That always has to do with the meant God, the thetic, propositional God of theology, with what Levinas calls *le dit,* the "overwhelming semantic event," which is for Derrida a nominal unity, around which the powerful institutions of the concrete "messianisms" are erected. But what the biblical tradition calls the living God (*TA* 9/*TO* 31) has to do with *le dire,* with *à-Dieu,* with *dire adieu,* with the pre-position before all propositions of being turned to God, with practice not thetics, with pragmatics not semantics, with the praxis of commending the stranger to God, with *saying* adieu, with *doing* adieu, *facere veritatum,* and writing the rest off as semantics. In short, with translating the name of God into hospitality. For in the semantic field, which is the field of being and manifestation, of proof and knowledge, we are, when it comes to God, enveloped in darkness and we are all a little lost. We see now, in the *khora,* through a glass darkly, and we are all a little blind. Deconstruction is a memoir of the blind—and so is ethics. "*Je ne sais pas,*" says Derrida at the beginning and end of *Memoirs d'aveugle,* "*il faut croire.*" Of the command that commands me to the Other, Levinas says, I do not know whence—*je ne sais d'où*—it arises (*AE* 189/*OB* 148–49).

That is why *adieu* is a holy word for Derrida, and why Derrida is a man of prayers and tears, of faith, hope, and loving hospitality, although he lacks a theology and a *Hinterwelt,* does not say *credo in unum deum,* and rightly passes for an atheist. "The *yes* of faith is not incompatible with a certain atheism or at least with a *certain* thought of God's *inexistence* (beyond being)" (*A* 111 n. 1). When I affirm the Other, I do not "know" what I affirm but I pledge myself to the Other *sans voir, sans avoir, sans savoir.* What do I love when I love my God? *Je ne sais pas—il faut croire.* What (*quid*) do I love when I love my God? God is not a what, a *quidditas,* but a *how.*

Then do deconstruction and first philosophy translate into each other without remainder? I would say that there are three main differences between Levinas and Derrida here, in this text, and elsewhere.

(1) First, as regards the ethics of hospitality: in Levinas, the notion of God functions as a kind of *ordo ordinans,* an overarching backup or ground which orders me to the neighbor or the stranger, which somehow or another is *au-delà dans,* a transcendence in immanence, a God who is a *tout autre* who is *autre qu'autrui,* commanding respon-

sibility and hospitality. In Derrida, on the other hand, hospitality is responsive directly and immediately to the *singularity* of the Other, so that every Other is wholly Other, *tout autre est tout autre*, and there is no movement of deflection from the Good to the neighbor, no *ordo ordinans* in the Levinasian sense of ordering my desire for the Good into a desire or affirmation of the neighbor. Rather than an overarching transcendence or *ordo ordinans*, Derrida's *adieu* transpires in a *khora* more like the *il y a* of Levinas, with which, says Levinas in a remarkable text, God, illeity, *l'autre qu'autrui*, slips into a "possible confusion" (*DVI* 115).

(2) Second, while Levinas always denounces the narcissism of the Same, I think—to Derrida's credit—there is always a residual narcissism in the deconstructive notion of hospitality. There is no one narcissism, Derrida says, but varying degrees of it, from the most closed-fisted and mean-spirited narcissism up to the most open-ended, "hospitable" narcissism.[16]

(3) Finally, and this is what the text of *Adieu* makes especially clear, Derrida presses the political paradox of hospitality more radically than does Levinas, presses all the more insistently to translate this ethics of hospitality into politics, to open the doors of this ethics to the demands of political hospitality, in particular, as regards the modern state that answers to the biblical name of Israel. Derrida wants to sound an international alarm about the demands of hospitality, to stress national and international political structures to the precise point at which, short of breaking, they become more porous. He wants to break down the walls and barriers that nations build against the strangers whose weary faces glow not with visible beauty—on the contrary!—but with God's glory, upon whom God makes his face to shine. Throughout the pages of *Adieu*, migrant and immigrant bodies pass us by, pressing their faces against the windows of our quiet academic studies, regarding us as we write and talk and think in the comfort of our academic refuges, soliciting not words but deeds, not the word "God" but godliness. For God is not a semantic event, however overwhelming, but a deed. Derrida would finally demand a more or less direct political translation of the ethics of hospitality, and hence of the name of God, a risky and formidable translation that fills us with fear and trembling, like daring to hold a dagger over one's own child, which would result in open doors, in nations without borders or national barriers. Derrida advocates the free movement of

human beings across the face of the earth, a daring policy that puts the various national identities and national languages at risk. The name of God translates into open doors and in*deed*, not simply as edifying ethical discourse but as a political deed, *facere veritatum.* Unconditional hospitality, not only as a word of honor of a personal ethics but as a political policy of unconditional admission of the foreigner into our land, sharing with them our jobs, our schools, the food out of our mouths. Opening national doors and lowering national barriers so that *we* are the ones who are "extradited," driven from our safe refuges, in order to make room for the stranger. Derrida would swing wide the gates of Jerusalem in order to make the stranger welcome. Indeed, the open doors of unconditional hospitality are what Derrida means by "Jerusalem," by the heavenly "gates of Jerusalem," and indeed, I dare say, by "God."

Bonjour, viens, oui oui, bienvenue, adieu. These are holy words, the words of travelers and wayfarers, of the weary and displaced, desert voices extending greetings to each other, ankhoral words wafting across the surface of an endless desert, disseminating into the darkness of an endless night.

> *Viens, oui, oui.*
> *Au nom de Dieu.*

NOTES

1. *A* = J. Derrida, *Adieu: à Emmanuel Levinas* (Paris: Galilée, 1997). The following abbreviations are also employed in this essay: *PdA* = J. Derrida, *Politiques de l'amitié* (Paris: Galilée, 1995); *POF* = trans. by G. Collins as *Politics of Friendship* (London: Verso, 1997); *BtV* = E. Levinas, *Beyond the Verse: Talmudic Readings and Lectures,* trans. G. D. Mole (Bloomington: Indiana University Press, 1994); *ITN* = *In the Time of the Nations,* trans. M. B. Smith (Bloomington: Indiana University Press, 1994). For further abbreviations, the reader is directed to the table of abbreviations for this entire volume. Where no Englith translation is cited, translation is furnished by the author of this essay.

2. "Circumfession" is to be found on the bottom half of the page of J. Derrida and G. Bennington, *Jacques Derrida,* trans. G. Bennington (Chicago: University of Chicago Press, 1993), 153–55. For a commentary, see my *Prayers and Tears of Jacques Derrida* (Bloomington: Indiana University Press, 1997), chapter 6, "Confession."

3. This last reference to a discussion of "*à-Dieu*" is to Levinas's 1982 essay "Diachrony and Representation," which has been published in translation in Richard Cohen's translation of *Time and the Other*.

4. Most recently in *Anne Dufourmantelle invite Jacques Derrida à repondre de l'hospitalité* (Paris: Calman-Lévy, 1997).

5. I doubt this will satisfy many feminists, who are at least as worried over the fate of empirical women as over the feminine, and who distrust schemata in which women are either less than fully human or more than human, but never precisely human.

6. J. Derrida, *Psyché: Inventions de l'autre* (Paris: Galilée, 1987), 53; trans. C. Porter, "Psyche: Inventions of the Other," in *Reading DeMan Reading*, ed. L. Waters and W. Godzich (Minneapolis: University of Minnesota Press, 1989), 55.

7. For more texts and further commentary on Derrida's distinction between the messianic and the concrete messianisms, see my *Prayer and Tears of Jacques Derrida*, chapter 3, "The Messianic"; and *Deconstruction in a Nutshell: A Conversation with Jacques Derrida* (New York: Fordham University Press, 1997), 20–25, 156–80.

8. E. Levinas, *Nouvelles lectures talmudiques* (Paris: Minuit, 1996), 63.

9. Levinas's essay first appeared in *Jérusalem: l'Unique et l'Universelle*, ed. J. Halpérin and G. Lévitte (Paris: P.U.F., 1979), 35–48.

10. *New York Times*, December 14, 1997.

11. Of course, Levinas would never agree that some *other nation or Book* was "elected" to be "unique," but would insist rather that election is to bear a "universal" message, meant for all people. *Adieu* is in part a eulogy, a work of filial *pietas*, and Derrida is not giving Levinas quite as much trouble as he might have.

12. Derrida is citing Levinas, "La conscience non-intentionelle," in *Emmanuel Levinas*, ed. C. Chalier and M. Abensour (Paris: L'Herne, 1991), 118–19.

13. The reader will recall that I have already touched briefly on this mention of "deconstruction" in the course of discussing Levinas's notion of "beyond the state in the state."

14. J. Derrida, "The Force of Law: 'The Mystical Foundation of Authority,' " trans. M. Quaintance, in *Deconstruction and the Possibility of Justice*, ed. D. Cornell et al. (New York: Routledge, 1992), 68–91.

15. The God beyond being not only does not have to be, but he does not have to give to me or pardon me. What sort of faith or devotion would there be if I were sure that God could not abandon me (separate himself)? Does Levinas think, Derrida wonders, that the *à-Dieu* is a prayer or a greeting addressed to a God who must respond, or might God abandon me? What elicits our admiration in this beautiful word, Derrida says, is its desire or

love of the stranger, its disproportion (A 182). "God who loves the stranger," beyond being, is not there. "Beyond and before the existence of God, outside of his probable improbability, pushed even as far as and up to the point of the most vigilant, if not despairing, the most cold [*dégrisé*] (Levinas loves this word) atheism, *le Dire à-Dieu* would signify hospitality." Not an abstract "love of the stranger," but the God *who* loves the stranger.

16. J. Derrida, *Points . . . Interviews, 1974–94*, ed. E. Weber, trans. P. Kamuf (Stanford: Stanford University Press, 1995), 199.

CONTRIBUTORS

Robert Bernasconi holds the Moss Chair of Excellence in Philosophy at the University of Memphis. A leading interpreter of Levinas and Derrida, he has also published widely in the fields of modern and contemporary thought. He is the author of *The Question of Language in Heidegger's History of Being* (1985) and *Heidegger in Question* (1993), and co-editor of *The Provocation of Levinas* (1988) and *Re-Reading Levinas* (1991). He is currently completing a book to be called *Between Levinas and Derrida* and is working on a study of the history of race thinking within philosophy.

Rudolf Bernet is Director of the Husserl Archief and Professor of Philosophy at the Higher Institute of Philosophy in the Katholieke Universiteit te Leuven. In addition to numerous articles in the fields of modern and contemporary philosophy, he has published *La vie du sujet: Recherches sur l'interprétation de Husserl dans la phénoménologie* (1994) and, together with I. Kern and E. Marbach, *Edmund Husserl, Darstellung seines Denkens* (1989).

Jeffrey Bloechl is Assistant Professor of Philosophy and Edward Bennett Williams Fellow at the College of the Holy Cross. From 1996 through 1999 he was postdoctoral research associate at the Katholieke Universiteit Leuven and the Belgian Fund for Scientific Research (Flanders). His book *The Liturgy of the Neighbor: Emmanuel Levinas and the Religion of Responsibility* is forthcoming, and he is completing another on the relationship between phenomenology and theology.

Roger Burggraeve is Professor of Moral Theology at the Katholieke Universiteit te Leuven. He has published several books on Levinas, as well as several more inspired by Levinas, in areas ranging from sexual ethics to biblical hermeneutics. An early interpreter of Levinas's work, he has also compiled *Emmanuel Levinas: Une bibliographie primaire et secondaire (1929–1985)*.

John D. Caputo holds the David R. Cook Chair of Philosophy at Villanova University and is Series Editor of Fordham University Press's Perspectives in Continental Philosophy. His books include *The Mystical Element in Heidegger's Thought* (1986), *Radical Hermeneutics* (1987), *Against Ethics* (1993), *The Tears and Prayers of Jacques Derrida* (1997), and, as editor with commentary, *Deconstruction in a Nutshell: A Conversation with Jacques Derrida* (1996).

Didier Franck is Professor of Philosophy at the Université de Paris X–Nanterre. A leading interpreter of phenomenology and Continental thought, his major works include *Chair et corps: Sur le phénoménologie de Husserl* (1987), *Heidegger et le problème de l'espace* (1988), and *Nietzsche et l'ombre de Dieu* (1998).

Jean-Luc Marion is Professor of Philosophy at the Université de Paris IV–Sorbonne and the University of Chicago. In addition to several important works on Descartes, he has published a series of books moving from Christian negative theology into the phenomenologies of Husserl and Heidegger. This latter group includes *Dieu sans l'être* (1982), *Prolégomènes à la charité* (1986), *Réduction et donation* (1989), and *Etant donné* (1997).

Paul Moyaert is Professor of Philosophy at the Higher Institute of Philosophy in the Katholieke Universiteit te Leuven and a member of the Belgian School for Psychoanalysis. In addition to extensive writing on psychopathology and Freudian theory, he has published books on Christianity, *De mateloosheid van het christendom* (1998), Lacan's Seminaire VII, *Ethiek et sublimatie* (1994), and, together with Jan Walgrave, mystical desire, *Mystiek en liefde* (1988).

Michael Newman is Senior Lecturer and Head of Theoretical Studies and Art History at the Slade School of Fine Art and University College, London. He studied philosophy in Essex, Paris, and Leuven, and was Visiting Research Fellow at the University of Tilburg. An accomplished and prolific art critic, he has also written widely in contemporary philosophy, and is completing a book to be entitled *Traces of Memory and Forgetting: Heidegger, Levinas, Derrida.*

Adriaan T. Peperzak is Arthur J. Schmitt Professor of Philosophy and Director of the Center for Advanced Study of Christianity and Culture at Loyola University in Chicago. He has published five books on Hegel and two on Levinas, as well as more than 150 articles. His most recent works include *Beyond: The Philosophy of Emmanuel Levinas* (1997), *Before Ethics* (1997), and *Platonic Transformations* (1997), as well as several essays on the intersection between religion and ethics.

Rudi Visker is Permanent Research Fellow of the Belgian Fund for Scientific Research (Flanders), and teaches philosophy at the Higher Institute of Philosophy in the Katholieke Universiteit te Leuven. In addition to numerous essays in the area of contemporary Continental philosophy, he has published *Michel Foucault: Genealogy as Critique* (1995) and *Singularity and Truth* (1999).

Merold Westphal is Distinguished Professor of Philosophy at Fordham University. In addition to a wide range of essays on modern and contemporary thinkers, including several on Levinas, he has also published *God, Guilt, and Death: An Existential Phenomenology of Religion* (1984), *Kierkegaard's Critique of Reason and Society* (1987), *Hegel, Freedom, and Modernity* (1992), and most recently, *Becoming a Self: A Reading of Kierkegaard's "Concluding Unscientific Postscript"* (1996).